KAMPFGESCHWADER 53
"LEGION CONDOR"

The Complete History of KG 53 in World War II

Heinz Kiehl

Schiffer

Translated from the German by David Johnston.

Printed in China.
ISBN: 978-0-7643-4475-6

This book was originally published in German under the title *Chronik Kampfgeschwader 53 "Legion Condor"* by Heinz Kiehl. Originally published as a Special Edition in 2010 by Motorbuch Verlag.

Published by Schiffer Publishing Ltd.
4880 Lower Valley Road
Atglen, PA 19310
Phone: (610) 593-1777
FAX: (610) 593-2002
E-mail: Info@schifferbooks.com.
Visit our web site at: www.schifferbooks.com
Please write for a free catalog.
This book may be purchased
from the publisher.
Try your bookstore first.

Contents

Preliminary Remarks

Many of the contributions to this chronicle were written from memory relate anumber of personal experiences.

Surely others have found that subjective reporting is often the most honest method of getting closest to the real events or – if one wishes to use the big word – the truth.

The Author

Acknowledgements

As representative of all of those who contributed in any way to the writing of this chronicle, I wish to thank:

Generalmajor (Rtd.) Karl-Eduard Wilke and
Oberstleutnant (Rtd.) Fritz O. Pockrandt

I also wish to thank my wife Barbara, who stood tirelessly by my side in the compilation of this chronicle, but especially in the writing of the manscript.

Foreword

This is the chronicle of a *Kampfgeschwader* compiled from the documents and reports provided by a number of former members of *Kampfgeschwader "Legion Condor" 53* who survived the war.

Roughly comparable to a regiment in strength, a Kampfgeschwader generally consisted of four *Gruppen* (comparable to battalions) and these in turn of *Staffeln* (comparable to companies).

The first, second and third *Gruppen* were operational units, each organized into three *Kampfstaffeln* and a *Stabsstaffel*, which was later reduced to a *Stabsschwarm*.

The fourth *Gruppe* was a creation in war that had not existed during peacetime. It was the training and replacement *Gruppe*.

During the war *Kampfgeschwader 53* saw action over Poland, France, England and Russia.

The title "Legion Condor" was awarded to the *Geschwader* in Berlin on 12 June 1939 after the end of the Spanish Civil War. Each member of the *Geschwader* wore the cuff title on his uniform.

This honorary title was simultaneously bestowed on a flak artillery and a signals regiment of the *Luftwaffe*.

Three *Kampfgeschwader* had previously been awarded similar honorary titles: KG 1 "Hindenburg", KG 4 "General Wever" and KG 27 "Boelcke."

The claim that units of KG 53 were deployed in Spain is legend. The volunteers who saw service in Spain came from all parts of the Luftwaffe.

This book is dedicated to our comrades who did not come back. We living owe a debt to the dead. This work shall thus be our thanks to them, who gave their lives true to their soldier's oath.

K. Ed. Wilke
Gen.Maj. (Rtd.)

I. The Period before the Second World War

1. VERSAILLES 1919

"This is no peace, it is a ceasefire for twenty years."

— *Marshall Ferdinand Foch at Versailles*

On 28 June 1919, representatives of the German government signed the harsh peace treaty in the Hall of Mirrors of the castle of Versailles, where the German Empire had been founded on 18 January 1871.

The few terms of the treaty concerning aviation were sufficient to throw Germany back to the status of the hot air balloons of the 18th Century.

The creation of an air force was forbidden. All military aircraft that had not yet been handed over to the allies were to be destroyed. Commercial aviation was seriously restricted because the advances made during the war could not be exploited. Article 201 said:

"The construction and importation of aircraft, aircraft components, aero engines and aero engine components is forbidden in all of Germany for a period of six months after this treaty comes into force."

The dictated peace took effect on 1 January 1920.

It was a matter of course, therefore, that in the years that followed repeated efforts were made, with varying degrees of success, to outwit the control commission.

One of the most significant opportunities to do this was the founding of the flying school in Lipetsk.

2. THE BEGINNINGS IN LIPETSK

During the Russian Revolution the airmen of the Red Army not only had to fight their former comrades of the White Russian side, but also met airmen of the Royal Air Force, who had come to Russia as part of the Allied expeditionary corps sent to crush the communist revolution. The Canadian Raymond Collishaw was particularly successful. The Red Air Force suffered such heavy casualties that it soon had few experienced pilots left. Faced with this situation, the Soviet leadership decided to work closely with the German *Reichswehr*, German designers, technicians and aviation specialists.

In Berlin *General* Hans von Seeckt formed *Sondergruppe R* (Special Group R, R = Russia) to work with the Russians and also create a German air force on foreign soil. Its commander was *Oberst* Nikolai, a former signals officer.

A number of other experienced officers joined the unit, such as *Oberst* Oskar von Niedermayer, *General* Otto Hasse and *Major* Kurt von Schleicher.

General von Seeckt dispatched a military mission, whose members were retired and disguised as civilians, to Moscow, where they remained on unspecified business.

Next followed an agreement that was signed in Rapallo on 16 April 1920. The way was clear, but it would be three more years before the first pilots could be trained in Russia. In July 1921 *Oberst* von Niedermayer visited Hugo Junkers in Dessau to discuss the production of aero engines and aircraft components. After initial hesitation Junkers agreed, but with the proviso that no military aircraft would be built, and on 15 March 1923 he signed a contract with *Sondergruppe R*. Junkers subsequently began building a small factory in Fili, near Moscow. Then, at the end of 1924, the Junkers factory, with a staff of 91 men, began building reconnaissance aircraft for the Red Army. On 28 May 1925 fifty Fokker D XIII fighter aircraft were loaded onto the freighter *Edmund Hugo Stinnes IV* in the port of Stettin. The freighter set course for Leningrad. From there the disassembled aircraft were loaded onto freight cars, the car doors were sealed, and armed guards climbed onto the roofs of the cars, manning improvised positions in preparation for a long trip in the open air.

Concerning the delivery and origins of these fifty fighter aircraft:

After the Versailles Treaty took effect, the German government tried to retain eight military airfields and at least a few squadrons of aircraft as part of the 100,000-man army. The counselor for the victorious powers, based in Paris, turned down the request, even though it was based on internal political justifications rather than military ones.

As a result of this decision, all of the army's aviation-related equipment, down to the last spare engine, had to be destroyed or surrendered, and the last flight engineers and aircraft mechanics had to be discharged.

An attempt to preserve some air force equipment and personnel in so-called Police Aviation Squadrons also failed, for in 1920 the squadrons had to be disbanded. Several years later – at the time of the Ruhr crisis in 1923 – this picture changed to a modest extent.

The German government was determined not to stand idly by in the face of French threats to march in and to meet such an invasion with force. Money from the so-called Ruhr Fund was used to order 100 fighter aircraft from the Dutch aircraft company Fokker.

Apart from the fact that the aircraft could not be delivered in time, there was no armed defense of the Ruhr.

But then a – to some extent unforeseen – use was found for the aircraft from Fokker: the German-Russian Rapallo Treaty. Fifty of the Fokker D XIIIs, then one of the most modern fighters anywhere, were dispatched to Lipetsk to the German "Stahr Flying School", named after its first commander *Major* (Rtd.) Stahr. After a brief stop in Moscow, the train headed south, crossed the Don Plain and arrived in Lipetsk, almost 400 kilometers south of Moscow and 1500 kilometers from Berlin. In that faraway region the *Reichswehr* hoped to create the nucleus of a new air force.

Lipetsk, situated near Voronezh, is an idyllic small town that had once been a spa town used by Peter the Great. The German soldiers, however, led a very ascetic existence.

Although the German technical staff had arrived in Lipetsk at the beginning of 1924, it wasn't until a year later that flying activities could commence.

The German flight cadets soon discovered, however, that from a military standpoint Lipetsk left nothing to be desired: two runways, an extensive infrastructure of hangars, maintenance facilities, workshops and all other types of administrative, technical and medical equipment, plus radio and telephone installations. By the standards of the day the entire installation could be described as up-to-date.

The size of the German group remained steady at about sixty throughout the year. As well there were about fifty flight students and 70 to 100 men engaged in testing. The installation was sealed off and guarded by Soviet military personnel. As well, there were many Soviet military personnel receiving training from German mechanics.

Among the first instructors were two First World War fighter pilots: Karl von Schönebeck and Werner Junck; however, they had fought against the Bolsheviks with the *Freikorps* in 1919 and were considered politically unreliable. Like all members of the *Reichswehr*, they travelled by a secret route that led from Stettin via Leningrad to Lipetsk. Reich President Ebert died on 28 February 1925 and was succeeded by 78-year-old *Generalfeldmarschall* von Hindenburg. At the same time Seeckt's star began to wane. He had harmed his position by going over the head of Minister of Defense Dr. Gessler at every opportunity and by doing so of course undermining his responsibility.

Seeckt resigned in October 1926. The domestic situation became even worse when, at a sitting of the *Reichstag* on 10 December 1926, Philipp Scheidemann, a Social-Democrat, complained that "... the *Reichswehr* has become a state within a state ..." and accordingly declared "... a Special Group R seems to exist ... we must put an end to this scandal. We can no longer tolerate a situation which conflicts with the creation of a truly republican and democratic army."

The aviation program continued to evolve. It was now also tightened up somewhat, with sixty pilots to be trained annually for the *Reichswehr* in future. Half were officers, ten of whom could have no flight training. The rest were officer candidates, who had received civilian flight training and only afterwards began their military careers.

These sixty flight cadets earned their B-2 flight rating in a one-year course in Schleissheim. The ten best graduates were sent to Lipetsk for fighter pilot training.

In Lipetsk the fighter training culminated in mock air battles between two squadrons, each of nine aircraft. "Victories" were confirmed on the basis of film from cameras mounted in the aircraft.

There were few accidents, which was largely due to the high performance level of the instructors, especially of the German *Werkmeister* Paul, who later became a *Generalingenieur* in the *Luftwaffe*, and the astonishing expertise of the Russian mechanics, fitters and specialists.

In summer 1928 *General* Werner von Blomberg, head of the *Truppenamt*, visited Russia for maneuvers near Voronezh.

He watched with satisfaction as the formations of Fokker fighter aircraft and the new Heinkel He 17 reconnaissance aircraft roared low over the heads of the Russian infantry and tanks.

Blomberg and his staff officers also visited the tank school near Kazan and then travelled on to Orenburg, where there was a test facility for poison gas.

After returning to Berlin he wrote a fifty-page report in which he expressed his enthusiasm over the reception given to the German officers by the Russians, which was everywhere friendly, often warm and very lavish. War Commissar Voroshilov had given instructions "to show us everything and grant all our wishes." He once again stressed the advantages of cooperation with the Red Army.

Lipetsk was not just a training center, but also a test facility for new machines produced by the German aviation industry. On 30 September 1929 Fritz von Opel took off from the Wasserkuppe in a rocket-powered glider and during a ten-minute flight – the burn duration of the rockets – achieved a speed of 160 kph.

At the same time designer Claude Dornier was watching the takeoff of his twelve-engine flying boat, the Do X, as it lifted off from Lake Constance with 169 persons, including nine stowaways, on board.

Then on 31 January 1931 the Do X, dubbed the world's first "air ship", took off from Lisbon with a crew of twelve on a flight to South America. It was the start of a goodwill flight of more than 40,000 kilometers that took it to the Bahamas, South America, Miami, New York and Newfoundland. Commander and director of the entire flight was *Kapitän* Friedrich Christiansen, a *Pour-le-mérite* hero and well-known seaplane pilot of the First World War, who later served for eight years as a captain for the Hamburg-America Line.

The flying boat's pilot was *Flugkapitän* Dipl.-Ing. Horst Merz, a naval pilot during the war. He had been made available for the flight by the airline *Lufthansa*.

Second pilots were: as far as Las Palmas the German-American Clarence Schildhauer, to Rio de Janeiro Cramer von Clausbruch, and from New York to Berlin Walter Diele.

The Do X received a jubilant welcome in New York on 27 August 1931. President Hoover received the crew in the White House. On 19 May 1932 the aircraft took off from New York to return to Berlin. The flight ended with a landing on the Müggelsee on 24 May. Because the Do X was too large for European routes and too small for trans-Atlantic flights, it ended up in the aviation museum at Berlin's Lehrter Station, where it was later destroyed by Allied bombing during the Second World War.

Between 1928 and 1930 new prototypes of military aircraft were tested in Lipetsk, far away from the League of Nation's disarmament commission and the suspicious eyes of some *Reichstag* deputies.

From the Arado Flugzeugwerken GmbH of Babelsberg near Berlin came the Arado Ar 64 and Ar 65, biplane fighter aircraft; from the Ernst Heinkel AG, Rostock-Marienehe, the He 38, a floatplane fighter aircraft (envisaged for trials with a wheeled undercarriage), plus the He 45 and He 46, tactical reconnaissance biplanes; and finally from the Junkers Flugzeug- und Motorenwerke AG of Dessau, the Junkers Ju (K) 47, an all-metal, low-wing two-seat monoplane fighter built by Junkers' Moscow-Fili plant in 1928. Incidentally 50 Napier Lion engines were used for a period of eight years. Each year the engines – which powered aircraft flown by Germans in Russia – went back to England for overhaul.

In keeping with the concepts of Italian General Giulio Douhet (Air Superiority), three prototypes of long-range bombers were developed in Germany and sent to Russia. The first was the Rohrbach Roland, which was nothing more than a developed version of the trimotor airliner used by *Lufthansa*.

The aircraft was not selected for quantity production, however. Dornier then developed the Do P, a four-engine bomber with a crew of six. The engines were installed in the wings a tandem arrangement similar to that of the Do X. This solution also proved unsatisfactory. Finally a compromise: Dornier produced the Do 11, which was based on the Do F cargo machine. There was no doubt that German designers could develop a four-engine machine, however the open production of a four-engined bomber would have been such a flagrant violation of the Treaty of Versailles that it would have meant, among other things, Germany's expulsion from the League of Nations, which in the existing situation would never have been allowed by the *Reichstag*. And so the Do 11 became the *Reichswehr*'s twin-engined heavy bomber. In 1931 the *Reichswehr* decided to gradually close the pilot and observer school in Lipetsk.

An agreement between the Federal Ministries of Transport and Foreign Affairs and the *Reichswehr* in November 1930 played a role in this decision. In strictest confidence the ministers agreed to disregard the provisions of the Treaty of Versailles which limited the production and stockpiling of aviation equipment. In practice this was equivalent to the formation of an air force within the borders of the German Reich.

A secret testing station was established in Rechlin, Mecklenburg. Lipetsk was abandoned within two years and the facility at Rechlin was systematically expanded.

During fall maneuvers in Silesia in 1931, small free balloons were supposed to simulate air support for the troops. This discrimination displeased the minister responsible for the *Reichswehr*, Wilhelm Gröner. Twelve pilots were subsequently sent to Germany from Lipetsk. They formed three *Staffeln* each with four Arado Ar 65 aircraft. These pilots did not return to Lipetsk, instead they and their aircraft were stationed in Berlin, Königsberg and Nuremberg. To conceal their true purpose they were rented out to private companies for advertising purposes.

The observer school in Lipetsk was closed at the end of 1932, while the last fighter pilot course took place in the summer of 1933. With high-level German-Soviet military cooperation functioning better than ever – Marshall Tukhachevsky attended the *Reichswehr* maneuvers of 1932 and was given a warm welcome by Reich President Hindenburg – the Soviets were less than pleased by the closure of Lipetsk. Moscow wanted to restore the Lipetsk operation to its original scope and also wanted to observe a demonstration of night bombing there. They were determined that the training and testing center should continue to exist.

Soviet pilots had been able to fly the latest German types in Lipetsk, their mechanics had learned from German experts, and the Soviets had been given access to manuals of a tactical and technical nature.

After several tough discussions the Russians finally gave in. The fixed airfield installations would be turned over to the air forces of the Red Army, while the prototypes of the German bomber were flown back to Germany. At the request of the Soviets, the remaining Do XIII aircraft were left there.

Thus ended the Lipetsk operation. It had lasted ten years, with six years of use as a training facility. During that time 120 fighter pilots and 100 observers had been trained there.

Last but not least:

Generalmajor (Rtd.) D.K.Ed. Wilke, born 1901, author of the foreword and *Kommodore* of KG 53 from November 1942 to March 1943, arrived in Lipetsk on 1 May 1928. Of those days he recalled:

"I was with the school from 1 May 1928 to 15 October 1929, initially as a 'student', and from 1 October 1928 as head of the photo section.

We were three Germans and nine Russians. The latter (very clever, modest and diligent) were trained according to our doctrine.

I had received my commission on 1/8/1926 and arrived in Lipetsk as an *Oberleutnant* (retired). We were discharged for the time we were there, and after my return I returned to service with the 1st (Prussian) Artillery Regiment in Königsberg (Prussia)."

3. FURTHER DEVELOPMENT AS A SECRET AIR FORCE

On 2 February 1933 Hermann Göring was named Reich Commissar for Aviation by Reich President Hindenburg.

At that time the Air Defense Office (*Luftschutzamt* or *LS-Amt*) already existed and was directly subordinate to the Defense Minister. This office had its origins in the days of *General* von Seeckt.

Effective 1 April 1933, the army and navy air operations staffs were combined in the *LS-Amt*. It is almost certain that this office would have been established even without the change of government on 30 January 1933, just as the *Reichswehr* would have established army and navy air units. At that juncture there had been absolutely no contact between any aviation office of the *Reichswehr* and Hermann

Göring. During an inspection of the aviation testing facility in Rechlin in March 1933, Göring was visibly astonished by the high level of research being carried out.

On 27 April 1933 the Reich President ordered the establishment of the *Reichsluftfahrtministerium* (State Aviation Ministry or RLM), which was formed from the Reich commissariat and placed under Defense Minister von Blomberg, who at that time had the title of "Reich Defense Minister" and Commander of the Armed Forces.

This fact of military subordination under von Blomberg could leave no doubt as to the official connection between the entire secret armed forces aviation branch and Göring and his state secretary Erhard Milch.

Effective 15 May 1933, von Blomberg ordered the transfer of the *Luftschutzamt* to the State Aviation Ministry. It was initially quartered in the inner city of Berlin before moving to its ultimate home on Leipziger Strasse.

This order by von Blomberg can be characterized as the starting point for the *Luftwaffe*, whereby, as it later turned out, the way was paved for the third branch of the armed services.

The other branches of the armed services were not exactly thrilled about the removal of aviation units from the army and navy. Keitel, then an *Oberst*, had to use his influence as head of the army's organizational department to prevent the army aviation units returning to army control. In November 1933 the naval staff also complained about the sole power of command of the State Minister of Aviation and argued that, "… a navy without an air arm is in no position to completely carry out its duties." All objections proved fruitless, however, as would be shown a few years later.

By August 1933 the RLM organized itself into two large ministries, one military and one civil.

The military section was the *Luftschutzamt* (LS or LA), with overall responsibility for air command and air organization, whereas the civilian branch was largely responsible for aviation technology.

Effective 1 September 1939, the *Luftschutzamt* was renamed the *Luftkommandoamt* and the ministry was reorganized. This reorganization meant the establishment of a secret general staff. The foundation for the creation of the *Luftwaffe* had been laid, all that was missing was aviation units.

In 1933 there existed three advertising squadrons, in Berlin-Staaken, Königsberg (Prussia) and Fürth. These served as military "forward outposts" for the training of pilots. At that time there were also military training installations at the civilian flight schools in Brandenburg, Jüterbog, Schleissheim, Würzburg and Warnemünde (for seaplane pilots).

In Rendsburg there were two troops of army motor transport battalions as cadres for non-commissioned and enlisted personnel, future flight engineers, radio operators, gunners and aviation ground personnel.

The first unit to be formed was a fighter squadron (*Jagdstaffel*), created from the advertising squadrons.

The establishment of an interim bomber wing (*Behelfsbomb-engeschwader*) began in October 1933. On the basis of mobilization preparations by the army department", the airline *Deutsche Lufthansa* (DLH) provided personnel and facilities.

As additional units were created, the number of training airfields gradually became inadequate. From the end of 1933, therefore, the air force administration office's main task became searching for new facilities.

What could be more logical then than to use and dispose freely of the existing airfields and seaplane bases of the German Commercial Pilot's School (DVS), Luftdienst GmbH, the German Aviation Sports Association (DLV) and the Reich Association of the German Aviation Industry (RdDLI). The airfields involved were located in Neuhausen near Königsberg, Staaken near Berlin, Rechlin, Tutow, Kottbus, Schleissheim, Lechfeld and Kitzingen. There were also the seaplane bases in Holtenau near Kiel, Warnemünde, Nordeney, List/Sylt and Travemünde.

In October 1933 the Aviation Technical School in Jüterbog assumed responsibility for the training of aviation technical personnel, originally trained in civilian maintenance shops, operational facilities and aircraft factories. The school had an annual capacity of 1,500 students. Its first commander was Kurt Student, who later rose to the rank of *Generaloberst*.

The *Luftwaffe*, like the rest of the military, expanded rapidly following the start of Germany's military buildup in 1933.

The reorganization of the RLM with the associated transfers of personnel in the various offices and departments was completed by the end of 1933.

Formation of the six *Luftkreiskommandos* (Air District Commands) in Königsberg, Berlin, Dresden, Münster, Munich and Kiel began on 1 April 1934.

As before, of course, there was still a need for concealment. For this reason the air district commands were called "senior air offices" and for the same reason their commanders were "presidents." They were *General* Wachenfeld in Air District (LK) I Königsberg, *General* Kaupisch in LK II Berlin, *General* Schweickhardt in LK III Dresden, *General* Halm in LK IV Münster, *General* Ebert in LK V Munich and Admiral Zander in LK VI (See) in Kiel.

At the same time the first air division (*Fliegerdivision*) was formed. Its commander was *Oberst* Sperrle.

The first flying units also underwent significant expansion. From the air advertising department with three squadrons (*Staffeln*) and DLH's interim bomber wing were created five reconnaissance squadrons, three fighter squadrons and five bomber squadrons, plus a maritime reconnaissance squadron, a floatplane fighter squadron, a multipurpose maritime squadron and an air service towing squadron.

Also on 1 April 1934, *Jagdgeschwader 132* was formed in Döberitz near Berlin under the command of the *1. Fliegerdivision*. This was the *Luftwaffe*'s first fighter unit and it was equipped with Ar 65 and He 51 aircraft.

In the course of 1934, *Kampfgeschwader 154* was established in Fassberg with three *Staffeln* (1. to 3./154) and *Kampfgeschwader 252* in Tutow with two *Staffeln* (1. and 2./252). The interim bomber wing was assigned the number 172.

Three reconnaissance squadrons, also created in 1934, were attached to the army's air division. They were based in Neuhausen near Königsberg (1/121), Prenzlau (2/121) and Grossenhain (3/121).

The two *H(Heeres)-Staffeln* (army squadrons) were based in Kottbus (1/113) and Gotha (2/114).

At the same time, training activity at the schools increased significantly. In 1934 the command responsible for air armaments schools and aviation technical schools had under it:

the aerial reconnaissance school in Brunswick and Hildesheim,

the bomber school in Lechfeld and Prenzlau,

the fighter school in Schleissheim,

air gunner's courses in Schleissheim and Lechfeld,

the Aviation Technical School in Jüterbog with branches in Berlin and Adlershof.

There was also a Pilot Training School Command, to which were attached the flight training schools in Kottbus, Neuruppin, Celle, Gotha and Kitzingen.

The first floatplane fighter squadron (1/135) was formed in Kiel-Holtenau, the multipurpose maritime squadron (1/286) in List on Sylt on 1 August 1934 and the maritime reconnaissance squadron (1/116) in Holtenau on 1 September 1934.

A fourth squadron was under formation on Nordeney at the beginning of 1935. Like the land-based units, the float- and seaplane units had their own schools.

In the spring of 1935, with no more need for concealment, the result was: 20 land and maritime squadrons, and 20 land and maritime flight training schools or courses.

By the time the veil of secrecy was lifted from the air force, the Air Force Administration Office had available 23 bases for land- and water-based units. Fourteen other airfields were under construction, including Gablingen and Schwäbisch Hall.

The following is a list of installations needed by a flying unit or flight training school for practice and training operations: landing field, runways, hangars, refueling installations, repair facilities, air traffic control, radio, DF homing and telephone stations, living quarters, classrooms, security installations and track systems. The Jüterbog Air Arsenal was created in 1934 to stockpile and supply the units with equipment, weapons, ammunition and fuel.

At that time there were about sixty officers serving in the Ministry of Aviation. In 1934 the intake of officers from the army and navy consisted mainly of young officers and officer candidates who had volunteered for flight training. In 1935 a growing number of active police officers also joined the *Luftwaffe*.

Particularly numerous were young civilian pilots, who joined the *Luftwaffe* and were promoted to *Leutnant* after a brief period of military training. Most squadron and flight leaders were flying officers who had received training in Lipetsk.

The first officer candidate course, still given by the Infantry School in Dresden, began in 1935. The first *Luftwaffe* officer training school (*Luftkriegsschule*) was set up in Berlin-Gatow on 1 April 1935. The various air sports associations and organizations were combined to form the German Air Sports Association (DLV). Under the State Minister of Aviation, it represented the *Luftwaffe* reserve.

4. THE *LUFTWAFFE* BECOMES AN INDEPENDENT BRANCH OF THE ARMED SERVICES

On 25 February 1935 von Blomberg authorized the State Minister of Aviation " to carry out the unveiling at a pace to be determined by him."

After the death of Hindenburg, Hitler became *Führer* and Reich Chancellor and thus supreme commander of the armed services.

On 26 February 1935 Hitler signed the decree making the *Luftwaffe* the third independent branch of the armed services.

Hitler originally wanted the air force to be called the "*Reichsluftwaffe*." This title never caught on, however, and it soon became just "*Luftwaffe*" in general parlance. The decree took effect on 1 March 1935.

The *Luftwaffe* was a special branch of the armed services. The British air arm only achieved similar independence after a three-year struggle following the First World War and the American air arm not until 1947.

The "Law for the Building of the Air Force" was enacted on 16 March 1935, and this was followed by a law for universal compulsory military service on 21 May. After 1 March 1935 basically nothing changed in the organization of the RLM as the supreme command authority – several new offices were created, that was all.

The rules revising the designation of offices took effect on 1 June 1935. Among the changes in titles was the switch from "*Reichswehr*" to "*Wehrmacht*."

The *Luftwaffe*'s building plan of 29 August 1935 envisaged the formation of 18 *Gruppe* headquarters (*Gruppenstäbe*) and 13 *Geschwader* headquarters (*Geschwaderstäbe*) of fighter, bomber and reconnaissance units by 1 October 1938.

A total of 126 air base garrison headquarters and a series of offices and institutions were created for the ground organization.

To disguise the true strength and composition of the air force, all of its units were designated *Fliegergruppen* (air groups) or *Fliegerstaffeln* (air squadrons). For example, the fighter group I/132 was designated *Fliegergruppe Döberitz*, the bomber group II/152 *Fliegergruppe Greifswalde* and dive-bomber group I/162 *Fliegergruppe Schwerin*.

The pace of formation of new units was accelerated in the spring of 1935. Existing units released personnel to form cadres for new units. This multiplication process was universally referred to as "mother units-daughter units."

In 1935 three air units were awarded honorary titles: in March *Jagdgruppe I/132* in Döberitz became the "*Richthofen Geschwader*." On 3 April 1935 bomber group I/154 in Fassberg became the "*Boelcke Geschwader*" and on the same day dive-bomber group I/162 in Schwerin assumed the title of "*Immelmann Geschwader*."

The described multiplication process continued until 1938, with 1936 going down as the year of cell division.

All of the newly formed units became fully operational in July 1936. The bomber wing headquarters were:

152	in Greifswald
153	in Merseburg
253	in Gotha
154	in Hanover
155	in Gablingen

In the spring of 1936 the following newly formed bomber groups were attached to these:

III/152	in Barth
III/153	in Altenburg
II/253	in Erfurt
III/253	in Nordhausen
II/154	in Delmenhorst
I/254	in Wunstorf
II/155	in Gablingen and
III/155	in Schwäbisch Hall

As a result of these moves, in 1936 the bomber arm's strength grew by five bomber wing headquarters and eight bomber groups. Total strength was now five bomber wings (*Kampfgeschwader*) and fifteen bomber groups (*Kampfgruppen*).

With respect to bomber units, this represented half of the units called for by the formation program by 1938, proof of the expansion program's efficiency.

On 1 June 1936 the concealment measures were finally lifted and unit designations were expressed openly – for example *Kampfgruppe I/155*. As in 1935, additional honorary titles were awarded: *Kampfgeschwader 152* was given the name "*Hindenburg*", while *Kampfgeschwader 253* was awarded the name "*General Wever*" immediately after the tragic death of the Chief of the General Staff on 3 June 1936.

The formation of airfield operating companies (FBK) began in 1937, in order to make the flying units less dependent on airfields, even in peacetime. These were supposed to be available to service and maintain the equipment of their respective *Gruppen*. Each FBK was organized into an aircraft maintenance group and three technical operations platoons. These were responsible for ensuring that the technical requirements of the *Staffeln* and *Kampfgruppen* were met.

The year 1937 saw the sharpest increase in the pace of expansion, particularly with respect to the bomber units. By the end of the year the bomber arm had eleven *Geschwader* headquarters and thirty bomber groups, each with three squadrons.

In 1938 the rate of increase in all types of units declined noticeably. In the bomber arm, however, the number of *Geschwader* headquarters grew to fourteen. Overall the *Luftwaffe* achieved its growth target in the year 1938.

By the autumn of 1938 there were eight flight training schools in Celle, Kitzingen, Fürth, Ludwigslust, Magdeburg, Neuruppin, Perleberg and Salzwedel, plus pilot courses in Celle, Brandis and Gablingen.

For tactical training there were the reconnaissance pilot schools in Brunswick and Hildesheim, the fighter pilot school in Schleissheim, bomber pilot schools in Fassberg, Jüterbog, Lechfeld, Prenzlau and Tutow, and for the fleet air arm the maritime pilot schools in Warnemünde and Travemünde.

A command and control office was created to oversee training of aviation technical personnel at the technical schools in Jüterbog and Berlin-Adlershof.

The training installations underwent another major expansion in spring 1938, especially the flight training, bomber and aviation-technical schools.

With respect to the signals troops, the reader is referred to the account by Heinz Waldhecker that appears later.

5. OPERATIONS PRIOR TO THE SECOND WORLD WAR

In the years 1935 to 1938 the *Luftwaffe* conducted operations which had a demonstrative nature. With the entry into the Rhineland on 7 March 1936, the demilitarized zone was remilitarized. Following a demonstration flight over the area, *Staffeln* of III/JG 134 and I/Stuka 165 landed at Cologne-Butzweilerhof, Frankfurt/Main and Mannheim.

On 31 July 1937, *General der Flieger* Milch, in his capacity of State Secretary for Aviation, bade farewell to 86 *Luftwaffe* volunteers bound for Spain to fight under the Nationalist flag in the Spanish Civil War. It was the foundation of the German unit which in November 1936 was named the "*Legion Condor.*"

At that time a bomber squadron, which ultimately became *Kampfgruppe K88* with about ten *Staffeln*, was formed from the air transport unit. The Legion also included a flak battalion with five gun batteries, searchlight batteries, signals units and supply installations.

Commanding the *"Legion Condor"* in Spain was *Generalmajor* Sperrle with his chief-of-staff *Oberstleutnant* Holle and, from 1937, *Oberstleutnant* von Richthofen.

Sperrle was succeeded as commander of the Legion by *Generalmajor* Volkmann Finally, in November 1938, von Richthofen became the last commander of the *"Legion Condor"*, with *Oberstleutnant* Seidemann as chief-of-staff.

The *"Legion Condor"* was subordinate to the commander-in-chief of the *Luftwaffe*. On average its personnel numbered 5,000 officers, non-commissioned officers, enlisted men, officials and employees. At no time did the Legion have more than 5,500 members. There was a continuous exchange of personnel. Much earlier in the war the Republican forces were bolstered by foreign volunteers of the "International Brigade", far outstripping the *"Legion Condor"* in numbers.

Hauptmann Lützow wrote about the action in Spain: "The struggle for a foreign people ... the responsibility for high-value personnel never allowed the passion of the fighter pilot to fully develop ... The fact that we suffered few losses despite being outnumbered can be attributed to the other side's inadequate training and poor planning as well as the superior speed of our fighters (Bf 109)."

The Legion Condor's deployment officially ended with a victory parade in Barcelona on 21 February 1939.

The Legion's losses totaled 420 men. 96 German aircraft were lost, 40 of them due to enemy action.

Göring welcomed the *Legion Condor* on its return to Hamburg. This was followed by a parade before Adolf Hitler in Berlin in which all of the soldiers who had served in Spain (about 20,000) took part.

The *Legion Condor* then ceased to exist. It was disbanded and its personnel returned to their original units.

It was at this time that the last honorary title was awarded to a *Kampfgeschwader*. On 12 June 1939 KG 53 was given the titled *Kampfgeschwader "Legion Condor" Nr.53*. Over the course of time the "Nr.53" was dropped. Other Geschwader were named after their unit emblem, for example KG 51 *"Edelweiss"* and KG 55 *"Greif"* (Griffon).

Even while the Spanish Civil War was still going on, the *Luftwaffe* made preparations for its next action.

On 11 March 1938 Hitler ordered preparations to begin for the military occupation of Austria. The *Luftwaffe* mobilized mainly bomber *Staffeln*, which on 12 March 1938 dropped leaflets over the Austrian capital city, while transport aircraft landed in Vienna. The *Luftwaffe* units taking part were under the command of *Generalmajor* Wolf of Air District V. After landing at Vienna-Aspern on 12 March 1938 he also assumed command of the Wels, Vienna-Aspern, Wiener Neustadt and Klagenfurt airports. Following the incorporation of the Austrian air force on 16 March, Göring named its last commander, Lohr, as commanding general of the *Luftwaffe* in Austria. *Oberstleutnant* Korten became chief-of-staff. 500 *Luftwaffe* aircraft took part in the entry into the Sudetenland by German forces on 1 October 1938. A few days later, on 10 October 1938, the *Wehrmacht* High Command reported that the *Luftwaffe* had taken over the installations and facilities of the Czech air force in the "occupied region" of Czechoslovakia.

Because of their success, these three operations created a great deal of respect at home and abroad. This was intended and desired, for the leaders of the Reich were very interested in an overestimation of German strength. This assessment by foreign powers helped Hitler achieve foreign policy successes.

Before the Second World War began, Germany occupied the rest of Czechoslovakia and the Memel District. The *Luftwaffe* participated in both actions. It made a demonstration flight over Prague with several hundred aircraft on 17 March 1939, and on 23 march units of *Luftwaffe* Command East Prussia crossed the East Prussian-Lithuanian border and circled over Memel for an hour. The aerial parade was repeated over the Memel District in the afternoon.

In June 1939 the *Luftwaffe* numbered 12,000 officers and 320,000 non-commissioned officers and enlisted men. The *Luftwaffe* Personnel Office planned to increase these numbers to 556,000 men by fall, but it came nowhere close to reaching this goal. Before mobilization swelled the ranks of the units, the air arm and parachute troops numbered 208,000 men, the anti-aircraft artillery 107,000 and the signals troops 58,000.

In August 1939 the number of aircrew stood at about 20,000 men, with a slight preponderance in pilots compared to observers, radio operators and flight engineers. The *Luftwaffe* had about 370,000 personnel, of which approximately 15,000 were officers, in August 1939. It had approximately 1,300 bomber crews (pilot, observer, radio operator and flight engineer) ready for combat plus 160 strategic reconnaissance crews, 150 seaplane crews and 450 transport aircraft crews. The majority of the pilots were ELF pilots, meaning they held the advanced pilot rating and were also qualified for blind flying (instrument flight at night and in bad weather). The observers and radio operators held similar qualifications in their fields.

Battle training for bomber crews included day and night navigation flights, formation flying and bomb-dropping from various altitudes.

The day before the war started, the *Luftwaffe* Quartermaster-General listed the air force's operational strength in a report:

1,180 bomber aircraft

771 fighter aircraft

336 dive-bombers

408 heavy fighters (*Zerstörer*)

40 close-support aircraft

552 transport aircraft

379 reconnaissance aircraft (strategic)

342 reconnaissance aircraft (tactical)

240 seaplanes

55 aircraft attached to special units

———

4,333 aircraft in total

In 1938 orders were issued for the replanning of air armaments for the period until 1942; just one year later, however, the *Luftwaffe* had to face its baptism by fire.

II. Building up the Air Force

1. THE FORMATION OF NEW UNITS

The formation of new units had begun rapidly in 1935. The men came from the army, from the navy and from the police. The experience of Gustav-Adolf Klüter, who describes his time at the "Geyerhorst" in Giebelstadt near Würzburg, is typical:

"More than 180 young graduates, students and pilots in training were trained by the *Kriegsmarine* in the period from 1 April 1934 to autumn 1936. When the new air force was created, its existing cadre of officers was supplemented by similar size groups from the army and the police.

The navy gave us tough, outstanding training and was confidently able to release the 'Göring cadets', as we were called, to the *Luftwaffe* as officer candidates. Our 'Crew 34' was split up and sent to observer and pilot schools for basic flight training. In October 35, I and about forty comrades arrived at the bomber school in Tutow, Pomerania, where our arrival as officer candidates in naval uniforms caused quite a stir. After being kitted out in *Luftwaffe* uniforms, we began theoretical and flight training to become bomber observers. Our first much anticipated flight was a familiarization flight in a Ju 52 so that we could get to know the local area 'from above'. Then we began scouting flights in He 45 and He 46 aircraft, during which we had to observe and record the number of trains at local stations, the number of cars, locomotives and their direction of travel. After many hours of training on the bomb sight, we nervously dropped our first cement bombs from a Do 11. It happened this way: the bombing instructor *Hptm.* Mehnert, called 'Max Pumpe' because he came from Saxony, bent over the students who lay on the floor bent over the bomb sight, and when in his opinion the drop point had been reached, gave us a sharp kick in the sternpost, whereupon the student had to immediately operate the bomb release lever; the results were what one would expect! I had the unusual good fortune to place my bomb in the middle of the target circle several times, as a result of which I received high marks from 'Max Pumpe'. During the war I never had a chance to try it out in the He 111, as by then I had become a pilot. The entry into the Rhineland happened halfway through our training, and the order was given for all officer candidates to be sent to the existing flying groups. We had the advantage of being able to choose from the existing flying groups, and about ten comrades and I, a northern-German, decided on Bavaria, specifically Giebelstadt near Würzburg.

We arrived at Würzburg station on a beautiful spring day, a great feeling after the wintry weather in Tutow. Of course, before leaving on the bus for Giebelstadt we tried our first *Boxbeutel* (a Franconian wine specialty) at the station. Many more were to follow in Giebelstadt. Then we set off through the spring-like Main Valley with the first peach blossoms towards our new home in Giebelstadt, where we were immediately divided among the *Staffeln*. *Fliegergruppe Giebelstadt*, as it was called before the *Geschwader* was formed, consisted of three *Staffeln* equipped with Do 23s, several Ju 52s and W 34s plus a few training aircraft. On the noses of the Do 23s was the 'Geyer (Vulture) Emblem', consisting of a vulture's talon in red on a white field, a sign that Florian Geyer (a knight who led during the Peasants' War of 1525) came from Giebelstadt, where he had a castle whose ruins still stand today and where 'Florian Geyer' is performed every year in competition with Jagsthausen:

> *'We are Geyer's black band,*
> *Heia, hoho!'*

At every opportunity this song of defiance rang out through the interim officer's accommodation building, which was called the 'plywood canteen'.

In the *Staffeln* we were welcomed by the *Staffelkapitän* and turned over to the more senior *Leutnants*, who had been there almost a year already, for further training as bomber observers. With crewmates Langer (†), Piecha (†) and Bartens (†) I was assigned to *Major* Heidenreich's 2. *Staffel*, and for the time being *Leutnant* Herbert Wittmann became our mentor and instructor.

Organizationally *Fliegergruppe Giebelstadt* was attached to the soon to be formed *Kampfgeschwader 155* whose headquarters were in Ansbach. Its *II. Gruppe* was formed in Gablingen near Augsburg and moved to Ansbach, the *I. Gruppe* was based in Giebelstadt, the *III. Gruppe* in Schwäbisch Hall. The *Geschwader*'s commander was *Oberst* Dessloch, who became a highly-decorated air fleet commander later in the war. In June 1939 the *Geschwader*, along with a flak and signals regiment, received the honorary title '*Legion Condor*'.

Oberstleutnant Speidel, the *Gruppenkommandeur*, who was relieved by *Major* Weber in February 36, was also air base commander. The organization was later changed a little when a dedicated air base garrison headquarters with all the associated units (air base company, maintenance facility, signals company, administration) was formed. This air base group was originally under the flying *Gruppenkommandeur*, but a year later it was attached to the newly-formed Airfield Command. This command agency was subordinate to the *Luftgau* (air region) and thus formed the lines of command of the ground organization (Air Region) and the flying units (Senior Air Command, later Flying Corps), all of which was subordinate to Air Fleet 3 in Munich.

Our training consisted of further theoretical study in the weapons and bombing fields, radio procedures, navigation classes and operational tasks in preparation for the observer test and flight training.

Each month the *Staffeln* were sent to Gelnhausen, an operational base near Bad Orb, for two days to put theory into practice by dropping cement bombs and firing from the air at ground targets. We always enjoyed these deployments, for living in tents and flying, combined with new, independent tasks, seemed appealing to us.

After the *Führer*'s birthday parade on 20 April 1936, we 15 *Oberfähnriche* were promoted to *Leutnants* and took over the tasks of weapons, radio and bombing officer along with technical and training functions. We now began to teach ourselves. Among veteran instrument-qualified pilots, we were initiated into the secrets of flying.

As I was responsible for continued military training in the *Staffel*, in the summer of 1936 I was given a platoon of reserve officer candidates for basic training, as we 'Göring cadets' had learned plenty about the infantry. I was later transferred to Aircrew Replacement Battalion 15 in Neubiberg and had no idea that I would see the 'Geyerhorst' again exactly two years later."

2. GIEBELSTADT-GABLINGEN-ANSBACH-SCHWÄBISCH HALL

On 18 December 1935 the Reich Minister of Aviation and Commander-in-Chief of the *Luftwaffe* issued the order "for the formation of air units in the third formation phase." As a result, effective 1 April 1936 bomber units were formed in Air District Commands II, III, IV and V. Within Air District Command V, the headquarters of *Kampfgeschwader 155* was formed in Ansbach, *Kampfgruppe* II/155 likewise in Ansbach and III/155 in Schwäbisch Hall. Until the base in Ansbach was ready to accept units, the formation of the headquarters of KG 155, *Kampfgruppe II/155* and *Kampfstaffeln 4-6/155* took place in Gablingen.

The newly-formed *Kampfgeschwader 155*, with the *Geschwaderstab* and *Gruppenstäbe II* and *III* with their *Staffeln* came from *3./ Kampfgeschwader 252* (Tutow). While the headquarters and *Staffeln* of the first *Gruppe* are not expressly mentioned in this order, many orders overlapped during the formation process and there were corrections. As well, many documents were lost in the postwar turmoil. We can assume that as of 1 April 1936, in addition to *Fliegergruppe Tutow*, *Fliegergruppe Giebelstadt* (formerly KG 455) also joined KG 155 and formed its *I. Gruppe*.

KG 355 was renamed KG 155 effective 1 April 1937. The unit received its ultimate designation on 1 May 1939, when KG 355 became KG 53. This development is illustrated by a chart on Page 33.

In the course of the "cell division" process, but also for reasons of concealment, other *Geschwader* were certainly created from *Geschwader 252, 155* and *355* (e.g. KG 76, KG 2, KG 55), however the formation process as described for KG 53 will suffice for this chronicle. The *Geschwader* designation adopted on 1 May 1939 remained unchanged until the end of the war.

As of 1 May 1939 the *Geschwader* were assigned numerically to the air fleets, specifically:

> *Luftflotte 1 Geschwader* Nos. 1-25
>
> *Luftflotte 2 Geschwader* Nos. 26-50
>
> *Luftflotte 3 Geschwader* Nos. 52-75
>
> *Luftflotte 4 Geschwader* Nos. 76-100

Thus there existed the *Geschwader* headquarters of KG 1 "*Hindenburg*", 2, 3, 4 "*General Wever*", 26, 27 "*Boelcke*", 51, 53, 54, 55, 76 and 77. The headquarters of *Lehrgeschwader (LG) 1* also counted as a *Kampfgeschwader*. Among these thirteen *Geschwader* headquarters, to each of which was attached a *Stabsstaffel* (staff squadron), there were 30 *Kampfgruppen* with a total of 90 *Kampfstaffeln*. KG 53's bases were now: *I. Gruppe* Ansbach, *II. Gruppe* Schwäbisch Hall, *III. Gruppe* Giebelstadt.

Before another personal account from the formation period, first a look back at KG 53's *Stabsstaffel* and the function of this special unit.

After the formation of the *Kampfgeschwader*, in 1938 a *Stabsstaffel* was attached to each *Geschwader*. Each had nine crews of five men, one of whom was an officer. The *Staffel* had its own servicing personnel and a mobile photo unit.

Like the rest of the *Geschwader*, the *Stabsstaffel* was equipped with He 111s, however its aircraft were all equipped with enhanced photographic and radio equipment.

The *Stabsstaffel* was a leadership organ of the *Geschwader* and was intended for day and night reconnaissance, target survey and target photography missions.

The *Stabsstaffel* was supposed to constantly monitor the *Geschwader*'s area of operations, provide photographs of targets and take and evaluate post-strike photos.

During its existence, the *Stabsstaffel* was commanded by *Hptm.* Kerber (1/5/38 – 1/7/39), *Hptm.* Wittmann (1/7/39 – 14/10/41) and *Hptm.* Von Horn (14/10/41 – 15/3/42, MIA).

The following information from Alfred Sticht's record shows what was involved in a move from the police to a flying unit:

4/4/34 – 30/9/34	Bamberg Police School
1/10/34 – 8/5/35	8th State Police Group of Hundred, Fürth
9/5/35 – 30/4/36	Air Base Garrison Headquarters Fürth
1/5/36 – 15/10/36	*Fliegergruppe (S) Lechfeld, Stabsstaffel*

Sticht was accepted into the *Luftwaffe* as an *Unteroffizier* and on 1 August 1939 was promoted to *Feldwebel*, and after reserve exercises with the *Bundeswehr* is now a *Major der Reserve*. He completed the bomber observer course at Lager Lechfeld on 15 October 1936 and was transferred to the 5. *Staffel* of KG 155 in Gablingen near Augsburg. Soon afterwards the unit was moved to Ansbach.

At Ansbach, Sticht carried out cross-country flights, navigation and DF homing flights, practice bombing and orientation flights, bomb dropping and simulated combat with Ju 52, W 34, Ar 66 and Fw 44 aircraft.

After his transfer to 1./KG 355 on 13 March 1937, he conducted additional cross-country, radio, navigation and homing flights, practice bombing with cement bombs, aerial combat, air gunnery and formation flying in the Ju 52.

In the period from 12 to 27 September 1937 the Ju 52 crew made up of *Fw.* Schimpl (pilot), *Uffz.* Sticht, *Uffz.* Schuster and *Fw.* Gewalt took part in the 1937 *Wehrmacht* maneuvers in the Merseburg-Schivelbein-Königsberg area. Each *Staffel* sent one aircraft to take part. At Gablingen there were further navigation flights until April 1938, when the unit was moved again, to Ansbach. There the *Staffel* was already largely equipped with the He 111, although four Ju 52s, three Fw 58s, one W 34 and one Go 145 remained. At Ansbach training was intensified and deepened. Then, at the beginning of

May, the crew of *Oblt.* Allmendinger, *Uffz.* Sticht, *Fw.* Schuster and *Uffz.* Paetau was sent to the Long-Range School in Köthen for the duration of one month.

For aircrew training, since 1938 the Air Signals Experimental Regiment in Köthen had been conducting flights abroad to Tripoli, Las Palmas (Canary Islands) and Debreczen (Hungary). These flights were intended to test new radio navigation aids and further blind flying training. The sorry state of blind flying training was illustrated by a radio navigation check flight from Ostfriesland to the Humber Estuary, in which the commander of *Luftflotte 2*, *General der Flieger* Felmy, took part along with his leading navigation experts. Although the weather was good, they missed their target point by fifty kilometers. A second attempt was made but the results were even worse.

It was obvious that a further period of intensive training was required before the air force could be considered ready for the worst case.

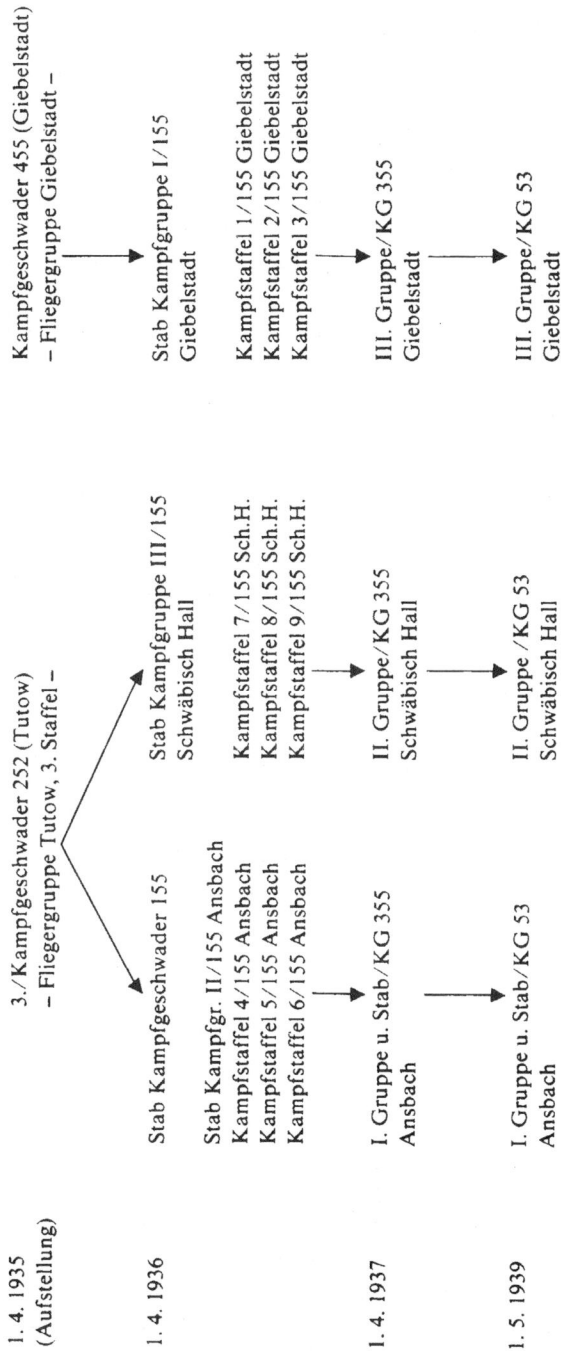

1. 4. 1935
(Aufstellung)

3./Kampfgeschwader 252 (Tutow)
– Fliegergruppe Tutow, 3. Staffel –

Kampfgeschwader 455 (Giebelstadt)
– Fliegergruppe Giebelstadt –

1. 4. 1936

Stab Kampfgeschwader 155

Stab Kampfgruppe III/155
Schwäbisch Hall

Stab Kampfgruppe I/155
Giebelstadt

Stab Kampfgr. II/155 Ansbach
Kampfstaffel 4/155 Ansbach
Kampfstaffel 5/155 Ansbach
Kampfstaffel 6/155 Ansbach

Kampfstaffel 7/155 Sch.H.
Kampfstaffel 8/155 Sch.H.
Kampfstaffel 9/155 Sch.H.

Kampfstaffel 1/155 Giebelstadt
Kampfstaffel 2/155 Giebelstadt
Kampfstaffel 3/155 Giebelstadt

1. 4. 1937

I. Gruppe u. Stab/KG 355
Ansbach

II. Gruppe/KG 355
Schwäbisch Hall

III. Gruppe/KG 355
Giebelstadt

1. 5. 1939

I. Gruppe u. Stab/KG 53
Ansbach

II. Gruppe /KG 53
Schwäbisch Hall

III. Gruppe/KG 53
Giebelstadt

31

3. KÖTHEN LONG-DISTANCE SCHOOL

Alfred Sticht described his assignment to the long-distance school in Köthen:

"On 21 April 1939, a beautiful spring day, I was advised by *Oberleutnant* Allmendinger, *Staffelkapitän* of the *1. Staffel*, that our crew (*Oblt.* Allmendinger, *Uffz.* Sticht, *Uffz.* Paetau and *Fw.* Schuster) was being sent to the long-distance school in Köthen.

We flew in civilian clothes, and our passports showed that we were a study group.

Flying a He 111 with the code 55 H 1, we took off at 12:15 on 2 May 1939 and landed in Köthen at 13:22.

Several crews had already arrived ahead of us. For several days we carried out navigation flights in conjunction with individual DF homings within Germany.

Then, on a sunny May day, it was 12 May 1939, the time came. We took off and headed out across Lake Constance and Kescemet to Debreczen in Hungary. The Hungarian airmen gave us a warm welcome and we were given accommodations and meals in a first-class hotel. A helpful lieutenant was our constant companion. There were plenty of surprises. When we entered a restaurant with our escort, the gypsy band promptly greeted us with a German air force march. The next day we set off on the return flight.

Other crews returned at the same time after flights to Rome and Seville, and there was much to tell and of course a lively exchange of stories.

On 17 May 1935 there was a flight briefing for a new assignment. With the same, now well-tested crew under the *Kapitän*, at 07:10 on 18 May we took off for Tripoli in North Africa, making en route stops in Rome and Littoria. Flight preparations were almost always the same. We prepared our maps carefully, marking our planned route, headings, altitudes, DF stations and alternate airports. According to the air force manual, the pilot, observer and radio operator are responsible for navigation during a flight, the flight engineer for ensuring that the aircraft is loaded properly, has sufficient fuel and is mechanically sound. An aircraft crew has to work together harmoniously, for a mistake by one can be fateful for all.

By 07:00 on 18 May 1939 we were ready for takeoff. We donned our parachutes and life vests and made sure that the life raft was in order.

We took off for the Dark Continent precisely at 07:00 and initially set course for Rome. There was light icing as we climbed through the clouds. The cloud dispersed as we neared the Alps and soon the mountains were visible in all their glory. There was a foehn wind with outstanding visibility. After crossing the Alps we descended below 4000 meters and were able to take off our oxygen masks. We left the Po Plain behind us and flew over the Eternal City. Later our enthusiasm over this magnificent panorama received a damper. Soon after landing we were presented a complaint from the Vatican. Apparently we had flown too low. But the Italian interpreter told us that that the matter had been dropped after it turned out that the "sinners" were the crew of a German aircraft.

We weren't on the ground long and took off again for Tripoli at 12:00. We climbed to 5000 meters. Blue sky, excellent visibility, below us Sicily, soon Malta then the Mediterranean in all its beauty.

Many ships crossed our course or we theirs. The coast of North Africa came into view after three hours flying time, and at 15:10 we landed at the Castell Benito airport in Tripoli.

We received a very warm welcome from Italian airmen and locals in the officer's mess. We were given excellent accommodations in the Hotel Del-Mehari, which translates loosely into Hotel of the Camel. The next day we took a stroll through the Libyan capital with its mosques, the harbor and Arab shops.

In the evening gun salutes suddenly rang out. Shocked, we froze. Everything stopped. The people turned to face Italy and raised their hands in the fascist salute.

In the evening we spent a long time with our Italian air comrades over excellent red wine. The interpreter was a Tyrolean from Bozen who had been sent to Tripoli as punishment for identifying himself as a German while speaking to the crew of a German aircraft.

We flew back on 20 May 1939 and carried out additional long-distance flights inside Germany until 31 May. On 1 June 1939 we left on another flight abroad, this time to Spain. We flew via Barcelona to Seville, the capital of Andalusia in southern Spain, a city rich in works of art and architecture, with the Late Gothic cathedral (15th-16th Century) and the Alcazar from Moorish times. There, too, we spent wonderful days. This ended our course at the long-distance school in Köthen. On 5 June 1939 we returned to Gablingen."

Often, after having become part of a group of like-minded comrades and accepted as one of the gang, one is forced to leave. There were new tasks, and transfers and reassignments came all too quickly during the formation period.

Gustav-Adolf Klüter, retired *Brigadegeneral*, who became known as the "Lion of Agadir" and as an *Oberst* commanded the *Bundeswehr* relief team after the catastrophic earthquake, described his return to Giebelstadt and his activities there until the outbreak of war:

"I had always stayed in touch with my comrades in Giebelstadt, and many cross-country flights by both sides allowed us to see one another. My most heartfelt wish was to get back to my old *Gruppe*. During the incorporation of Austria I was assigned as pilot of a W 34 and supplemented the courier *Staffel* of the commander of the XVII Army (*General* Ruoff). After two pleasant months in Vienna I was recalled to Neubiberg. There the *Kommandeur* informed me that I had been transferred to KG 255 in Leipheim near Ulm and had to report there by 1 June. I bade farewell to Munich and was picked up by a Do 17. This aircraft from the Dornier company, called the "flying pencil", was in service with several *Geschwader* and popular with its crews. As I had earned the observer's badge in Giebelstadt, but was not yet qualified as a pilot on the Do 17, I was made an observer. *Oberleutnant* Fritz von Schrötter, the *Staffelkapitän*, was a splendid fellow, full of humor with a fine touch as commander. Despite this, I left him in no doubt that I would like to return to Giebelstadt. With the help of an uncle in an influential position in the RLM I got my transfer on 1 July 1938. After a move to Insterburg, East Prussia for live bomb dropping and firing at water targets, during which we all enjoyed extracurricular activities such as swimming in the Baltic near Cranz and Rauschen, on 30 June they put me into a Do 17 which transported me to Giebelstadt. I was back at my first home as an airman. Much had changed, the base had been further expanded, the new officer's quarters were finished. The bases that Göring had built at that time were magnificently equipped. The circle of comrades had changed, with new *Gruppe* and *Staffel* commanders. The *Gruppe* was now part of *Geschwader 355*, which was renamed KG 53 on 1 May 1939, based in Ansbach. The *Kommodore* was *Oberst* Stahl, and our *III. Gruppe* was led by *Oberstleutnant* Behrendt with *Oberleutnant* Thon as adjutant. Half of the officer corps had been transferred as a result of the formation of a new *Geschwader* in Austria (KG 76), while some of the crews were in action with the "*Legion Condor*" in Spain. When I arrived I was assigned to the *8. Staffel* led by *Major* Baron von Falkenstein. I had to complete my flying training immediately and converted onto the Ju 52 and He 111. The He 111 Type B had since been supplanted by the He 111 Type H with a fully-glazed nose, a safe bomber that was pleasant to fly. As I remember, the *Gruppe* leadership in the summer of 1938 was as follows: *Gruppenkommandeur Oberstleutnant* Behrendt, who soon went to Wunstorf as *Kommodore* and was relieved by *Major* Edler von Braun, adjutant *Oberleutnant* Thon, then *Leutnant* Gehrke. The *7. Staffel* was led by *Hauptmann* Zorn. The *8. Staffel* was commanded by *Major* Baron von Falkenstein, who was transferred to a general staff position and replaced by *Hauptmann* von Melgunoff, who in turn was succeeded by *Hauptmann* Fabian in autumn 1938. The *9. Staffel* was under *Oberleutnant* von Lösch, who was succeeded by *Major* Franz Reuss, who came from a general staff position.

New crews were created for the individual bombers and through practice learned to work together. Formation exercises in *Kette* and *Staffel* strength took us on long cross-country flights and landings at distant airfields. I remember a *Staffel* exercise in early 1939, when we took off from Giebelstadt at 05:00 and flew in formation over Cologne-Münster-the North Sea-Helgoland-Königsberg, East Prussia, where we landed for fuel. After lunch we returned over the Baltic Sea – the corridor was restricted airspace – Stettin-Berlin-Dresden to Ainring in Upper Bavaria, where we landed in *Staffel* formation at the small "*Führer* airfield." After coffee we took off again in *Staffel* formation and landed at Giebelstadt precisely at 18:00. All aircraft and crews had completed their mission without incident, a sign that out flying and technical training had already achieved a level of efficiency. Most pilots were instrument qualified, some were blind flying instructors. Most of the radio operators and flight engineers were old hands who could look back on lengthy experience with the unit or the "*Legion Condor*."

The *Gruppe* was not spared its share of high-ranking visitors. *General* Sperrle, the air fleet commander, and *Generaloberst* Milch, the *Luftwaffe's* Inspector-General, visited the *Gruppe* in autumn 1938. I recall a pleasant experience during Milch's visit. Following a successful inspection, during the usual gentlemen's evening with music the *Gruppenstab* tried to talk the *Generaloberst* into building a swimming pool. As the Karthäuser beer and the Boxtbeutel were making the rounds and the mood was jovial, Milch almost agreed. Later that night the *Generaloberst* was escorted to the general's quarters with gruesome songs about Florian Geyer and the 'old Germans', who always drank to both banks of the Rhine. The cheeky *Leutnante* kept celebrating, and because nothing was sacred to us, in a playful mood the *Generaloberst's* uniform was quietly fetched from the dressing room and hung in the big tree in front of the mess. In the morning there was a big fuss, nothing came of the swimming pool – although we got one a year later – and Milch never visited Giebelstadt again. He had too little understanding of fun and had never been a *Leutnant* in Giebelstadt!

In autumn 1938 our *III. Gruppe* was moved to airfields in the southeast for the Sudeten and subsequent Czech actions. I have forgotten their names, but I will never forget the flights over Eger, Brünn, Prague, and we were very pleased that it came off with no shots fired. We all had the feeling that things wouldn't continue so peacefully and it was regarded by many as a sort of preparation for war. After the winter of 38-39 passed uneventfully, beginning in the spring of 39 the pace of flying and weapons training was stepped up. The *Staffeln* took turns flying to Bonn-Hangelar for live bomb dropping and in June 39 to Wangerooge and Oldenburg for gunnery and bombing against sea targets, accompanied by lengthy overwater flights and lectures on maritime knowledge and navigation by naval officers under *Kapitän* von Borries. We still enjoyed these moves as diversions, visited the wine towns on the Rhine and the Ahr, played on the beach at Wangerooge or wandered the town of Oldenburg. When we returned to Giebelstadt we found several new installations. Strange fueling stations and 'secret barracks' had been erected, and a detachment appeared under *Hptm.* Mattenklodt. Several He 111s were fitted with water tanks, which were filled, and the first flights with 'power eggs', preliminary practice with takeoff-assist rockets for use from small airfields, were carried out. The takeoff was the most difficult part, everything depended on properly trimming the aircraft, and of course the 'power eggs' firing. After a successful takeoff, on reaching a specified altitude the empty rockets were jettisoned by parachute over the airfield and the water tanks drained. Each crew made three takeoffs, after which the trials were stopped. I personally never had to try it out during the war."

5. ANECDOTES

The following two accounts shall provide a final look back at peacetime:

The Captain of Köpenick
While *Obergefreiter* Reich did not duplicate the actions of the Captain of Köpenick, his escapade is itself worth telling about. *Uffz.* Alfred Sticht described what happened:

"The *I. Gruppe*, then part of *Kampfgeschwader 355*, was stationed at Gablingen air base near Augsburg. It was the end of July 1937. The crews of the *1., 2.* and *3. Staffel* were being trained for increasingly difficult flights. For example the younger, less experienced crews were sent to Germany where the prevailing weather was favorable, while the more senior, experienced airmen had to carry out more difficult flights, for example into areas of bad weather with heavy icing. Our *I. Gruppe* was equipped with Ju 52s.

All of the Ju 52 crews had gathered in the lecture room for a flight briefing. The meteorologist reviewed the overall weather picture and conditions on various routes. The crew of *Hauptmann* Lange, an experienced instrument pilot, had the assignment of flying into the bad weather region with a stop in Liegnitz. The crew, with *Hptm.* Lange as pilot and flight instructor, *Leutnant* Göhring as copilot and instrument flight instructor, *Feldwebel* Buchholz, an experienced bomber observer, and *Feldwebel* Vetter, a senior, good and conscientious radio operator, was supposed to gain experience. Altogether the machine was crewed by nine men. At first everything went well and according to plan, but over the Riesen Mountains, with the 1603-meter Schneekoppe, *Hptm.* Lange gave the order to descend through cloud to obtain visual contact with the ground and the aircraft struck the tops of trees and crashed. Three of those on board were killed, namely *Lt.* Göhring, *Feldwebel* Buchholz and a third whose name I unfortunately cannot remember. Six comrades were also seriously injured.

My comrade Fritz Seiler, who was later killed in the Spanish Civil War, and I, *Uffz.* Alfred Sticht, were ordered by the *Gruppe* navigation officer, *Oberleutnant* Schwarz, to reconstruct the entire flight up the crash using the radio log, in which were recorded all radio traffic, DF bearings from the aircraft and ground stations, position reports, etc. We determined that *Hptm.* Lange had chosen his descent point based on air and ground DF bearings used to establish his position. Because of heavy icing, the DF loop, which was mounted atop the Ju 52's fuselage, had twisted approximately 30 degrees, causing the bearing to be out by 30 degrees. This was confirmed by photos of the aircraft at the crash site. That was the cause of the crash. We buried our three dead comrades with military honors, while the other six crewmembers, including pilot *Hauptmann* Lange, began their lengthy convalescence in civilian and military hospitals.

Several weeks after the tragic crash a report was received from the Cologne police: air force *Hauptmann* Lange had just been in an auto accident in Cologne! Everyone thought it must be a mistake. A call was made to the Cologne traffic police, who confirmed the report. Impossible, *Hptm.* Lange was in hospital with serious injuries. But the report from Cologne also contained a great deal of truth. According to the uniform and driver's license it was a dashing young, perhaps too young, air force *Hauptmann* named Lange. It turned out that beneath the uniform was the batman of the real *Hauptmann* Lange, one *Obergefreiter* Reich, a young man from Cologne who decided he would show off in his home town in a dashing uniform with pilot's badge and two stars on the shoulder boards – albeit without an officer's commission.

This was only discovered later on, and the commander was at first speechless and could only shake his head. Soon afterwards the bogus '*Hptm.* Lange', in other words *Obergefreiter* Reich, was brought before him. The story made the rounds of the base; we had *our own* Captain of Köpenick in Gablingen. [*Translator's Note: The Captain of Köpenick is a play by German dramatist Carl Zuckmayer. Based on a true event that happened in 1906, it tells the story of a down-on-his-luck ex-convict shoemaker who impersonates a Prussian Guards officer.*] Many laughed at his inventiveness, others his audacity, while still others, when they thought about it, regretted what lay in store for him: a police report followed by a court martial. However things are not always as bad as they seem. The real *Hauptmann* Lange had his good heart back again and decided not to bring the *Obergefreiter* up on charges. *Obergefreiter* Reich therefore got off easily and was given three weeks under close arrest. But that didn't shake our buddy Reich. He is supposed to have told his comrades, 'I'll sit out the three weeks on one cheek.'"

The second story comes from *Fw.* Siegfried Gaedke and took place shortly before the outbreak of war:

"On 24 August 1939 the *3. Staffel* moved from Ansbach to Schönwalde. The He 111 with the code A1+FL, pilot *Unteroffizier* Gaedke, took off from Ansbach at 14:45 and landed in Schönwalde at 16:09. The *Staffel* had the next day off, and the men were enjoying a sunbath when the duty officer appeared and informed *Uffz.* Gaedke that he was to immediately leave for Kolberg in a Ju 52, accompanied by a *Gefreite* as flight engineer, to pick up spare parts. It was urgent and he had to take off immediately. The men were only wearing casual clothes and athletic shoes with no headgear.

Gaedke and his flight engineer were driven by car to the Ju 52, which was waiting ready for takeoff. He took off immediately. After landing in Kolberg they were immediately marshaled in the direction of the control tower. An *Oberfeldwebel* in uniform gave the final signals in front of the control tower, followed by the sign to shut down." *Uffz.* Gaedke continued: "We were amazed by this service. Officers by the score stood in front of the control tower. A red carpet was laid out. In the background troops had formed up in an open square. We became very queasy. I hardly dared shut the machine down. But when the duty Oberfeldwebel from the control tower gave me the sign to shut down the engines and an officer officiously opened the door of the Ju 52, we found ourselves looking into an appalled face. We weren't the guest they were expecting – they were expecting no one less than the *Führer* in person. We told the officer that we had come to collect spare parts. All he said was: 'Start up as quickly as possible and get out of here!' By then the air traffic control officers had realized the mistake and broken out into peals of laughter.

We quickly taxied to the maintenance hangar, loaded the waiting spare parts and left the Kolberg airport."

III. The Second World War

On 3 April 1939 Hitler issued the first "Case White" directive as the planning basis for the high commands and branches of the armed forces in the event of war with Poland.

20 May 1939 saw the start of secret negotiations in Moscow between Germany and the Soviet Union, which on 23 August concluded in a non-aggression pact with a secret supplementary protocol.

On 25 August 1939 Hitler postponed the attack on Poland, which was supposed to begin the next day. Why did he do this? First, England had once again and unmistakably affirmed its guarantee to Poland through the British-Polish mutual assistance pact. At the same time Mussolini informed Hitler that he could not provide any military assistance to Germany in the event that the western powers declared war on Germany.

Then, at 12:40 on 31 August 1939, Hitler issued the final attack order. The invasion would begin at 04:45 on 1 September 1939.

Two German army groups had been in position to attack for some days: Army Group North, with the 4th Army in Pomerania and the 3rd Army in East Prussia, under the command of *Generaloberst* Fedor von Bock; Army Group South with the 8th Army in Lower Silesia, the 10th Army in Upper Silesia and the 14th Army in Moravia.

The commander-in-chief of the army intended to "forestall an orderly mobilization and massing of the Polish Army, in order to destroy the enemy's main force, which was expected to be west of the Vistula – Narew line, through a concentric attack from Silesia on the one hand and Pomerania/East Prussia on the other."

The 10th Army would drive towards Warsaw, while its flanks were covered by the 8th Army in the north and the 14th Army in the south. From East Prussia the 3rd Army, with the XIX Panzer Corps under *General* Heinz Guderian as its spearhead, would attack towards the 10th Army from the opposite direction, while weaker elements of the 3rd and 4th Armies had been given the task of linking up and pinching off the northern part of the Polish Corridor. This campaign plan was based on the *Luftwaffe* achieving air superiority over all of Poland early on, if possible on the first day, so that it could then turn its full attention to supporting the army.

Two air fleets had been assembled for this task: *Luftflotte 1* with *Luftwaffe* Command East Prussia under *General* Albert Kesselring to support Army Group North; and *Luftflotte 4* under *General* Alexander Löhr supporting Army Group South.

In East Prussia the *Luftwaffe-Lehr-Division* was directed to support the 3rd Army. From Pomerania the *1. Flieger-Division* operated with the 4th Army. The *2. Flieger-Division* under Loerzer and the *Fliegerführer z.b.V.* had been assembled in Silesia mainly to support the 10th Army. The 8th and 14th Armies would receive air support as required.

On the first day the *Luftwaffe* found itself facing unfavorable weather conditions. Fog and cloudy skies stretched over the entire front.

"Operation *Wasserkante*" (Seaboard), a massed bombing raid against Warsaw planned by Göring, had to be called off as the ceiling was below 1000 meters.

The weather improved as the day went on, and *Luftflotte 4* began large-scale attacks against air bases in the south of Poland. Reconnaissance aircraft reported that there were numerous aircraft on the airfields and that visibility was good. A total of twelve airfields were attacked on the first day, including Lodz, Kattowitz and Krosno. The heaviest attack struck Cracow. In the first phase of the attack sixty He 111s carpet-bombed the airfield.

After the first day of the attack it looked as if the Polish Air Force had been destroyed on the ground. This proved to be incorrect, the reason being that many of the aircraft destroyed on the first day were trainers or non-combat machines.

On the first day of the war ninety He 111s of KG 27 arrived over Warsaw and were engaged by thirty PZL P 11 fighters. The Polish defensive effort was ineffective, however, and five fighters were shot down. The Polish fighters were powerless against the superior Messerschmitt Bf 109 and were literally swept from the skies. With growingly frequency, returning Polish pilots found that their airfields had been destroyed by German bombers.

The *Luftwaffe* also intervened in the land battle.

When the weak rearguards of the 8th Army became involved in tough fighting in the area of the Vistula and Bzura Rivers, the commander-in-chief of Army Group South, *Generaloberst* von Rundstedt, telephoned *General* Kesselring and asked for air support. Kesselring initially committed von Richthofen and his close-support units, followed by massed employment of Do 17,

He 111 and Ju 87 level- and dive-bombers. The threat to the 30th Infantry Division was eliminated. Squeezed into an area of approximately 30 by 40 kilometers, the Polish Posen Army became a practice target for the *Luftwaffe*.

The Poles fought back with rifles, machine-guns and light flak and shot down a few German aircraft; but the German forces attacking from all sides were overwhelming.

Polish General Kutrzeba later declared, "The heavy air attacks on the river crossings near Wittkowitz were unprecedented, both in the number of aircraft employed and the fierceness of the attacks and the acrobatic skill of the pilots. Every movement, every troop concentration, every march route came under a crushing bombardment. The bridges were destroyed, the fords blocked and the stalled columns decimated. We took cover in a small birch wood outside the village of Myszory. There we stayed, unable to move, until the air attacks temporarily stopped at about midday."

The only element of KG 53 to see action in Poland was the *I. Gruppe* under its *Kommandeur Major* Mehnert.

It was attached to *Kampfgeschwader* Siburg, which operated in the sector of *Luftflotte 4* "Southeast" (Löhr) as part of the *2. Flieger-Division* (Loerzer).

The entries in the *1. Staffel*'s war diary may be seen as representative of operations by the entire *Gruppe*:

1/9/39	*Takeoff* Schönfeld airfield, takeoff readiness from 02:30, *Gruppe* takeoff at 11:50.
	Takeoff sequence: command flight, 3., 2., 1. Staffel.
	Objective: Gnesen, Wreschen, Schroda airfields.
	Attack altitude 3000 m
	Bomb load 96 SD (fragmentation bombs, thick-cased, 50 kg)
	160 SC 50 (fragmentation bombs, cylindrical)
	Takeoff by nine bombers
	Time over target: Gnesen 12:34
	Wreschen 12:58
	Schroda 13:20
	Weather 8/10ths cloud, heavy mist at 800 m
	Mission uneventful
	Anti-aircraft fire light flak over Schroda
2/9	*Takeoff*: 13:10
	Objective: destruction of Polish bridge construction over the Vistula near Schwetz and Graudenz.
3/9	*Takeoff*: 17:10
	Objective: destruction of railway installations Zgierz-N of Lodz

4/9	*Takeoff*: 13:05
	Objective: ammunition dump E of Koluski
	Koluski railway station, Widzew station,
	airfield 25 km W of Lodz bearing 290°
5/9	*Takeoff*: 05:17
	Objective: railway crossing 5 km E of Kolo,
	2nd mission: takeoff 10:17,
	Objective: as before
6/9	*Takeoff*: 15:27,
	Objective: attack columns on roads:
	Dabic-Lecyzca-Lowicz with bombs and machine-guns
7/9	*Takeoff*: 12:35
	Transfer flight to Neudorf
8/9	Operations base Neudorf
	Takeoff: 11:20
	Objective: Przemsyl-Preseworsk and Jaroslaw-Lubaczow rail lines
9/9	*Takeoff*: 07:35
	Objective: columns and trains on roads and railroads SW of Lvov.

At 14:25 on 9 September the *1. Staffel* took off again and flew to the peacetime airfield at Giessen. It was replaced by the *6. Staffel*, however on 12 September all of *Kampfgeschwader Siburg* ceased operations and the Mehnert *Gruppe*'s part in the Polish campaign ended. That same day the units returned to their home bases.

The *I. Gruppe*, in the end supplemented by the *6. Staffel*, flew a total of 19 combat missions without loss.

The remaining units of the *2. Flieger-Division* continued combat operations until the fighting in Poland was over. These were KG 55, which moved to Cracow on 13 or 14 September, plus I./KG 77, I./ZG 2 and I./JG 77.

2. ENGLAND AND FRANCE DECLARE WAR

On 3 September 1939 Great Britain and France declared war on Germany. Then *Staffelkapitän Oberleutnant* Herbert Wittmann wrote of this:

"The *Stabsstaffel* was mustered on 3 September 1939. I informed the *Staffel* that England and France had declared war on Germany. Everyone was deeply shocked, and the mood was anything but one of enthusiasm for the war.

The *I. Gruppe* of KG 53 had already seen action against Poland, while the *Stabsstaffel* plus the *II.* and *III. Gruppe* had been held back as operational reserve against the west.

The success achieved by the air force in Poland filled us with envy. Soon we would learn better.

On 4 September 1939 we flew the first reconnaissance missions over France. The crew of the very first reconnaissance mission, in clear weather, failed to return.

During these missions, in addition to reconnaissance we were supposed to drop leaflets over the front lines and the French rear.

Daylight missions in good weather had to be stopped because of heavy losses and were changed to night and bad weather flights. In order to shorten the flights to France, the *Staffel* was moved to Schwäbisch Hall. Because of the blackout in Germany and France, these first night sorties involved more flying around than precisely locating a target and finding the way home. It turned out that while we had been able to make wonderful formation and long-distance flights in peacetime, radio navigation, DF homing and the like were in a sorry state.

Sometimes the leaflets were not dropped over Paris or other French cities, but instead over neutral Switzerland. One crew that made an emergency landing there was interned and thus sat out the war in Switzerland."

The *II. Gruppe* moved to Roth, from where it also flew leaflet-dropping missions over France.

After returning from operations over Poland, the *I. Gruppe* remained in Ansbach until 6 February 1940.

The *III. Gruppe* moved its *8.* and *9. Staffel* to the frontline base at Gross-Ostheim near Aschaffenburg, while the *7. Staffel* went to a nearby airfield.

A picture drawn for us by Gustav-Adolf Klüter from those days shows the mood of the *III. Gruppe* in 1939 after the war against Poland:

"The political tensions increased and on 1 September 1939 the war against Poland broke out. Two days later France and England followed with declarations of war on Germany. Our *Gruppe* was supposed to remain in the west in a defensive role. The *8.* and *9. Staffel* moved to the operational airfield at Gross-Ostheim near Aschaffenburg, while the *7. Staffel* was at another nearby airfield. One of the *Gruppen* of the *Geschwader* saw action in the Polish campaign and everyone envied our comrades, not suspecting that we would be given plenty of opportunities to put what we had learned to use. But what idea did we have in 39?! Everything stayed quiet in the west and we passed the time building positions and huts as well as picking mushrooms, huge quantities of which were fried in washbasins. Our 'mushroom master', *Oberleutnant* Neumaier, was so knowledgeable that we all survived. Once a week there in the barrack hall was a *Staffel* evening under the direction of *Hptm.* Fabian, who, after a short breaking-in period, turned out to be an excellent commander and comrade. On 1 October 1939 the *Gruppe* returned to Giebelstadt and training resumed. During that very cold winter of 1939-40 several comrades and I took part in an instrument flying course in order to earn our instrument (B) ratings. The *Gruppe*'s own blind-flying instructors gave the course, and later, in difficult situations, I was very grateful to our capable instructors Ludwig Eck and Fischback for what they had taught me. I had to take the examination itself in Manching from the strict 'Grampa Fischer', who was responsible for the 'Fischer blind flying method'. When I graduated I was instrument qualified on all types."

The long winter of waiting finally ended. Before sunrise on 10 May 1940, the airmen of the *Luftwaffe* were alerted at bases along the frontier. They were summoned to the command posts, where they heard that the attack against France, Belgium and Holland was going to begin at daylight.

The many training flights, the long-distance blind-flying exercises, the studying of thousands of reconnaissance photos were over. The aircraft crews were filled with determination to locate airfields, railway stations, transportation and other practice targets and play a decisive role in the battle.

Once again we turn to Gustav-Adolf Klüter, then an *Oberleutnant* who left the *Geschwader* in 1940, for his impressions of the period from the winter of 1939-40 to the attack on the west as a member of the *III Gruppe*:

"To the extent that the war permitted, the social gatherings resumed, but not much happened after the Polish war and we were able to have a good time and celebrate Florian Geyer and the 'old Teutons'. I met my wife, with whom I celebrated my 40th anniversary in 1980, at a dance in Giebelstadt. In February 1940 we celebrated what was probably one of the last happy military weddings of the war. There was a beer call with the *Staffel* following the civil marriage in Giebelstadt, and the church service on a sunny but cold winter day in Würzburg with officers of the *Staffel* and other officer friends in the Lämmle Hotel. Late in the evening my witnesses Franz Reuss (now a retired *General* in Munich) and Peter Gleue (killed in the Mediterranean) discovered Lale Andersen in the hotel. Of course they brought her in and to everyone's enjoyment she sang the song 'Lili Marleen', the first time we had heard it. It was unforgettable.

The *Gruppe* gave us a magnificent silver bowl as a wedding present. The names of all the officers were engraved on it, which makes it possible for me to reconstruct the staffing at that time:

Staffing and officers of III./KG 'Legion Condor' 53 Giebelstadt at the outbreak of war 1 September 1939

(Kommodore: Oberst Stahl)
(Adjutant: Oblt. Joachim)

III. Gruppe

C.O.:	*Major* Edler von Braun
Adj.:	*Oblt*. Gehrke
T.O.:	*Lt*. Gäbler
Sig.Off.:	*Oblt*. Kallass
7.F.B.K.	*Oblt*. Pfeiffer
8.F.B.K.	*Hptm*. Klosinski
Admin.Off.	*OberInsp*. Schulz

7. *Staffel*:	*Hptm*. Zorn
	Oblt. Langer
	Oblt. Repenning
	Lt. leonhardi
	Lt. Kupfer
	Lt. Büchler
	Lt. d. Res. Lütticken

8. *Staffel*:	*Hptm*. Fabian
	Oblt. Klüter
	Oblt. Neumaier
	Lt. Anders
	Lt. Leber
	Lt. d. Res. Woldmann

9. *Staffel*:	*Major* Reuss
	Oblt. Gleue
	Oblt. Wilhelm
	Oblt. Meinicke
	Lt. Linke
	Lt. Huhn
Air Base Group:	*Oberstleutnant* Christen
Air Base Company:	*Hptm*. Kneuer
Hptm. B. Stabe	*Hptm*. Bauer
Sig.Off.:	*Oblt*. Wherek

In March our *Gruppe* moved to Schwäbisch Hall. The Haller *Gruppe* had previously moved to another airfield. The practice alerts became more frequent, and when 9 May 1940 dawned we had no inkling that things were about to get serious. Several crews, including mine, had already made night flights over Paris and dropped leaflets. It was a strange feeling to fly over enemy territory for the first time at night. For safety reasons we flew at altitudes of 5,000 to 6,000 meters. What little flak there was, was far away, and there were no night-fighters as yet, consequently we all made it back safely to Schwäbisch Hall. On 9 May 1940 we again had the usual practice alerts. The aircraft were fully loaded, usually with 50- and 250-kg high-explosive bombs, and the drums filled with live machine-gun ammunition. The crews stayed in the takeoff shack. The alarm was usually cancelled in the afternoon, but not this time, and so we felt 'here we go'.

The *Staffelkapitäne* were briefed by the *Kommandeur*, and the mission order was: 'Dawn attack against French airfields in the Sedan-Charleville area, night takeoff in *Kette* formation, individual approach to designated targets,'

My good crew (*Uffz.* Noe as observer, *Fw.* Mank as flight engineer and 'Spezi' Hofbauer as radio operator) and I as pilot and *Kette* leader were extremely tense before our first combat mission, but we had nothing to worry about. Once again a higher power took me and my crew under its wings, and it carried me safely through all of my flights over France until my transfer. The lights were switched off as we taxied out, bad for the *Kette* leader, but we took off anyway. After we lifted off one of the engines sputtered and then quit completely, and this with a full bomb load and pitch blackness. I reacted as we had been taught: 'Throttles closed, stick back into the stomach and wait for the crash. Ignition off!' There was a crash, it stank, but after bouncing 50 meters there was absolute quiet. I shouted: 'Everyone out and get down!' We scrambled out of the machine and threw ourselves down on the ground, but nothing happened. After ten minutes we began walking in the direction of the base, where our *Kommodore* 'Spezi' Stahl greeted us with the words: 'I was watching from the tower, thank God you're alive. Go to the mess and drink a bottle of champagne on me.' The reason: he had just received news that two aircraft had collided while taking off from Ansbach and their bomb loads had exploded. Both were total losses. When we inspected the damage the next morning, we saw that we had made a perfect belly landing. The bombs – unarmed – were still in the cells and we were five meters from a wood. The aircraft was recovered and after eight days in the repair shop it was returned to service.

At noon on 10 May I took off in another aircraft. Once again it was not to be. We lost a bomb, which struck the tail and badly damaged it.

With full use of the trims and full rudder, I landed again with the full bombload, something initially thought to be impossible. The head of the maintenance shop came running. It had made his hair stand on end, but it was a smooth landing. So, we thought, all that's missing now is the third thing – and it wasn't long coming! Our third takeoff was uneventful – finally – and we headed out to attack armor concentrations in the Sedan area. For the first time we experienced fighter attack by French Moranes and heavy but inaccurate anti-aircraft fire. To defend against fighter attack we closed up into tight formation. The radio operator and dorsal gunner had plenty of opportunities to busy themselves. A bullet must have hit our starboard engine, because it lost power and the Moranes closed in. But suddenly our Me 109s appeared and the danger was past. We had survived the third thing. We landed with reduced power, the last to return. After landing someone told me that airmen weren't superstitious. I can't remember all of my missions over France, because unfortunately American soldiers 'confiscated' my diary and logbook at the end of the war. I would like to emphasize that KG 53 and with it the *III. Gruppe* played an important part in the breakthrough at Sedan by attacking armor concentrations, troop assembly areas, railway junctions and other lines of communication in the rear areas. Long flights to Marseille, in some cases in the face of numerous enemy fighters and bad weather fronts, some of which we flew through in formation, resulted in the first casualties but also successes. We suffered our first losses in men and machines, but the first decorations, the Iron Cross, Second Class, were also awarded to crews of the *II. Fliegerkorps* (Gen. Loerzer). As the front advanced, at the end of May we moved to Frankfurt-Rhine/Main airport, which we shared with Ju 52 *Staffeln* and Ju 88 *Gruppen*. From there we were able to take off in *Staffel* formation, which of course significantly reduced the time required to form up. The *Gruppe* took off in all sorts of weather and the combat missions became longer, into the area around Paris, the Loire Valley and soon to the next focal point, the area of Reims-Metz-Verdun. By the time of the ceasefire on 25 June each crew had flown 25 to 30 combat missions and had been decorated with the Iron Cross, First Class (*Luftflotte 3, Generaloberst* Sperrle).

With a heavy heart, after the French surrender I was forced to take leave of my crew and *KG 'Legion Condor' 53*. I was transferred to KG 30 as a *Staffelkapitän* and had to retrain on the Ju 88, beginning a new chapter for me. My time with my original *Geschwader*, with which I remain in closer contact than the other two *Geschwader* I flew with during the war until general staff duty took me on another career path in 1943, came to an end. I am happy that I was allowed to return to Würzburg after I was released by the Americans in 1947 and soon began to establish the 'Florian Geyer' comrades group in the Würzburg area. It lasted for many years until the old *Geschwader* KG 53 again closed ranks with those who today still take pride in their association with the old and proven *Kampfgeschwader 'Legion Condor' 53.*"

3. LEAFLET MISSIONS – PROPAGANDA FLIGHTS OVER FRANCE

Leaflet missions have already been mentioned in the previous accounts by members of KG 53.

The purpose of these missions was, of course, to undermine the morale of the enemy troops and the French enemy's will to fight. These missions were certainly not as risky as those later in the war. The mission reports submitted by several crews will be representative of all the crews of the *I. Gruppe*:

Evening dispatch:	Sent to *Kampfgeschwader* 53 at 14:15 on 21/11/39, received by *Uffz.* Fischer.	
Crew:	Pilot:	*Obfw.* Klaue
	Observer:	*Oblt.* Pröbst
	Radio Operator:	*Fw.* Wagner
	Flight Engineer:	*Fw.* Wagner
03:55	Takeoff by 1 He 111 A1+CB to drop leaflets in the Paris-Le Havre area	
04:40	Flight aborted between Saarlautern-Metz because the radio operator developed altitude sickness and heart trouble at an altitude of 7200 m. DF and radio equipment failed. Navigation by means of the Hilde light beacon	
06:32	Landing in Illesheim.	
07:10	Landing in Ansbach.	
Payload:	8 bundles of leaflets (Molotov-Ribbentrop speech) Leaflets not dropped.	
Enemy defenses:	Flak:	none
	Fighters:	none
	Searchlights:	numerous searchlight positions active along the front (Metz), aircraft was not coned by
Unusual incidents:	None	
21:15	Landing at Giebelstadt.	

Report from same day:

23:11   Takeoff by 1 He 111 A1+BB to drop leaflets in Area
D (Paris-Le Havre

Crew: Pilot: *Fw.* Grünke
                      Observer: *Oblt.* Plank
                      Radio Operator: *Uffz.* Biller
                      Flight Engineer: *Obfw.* Weyers
01:10   Time over target.
Payload: 8 bundles of leaflet No. 107
                      Leaflets dropped in assigned area.
Enemy defenses: Flak: near Paris
                      Fighters: none
Searchlights: searchlights along entire route, aircraft not coned
                      by searchlights.
Casualties: none
Reconnaissance Results: none.
Unusual incidents: Two bundles of leaflets jammed, causing the
                      detonator to explode. No damage to the aircraft.
                      Direction finder unserviceable, (continuous buzzing
                      tone). Frequency selection made difficult – and the
                      DF loop crank (frozen).
03:41   Landing at Giebelstadt.

Leaflet missions continued in the period that followed. The targets were the
following areas:

Amiens-Arras-Cambrai

Paris

Metz-Diedenhofen.

The only information we have concerning these flights concerns the crews
that took part:

PT	*Fw.* Burger	PT	*Fw.* Burger	PT	*Oblt.* Grosholz
OV	*Oblt.* Weber	OV	*Hptm.* Schwarz	OV	*Oblt.* Amende
RO	*Obfw.* Fegert	OV	*Lt.* von Goertz	RO	*Obfw.* Müller
FE	*Fw.* Puth	RO	*Obfw.* Weidenhammer	FE	*Fw.* Kempgens
FE	*Uffz.* Bott				
PL	*Oblt.* Allmendinger	PL	*Obfw.* Krause		
OV	*Obfw.* Seidel	OV	*Oblt.* Pröbst		
RO	*Fw.* Schuster	FE	*Fw.* Wagner		
FE	*Uffz.* Marbach				

In the meantime on 3 February 1940 the *Geschwader* moved to the following airfields:

> *Stabsstaffel to Schwäbisch Hall*
> I. *Gruppe* to Roth
> II. *Gruppe* to Manching
> III. *Gruppe* to Schwäbisch Hall

Leaflet missions were flown from there until the end of April 1940.

4. THE FRENCH CAMPAIGN

Hitler had originally intended to attack France in autumn 1939, after the Polish campaign.

On 29 October 1939 the final plan was presented to Adolf Hitler in the form of an OKH organization plan. The attack date was put back several times, and the early onset of a difficult winter forced its postponement until the spring of 1940.

Essentially the plan was a revised version of the Schlieffen Plan of 1914. With a strong right wing, German forces would advance through Belgium into northern France and then swing south, outflanking the French and British armies.

This plan was never implemented, however, for two reasons: a German courier aircraft with two German officers and the complete operations plans on board, became lost and was forced to land in Belgium. The officers were only partly successful in destroying the plans.

The second reason was the arrival of *General* von Manstein as *Generaloberst* von Rundstedt's chief-of-staff of Army Group A. The new plan of attack called for the main effort to be shifted to Army group A, the central army group. It would drive through Luxembourg and southern Belgium with powerful armored forces, from Namur in the direction of Sedan, to breach the Maginot Line, which was weaker there, and then advance in the direction of the Channel Coast to trap the bulk of the Allied forces positioned there. Only then would the attack into the French heartland take place.

In practice, this plan would prove so successful that, at the outset of the campaign against France, it would vastly overshadow the experiences of the early days of the Polish campaign.

The breaching of the vaunted Maginot Line alone was achieved with unexpected ease. The organization of the *Luftwaffe*'s units followed that of the army. *Luftflotten 2* (Kesselring) and *3* (Sperrle) fielded 1,300 bomber aircraft, 380 Stukas and 1,200 fighters, plus about 640 reconnaissance aircraft, 475 transport aircraft and 45 gliders. The *Luftwaffe* had three assignments in this campaign: heavy attacks against enemy airfields, especially in support of airborne landings, interdiction and destruction of supply lines, and support for the ground forces.

The German attacks on airfields in Holland and Belgium and the British and French air fleets in France began at dawn on 10 May 1940. The *Luftwaffe* enjoyed air superiority from the very first day and maintained it for the duration of the campaign in France.

On 13 May the *Luftwaffe* delivered devastating attacks against the French positions along the Meuse River in preparation for the attack by the army. Under an air umbrella provided by the *Luftwaffe*, the first armored division crossed the Meuse over a hastily erected pontoon bridge and fought its way through the French defense front. The crossing of the Meuse proved to be the decisive turning point of the entire campaign.

After the armored thrust in the direction of the coast really got going, neither the British nor the French were able to stop it. As soon as air or ground reconnaissance discovered nests of resistance, they were attacked and destroyed by German bombers and Stukas. On the evening of 20 May, just one week after the crossing of the Meuse and 400 kilometers away, the German armored spearhead crossed the Amiens-Abbeville canal and reached the Channel. The plan of splitting the British and French armies had worked; it was the beginning of the end of the Battle of France.

Now we once again turn to accounts by the crews of KG 53. First *Major d.R.* Alfred Sticht, then a *Feldwebel* and observer in the crew of the commander of the *1. Staffel*:

"Today is the 10th of May, and since 7 February we have been stationed at the forward airfield in Roth-Kiliansdorf. It is shortly after midnight when the duty officer wakes the men of the first *Staffel*, operational readiness. Our 'black men', the soldiers of the ground personnel, go to the machines, load them with bombs and ammunition. Then the aircraft are fueled and made ready for takeoff. The aircrew make their way to the flight briefing: target, navigation method, weather. Each member of the crew supplies himself with operation-specific documents, as required, and then it's off to the aircraft.

It is 03:30 in the morning, and from all sides aircraft taxi to their respective takeoff positions. The night stillness is shattered by the roar of engines.

We are flying the command aircraft of the 1st *Kette*, *1. Staffel*, with *Staffelkapitän Hptm.* Allmendinger, observer *Fw.* Sticht, second observer *Fw.* Seidel, radio operator *Fw.* Schuster, flight engineer *Uffz.* Marbach and gunner *Gefr.* Lehner.

The takeoff director gives us the green light, directing us to taxi into position right behind the commanding officer's flight (*Stabskette*). Horizontal visibility is poor, we will take off blind. The second and third *Ketten* have moved into position behind us. The airfield lighting is switched on briefly, the sign to the *Kommandeur* that we are cleared for takeoff.

The *Stabskette* begins to move, picks up speed and almost immediately lifts off the ground. My *Staffelkapitän* takes one last look at the instruments, our He 111 A1+BH is ready to go. A few more seconds and the takeoff run will begin. The other two members of our *Kette* on our left and right report that they are also ready to take off.

And then – full power – the rumble of hundreds of horsepower rings out through the night … But now – what's happening in front of us? Throttles back. A call over the intercom rings out in my headset. The brakes squeak. We almost nose over.

Two aircraft in front of us have collided. They turn in a circle and one of the incendiaries in one aircraft explode. Taxi away from the burning aircraft as quickly as possible. The entire taxiway is filled with aircraft. The pilots quickly taxi their machines out of the way, and the crews leave their aircraft and take cover. At any minute the high-explosive and fragmentation bombs might go off.

Fire trucks and ambulances race across the airfield. In Roth the sirens howl, air raid warning. Then more bombs explode, and we can feel the shock waves.

Finally there is quiet. One machine is completely burnt out, the other is heavily damaged.

The cause of the trouble: the port engine of the *Kommandeur*'s machine failed and the aircraft swung to the left."

The then *Oberfeldwebel* Winter, pilot of the *Kommandeur*'s aircraft, described the incident:

"… I begin the takeoff roll and suddenly notice that the rudder forces are increasing. I immediately look at the port rpm indicator, which drops to zero. Repeated pumping of the throttle lever does nothing. I try to keep the machine straight by applying the right brake, but it is already drifting left … Suddenly I see the aircraft on the left of the *Kette* coming straight towards me. I hope that he might be able to pass by. But then everything happens very quickly. His port wingtip scrapes against the bottom of our glazed nose, the observer sustains a head injury … The other aircraft's wing breaks off at the port engine and flies on another 50 meters, and the machine immediately bursts into flames. The burning machine turns three times around its own axis, the starboard engine still running at full power, then the tires burst. The engine stops, the machine ends its gyrations and burns out completely. It is placed under guard as sabotage is suspected.

Another takeoff is scheduled two hours later.

I am still a little unsettled, but there isn't a lot of time to dwell on one's own thoughts. The commander has committed the reserve *Kette*. Then, over the intercom, I hear the radio operator: radio equipment functioning, out! After takeoff our course is west. Together with the *1. Staffel*, our mission is to bomb the training field at Sarralbe with high-explosive and incendiary bombs.

The visibility is poor, there is plenty of anti-aircraft fire, attack height 5000 m. We complete our mission without incident. At 09:27 we land at our new base in Gelchsheim (S of Giebelstadt).

It is the 11th of May. Our *I. Gruppe*, in *Luftflotte 3*'s area of operations, has been ordered to attack and destroy the airfields at Sommesous and Vasincourt, plus anti-aircraft positions near Metz and Verdun. The command flight with the *Kommandeur Oberstleutnant* Mehnert takes off at 05:20, followed by the *3.*, *2.* and *1. Staffel*.

The *Kapitän*'s aircraft takes off at 05:39 with the same crew as on 10 May. Attack altitude is 5100 meters and we cross the French border near Merzing. North of Metz and Verdun we encounter heavy anti-aircraft fire. The weather conditions are hazy, visibility poor. Over the Argonne we change course and fly straight towards the target. Above us there are several aircraft which we soon identify as Me 110s. They are on a fighter sweep in the Sedan – Verdun area.

We can see well the *2.* and *3. Staffel*, but of the command flight there is no sight. South and north of us we can make out several *Staffeln* of other units flying west – there is plenty going on in the air.

Then we arrive over the assigned target, bomb doors open, ZSK (bomb fusing panel) on. I acquire the target in the Lotfe 7 B and, after issuing a steady series of course corrections to the pilot, drop the bombs. The anti-aircraft fire is too low. There are no fighters and we set course for home. Between Metz and Verdun we are again fired on by anti-aircraft guns of every caliber but without effect.

But then the radio operator suddenly reports: enemy fighters behind. They are six Morane 204s (sic). They attack our *Staffel* and we close up to concentrate our defensive fire. A life and death struggle develops. We fight for our lives, taking a number of machine-gun hits in the wings and fuselage.

The aircraft on the left of our *Kette* (A1+FH) is shot up, its port engine is smoking.

We reduce speed to provide cover for the damaged machine. The French attack again, this time from the front. The first Morane flies right into our machine-gun fire. It begins to smoke, rears up and bursts into flames. The pilot saves himself with his parachute. The anti-aircraft guns cease fire to avoid hitting their own man. The damaged machine from our *Kette* is losing altitude steadily and heads toward Longwy, trying to reach the front at the German border. Then its second engine is hit by anti-aircraft fire and the pilot is forced to make a belly landing in French territory. The crew was later rescued by a German patrol.

A member of the aircraft's crew described what happened:

'... as we fly over the Maginot Line near Longwy, our second engine is hit by light anti-aircraft fire. We immediately make a belly landing in front of a French bunker. The crew leaves the aircraft with three MG 15s and plenty of ammunition. There is no time to set it on fire. All five men run up a slope, find a shallow depression at the top and take cover. Artillery shells are falling near a road with traffic farther east and northeast. Several shells hit the road. We must assume that we are between the fronts and take cover. After many hours a German patrol appears from an easterly direction – we are saved.'

The operations order for the entire *Geschwader* for 11 May 1940, sent by teletype, illustrates the situation on that day. The report on the *I. Gruppe*'s actions, including the downing of aircraft A1+FH described here, also reflects the sobering numbers."

The mission on 11 May produced other dramatic events. Retired *Hauptmann* Martin Winter, then an *Oberfeldwebel* and the *Gruppenkommandeur*'s pilot, wrote:

"... the procedure after takeoff was as follows: the command *Kette* would fly straight ahead for seven minutes, then made a 180-degree turn; the following *Staffeln* would then join up with the command *Kette* in a left turn, so that the unit was in close formation by the time it reached the field at the latest. A young, ambitious *Staffelkapitän* ignored this order, which had grave consequences.

We took off in *Kette* formation at 05:30 on 11 May 1940, target Trondes near Toul. As described, I took off with my *Kette*, flew straight for seven minutes and then made a 180-degree turn to reverse course. We ought to have seen the first *Ketten* one minute after the turn, but we saw nothing, even after a few minutes. The *Kapitän* of the 3. *Staffel* must therefore have headed straight towards the front, followed by the other *Staffeln*.

As my *Kette* and I were faster than an entire formation and had a better climb rate to the attack height of 5100 meters, I still hoped to find the *Gruppe*. Unfortunately in vain.

Now we were one *Kette* on its own. Then, suddenly, three condensation trails – fighters! I advised the *Kommandeur* that we had no chance; all we could do was dive away and save the crew and the aircraft. His response, however, was: 'We will complete the mission.' No sooner had he said this when six more fighters appeared. There was no changing the *Kommandeur*'s mind, however. Then the fighters spotted us and our battle against six Moranes began. The aircraft on the right suddenly peeled off – hit.

There were bangs in my aircraft. The undercarriage lock was hit and the landing gear fell down. There went our speed. To make matters worse the port engine was hit in the radiator, causing it to quit.

I immediately set course for the German border by the shortest route. But suddenly there was a loud bang in the cockpit, our observer had been fatally hit by a bullet. The *Kommandeur* pulled him from the cockpit, placed him in the right seat and took his place. The fighter was still nearby, however it held its fire, although it sometimes came so close that it seemed it intended to ram us.

Meanwhile we had lost a great deal of altitude and were only 150 meters above the ground. I had to find a place to make an emergency landing and quickly. We came to a stop in a field, fifty meters from a road. During the emergency landing we struck a pole, the fuel tank was ruptured and the aircraft caught fire. We wanted to retrieve the observer's body, but the Frenchmen, who were standing on the road, had already raised their rifles. We ground our pistols into the mud and were then taken prisoner. The French led us to a guard room and after a short time brought in the body of the dead observer.

Then, outside, there was a frightful explosion, our aircraft had exploded.

After being transported away, I spent the first day of Pentecost in the military jail in Nancy, where I was interrogated by a French *Captaine*, a veteran of the First World War. He told me about sabotage at our base of operations. The failure of my aircraft on 10 May had been caused by a saboteur (an *Obfw.* who was later arrested). He had inserted a disc into the fuel filter which was set to allow the aircraft to take off, but then cut off the flow of fuel. But I had run up both engines at full power a second time while in takeoff position, something the saboteur hadn't counted on."

On 12 May the entire *Geschwader* was committed against airfields and road and railway traffic.

The mission order from the *Kommodore, Oberstleutnant* Stahl, for 12 May was transmitted to the *Gruppe* by teletype. Essentially its contents were:

Targets for each *Gruppe*,
instructions for assembly or forming up by the *Gruppe*,
rendezvous with the escort,
return flight route,
bomb load, target photos, weather situation.

The *I. Gruppe* was at the forward airfield in Gelchsheim, the *II.* at the forward base in Ödheim, the *III.* at the Rhine-Main airport in Frankfurt.

Alfred Sticht described the *I. Gruppe*'s mission:

"Target:	Mourmelon airfield, two alternate targets,
formation:	*Staffel* column, *Gruppe* wedge,
attack altitude:	5300 – 5800 m,
time over target:	07:55,
bomb load:	50- and 250-kg high-explosive and incendiary bombs,
defenses:	heavy flak and fighter defense to be expected. Flight route
Gelchsheim-Kirn.	At 07:00 rendezvous with a *Gruppe* of Me 110 *Zerstörer* of ZG 2 over Kirn at an altitude of 3000 m.

II. and *III. Gruppe* to rendezvous with a second *Zerstörer Gruppe* over Trier at an altitude of 4000 m at 07:15. After rendezvousing with the *Zerstörer*, the *Geschwader* is to proceed straight to the target. *Geschwaderkommodore Oberstleutnant* Stahl will fly with the *III. Gruppe*.

Should bad weather be encountered and the *Zerstörer* unable to follow, return flight from the target with course towards Stenay on the Meuse. Rendezvous with the *Zerstörer* there and head for home.

Synchronization of watches – navigation aids – valid recognition flares – the mission briefing by the *Kommandeur* was over. We took off at 06:01, the *Staffelkapitän*'s A1+LH with the other two aircraft of the *Kette*. The other flights followed at brief intervals.

We arrived over Kirn at 3000 meters punctually at 07:00. The escort was waiting and we flew on to Trier, and at precisely 07:15 we rendezvoused with the *II.* and *III. Gruppe* at an altitude of 4000 meters. The *Geschwader* turned onto the heading for the target in an extended left turn with the comforting feeling: there were two *Gruppen* of *Zerstörer* above us at an altitude of 5000 meters to watchfully escort us into enemy territory. It was still around 200 kilometers to the target. At first everything went quietly and according to plan. We overflew the Maginot Line and below us we could see the fortifications. There was moderate flak but it was ineffective. The Maginot Line was well-camouflaged, but we could see the considerable destruction caused by earlier Stuka attacks.

We crossed the Meuse north of Verdun, flew over the Argonne Forest and were within seventy kilometers of the target. The *Staffeln* were flying in *Staffel* column, this means three *Ketten* one behind the other, with the 2. *Staffel* on the right and the 3. *Staffel* on the left, both in the same formation. The three *Staffeln* thus formed the *Gruppe* wedge.

We ran into heavy anti-aircraft fire while still some distance from the target, and the closer we got to Reims the heavier it became. The French fighters were dangerous and the first appeared at this point, Moranes and Curtisses. They attacked us in a dive while another group engaged the *Zerstörer*. But we had to carry out our mission. The *Staffelkapitän* gave his orders: bomb bay doors open, bomb fusing panel on, maintain precise altitude and speed. The bomb run began. We were flying at an altitude of 5400 meters, while above us a fierce dogfight raged between Moranes, Curtisses and our *Zerstörer*. The crisscrossing white condensation trails became more numerous. The bomb aimers acquired the target in crosshairs of their Lotfe 7 B bombsights. The bombing mechanism was running, there were many aircraft and hangars in the sight.

Our aircraft flew straight and level, no one in the crew spoke, then the awaited words from the observer: 'Bombs gone'. The machine-guns and cannon fell silent for a moment. The bombs were armed as they left the aircraft. It had happened that a bomb was hit by one of our bullets and took the aircraft down with it.

We could see the results of our bombing as we flew away. They exploded among the approximately 50 aircraft parked on the airfield. Several tried to get airborne, too late. The effect of the bombs was devastating. Our mission accomplished, we turned for home. North of Mourmelon more enemy fighters appeared and attacked our formation. The 3. *Staffel*, in particular, came under heavy attack. Another enemy machine was shot down in flames. The pilot did not bale out. The enemy fighter crashed and exploded.

We also suffered losses. At that moment I saw an aircraft, A1+EL of the 3. *Staffel*, attacked and hit by fighters. It literally blew apart in the air. It was the crew of *Leutnant* von Satzenhofen-Fuchsberg.

The aircraft went down. Several members of the crew spun through the air. Thank God, at least two parachutes opened, but of the other three crewmen nothing was seen. During a brief pause in the fighting I thought of the men of the crew, who yesterday had been so close and present. Before long the other aircraft in our *Kette* was also hit and it peeled off. We called the lead aircraft of the third *Kette*: 'A1+AD from A1+LH: please assume command of the *Staffel*.' Anton Dora acknowledged. We descended slowly and escorted our shot-up wingman, whose port engine was out, to Wiesbaden, the nearest operational base."

The reports submitted by the *I. Gruppe* provide eloquent testimony as to the costly missions on 12 May 1940.

As in Alfred Sticht's account, the report concerning the first mission on 12 May also mentions the shooting down of aircraft A1+EL flown by *Lt*. von Satzenhofen-Fuchsberg. The only survivor was the observer, *Fw*. Karl Ulrich. Here is his account:

"We were part of the *3. Staffel* and were flying He 111 A1+EL. The members of our crew were: pilot *Leutnant der Reserve* E. von Satzenhofen-Fuchsberg, observer *Fw*. Karl Ulrich, radio operator *Uffz*. Georg Eisenmann, flight engineer *Fw*. Georg Stadler, gunner *Gefr*. Sigfrid Holbein. The latter was not actually a member of the crew but had wanted to take part in a combat mission.

After the misery of 10 May, a 'Black Friday' for our entire *Gruppe*, on the second day of the campaign we flew attacks on Sommesous and in the afternoon a relief attack against French armored units in the Sedan area. We had since moved to the forward airfield in Gelchsheim.

On the evening of 11 May we sat having a glass of beer together, Edi von Satzenhofen and I. He had been promoted to *Leutnant der Reserve* a few days earlier. For him, too, it now became deadly serious. He had first joined us after the campaign against Poland. During our conversation he admonished me to do a good job as observer, for his two children wanted to see their father again. My reply: we certainly won't fall on our face because of me.

Pentecost Sunday, 12 May 1940

Takeoff at six in the morning. Target Mourmelon airfield. We flew in *Gruppe* formation. The *3. Staffel* had just eight aircraft, enough for two *Ketten* and a *Rotte*. Our A1+EL flew in the pair. The day before we had flown well ahead in the formation, today we were at the rear. But, as the saying goes, the devil take the hindmost. God knows this saying came true. There was an order which stated: a complete *Kette* must always fly at the rear of a bomber formation. Since we were only a *Rotte*, we flew in the second-last position in the formation. After reaching attack altitude we settled into cruise speed, adjusted propeller pitch to 5 before 12, boost pressure, etc. We initially headed toward the forward airfield at Kirn in the Pfalz. There we were supposed to pick up our escort of Me 110 *Zerstörer*. It was a magnificent sight to have an entire formation in front of and below one, the lead aircraft at 5500 m and we, in the rear, at 6500 m. We overflew Kirn and a smoke signal was dropped. Below I could see Me 110s leaving their dispersals and taking off higgledy-piggledy across the field. I thought to myself that that was something we couldn't do in bombers.

Would our fighter escort at least be waiting today? Unfortunately it hadn't been yesterday. We were approaching the border of the Reich heading for Stenay. The last *Kette*, led by *Oblt.* Wegener, suddenly flew overhead and positioned itself in front of us. We cursed. The Maginot Line was overflown, the enemy flak made its presence felt, then fighters were seen approaching. We breathed a sigh of relief – until we came under a hail of fire, they were enemy Morane fighters. We were already isolated. The formation in front of us opened up on the fighters attacking us from behind. Streams of tracer zipped past us on the left and right, above and below. It was a gruesomely beautiful sight – but damned uncomfortable. At that moment I was more afraid of our own bullets, which were much too close to our machine. From the smoke trails I could tell exactly whether the fighter was attacking from left or right above. The formation in front of us initially provided massive covering fire, but the interval between us steadily lengthened.

At the mission briefing we had been instructed not to fly over Diedenhofen or Verdun, as the fortifications there included anti-aircraft guns. Now, with six French fighters at our throats, the flak was unlikely to fire. Whereas this was the prescribed and followed practice in the German air force, it soon turned out that it was not the case in the French. Anti-aircraft shells detonated in front of, beneath and above us, while at the same time six Moranes made repeated firing passes.

The gap between us and our formation had become so great that the defensive and relief fire had stopped. The crew in back fired like mad. The French tactic was to position one fighter above us on the left and right, from where they peeled off and attacked. I sat looking rearwards, watching the fighters. As they approached I guessed when they would open fire and ordered a left or right turn as appropriate. At first I gave my orders too soon and saw that the fighters turned with us. I had to stay calm and let them get close, so that we could turn out of their sights at the correct moment. This was the only way we avoided being shot down immediately. The combat went on for about 35 minutes, during which I counted about 25 attacks, then it ended.

The radio operator reported that his breathing apparatus had been hit. I instructed him to don the portable reserve equipment, but we couldn't afford another hit in anyone's oxygen gear. No sooner did this happen than the gunner reported that *Fw.* Stadler, our flight engineer, had been hit in the upper arm. He was bleeding badly, and it looked as if all that was holding his arm on was a piece of tendon. I advised him to apply a tourniquet above the injury. Looking back between the bomb cells, I could see *Fw.* Stadler at the side window, still operating his machine-gun with his good hand, firing at the attacking fighters.

By now we were near our target; about 15 kilometers to our right we saw our *Geschwader* calmly heading for home, unmolested by fighters. We had long since accepted that we weren't going to make it back. We were, however, determined to reach out target, as we still had our full bomb load on board.

The radio operator reported that his gun had jammed. *Lt.* von Satzenhofen called to me: 'The radio operator's gun has jammed, what can I do?' I transmitted to the back: 'Clear the jam. If you can't, remove the machine-gun and install the seventh spare weapon, which is in the tail compartment'.

Suddenly the radio operator reported that the port engine was on fire. I looked at the port wing and saw black smoke pouring from the engine. The wing itself looked like a grater because of the countless bullet holes. Another glance at the oil temperature gauge confirmed it: the pointer was showing 150°, as high as it would go. The normal temperature was 80°. Nevertheless the engine continued to drone at full rpm. Flames flickered from the wing, but it looked as if the airflow would extinguish them at any moment. We decided to bale out. I passed the word to the men in back. At that moment *Leutnant* von Satzenhofen pointed to a spot on the ground from which heavy smoke was rising. We were looking at Mourmelon, which had been heavily bombed. We decided to first get our bombs to the target, which was right in front of us, and then bale out.

Everything happened quickly. I had switched on my Lotfe 7 c bombsight, aimed at a secondary target, and turned on the bomb release and fusing controls. This process so engrossed and busied me that I initially forgot about the dangerous situation we were in. *Leutnant* von Satzenhofen had previously handed me his aviator's glasses because the wind blowing through a hole in the glazed nose had blown stirred-up dirt into my eyes. I had first tried jamming a parachute into the hole, but the draught kept dislodging it.

Before me lay aircraft hangars, laid out in pairs at right angles to each other. Several aircraft sat on the apron, behind that several rows of billets. I had everything perfectly in my sight. The bombs fell and I followed their path. I picked up my binoculars and waited for them to land. As long as the bombs were in the cells, the two of us up front were shielded. During the bomb run, of course, we couldn't take evasive action. Many of our instruments had already been knocked out by hits. The fighters could now attack unhindered.

As soon as the bombs left the aircraft everything suddenly changed. I felt a slight impact on the top of my head. It later turned out that I had been grazed by a bullet, which created sort of a peak on my head and undid my headset. It wasn't until blood began running down my face that I became fully awake again.

The men in the back were ordered to bale out immediately. Sweat was running down von Satzenhofen's face. He was staring straight ahead. We agreed that he would keep the aircraft straight and level until we had baled out. I stood up to snap on the thigh belt of my parachute harness; but it didn't work so well. Overcome by the entire situation, I became nervous. We had probably waited too long. The bombing run had cost precious minutes, perhaps our lives. After some tugging I finally brought my harness together and clipped on my parachute. At that instant an explosive bullet struck the cockpit; as it later turned out twelve of its fragments struck me. I tapped von Satzenhofen again and tried to make my way to the back, but at first I was hindered by my oxygen mask, which had frozen together at the attachment point. Hard as I tried, I couldn't pull the hose off. Unhooking it from my helmet was also out of the question as it would take too long. Despite my fur-lined gloves, my hands were frozen numb. I therefore forced myself between the bomb cells with my oxygen equipment still in place. I didn't dare look around, as the hose might tear off at any minute and the ring with the metal clip might shoot into my face and put out an eye. I therefore reached back again, without turning my head that way, pulled hard, and somehow the hose came off. I expected to find that the crew in back had long since left the aircraft; but they were all still there, standing around the open hatch in the ventral bath. All had been hit in some way. The radio operator was standing with his back to me. I debated whether I should give him a shove to finally get things started. But baling out of the ventral hatch wasn't all that easy and involved risk. At that moment the machine lurched violently to the side and began to spin. My first thought was: Satzenhofen has lost his nerve and put the machine into a dive too soon. I fell face first over the floor mount of the radio operator's seat with its metal hooks and into a corner of the aft compartment. I could tell that I had sustained facial injuries. I also felt all sorts of pieces that had been lying about in the aft compartment falling on my back. In the rear were the wheel chocks, the spare machine-gun, numerous empty magazines, etc.

As the machine spun, it made strange uneven rotations, so that in my position, squeezed into the corner, the pressure repeatedly eased somewhat before I was pinned there again by greater force.

I hadn't been able to see for quite some time. As a result of my numerous head injuries blood had run into my eyes and filled them.

Despite this I knew what was front and back, but not what was up and down. I also knew that the open ventral hatch was not far away and I repeatedly tried to pull myself there so that I would be hurled from the spinning machine, but in vain. The centrifugal forces were so great that I couldn't even extend my arm towards it. I now knew that I was never going to get out of the aircraft. I accepted that I was going to die, completely without fear, it was more resignation: pity that you are all of 21 years old, will never see the end of the war and victory. Yes, we were such idealists in those days.

Suddenly there was a bang louder than all the other noises. I felt that my body was being pulled over some kind of precipice and then I was completely free and falling through space. It was an unreal feeling that is hard to describe. I seemed to me that after this impact, which I had been expecting to come at any minute, I was dead and my soul would leave my body and disappear into the hereafter. But soon, however, I regained my senses and gradually realized that I was still alive. My arms were flapping around, something was tugging at my feet and it was frightfully cold. I had the strangest feeling in my face, as if the air was streaming into my mouth and out again through a hole in my cheek.

My spirits revived very quickly. I realized that I was no longer in the aircraft but was alive and in free-fall. Only then, with this realization, came the terror and fear one would expect with a crash. It seared through me that I must hit the ground at any second. Before I had waited for an eternity for the impact, completely resigned and having long since abandoned any hope of living, but now I clung to life, I could make it, I had a chance.

This will to live returned with full force, but I couldn't see, didn't know how high I was. I became fearful that my parachute might not open in time. Where was the handle to pull? Usually I knew in my sleep where it was. I searched desperately for it, but I couldn't feel anything with my frozen hands. I still had my thick fur-lined gloves on and felt my chest. It had to be there. Then I found it. In a flash I grasped the handle, pulled, and soon I felt a powerful jerk and the canopy was open.

My next concern was to open my eyes so that I could see. I was worried that pieces of my aircraft might land on the parachute and undo everything. Then I opened my eyes and saw that I was still at about 600 meters, but – the next shock – I saw a fighter flying straight towards me. I could see the muzzles of his cannon and machine-guns. I grew ice-cold, it could be over at any minute. A thought seared through me: the day before I had heard that the crew of a German aircraft had been shot in their parachutes by a fighter not far from the Swiss border. The muzzles remained still but the machine came ever closer, as if the pilot intended to fly right through me. I became frightened that the pilot would misjudge his pass and cut through my parachute lines with his wing. When he flew past he waved at me, and I could breathe easy. My parachute now began to oscillate and I swung beneath it. The fighter turned round and again flew close by. The turbulence from the fighter, which had circled me twice, made me swing so wildly that I almost swung as high as my chute. The next fright came: what would happen if I swung higher than the canopy, causing the pressure on the lines to slacken and possibly making me fall back into the parachute? I quite simply had to put an end to these thoughts, think through to the end. Of course all of this happened much faster than I can express it here. While all of this was going on, I realized that apart from the fighter and me there was nothing in the air. Kilometers apart I saw burning parts of an aircraft. At first I even had the impression that a second aircraft, most likely an enemy fighter, had gone down too. But later I realized that it was just widely scattered parts of our He 111 that were burning. The ground came closer quickly, increasingly quickly. I landed as we had been taught, touching down on my left knee and left shoulder and rolling. At the moment I touched down my gyrating parachute was swinging high, which reduced the impact somewhat. I was in sock feet, having lost my flying boots when I was thrown out of the aircraft. When I touched the ground I tumbled face first several times. It felt like my feet had been knocked off. My intention, to jump up immediately, run towards the parachute and fall on it, remained just that – it was a good thing that there was no wind on that fine spring day. It was 07:30 on Pentecost Sunday, the name of the village was Sommepy. I was deep in enemy territory, about 40 to 50 kilometers from Paris. My face had been terribly mauled, I couldn't make any sort of expression. Most of the eleven fragment wounds were in my head and my spine was injured, I could barely move. My feet were badly swollen and my nose was broken. I had a hole in my right check through which I could stick my tongue. I was in bad shape. From far away a voice called: 'Hello, Englishman?' The thought went through me that they didn't know that I was German and took me for a downed British airman. The fighting had all taken place at a great height and the men on the ground had no idea who was shooting at whom up there.

But this was just a sudden inspiration. If they opened my flight suit they would quickly recognize me as a German airman. I called to them: '*Non, aviateur Allemagne.*' And promptly came the answer in German: '*Hände hoch!*'

In no time I was surrounded by Frenchmen. Their number grew steadily as the news went round that a German airman had been captured. Eventually there were enough soldiers there plus someone who was in command. *Lt.* von Satzenhofen lay in a wheat field. It was a gruesome sight. His body had landed feet first and accordioned. The head was slightly buried in the body and it in turn was imbedded in the ground. It was only a brief look, but I will never be able to forget it.

Accompanied by jeering, I was taken to a police station. The police gave me less than a warm welcome. All of my badges and shoulder straps were torn off, and everything I had in my pockets, including my handkerchief and watch, were taken from me. The entire nightmare was interrupted several times by air raid warnings. I was rushed to the village jail, which was only large enough for a wooden bed.

During a break between alarms the door opened and a slender, dark-haired French airman with the rank of sub-lieutenant extended his hand in greeting. In broken German he congratulated me on my survival and for our having put up a good fight. He had been flying one of the six fighters and had been forced to make an emergency landing nearby as he was out of fuel and had expended all his ammunition.

He was the one who had circled me in my parachute and from him I learned that our burning machine had first lost its port wing, then went into a spin and finally blew up at an altitude of 3000 meters, which is when I was thrown out.

As a souvenir the fighter pilot had been given my shoulder straps, one of which still had the three wings. I found my aerial opponent's behavior towards me particularly fair and pleasant; for all of my experiences up to that time had been negative, although I had no idea that much worse was to come. For all of my life I will remember this young French fighter pilot as a chivalrous opponent.

Later in the day a detachment from the *Garde Mobile* took me to various military and command posts. When I was placed in a big Citroen convertible I got a big surprise. My radio operator *Uffz.* Eisenmann was lying on the back seat and tried to smile at me. He was wounded and his leg was broken in several places. I never saw him again.

The drive continued in breakneck fashion. I sat between two members of the *Garde Mobile*. Every bump caused me pain. Each interrogation was accompanied by blows and verbal abuse. They used this method everywhere in an attempt to extract military and technical information from me. In Châlons-sur-Marne I was taken to a barracks. The drone of aircraft could be heard, interspersed with the dull thump of heavy anti-aircraft guns. These two dragged me up the stairs to a flat roof. There they left me lying all alone. All around I heard a sort of clinking, caused by shrapnel falling on the surrounding roofs. I experienced my first German air raid there. After the all-clear was sounded three *Garde Mobile* soldiers brought me down and dressed me again. Our open car passed through hostile crowds of people. They threw things at us and it looked as if they were about to rush the car. Even my escorts ducked their heads. We just got through. I was certain that my final hour had come. As we drove on, I saw a road sign with the name Sommesous, where I had bombed the airfield. All I had that first day was a cup of coffee given me by a nurse. My face was so battered and blood-smeared that I thought I would be disfigured for life. My many wounds remained untreated, no bandages, no medical attention. It continued from one interrogation to another, with all the described accompaniments. Mentally I was almost finished. I envied my comrades who had left everything behind. That should say it all. For at 21 one normally clings to life, especially after almost losing it.

It must have been after midnight when they delivered me to the jail in Nancy. After a frightful day there was a frightful night. The special interrogations by specialists began.

It was hard to believe how much they already knew. The documents and possessions carried by members of the crew were lying on the desk. We were never supposed to reveal our home base or operational airfield, but they already knew both. I complained to an RAF interrogation officer about my miserable treatment. He promised to see to it that I received medical care and dressings for my wounds. Soon afterwards this was done by a French medic, who gave me a cursory examination, spoke German with a Hessian accent and who saw his primary task as talking to me about us Germans, Hitler and the war. I received no treatment for my wounds or dressings. He observed that it wasn't all that bad and that my system would have to heal itself.

Another interrogation took place the next day by a French intelligence officer, a captain. It, too, was quite mannerly and without drama. I was very surprised by his detailed knowledge about Ansbach and his excellent German. From him I learned that the wife of our former *Staffelkapitän Major* Alarich Hoffmann had given birth to a daughter a few days earlier and that she was doing well. He knew certain drinking establishments in Ansbach, Katterbach too, and must have been active there for some time.

The interrogations continued on the third day, after they had first shaved my head. The journey ended outside the city of Metz in an outwork of the old fortress called Deroulede. I was to spent more than a week there, locked in a dark, damp room under the fortress wall. It was dank and there were rats. The area lay under German artillery fire. There I also experienced the frightful and demoralizing effects of

German Stuka attacks. They dropped bombs with screaming sirens, a horrible, unnerving thing. I lay completely alone and chilled through, afraid that the rats would gnaw on me as I slept. At the very end I was joined by another airman who had been shot down. He was *Fw.* Karl Kramer of our *Geschwader*'s *II. Gruppe*, whose peacetime base was in Schwäbisch-Hall. At night it was so cold that we sometimes lay close together for warmth.

The sound of fighting became louder as the front drew nearer. One day we were brought out and formed up in rows of five. The guard was huge. There were 51 Germans, mainly airmen. They took us to Bar-de-Luc in a crowded cattle car. Overhead we heard the drone of German aircraft, accompanied by the constant rumble of artillery and the rattle of fighter machine-guns. After an extremely uncomfortable 24 hours in Bar-le-Duc we continued southwards. I had been a prisoner of the French now about ten days, and almost always in solitary confinement, before I arrived in a prepared and regular prisoner of war camp for the first time.

It was Depot 601 near Auxerre. There I was registered and given *prisonnier de guerre* number 168. They used a stencil and white oil paint with a brush to put PG 168 and a large white disc on the front and back of my flight jacket and pants. Then I was shown to a barrack. The only light came from tiny skylights high on the walls. A central walkway separated the wooden bunks on the left and right, similar to a rabbit pen, one above the other. The sleeping surface was rough wood plus a wool blanket. I had just taken a few steps down the walkway and my eyes had begun to become accustomed to the half light when I heard a cheerful call of 'Karle-Karle' and radio operator *Fw.* Gustav Fegert came up and threw his arms around me. In seconds I was surrounded by the surviving members of the aircraft from the command *Kette*, pilot Jupp Schimpl and his flight engineer Fritz Puth. They had been shot down the day before me and had only lost their observer *Fw.* Bühler. *Oblt.* Hufenreiter had been separated from them and subsequently taken to another camp. Before they had been shot down, radio operator *Fw.* Fegert had shot down an enemy fighter. There were also two men from the crew of pilot *Fw.* Leo Etzel. There was a warm welcome all around and mutual satisfaction that we had survived. Of course everyone wanted to hear the latest about what was happening outside, the fate of other crews and how the war was going. Among those gathered round me I also discovered comrade Boiselle, who had been with me at Bomber Observer Course N at the air weapons school in Neuburg/Donau and the Central Bomber School in Lechfeld, but who was with another *Geschwader*. There were also several crews from the *Stabsstaffel* of KG 53.

Surrounded by these old comrades, I suddenly felt quite differently, almost saved. After a few days I was permitted to write home for the first time. The camp was laid out to accommodate many thousands of prisoners and consisted of about ten individual camps each with three barracks. We occupied just one, with about 200 men. Our main task was roll call, which was held three times daily. We did everything we could to find out about the state of the war and our chances of liberation. We organized an intelligence service, whose job was to determine where the front was, casualties on both sides and other usable knowledge, based on conversations and remarks by the guards, from French newspapers we could lay our hands on and information from new arrivals. Now and then we succeeded in getting hold of the official war communiqué from the French Army high command from a newspaper.

When one hears about the individual experiences and fates of downed German airmen, often one must be grateful to have gotten off so easily. Others had to endure much worse. One night there was an air raid warning and the two barrack doors were locked shut. We were completely helpless against our own attack. A sigh of relief went through the room when the sound of the engines faded and the German aircraft flew away. On one occasion the far end of the camp, which, thank God, was unoccupied, was hit. We protested to the camp commander, a captain, and asked for a visit from the International Red Cross and requested that the camp be clearly marked to prevent further attacks. The only concession we received was permission to make the word 'Depot 601' in front of our part of the camp in light-colored gravel. The characters were about two meters in size.

The days themselves were filled with frequent lengthy roll calls, during which we had to stand at attention. They frequently miscounted and had to start all over again. The main actor in this at least thrice-daily ritual was a sergeant, who we called 'swineherd' on account of his harsh tone; for to these people we were the '*Boche*'.

Despite everything, the time spent in this camp was relatively easy to bear. The rumble of guns grew louder, and of course we hoped that we would be overrun by German troops and freed. But then without warning we were forced to leave the camp and move south. It was the beginning of a terrible time, between refugee columns, retreating troops and frequent air attacks. The sun shone down mercilessly on our shaven heads. Water, water was the biggest problem. Our number had grown to about 1,900 German prisoners. Food remained almost non-existent. Our daily rations consisted of watery soup and a little bread. We all became very weak.

Our destination was the small city of Mazères at the foot of the Pyrenees. We were quartered in a half-fallen-down brickworks nearby.

Among us prisoners, hopes grew that France was finished and that the war would soon end. We noted this particularly in the behavior of the guards and the way they stood up to superiors. The food problem was catastrophic. One night, it might have been at about three in the morning and totally dark, the airmen were told in a whisper to assemble outside and fall in. Our hopes rose: we airmen were the first to be going home.

Outside an unusual scene: buses filled with German airmen left the camp. We had to wait and did so with excitement. But soon we learned from French soldiers that we were being taken to a Mediterranean port on the coast, from where we were to be shipped to Africa. France and its allies had reached an agreement whereby all airmen and specialists from other branches of the military would be sent out of the country before a ceasefire. We protested and became mutinous. We threatened the guards that we would tear down the barbed wire and smash everything to bits if a delegation from the prisoners was not allowed to immediately contact French commands and German troops.

The guards were already so demoralized that they put away their weapons and shouted: '*La guerre fini – Schiessen nix gut.*' We know knew that there must be a ceasefire. The camp commander had meanwhile rushed to the scene, and we were permitted to send a three-man delegation with him and his people to Toulouse. There we were able to establish telephone contact with German troops of Panzer Group Kleist in Bordeaux. The French command was instructed to leave us where we were and was told that there would be reprisals for any missing airmen. Our delegation was taken back to the camp. Soon, however, there came news that we were to be taken by special train to a designated point several kilometers from Bordeaux, where we would be handed over to German troops.

In Mazères a train of freight cars was hastily assembled and we were put aboard. Suddenly there was also enough to eat. There was plenty of bread and cheese and a large milk can full of red wine was placed in each car.

Somewhere, about forty kilometers from Bordeaux, our train pulled into a small station. The place was empty, no people anywhere. To the left and right, however, there were anti-tank guns pointing towards us menacingly. The train was signaled to stop. Suddenly from behind the gun shields appeared German helmets, commands in German rang out and before we knew it the entire train was surrounded. There was jubilation. We were taken in front of the station, where we were separated by branch of service and immediately assigned to waiting

Wehrmacht trucks. We then drove through Bordeaux. Our guards, as we later learned, were all taken prisoner.

On reaching Bordeaux we and four men of the *3. Staffel* were each assigned to two men of an artillery battery as so-called sponsored children. There we were given uniforms and felt a little better.

With four men of the *3. Staffel*, pilot *Fw.* J. Schimpl, radio operator *Fw.* G. Fegert, flight engineer *Fw.* Puth (all from the *Gruppe* command flight) and I as the last survivor of *Lt.* von Satzenhofen's crew, after some time we made our own way to the aircrew assembly group in Brussels and reported to the Processing Center for the Reassignment of Aircrew.

Our *Geschwader* was soon informed and a vehicle from the *I. Gruppe* collected us and took us to the command post on the Lille-North airfield.

Our odyssey through France had come to a temporary conclusion."

This account by Karl Ulrich found its conclusion thirty years later, when he discovered the identity of his former enemy: "Thirty years later – long after the war, my thoughts kept returning to that chivalrous *Sous-Lieutenant*. I was able to find out the names of the six fighter pilots. Two of those who had helped shoot down my machine were still living, but the one who had circled my parachute and who had shaken my hand in Sommeby prison was no longer alive. His name was *Lt.* Hebrard. A cordial exchange of ideas developed with his squadron commander, *Lt.* Angiolini. The key sentence of a letter dated 9 February 1971 and another from 28 June 1971 contained the statement which expressed in simple and moving words how the chivalrous gesture from that time symbolizes the present relationship between our two peoples: '... the former enemy, apologizes to the friend of today ... Should you ever come to France, I would be very pleased to welcome you into my home, for despite the fact that we were once enemies, we will remember just one thing: we are, after all, just two airmen who at that time simply did our dut.'

For me there was no question that in my answering letter to reply to him: '... there is certainly no need for you to apologize to the former enemy, rather I should and must do the same to you ... I would be happy ... and would very much like to meet you in person and with a handshake bury the hostility once forced upon us and begin a new friendship like that begun between France and Germany and therefore we two.'

The chivalrous spirit of which the air force boasts is found on both sides."

This ends Karl Ulrich's account.

But the war went on relentlessly. The mission orders for 13 May were aimed at positions in the Sedan area. One day later the *Gruppen* received advance information for the 14th of May concerning the advance by the XXXXI Army Corps:

The XXXXI Army Corps has crossed the Meuse near Mothermeau north of Charleville. Bridgeheads established NW and SW of Sedan. 1st Panzer Division has broken through on a general line Cheheris-Boullion. Intended advance in general direction with Rethel as objective of the day.

Line of Security:

Attigny-Stenay – do not bomb north of this line.

Expected Mission:

Attacks against identified march and transport movements on roads and railways south of the line of security. To follow own reconnaissance.

Action to be expected during the morning.

Readiness as ordered.

Weather in the area almost clear. North of Sedan hazy, a small disturbance is expected to pass through.

The advance order for the morning mission on 14 May 1940:

1. KG 2 and KG 53 to attack transport in the following area

   right boundary:

   Montmedy-Stenay-Avennys-Rethel

   left boundary:

   Esch-Spincourt-Verdun.

   Separation KG 2 (right) and KG 53 (left) Stenay-Dun-Varenne (towns to KG 2).

   Rear border:

   Rethel-Chalerange-Verdun.

   Bombing line of security:

   Maginot Line to Montmedy-Stenay-Rethel. No bombs must be dropped north of this line.

2. 5./LG 1 is directed to work closely with KG 53.

3. The *Stabsstaffel* to conduct reconnaissance in the *Geschwader* combat area with 1 He 111 and 5 He 111s of KG 53.

   The objective is to locate march columns and rail transports. March columns and transports are to be attacked as soon as located. Take off immediately.

4. Attack altitude 2000-2500m, provided defenses permit.

5. I., II. and III./KG 53 are ordered to Readiness Level I as of 12:00. *Staffel* commanders and flight leaders to the *Gruppe* commander. Expect immediate action based on reconnaissance results.

6. For orientation:
   Reconnaissance results 07:00:
   Heavy rail traffic from Metz and Verdun to the north.
   Fuchs
   Oberleutnant and adjutant.

As per the advance order of 17 May, on 18 May 1940 the Geschwader moved as follows:

Headquarters with headquarters Staffel to Wiesbaden-Erbenheim
I. Gruppe operations base Gross-Ostheim
II. Gruppe operations base Zellhausen
III. Gruppe operations base Rhein-Main

Under growing threat of encirclement, the French and British armies tried to escape by withdrawing to the north and northwest. The *Luftwaffe* tried to hinder the enemy's retreat by attacking road and rail transports, especially in the area of Amiens and Abbeville. The mission orders and reports of 18 and 20 May 1940 reflect the toughness of the fighting:

Operations order for 18 May 1940:
1. KG 53 to inflict lasting destruction on assigned targets.
   I./KG 53 to attack and destroy line
   (a) Abbeville-Boulogne near bridge south of Neuyelle,
   (b) arc to the north near Beauvais near point due south of Aumale,
   (c) Boulogne-Rouen-Amiens due west of Fouilloy.
2. Zerstörer cover by ZG 2. Rendezvous en route to line Charleville-Oflize at 2500 m or under cloud base at 16:30. Rendezvous during return flight Reims-Chaulnes (35 km SW Amiens) -Troyes (15 km S Chaulnes).
3. Destroy rail lines, even if not in use.
   Report by I./KG 53 of 18 May 1940:
   Target: rail installations near Noyelles and Aumale, Nahn near Fouilly.
   Attack altitude: 2000 m
   Defenses: anti-aircraft fire near Amiens-Poix-Fouilly
   Results: 7 direct hits on Fouilly station. Other hits and direct hits on stations in Gouemirous, Vieux and Roues, Aumale station and road, St. Germain-Fernapon road, Noyelles turntable and station buildings in Noyelles, Amiens-Fouilly line, Noyelles-Buc line, Aumale-Eu-Mers.

Reconnaissance results: light southbound motorized column traffic on Amiens road.

Moving traffic at close intervals only in railway stations. At least 20 multi-engine aircraft on Poix airfield.

Mission order for reconnaissance aircraft on 20 May 1940:

5 He 111s and 1 He 111 of the headquarters Staffel to take off on reconnaissance mission at 06:30. Rendezvous with a Staffel of twin-engined fighters over Neufchâteau at 07:30.

Geschwader – Combat Area:

Abbeville-Le Treport-Plangy-Aumale-Abaucourt-Grandvillers-Amiens.

The 3. Staffel to reconnoiter this area with 5 He 111s plus 1 He 111 of the headquarters Staffel at 06:30. Rendezvous with a Staffel of twin-engined fighters over Neufchâteau at 07:30. Locate and destroy troop concentrations and movements on railways and roads in that direction. Also observe airfields at Amiens-Glissy and Poix and attack if occupied.

Reconnaissance results to be transmitted by radio immediately.

Takeoff: Individual takeoffs at 06:30. Rendezvous with a Staffel of twin-engined fighters over Neufchâteau at 07:30. (Fire 3 red flares as recognition signal.) Flight altitude depending on weather situation.

Report on 2nd mission of 20 May 1940 by I./KG 53:

Takeoff: 10:30 by 12 He 111s.

Landing: 14:15 – 14:30 by 9 He 111s.

Targets: Road and rail transport in the Amiens-Abbeville area.

Attack altitude: 2500m.

Defenses: Heavy medium and heavy anti-aircraft fire near Amiens and Abbeville.

Fighters: 16 Moranes and 6 Potez (Potez did not attack.)

Results: Direct hits on road-rail crossing near Piquigny. Other hits and direct hits on Longpré station, Amiens-Abbeville rail line, busy road fork at the southern exit from Fontaine sur Somme, troops in Airaines, busy station in Piquigny, busy road fork west of Conde Folie, rail line 500m west of Abbeville ion the south side of the Canal de la Somme, road and exit from town of Fontaine sur Somme, road in Hangest sur Somme.

Unusual Occurrences:

A1+EH starboard engine hit and set on fire east of Amiens. Bale-out not observed, may have force-landed in own territory.

A1+CK shot down by fighters due east of Amiens..

A1+FK shot down by flak due east of Abbeville. Aircraft spun down, no parachutes seen, this aircraft was observed to crash and explode.

Two Moranes sent down damaged east of Amiens.

Amiens-Glissy airfield unoccupied during outward flight, 6 multi-engine aircraft (probably Potez 63) observed during return flight.

Heavy troop movements on Albert-Amiens road (direction of march southwest). Also on Abbeville-Beauvais road, direction of march south.

The *Geschwader* was again sent to attack transport and movements in the Blangy-Rouen-Etrepagny-Poix area on 21 May.

The German advance continued irresistibly.

Geschwader order for 24 May 1940: Gross-Ostheim teletype office 23 May 1940, 00:00, to II./KG 53 Zellhausen – to III./KG 53 Rhein-Main:

1. *Situation:* The ring around the encircled English-French-Belgian armies has closed tighter. Kleist Group has taken Boulogne and St. Omer and advance elements are engaging English troops in Calais.

2. *Mission:* KG 53, as part of Fliegerkorps II, is being committed to secure the left flank of the right wing of the 12th and 4th Armies in the line Abbeville-Amiens-Peronne-Ham-La Fère.

3. *Combat Area:* Le Havre-Brionne-Rouen-Forges les Eaux-Poix-Le Treport (towns to KG)

4. *Bombing Line of Security :* Le Treport-Blangy-Poix-Roye-Noyon.

5. *Committed are:* I./KG 53 with 1 He 111 of the headquarters Staffel in the eastern combat area. Line of separation: Dieppe-Rouen (including city). Takeoff to be time to permit rendezvous with Zerstörer at 2000 meters or below cloud over Neufchâteau at 07:00. One He 111 ten minutes in advance. Mission: free hunt for road and rail movements, plus reconnaissance in designated area. Objective is to ascertain whether enemy forces are being moved north against our left flank from the direction of Paris and Rouen. The He 111 of the headquarters Staffel is to transmit reconnaissance results by radio on the Geschwader frequency. New orders will be issued should weather not permit group operation. II./KG 53 to Readiness Level 2 at 08:30. Anticipate mission in Geschwader combat area against transport movements on roads and rail lines base don reconnaissance results from the first mission. III./KG 53 to Readiness Level 3 at 08:30. Overhaul work can be carried out.

KG 53 Operations Section No 690/40 Secret.

The missions recorded in the logbook of Alfred Sticht, then an observer in the aircraft of the commander of the *1. Staffel*, may be seen as a representative overview of the operations by the *Geschwader*:

From 10-12 May 1940 systematic attacks on the French air force and ground organization and French transportation targets. First combat mission, takeoff from Roth, landing in Gelchsheim (near Giebelstadt). Six more combat missions by the *1. Staffel* from Gelchsheim.

10/5/1940	Attacks on Maginot Line near Sedan-Charleville
11/5/1940	Attack on Mourmelon airfield near Reims
12/5/1940	Attack 10 km S of Chalon sur Marne
12/5/1940	Attack on railroad and columns near Sedan
13/5/1940	Attack on Maginot Line near Sedan
14/5/1940	Attack on railroad and columns near Verdun
15/5/1940	Night mission 20:40 – 00:15. A1+LH made forced landing near Deiningen
18/5/1940	Transfer: Gelchsheim-Gross-Ostheim (near Aschaffenburg)
18/5/1940	Attack on railroad and columns Aunnale-Le Treport – Eu
19/5/1940	Attack on Clermont-St. Just-Beauvais
20/5/1940	Attack on rail line and troops Amiens-Abbeville
24/5/1940	Attack on rail line and troops Dieppe-Rouen
24/5/1940	Attack on rail line and armored troops Aunnale-Neufchâteau
25/5/1940	Attack on rail line, breakthrough to the sea
25/5/1940	Attack on tanks in the Amiens-Poix area
25/5/1940	Attack on port of Dieppe and Blagny station (flak and fighters)
26/5/1940	Attack on railroad and troops NE of Paris
27/5/1940	Attack on railroad and troops Marseille/Neau Monte
1/6/1940	Attack on Grenoble rail junction (Swiss Me 109)
6/6/1940	Attack on enemy troops SW of Reims
8/6/1940	Attacked enemy troops Beauvais-Clermont
9/6/1940	Attacked troops and positions N of Reims (flak and fighters)
10/6/1940	Attacked railroad south of Epernay (flak and fighters)
11/6/1940	Attacked positions S of Vouziers (flak)
13/6/1940	Attacked rail installations Neufchâteau (flak and fighters)
13/6/1940	Attack on Neufchâteau-Verdun road and rail line (flak and fighters)
14/6/1940	Attack on Epinal-Nancy road and rail line (flak and fighters)
14/6/1940	Attack on Belfort station (flak)
15/6/1940	Attack on Langrest-Merrey rail line (flak)

On 21 June 1940 the *Geschwader* moved from Gross-Ostheim to Evreux le Courdray. In Artois Panzer Group Kleist turned north then northwest. On 23 May it cut off Boulogne and Calais and on the 24th it reached the As (river between St. Omer and Gravelines) with its front facing east. The formation of a large pocket was unmistakable. The fate of the British expeditionary corps and elements of the French Army was sealed at Dunkirk on 26 May. The panzer division commanders pressed for an immediate advance to smash the expeditionary force

gathered there. Hitler, however, ordered the panzers to halt. The *Luftwaffe* would finish off the English at Dunkirk. The ultimate reason for Hitler's decision is still debated today. In any case there was a considerable discrepancy between what Göring wanted and what the *Luftwaffe* was really capable of.

Luftflotte 2 under Kesselring was given the task of destroying the port facilities and the British expeditionary corps. Kesselring telephoned Göring to express his reservations. He pointed out to Göring "that he was well aware of the effects on the airmen of almost three weeks of constant action and knew better than to order missions that could scarcely be accomplished with fresh forces." He also pointed out to Göring that the English were committing their new Spitfires from airfields in the south of England and that consequently heavy losses could be expected. Finally Kesselring declared that the operation was not feasible, even with the support of *VIII Fliegerkorps*. Although Jeschonnek shared Kesselring's views, he shied away from expressing this to Hitler.

While the English were only able to commit 200 Spitfires, they attacked our bombers 'with the fury of the crazy'. *II Fliegerkorps* alone lost 23 aircraft and 64 men on the first day. That was more than in the ten preceding combat days. Then the weather deteriorated, virtually grounding the air force. The rain continued until 29 May. Then the weather cleared and our bombers again appeared over Dunkirk. The heavy attacks destroyed much materiel, but the *Luftwaffe* was unable to achieve the destruction of the bridgehead and prevent the evacuation, allowing the core of the British Army to be saved.

By 4 June a total of 338,226 Allied troops (including 123,000 French) was evacuated from Dunkirk on 848 ships. Losses totaled 272 ships, including 9 destroyers. Dunkirk fell on 4 June 1940.

Even while the Battle of Dunkirk was still raging, German units assembled on the Somme and the Aisne in order to continue the attack as soon as possible.

The French tried to reduce the German bridgeheads, but in vain. The German attack across the Somme began on 5 June, one day after the fall of Dunkirk. French resistance was so strong that initially the attackers only succeeded in breaking out of the Abbeville bridgehead.

Panzer Group Hoth attacked there and Rommel's division outflanked the enemy and drove deep into the hinterland. At Amiens and Péronne, however, the German attack initially made no progress. Then, however, the way was opened for operations by larger panzer units.

KG 53's Geschwader order of 8-9 June 1940 read:

Teletype Center Gross-Ostheim – Secret – 9 June 1940 to I./KG 53 Gross-Ostheim, II./KG 53 Zellhausen, to III./KG 53 Rhein-Main.

Geschwader order for operations on 9 June 1940

1. Fl.Korps. II is supporting the major attack by the 2nd and 3rd Armies plus Group Guderian, which crossed the Aisne at 04:30.

2. Unit standby: II. and III./KG 53 at Readiness Level 2 from 07:00, I./KG 53 at Readiness Level 2 from 08:00.

3. Geschwader combat area: Pont Arry (23 km E of Soissons) -Epernay-Bergères-Pogny- (12 km SE of Chalons sur M.) -Givry en Argonne (15 km S of St. Menehould) -Suippes-Juneville-Chateau-Persien. KG 2 is also committed in the Geschwader area.

4. Bomb Load: 1 row of cells SC 10 and 1 row of cells ½ SD 50 and ½ SBE 50.

5. At 04:00 Headquarters Staffel will move two He 111s to Soissons and from there reconnoiter the Geschwader area, orders to be issued verbally.

Kampfgeschwader 53

Three days later Hoth reached Rouen. Rommel drove 12,000 British and French troops to the coast and occupied the major war port of Cherbourg. Reims fell on 10 June.

Paris could no longer be defended and the French government declared it an open city. The 18th Army (Küchler) occupied the city on the 14th. On 17 June Guderian reached the Swiss border. The French collapse was complete, and the government asked for a ceasefire.

The ceasefire agreement was signed at 18:50 on 22 June and at 01:35 on the 25th the guns fell silent.

Concerning the conclusion of the French campaign, a look at neutral Switzerland is warranted.

Border incursions by the warring powers "all around", especially when a relatively small nation like Switzerland is involved, are not uncommon. Most of the combatants probably experienced this. We must assume that the border violations were unintentional, at least until the contrary is proven.

For the reader's consideration the *Geschwader* order of 31 May 1940:

Teletype Center Gross-Ostheim – Secret – 31 May 1940.

To be treated as a 'Secret Command Matter' after receipt. To II./KG 53 Zellhausen I./KG 53 Gross-Ostheim, III./KG 53 Rhein-Main.

Order for the mission on the morning of 1 June 1940.

1. KG 53 is attached to Fl.Korps IV for 1 June 1940.

2. Fl.Korps IV will attack rail lines from Marseilles to the north with the objective of cutting deliveries of fuels to northern France.

3. KG 53 will attack as follows, with the objective of inflicting lasting

damage: I./KG 53 railroad junction near Rives (20 km NW of Grenoble), II./KG 53 rail line near Aix les Bains. III./KG 53 Amberieu railroad junction and rail line.

4. Bomb Load: 4 SC 250
5. At 06:00 the Headquarters Staffel will place three aircraft at Readiness Level I, so that one per Gruppe can be dispatched for target reconnaissance on a timely basis.
6. Operational readiness for KG 53: Readiness Level 1 from 06:00.
7. Defenses are expected to be weak over the target, caution when overflying the Swiss border. Attack by Swiss Bf 109 fighter aircraft is to be expected.
8. I will be flying in the aircraft of the flight leader of the 3rd Kette of III./KG 53. From Langendiebach to Rhein-Main in the aircraft of the Headquarters Staffel.
9. Weather briefing by telephone from the Geschwader meteorologist at 05:00.

Kampfgeschwader 53 No.184/40 Secret Command Matter.

The following is the *I. Gruppe*'s report on the mission:

Report on the first mission by I./KG 53 on 1 June 1940, takeoff by 12 He 111 at 15:30 – landing 19:50 to 20:00 by 11 He 111s.

Target:	rail junction near Rives
Attack altitude:	5500 m
Defenses:	Flak: heavy and light flak near Lyon (at another Gruppe). Heavy anti-aircraft fire near Belfort-Mühlhausen-Basel (accurate).
Fighters:	6 – 8 Bf 109s (with Swiss nationality markings observed).
Results:	rail junction not hit. 1 bomb fell short, the rest beyond and to the right of the rail line. 1 direct hit on the crossroad east of Rives.
Unusual incidents:	A1+EH aborted as accompanying aircraft returned to Langendiebach with undercarriage trouble.

It is strange that the incidents in the following account were not mentioned in the report:

"At 15:00 on 1 June 1940 we were ordered to the command post for a briefing by the *Kommandeur*. Attack on the railroad junction at Grenoble.

We took off at 15:36: *Hauptmann* Allmendinger, *Obfw.* Sticht, *Obfw.* Schuster and *Uffz.* Marbach in He 111 A1+LH.

We set course for Grenoble.

After we had completed our mission, we were on our way home along the French-Swiss border. Suddenly the radio operator in the last *Kette* shouted through his throat microphone: 'Attention, fighters from behind!' There may have been about 10 to 12.

The *Staffel* closed up tight, and the safeties were removed from the machine-guns and cannon. We prepared for a tough fight. Suddenly the radio operator in the last *Kette* called again: 'Attention, don't shoot. They're Me 109s, our fighter escort.' Thank God, for it would surely have been an unequal battle and we would undoubtedly have lost a few feathers.

Relieved, we secured our weapons again. The Me 109s came closer and closer. It was then that we realized our fateful mistake. When they were very close to our formation they suddenly opened fire.

Only then did we realize that they were Swiss fighters, their air force being equipped with our Me 109. We were more than a little surprised. By the time we were able to return fire, three of our aircraft had already been so badly hit that they were on fire and leaving smoke trails. The crews of the three aircraft had to make emergency landings or bale out of their burning aircraft. The survivors and wounded were taken prisoner by the French. This was a sign that we were over French territory and that the Swiss fighters had had no reason to attack us.

We swore revenge for our comrades, who had been shot down without justification. We landed in Großostheim at 19:52.

We later learned that this behavior by the Swiss pilots resulted in a single He 111 being sent on the same route several days later. This time, however, it was well watched by a *Staffel* of Me 110s at high altitude. When the Swiss Me 109s rose again to intercept the lone He 111, the escorting Me 110s dove on the Swiss fighters and shot down most of them. The rest dove into cloud and disappeared. Our Me 110s and the He 111 returned to their bases without loss."

Then *Staffelkapitän Oberleutnant* Wittmann provided the following summary of the Headquarters *Staffel's* actions during the campaign in France:

"We hoped that a political solution would prevent a continuation of this senseless war, but on 10 May 1940 the attack on France began.

The Headquarters *Staffel* suffered casualties on 10 May 1940. As we crossed the border near Charleville our formation was attacked by French or British fighters. A burst struck the cockpit. Bullets pinged, the whole cockpit was riddled and pilot *Oberleutnant* Schmitz was hit in the chest several times. We pulled him from the pilot's seat and laid him between the bomb cells. As the aircraft was going down, I took the controls and managed to level out at about 1000 meters. We abandoned the mission and set course for Frankfurt/Main, calling ahead for an ambulance. It was in vain, however, for that evening our *Oberleutnant* Schmizt was dead.

We flew mission after mission. Our command had photos of the targets and bombed airfields within about two hours after landing. As well, we had to fly regular photo-reconnaissance missions over the front to monitor movements, artillery positions and also the Maginot Line.

Because of our 'lightning victories', after several days the *Staffel* was moved to Langendiebach/Gelnhausen and then on 25 May 1940 to Lille-North. We were on French soil, in Flanders, where Richthofen, Boelcke and Immelmann had flown in the war of 1914-1918.

Because of our great success there were high spirits everywhere and we were continuously inaction, also attacking targets in the southern half of France.

The French and English fighter arms were excellent. The armament of our bomber aircraft was inadequate. It was very soon realized that a fighter escort was needed by our bomber formations and even reconnaissance aircraft.

Unfortunately because of the weather situation the *Luftwaffe* could not be used as required at Dunkirk and so England succeeded in evacuating almost all of its troops, at the loss of virtually all of their equipment, to England. This was a decisive accomplishment by the English, and we were not in a position to pursue the beaten English army.

The war moved quickly and France surrendered.

Once again, everywhere there was hope that perhaps the war might be over, but, as we know, in vain."

5. BETWEEN THE FRENCH CAMPAIGN AND THE BATTLE OF BRITAIN

Only a few days passed before the next battle began, the air battle for England, or the 'Battle of Britain'. First, however, we would like to take another look back at Dunkirk and what resulted, perhaps fatefully, for Germany and England.

Had Rundstedt caused Hitler to issue the halt order? After the British escaped, Hitler would surely have laid the blame at Rundstedt's feet, for he liked to blame others for his mistakes. If Hitler was influenced, it could only have been by Keitel or Jodl, the top military men in his staff. Another reason for the halt order of course was Göring, who overestimated the striking power of his air force.

There are also clues that it was Hitler who applied the brakes, particularly as the *Luftwaffe* was obviously not committed as strongly as would have been possible. It is therefore obvious to at least suspect that a political motive lay behind Hitler's military reasons.

Blumentritt, Rundstedt's operations planner, associated this with curious statements by Hitler in his headquarters. Hitler was in the best of moods. The war with France was almost over, a reasonable peace would be concluded with France and then the way would be open for an understanding with England.

Furthermore he surprised his generals when he expressed admiration for the British Empire, which he compared to the Roman Catholic Church; both were vital stabilizing elements. He declared: "All I will ask of Great Britain is that it acknowledge Germany's dominant position on the continent. Of course the return of our colonies would be desirable but not essential. That would be a matter of prestige. I am also prepared to offer England the support of my army if it should run into any sort of difficulty." In conclusion Hitler stated that he was prepared to conclude a peace with England under conditions "which it could accept in compatibility with its honor."

From this Blumentritt concluded that the halt order at Dunkirk meant nothing else than not offending England's sense of honor, for which it would then show its gratitude.

But Hitler's calculation didn't hold up. It must also be said that his character was so complicated that a simple explanation can scarcely get close to the truth.

6. THE BATTLE OF BRITAIN

a) The Starting Point

After the fall of France, Udet declared: "The war is over, we no longer need our production plans, they're worthless!" His euphoria disappeared, however, when the *Luftwaffe* found itself forced to wage a strategic war with tactical forces in the aerial campaign against Britain.

In Great Britain the aerial campaign of 1940 is called the "Battle of Britain." It began on 13 August 1940 with 485 bomber and 1,000 fighter sorties against the ports of Portland and Southampton plus airfields in Hampshire and Kent.

By the end of the day the *Luftwaffe* had lost 45 aircraft, the RAF 13. Two days later the *Luftwaffe* struck harder. There were 1,768 sorties, 520 of them by bombers against British airfields. The outcome: 75 aircraft shot down by the RAF against the loss of 34 British fighter aircraft. Subsequent attacks resulted in further significant losses. On 16 August the *Luftwaffe* lost 16 aircraft, on the 18th another 71.

After these failures in daylight attacks, the focus was shifted to night raids against England. This began on 28 August with three consecutive night attacks by large forces of bombers against Liverpool. The so-called "London blitz" began on 7 September. Until 13 November an average of 130 bombers attacked London night after night.

The aerial offensive against the British Isles was begun halfheartedly and without a clear objective.

What was actually supposed to be achieved? The Royal Air Force was supposed to be eliminated as a prelude to invasion, political pressure placed on England to surrender, revenge exacted for British attacks on German cities – almost all simultaneously, sometimes consecutively.

The name of this chapter of the war says little, in fact it has no name that can adequately describe the confused, improvised, haphazard but bitter battles, with thousands of terrors, air battles and bombing raids, that raged between the German and English in the period between August 1940 and May 1941. Adolf Galland even called it "a crazy, disorganized battle"! The first attempt in the history of warfare to defeat an enemy through air power took place in several phases:

Phase 1: 13 Aug. – 23 Aug. German air attacks on coastal targets in southern England, especially against the British fighter arm, airfields and aircraft factories.

Phase 2: 24 Aug. – 6 Sept. 40. Widening of the attacks to include the London area.

Phase 3: 7 Sept. – 19 Sept. 40. Day and night attacks against targets in the London area.

Phase 4: 20 Sept. – 13 Nov. 40. Day and night fighter-bomber attacks, focusing on London.

Phase 5: 14 Nov. 40 – May 1941. Night raids against targets in all of England.

In phase one the *Luftwaffe* tried and failed to achieve air superiority over the south of England. Göring then tried to strike at the economic potential and morale of the English civilian population. It came as no surprise to the responsible commanders that, for the first time, the *Luftwaffe* was unable to accomplish its mission.

Generalfeldmarschall Kesselring, whose *Luftflotte 2* lost almost 1,000 aircraft, observed: "Just as we entered the Polish war unprepared in 1939, we were not equipped for the economic war against England in its depth and diversity. We certainly made life on their island difficult for the English, but we were unable to sever Great Britain's lifelines."

Göring boasted to Hitler before the battle began. Now he frequently withdrew to the dream world of his East Prussian hunting lodge, before appearing near the end of the battle to make reproaches against the surviving crews for having made him look bad in the eyes of the *Führer*. The following example illustrates how sensitively the unit commanders reacted to the supreme command's total misreading of the situation: when *Generalfeldmarschall* Milch, behind whom Göring in reality stood, visited a unit in Holland, the crews of KG 30 made no secret of their displeasure. The *Staffel* commander, himself constantly in action, bluntly told the *Generalfeldmarschall* that it was impossible for him to achieve the results demanded of him with the aircraft, bomb sights and weapons available to him; he declared that the British fighters were superior to the German bombers.

Generalfeldmarschall Milch, apparently grateful for these frank statements, promised immediate remedies. These turned out to be the disbandment of one the *Geschwader*'s *Gruppen* for "mutiny and defeatism." The unit's officers were transferred and demoted.

During the month of July the fighter and bomber units of *Luftflotten 2* and *3* were assembled along the Channel Coat. The German air force massed 1,200 bombers, 280 dive-bombers, 760 single- (mostly Bf 109s) and twin-engined fighters (mainly Bf 110s) plus 140 reconnaissance aircraft. During this period *Luftwaffe* activity was restricted to reconnaissance flights.

b) Armed Reconnaissance

Alfred Sticht of the *1. Staffel* described an armed reconnaissance flight over the east coast of England:

"The crews of the *Staffel* commanders of the 1st, 2nd and 3rd *Staffeln* were given the task of conducting armed reconnaissance along the east coast of England from Dover through the Wash up through Scapa Flow to the Orkney Islands.

We received weather reports from the meteorologists, who warned that the effect of the Gulf Stream could result in rapid changes in the weather.

We took off in A1+LH at 14:00 carrying 36 50-kg bombs. Initially setting course for Radio Beacon 729 at Ruddervoorde south of Brugges, Belgium, we made a brief position report by radio and then signed off. We climbed at a rate of 2 to 3 meters per second to the cloud base, which was at 3000 meters, heading 290 degrees in the direction of Harwich on the English coast. After crossing the coast of Belgium and reaching the base of cloud, we climbed up into the clouds to check for icing. It was excellent bomber weather. In the event of fighter attack we could duck quickly into the clouds for protection.

On reaching the area of the English coast we dropped below cloud again and regained ground contact at an altitude of 3000 meters. At the same time we turned onto a heading of 050 degrees to avoid the flak belt. Abeam Great Yarmouth we spotted a convoy of 25 ships sailing north.

Over England the cloud cover broke up and we were forced to fly farther out to sea. We continued to head north and after a while turned onto a NNW heading in the direction of The Wash. Below on our left lay Grimsby with its oil tank farms. My fingers itched to drop a couple of eggs there, but the blue sky would mean the end of a lone aircraft. We would be easy meat for scrambling fighters, which were faster than we were.

We flew over Hull on the Humber estuary, Middlesborough, Newcastle (codename Chimneysweep), then over the Firth of Forth towards Scapa Flow. The balance of our reconnaissance: the convoy sighted off Great Yarmouth. On the return flight we faced the question: should we attack the convoy of 23 ships with several escorting warships? Did it make sense, could we risk it or were we gambling too much?

Finally we went into a slow descent and reached a favorable attack altitude.

A few minutes later we heard the voice of *Staffelkapitän* Allmendinger: abort the bomb run, bomb fusing controls off, close bomb doors, we're climbing back up to the base of cloud, set course for home.

The correctness of this decision was confirmed by the sad fate of the crew of the *Staffel* commander of the 3rd *Staffel*: pilot and *Staffelkapitän Oblt.* Kolmer, observer *Oblt.* Fritz, radio operator *Uffz.* Huber. flight engineer *Uffz.* Neuburger, gunner *Gefr.* Stiller. They were shot down and the bodies of *Oblt.* Kollmer and *Oblt.* Fritz washed ashore near Nordeney six months later.

We landed at our airfield in Wevelghem, near Courtray in Belgium, at 19:28."

Targets of opportunity were of course attacked during the period leading up to the offensive, however reconnaissance missions dominated.

On 12 July the *I. Gruppe* moved to Vitry en Artois, the rest of the *Geschwader* to Lille-North-Vonderville.

It was time for the radio beam navigation system to prove its worth, especially at night.

The *Luftwaffe* signals battalions had set up a total of nine "*Knickebein*" (Knock-Knees) transmitters from the coast of France and Holland to the far north. These transmitters made it possible to pinpoint any target in the British Isles.

When it came time to demonstrate its effectiveness, the *Knickebein* system proved a failure. On the bright nights after Dunkirk our aircraft used the radio beams for trial attacks. British signals intelligence discovered the secrets of the system before the major attacks began and had time to set up countermeasures.

From this new situation was developed the idea of illuminating targets with incendiaries.

c) Radio Beam Systems/Criticism from Göring

Kampfgruppe 100 was formed as a pathfinder and target-marking unit and was equipped with the special *X-Gerät* bombing system. Its first mission in this new role was the attack on Coventry. A few words about this radio navigation system:

The origins of the X-method can be traced back to Rechlin in 1934(!). It was derived from the technology used in the beam instrument landing system.

The X-method required three radio beams, one of which was aimed at the target, while the other two intersected the guide beam at almost right angles at two crossing points before the target. In this way an optimal point for bomb release was found.

Before the war a mobile X-station was tested on the Feldberg in the Taunus Mountains. Camp Grafenwöhr was used as a practice bombing range.

It was quite clear that the British would eventually begin jamming the X-system, but at the time they had no transmitter with a frequency of 70 Megahertz. Then chance came to their aid: on 6 November 1940 a He 111 of *Kampfgruppe 100* was obliged to make a forced landing on the south coast of England and its *X-Gerät* receivers fell into their hands. X-beams were still transmitted in June-July 1941 as a bluff; no more attacks were carried out however. Actions involving the *X-Gerät* thus ended in June 1941.

Our bombers could only operate in daylight with fighters escort, however the fighters had also suffered significant losses. The balance sheet that was placed before Göring on 19 August was catastrophic:

1. The British fighters arm, especially the Spitfires and Hurricanes, did not engage the German fighters as expected, but instead concentrated on the German bombers.
2. Our air attacks against the fighter airfields were mostly ineffective.
3. Our bomber losses were extremely high, casualties among aircrew considerable. 1 Geschwader commander, 2 air corps chiefs-of-staff, 6 Gruppe commanders, 12 Staffel commanders and 114 other officers were killed within the space of just ten days.

Göring thundered: "The fighters are to blame, they haven't protected the bombers well enough; they haven't stayed with the bomber formations, instead they went into business for themselves in order to wage their own war and score as many victories as possible."

It was the first of many unwarranted accusations made by Göring against the fighter arm, which became more frequent as the war went on.

And then the first heads rolled. Older *Geschwader* commanders from the First World War, most wearers of the *Pour le mérite*, were replaced by younger men.

d) Daylight Attack against Luton Airfield

Obfw. Sticht described a daylight raid on Luton airfield on 30 August 1940:

"Luton airport is located about 40 kilometers north of London. Our alternate target is industrial facilities in that city.

The ground personnel, our black men, have been working on the machines for hours. They bear the responsibility for the operational fitness of the aircraft and thus the lives of the crew. The aircraft crews know that they can rely on our comrades on the ground, this creates close ties between us. Between the ground personnel and the aircrews there is a bond of honest comradeship.

At 14:30 we are ordered to Readiness Level II. A few minutes later the assigned aircraft crews, in flight suits and life vests, are standing by the bus that will take us to the *Kommandeur* at the command post.

The flight briefing follows the customary pattern. The commander, *Oberstleutnant* Kaufmann, ends it with the words: '*Hals und Beinbruch*, and a safe return.' We head out to the aircraft.

We all know that it will be a difficult mission and that some of us won't be coming back. That is war. We know that, we are soldiers.

We – the first *Kette* of the Headquarters *Staffel* – take off at 15:36. The takeoff is by *Kette*, with the formation led by *Hauptmann* Allmendinger, commander of the 1st *Staffel*. The pilot is *Obfw.* Haug, observer *Obfw.* Sticht, radio operator *Obfw.* Schuster, flight engineer *Fw.* Marbach, gunner *Uffz.* Lehner. During our first unit-strength daylight missions, the British concentrated their fire on the lead aircraft carrying the *Kommandeur*. Later the *Kommandeur* flew in the third of fourth *Kette*, but even then the unit too frequently lost its commander. The higher ups therefore issued orders that *Kommandeure* were no longer to fly daylight missions and that each *Gruppe* was to be led by a *Staffelkapitän*, as was the case today.

The *Staffeln* have formed up and we are flying on a heading of 350 degrees – towards Cap Gris Nez. There we pick up our fighter escort and head for England.

Over Cap Gris Nez we reach an altitude of 4800 meters and can already see the Me 110s, twin-engined fighters of the 'Shark *Geschwader*'. They waggle their wings as they pass, signaling that they are our fighter escort. Soon they disappear from our view, taking up position several thousand meters higher, from where they are in better position to attack. We can, however, reach them by radio. The fighters' call sign is 'Marabu', ours is 'Owl'.

In tight-knit formation, the 1st *Gruppe* heads out across the Channel. In the distance we can see the shining chalk cliffs of Dover. We pass south of Canterbury, over the northern edge of Chatham and north of London.

Over Dover we begin taking medium and heavy anti-aircraft fire, while barrage balloons hang menacingly over the Thames and London.

The first Spitfires appear in the area of the Thames Estuary. In my headset I hear the call: 'Fighters from below!' Like tiny mosquitoes they climb towards us, growing ever larger. We – the flight engineer, the dorsal gunner and I, the observer in the glass nose – fire short bursts at the Tommies. Of course the Spitfires are faster and more maneuverable than we are, and their armament is also superior.

The call goes out: 'Marabu from Owl – request fighter protection, ten Spitfires are attacking our formation.'

Our *Zerstörer* and also Me 109s engage the English fighters and we can breathe a sigh of relief. Vapor trails in the sky bear witness to the fierce air battle. Several aircraft fall from the sky like blazing torches, though whether friend or foe we cannot tell. We should be over the target in 15 minutes. I watch as English and German fighters dive through the clouds and disappear. We have survived the first attack; the *Zerstörer* of the 'Shark *Geschwader*' have protected us well.

We are now very close to the target, which is visible through breaks in the cloud: a large airfield with several runways, large hangars, blast pens and around the airfield a large number of anti-aircraft positions, which immediately open fire as we approach.

The bomb cells have long since been opened, the bomb fusing master panel switched on. I have already acquired the target far ahead in order to determine our ground speed and prevent the bombs from overshooting. The pilot must maintain a precise heading, holding the machine absolutely steady. He cannot take evasive action, even if we are attacked. Suddenly more enemy fighters dive on us, coming from out of the sun. We fight back desperately. The observer works feverishly at the *Lotfe* (bomb sight).

Anti-aircraft shells burst dangerously near, and several fighters dive on our *Kette*. The aircraft on the right of the third *Kette* begins trailing smoke. It has been hit and is losing fuel. Once again the radio comes alive, this time it is formation leader Allmendinger: 'Marabu from Owl, request help for one He 111 flying behind the formation.' Our 'Marabus' immediately dive on the Spitfires and once again a life-and-death struggle erupts.

The aircraft is lost. Pilot *Uffz.* Gall and observer *Lt.* Rösler are posted missing but later turn up in a POW camp in Canada. Radio operator *Fw.* Künheim, flight engineer *Uffz.* Saam and gunner *Obgefr.* Fischer are killed.

The British pilots exhibit daring and bravery. They fly right through our formation and for seconds we cannot fire for fear of hitting our own machines.

Finally we are over our target. Through my throat microphone I say: 'Flight engineer cease fire', and then: 'Attention, bombs gone!' At that moment 36 fragmentation and high-explosive bombs each weighing a hundredweight and one 250-kg bomb leave our aircraft. The other aircraft have also dropped their bombs. I am able to observe the fall of our bombs and their effect. Mushroom clouds of smoke and fire rise up. The hangars, the parked aircraft and the landing field have been hit. Our bombs were on target.

We immediately peel off and assume a southerly heading.

With a somewhat uneasy feeling I realize that our Me 109s have left after running low on fuel. Thank God the Me 110s of the Shark *Geschwader* are still there. One He 111 has been hit. It rolls onto its back, engines burning, and goes down trailing smoke and fire. For anyone not engaged in firing, it is a scene we often have to endure.

But the wild fight goes on. The English attack doggedly and we fight back with the courage of desperation.

Another Spitfire is hit and goes down like a blazing torch.

But we have paid a heavy toll in blood. By now between 10 and 15 aircraft have fallen from the sky in flames. In the heat of battle it is impossible to tell how many of ours and how many of theirs. We are happy when we see an open parachute, appearing in the sky like white mushrooms, no matter whether friend or foe.

Near the Thames Estuary, south of Southend on Sea, *Fw.* Sünderhauf's crew reports: 'Engine trouble, flying on one engine, pilot badly wounded.' We immediately call the *Zerstörer* and urgently request fighter cover for one He 111. 'Flying on one engine behind the formation.' We ourselves reduce speed so as to remain in visual contact and be able to contact air-sea rescue if necessary.

We have left the English mainland behind and set course for Calais. Near St. Omer we say goodbye to the Shark *Zerstörer* by waggling our wings. We radio to say thanks for the fighter escort, without which things would have been much worse.

After landing we see that the English have made a mess of our aircraft too. We have no casualties but our bird has more than 100 bullet holes.

One of the aircraft of our 1st *Staffel* has a wounded man on board. Though seriously wounded, he remained at the cannon and fought off British fighters attacks until he collapsed. He was *Obfw.* Max Zieringer. The doctors worked on him for days until he was called away to the big army. He was buried with military honors in the military cemetery in Calais, where so many of our comrades have found their final resting place.

His death hit me particularly hard, for we were old friends. We had joined the Bavarian State Police together on 4 April 1934 and volunteered for the air force at the same time. He became a flight engineer, I an observer. We flew side by side during the wars in Poland, France and now England until his death separated us forever after six years of close ties and comradeship. My comrades and I of the 1st *Staffel* of KG 53 will never forget him, he lives on in our hearts."

e) Daylight Raid on the King George Dock/Ditching in the Channel

Retired *Hauptmann* D. Martin Winter, then an *Oberfeldwebel* and aircraft commander in the headquarters flight of the *I. Gruppe*, was unable to reach the French mainland during a mission on 7 September 1940 and was forced to ditch in the Channel. This is his account:

"Takeoff 15:40, target: the King George dock on the Thames. Crew: pilot *Obfw.* Martin Winter, observer *Oblt.* Albin Weber, radio operator *Obfw.* Gerhard Müller, flight engineer *Fw.* Friedrich Kempgens, gunner *Flg.* Hans König. Cruising altitude 3000 meters, heavy anti-aircraft fire. Just short of the target I spotted 15 Spitfires climbing towards us.

We had just dropped our bombs when I heard a clattering sound on the right side of the aircraft: a burst of machine-gun fire had struck the leading edge of the starboard wing, strips of metal were standing up at the exit holes. Soon afterwards I saw the coolant temperature rising towards 140 degrees, meaning we had been hit in the cooling system. I throttled the engine back to idle and was forced to drop out of formation.

The left aircraft in my *Kette* stayed by my side until just before Dover. Then I set course for Douai, staying low to avoid British radar. We were not bothered again by fighters and soon we saw the coast of France.

Then, suddenly, the radio operator called: 'Two Spitfires from behind.' No sooner had he said this when bullets began striking our machine. The fighters concentrated on our starboard engine. Then everything happened very quickly. By the time we reached 50 meters there wasn't much left to think about. The starboard engine quit. The sea had heavy swells. I lowered the flaps all the way and decided to ditch perpendicular to the waves, to prevent the wings from undercutting.

I let the first wave pass, dropped into the wave trough, applied full power to both engines – I had reduced both to idle – and two pulled the machine up the slope of the approaching wave. I put the aircraft down on the crest of the wave. There was a brief jolt and we were floating.

The flight engineer immediately jettisoned the life raft, which lay flat upon the water. I pulled off my fur-lined boots and jumped into the water which, thank God, wasn't cold.

I checked the raft and found that it hadn't been hit. When I came to the valve, however, I found to my dismay that the compressed air bottle wasn't attached. By then the crew had left the machine. It sank after five minutes.

My attempt to blow up the boat by mouth expended a great deal of effort, but at least I managed to inflate it enough so that it took on a little shape. But then I couldn't do any more. I was out of breath and had also swallowed too much seawater.

I helped the flight engineer into the raft. Not having to swim anymore, he was able to unhurriedly continue blowing up the raft.

We had unfortunately suffered a fatal casualty in the final fighter attack. He was a young mechanic of the ground personnel, a Sudeten German. He wasn't part of the crew, but as the *Kommandeur* wasn't allowed to fly with us, he had authorized the man to come along.

The radio operator had meanwhile disappeared. He was determined to swim to the lightship we had flown over shortly before ditching. I simply couldn't stop him. We never saw him again. About nine months later, as I learned after I was released from captivity, his body was found washed up on the French coast.

There were just three of us left. The raft was stable; we climbed in and waited for what was to come.

Suddenly a red and white aircraft, a Fw 58 (twin-engined Focke-Wulf 'Weihe'), appeared and began circling us. Soon, however, it was driven off by a Spitfire that was nearby.

It was beginning to get dark when a floatplane (He 59) appeared on the horizon. I fired a red flare. The crew of the Heinkel saw it and turned towards us. As it appeared to be on the wrong heading, I fired once again. It flew over us at ten meters and we waved. The aircraft then tried to land, however the waves were too high.

It flew over us once again and then turned away in the direction of the French coast. The night was pitch black, but at least we were happy that we had been found.

But then 36 hours passed with absolutely nothing happening. Then at 06:20 on Monday, the 9th of September, two motor-torpedo boats approached. When we saw the Union Jack flying from their masts we realized that we were going to be captured.

The English gave us a very good reception and fed us well. We sailed for two hours at high speed and arrived in Harwich. From there we were taken to another camp, and in January 1941 we were transported to Canada in a convoy of about twenty ships. For the German prisoners of war the trip on the Duchess of York was the start of almost six years in captivity."

An account by later *Geschwaderkommodore* Pockrandt illustrates how the units were decimated in the murderous air battle over England. Fritz O. Pockrandt, born in 1911, was a young *Leutnant* when he transferred to the *Luftwaffe* from the Saxon State Police in Dresden in August 1935. There he trained as a pilot.

After promotion to *Hauptmann* on 1 February 1940, in August he was transferred from the Bomber Crew Replacement Group in Quedlinburg to KG 53, joining the training *Staffel* in Giebelstadt.

On 1 September 1940 he was assigned to the *III. Gruppe* in Lille-Mouvaux, where he was given command of the 9. *Staffel*. On 11 April 1942 he took over as *Kommandeur* of the *I. Gruppe* and on 14 April 1943 he became the *Kommodore* of KG 53, a position he held until the end of the war.

Pockrandt rose from *Hauptmann* to *Oberstleutnant* in the same *Geschwader* he had joined as a pilot and served as *Staffelkapitän*, *Gruppenkommandeur* and *Geschwaderkommodore* until the end of the war.

And now his description:

"On 1 September 1940 I was transferred to the 3rd *Gruppe* in Lille-Mouvaux (*Kommandeur Major* von Braun) and placed in command of the 9th *Staffel*, which had been completely decimated in operations against England. My predecessor was among those who had been lost. My *Staffel* consisted of the general and technical personnel and several observers, radio operators, flight engineers and gunners. Apart from my crew there were no others. My initial impression was therefore downright depressing, but I had to suppress this as quickly as I could in order to improve the morale of the *Staffel*. In fact I didn't have much time to do this; I quickly met all the men and our first mission was scheduled.

My first combat mission with the *Geschwader* took place on 4 September 1940. At the mission briefing in the *Gruppe* command post I was assigned one crew from the 7th *Staffel* (*Hptm*. Zorn) and one from the 8th *Staffel* (*Hptm*. Wienholtz), so that I had at least one complete *Kette*. The target of this mission was Luton, an English fighter base north of London. After the *Gruppe* and then the entire *Geschwader* had formed up, we climbed towards our rendezvous point with the fighters near Calais. And our escort arrived punctually. The *Geschwader* made an imposing sight as it set course for England in excellent weather. In the distance other units were also in the air, something I had never seen before. But there was no time for sightseeing; I had to dedicate my full attention to the task at hand, close formation flying. This was the first time in my flying career that I was doing so in a fully loaded and fully fueled machine at 5000 meters. I must confess that, flying at the back of the *Gruppe*, I had my difficulties staying with the aircraft in front of me. I can still remember well seeing the chalk cliffs of Dover and Cape Dungeness, but then all hell broke loose. Our fighters were above and below us, and one could have had the feeling that not much could happen. But all of a sudden the English were there and cleverly lured our fighters away from the formation. After they had succeeded, the English dove on us. They came from all sides, blazing away, including some who attacked from the front in an effort to get the formation leader. We flew on undeterred in order to carry out our mission, but our ranks thinned after the very first attacks by the English. My crate, too, was hit, but at first nothing vital was damaged. The first aircraft jettisoned their bombs and then dropped out of formation with smoking engines and stationary propellers. I don't remember any He 111s being shot down during that period. I only know that by the time we approached the target my position in the formation was much further forward. After dropping our bombs on the fighter base, which was difficult to make out in the summer haze, we quickly reversed course and headed for home. I myself could not make out whether the airfield had been hit, and none of my crew had time to worry about where our bombs fell. There was fighter attack after fighter attack as we withdrew, also heavy anti-aircraft fire. There was almost nothing to be seen of our own fighters. They had shot all their powder and lack of range had forced them to head home. So we hung over England, trying everything we could to stay in formation, which we more or less did until we neared the coast. There was more heavy anti-aircraft fire over the coast, after which we went into a steep dive to avoid the last fighter attacks. This caused our formation flying to more or less fall apart. We headed out across the Channel at wave-top height. There were few intact *Ketten* to be seen but plenty of machines flying on one engine or with smoking engines, bullet-riddled tails and large holes in their fuselages or wings. My machine had also been shot up, but no vital parts had been hit, and after reaching the mainland we were able to climb a little higher to be ready for any eventuality or at least be able to prevent them in time. I cannot say that we froze on this first combat mission, on the contrary we were all sweat-soaked and now happy to be on our way home. The interior of the aircraft was a wasteland, almost all of our ammunition had been expended, the ventral bath was full of shell casings and it smelled of burnt powder. After landing we congratulated one another and then received a warm welcome from the ground personnel. The first combat mission of my life was over and all had gone well. So many had failed to survive their first mission against England. The proud armada that had taken off at about noon came home battered and bedraggled looking. If I remember correctly, aerial reconnaissance even showed that the *Geschwader*'s attack had been a success.

In the weeks and months that followed, I flew a total of 10 to 12 more missions against airfields around London, port and dock facilities on the Thames and oil storage sites. We then switched to individual sorties against special targets during bad weather and night raids. The *Staffel* was soon back up to strength and morale rose again. After daylight missions were abandoned, losses stayed within limits and could once again be made good.

Night missions followed against London, Birmingham, Liverpool, Coventry and other targets in central England.

Then *Major* Rohrbach took over the 3rd *Gruppe*. This was followed by my transfer to the 2nd *Gruppe* under *Major* Steinweg and command of *Hauptmann* Mundt's 6th *Staffel*; with this *Staffel* I flew further night missions against the familiar targets.

For a brief period at that time the 3rd *Gruppe* under *Major* Rohrbach became the training *Gruppe* on account of continued heavy casualties which Giebelstadt could not make good, for the purpose of bringing the *Staffeln* up to strength and training new crews. The original crews continued flying night missions and line daylight sorties.

I retuned to the 3rd *Gruppe* in mid-November and to my old 9th *Staffel*, which made me happy. After almost 30 combat missions, all of which I survived more or less intact, I was given the task of training replacements while still flying missions. Because of the losses in those three months, I was already almost one of the veterans.

Major Rohrbach was killed in an automobile accident and was replaced by *Hptm.* Fabian. The Giebelstadt training *Staffel* was disbanded."

g) Mission against Lodge (London)

The mission order for the entire *Geschwader* for 14 September 1940 shows once again the planned sequence of a mission against England with fighter escort and navigation aids:

Telex of 13 September 1940, 23:38

Mission order for 14 September 1940

one 1.   KG 53 will prepare for mission against Lodge targets No. 566, 453, 565 and 455.

2.   Attack leader *Kommandeur* two/KG 53

To be committed are: I./KG 53: 9 He 111; II./KG 53: 17 He 111 (6 He 111 are to be collected from III./KG 53); III./KG 53: 6 He 111. *Stabsstaffel:* 1 He 111

3. Time same as attack time.

4. JG 3 will provide close fighter escort, also JG 54
   Rendezvous line: Aire – Boulogne.
   Departure Boulogne: X – 30 min. At 5500 m.
   Attack altitude: 5500 – 6000 m, left turn after the attack.

5. *Bomb load:* 6 SC 250 (2 with delayed fuses) and if possible 1 incendiary bomb.

6. The aircraft of the Stabsstaffel, one/KG 53 and three/KG 53 to move to Vendeville by 07:00. Two/KG 53 to provide payload.

7. Readiness Level 2 from 07:00, takeoff not expected before 08:30.

two 1. In the event that the Lodge attack is not possible because of bad weather, II./KG 53 to send 10 He 111 on nuisance attacks on targets in photo (Nos. 7348, 7461, 712, 714, 7450). Decision to be made by the *Geschwader*.

2. For this purpose the *Stabsstaffel* will deploy 1 He 111, takeoff at 06:30 for weather reconnaissance.

3. Flight altitude over England not below 2500 m (barrage balloons). *Principle:* cover takes priority over effect.

4. *Navigation aid:* Knickebein 1: 07:00 – 20:00 on Sword.
   Knickebein 2: 06:00 – 15:45 on Picture.
   16:00 – 20:30 on Lodge.

All radio beacons activated as required by the *Gruppe*. The radio beacons are only to be overflown visually during the outbound and return flights, as they are also being used by aircraft of KG 3 and KG 26 for nuisance raids.

KG 53 operations section No.1520/40 Secret.

This mission order was issued during the phase 'day and night attacks on targets in the London area'.

The day that followed, 15 September, was to be a black day for the German units. Fierce air battles raged over the metropolis of the Empire. German losses were fifty-six aircraft, the British twenty-six. Today the 15th of September is still celebrated as Battle of Britain Day.

But high-explosive and incendiary bombs continued to fall on London for sixty-five nights. Coventry, an armaments production center, was devastated by a raid on the night of 14-15 November 1940. Birmingham, Southampton, Manchester and Liverpool-Birkenhead were also struck, but the principal target remained London (codename Lodge), with occasional raids on Portland, Portsmouth and Plymouth.

In those days BBC London could not but admit: 'Whenever the weather is favorable, waves of German bombers protected by fighters appear over the island, often 300 to 400 at one time. The German effort to achieve air superiority over England is the cross of this war!'

On 7 September Göring met with Kesselring and Loerzer near Cap Blanc Nez on the Channel Coast. He told the reporters who were present that he had taken personal control of the air force in the battle against England.

The Battle of London had begun. The British fighters certainly had the advantage of fighting near their bases. They also had effective ground control, which guided them onto German attackers and enabled them to concentrate their efforts.

On the basis of equality of the German and British pilots, in the existing situation the outcome of the battle could not be in doubt. It was thus also clear that, given the way in which Göring was going to employ the air force, that the destruction of the RAF could not be achieved. In the long run the *Luftwaffe* could not endure the war of attrition, which from 10 July until 31 October 1940 had cost 1,733 German aircraft. British losses in the same period were 915 aircraft.

h) War Diary of the I. Gruppe from 21 September 1940 to 30 May 1941

Parts of the war diary of the *I. Gruppe* of our *Kampfgeschwader* covering the period beginning late September 1940 have survived. The information about the missions provides an overview which is also representative of the other *Gruppen*:

21/9/1940

Vitry

00:48 – 01:12	Takeoff by 9 He 111 for an attack on London. One He 111 (A1+DH) dropped its bombs prematurely due to engine trouble.
11:20	From KG 53: mission order for 21/9/40: single daylight sorties by selected crews.
13:26 – 16:20	A1+EH took off to attack 7319 (Derby). Mission aborted due to bad weather.
15:28 – 17:42	A1+HH took off to attack Birmingham. Attack aborted, alternate target convoy, no effect.

23/9/1940

Vitry

11:55 – 15:52	11 He 111 attack on London, aborted because of cloudless sky.
24/9/1940	
Vitry	
12:18 – 13:20	Transfer of 9 He 111 to Vendeville.
	Individual attacks on Birmingham, 11 He 111 against London.
25/9/1940	
Vitry	
00:30 – 01:43	Attack on London by 4 He 111.
27/9/194	Individual attack on Morris (Birmingham factory) by He 111 A1+HH, Oblt. Leonhardi crew. Direct hit with one SC 1000.
28/9/1940	
02:42 – 03:00	Takeoff by 5 He 111 to attack London and individual attacks on 7319 (Derby).
29/9/1940	
03:15 – 03:36	7 He 111 to London.
16:17	He 111 A1+FH, *Oblt.* von Buttlar's crew, target Derby (Rolls-Royce engine factory). Approach to target at low level, 1000-kg bombs dropped from a height of 600 meters onto the southeast part of the factory.
30/9/1940	
Vitry	
02:30 – 02:51	6 He 111 to London.
1/10/1940	
20:33 – 21:30	8 He 111 to London and Birmingham.
	He 111 A1+HH took off to attack Birmingham. Target could not be bombed because of barrage balloons.
02/10/1940	
16:34	During attack on Birmingham, He 111 A1+CH transmitted in plain language that it had to make a forced landing in England, did not return. Crew probably taken prisoner.
20:00	Mission against London cancelled because of bad weather.
03/10/1940	Individual attack on Birmingham, aborted due to bad weather.
04/10/1940	Individual targets not attacked because of bad weather.
15:45	15 He 111 to London.
05/10/1940	5 He 111 to London, various individual attacks.
06/10/1940	
Vitry	Individual attacks on London, I./53 nuisance raid on London, government quarter.
07/10/1940	Individual attacks on various targets.
04:12 – 04:23	Attack on London by 3 He 111, government quarter. Bombs on target, explosions seen.

09/10/1940

03:30 – 03:43   Revenge raid on London by 5 He 111. 5x1000-kg bombs dropped using radio navigation, DF bearings and dead reckoning.

10/10/1940

Vitry   5 He 111 to London, individual attack.

11/10/1940   4 He 111 to London

The daily sequence of night missions, with London as the primary target and individual targets in Derby, the Rolls-Royce factory and Birmingham, continued until 13 November 1940.

14/11/1940

Vitry

11:08   1 He 111 took off on weather reconnaissance and nuisance raid on London. Returned due to weather.

17:00   KG 53 took part in major raid on Coventry (Corn), time over target 23:00 – 23:45.

21:24   Takeoff by 8 He 111 to attack Coventry. Very good success, many large fires, bombs clearly on target.

15/11/1940

17:00   Night attack on Corn (Coventry), individual nuisance attacks.

21:20 – 22:23   8 He 111 took off to attack Coventry. Because of heavy cloud cover, some 00:04 – 02:32   aircraft   attacked secondary targets London and Sherness. Bombs dropped by radio navigation and dead reckoning.

16/11/1940

16:10   Individual night nuisance attacks on Coventry. In the second half of the night on London.

19:07 – 23:24   Takeoff by 1 He 111 for Coventry and 3 He 111 for London. Bombs dropped on Coventry. Bombs dropped over London by radio navigation and dead reckoning.

In the period that followed, the attacks on London, as well as Derby Birmingham and Hamswell airport – usually by single aircraft – continued. Liverpool (codename Pantry) and Manchester (codename Wardrobe) were added to the target list on 26 November, while attacks on London continued.

Sheffield was added as a new target on 15 December. An effective attack on the city was made on the 15th, while at the same time raids on Manchester and Liverpool were intensified.

Cardiff was bombed on 2 January 1941, followed on the 4th by the first raid on Bristol. On 31 January there was a very successful attack on a large oil storage facility in Southampton, which received mention

in the *Wehrmacht* communiqué. This was followed by a raid on the public shipyards in Chatham. The West-Raynham and Hamswell were also subjected to repeated heavy attacks at this time.

The war diary entry on 16 February 1941 read:

Vitry

11:41	Takeoff by 3 He 111 to attack target 10242 (Hamswell).
	2 aircraft reached the target and scored hits on quarters and hangars.
	1 He 111 was forced to abort due to engine trouble.
14:24 – 15:07	Takeoff by 5 He 111 to attack West-Raynham airport and Hamswell.
	2 He 111 put bombs on the target. *Oblt.* Ziegler's crew was particularly successful during the 6½ hour flight, scoring hits on hangars, parked aircraft and the main railway line. The aircraft landed in Antwerp as its radio system had been shot up.

There now follows the report submitted by *Lt.* Mayer, who took part in this mission:

23/2/1941	Heavy attack on Hull.
27/2	Attack on Great Yarmouth and oil storage facility in Hull.
3/3	Heavy raid on Newcastle, Tynemouth and South-Shields. 9 aircraft reached the target and dropped their bombs from an altitude of 2500-4000 meters. Small persistent fires were observed. 1 aircraft was attacked by a night-fighter during the return flight to Merville. Smooth landing with 50 bullet holes and 1 engine. Pilot and radio operator slightly wounded. 2 aircraft were forced to turn back on account of engine trouble and failure of the fuel transfer system, respectively.
8/3	

Vitry and Wittmundhafen Partial transfer to Wittmundhafen.

12/3 Vitry	Night mission against Liverpool.
13/3 Vitry	Attack on Glasgow.
14/3 Vitry	Heavy attack on Glasgow. Large fires were started which were visible from 100 kilometers.
16/3	Transfer back to Vitry.
18/3 Vitry	Heavy attack on Hull.
19/3 Vitry	Heavy attack on London.
21/3 to 24/3	No missions because of weather.
25/3	By order of the Supreme Commander of the Armed Forces, effective immediately and until further notice all attacks on Sea Snake (London) and overflights of the city are forbidden. No missions because of weather.

Weather reconnaissance and individual sorties were flown beginning on 26 March. On 30 March the *Gruppen* were given a new assignment – attacking British night bases. The following were identified as principal targets:

Target	1069	Duxford (the English Rechlin)
	10249	Wattisham airfield
	10107	Honnington
	10218	Stradishall
	10154	Newmarket
	10146	Mildenhall
	10152	Wyton

On that same day 7 He 111s were sent against night bases, however little was achieved. On 31 March, therefore, another mass attack was scheduled against Hull.

5/4/1941	Visit by the commander of Luftflotte 2, *Generalfeldmarschall* Kesselring, to check on preparations by the crews for the coming full-moon periods. After a brief conversation on the airfield, where the commanding officer outlined the *Gruppe's* preparations to the field marshal, from 16:00-17:30 the Generalfeldmarschall sat in on a preflight briefing for the men of the 3. *Staffel* in Monchy le Preux. The field marshal was extremely satisfied with the detailed preparations that had been made and expressed his special appreciation to all who had taken part.
6/4	Heavy raid on Cannon (Nottingham). Alternate target Daimler (Derby).
7/4	Attack on Cemetery (Dumberton, Glasgow). For the first time our airfield was attacked by an English night-fighter. It dropped bombs and subsequently attacked landing aircraft with guns. Two aircraft were damaged by cannon fire.
8/4	Attack on Hull.
9/4	
00:45 – 02:05	Takeoff by 15 He 111s to attack reported convoys. Difficulty locating targets due to absence of moonlight. 5 machines attacked. One freighter took a direct hit amidships and sank. *Hptm*. Dreher's crew. Because of darkness none of the other aircraft were able to see the effect. The remaining aircraft attacked secondary targets, such as Great Yarmouth, Harwich, etc., visually. 2 aircraft returned with their bombs after failing to locate suitable targets. Heavy return fire from the ships. *Hptm*. Dreher received a grazing wound in his right hand.

15:00	Visit by the commanding general of II. *Fliegerkorps, General der Flieger* Loerzer.

15:00 Visit by the commanding general of II. *Fliegerkorps, General der Flieger* Loerzer.

22:30 – 24:00 21 He 111s attack on Newcastle. Clear conditions over the target, 17 aircraft bombed. Good results, several large fires. Two new crews dropped their bombs over Great Yarmouth as directed without problems. 2 aircraft had to jettison their bombs because of fighter attack and engine trouble, respectively.

10/4/1941 Heavy raid on Nottingham.

11/4 Heavy raid on Portsmouth. Very good results.

15/4 Large-scale night raid on Belfast (Stage).

16/4 Two attacks were ordered against London in reprisal for the bombing of Berlin. Weather extremely suitable.

21:14 19 He 111s to London.

01:59 – 02:40 15 He 111s to London.

34 of the *Gruppe's* aircraft reported a resounding success. The last aircraft counted 80 large fires. At the beginning of the 2nd takeoff 1 He 111 aborted takeoff after its undercarriage was damaged by an SC 1000 dropped onto the runway by the previous aircraft. Machine heavily damaged, crew unhurt.

17/4/1941 Night raid against Portsmouth.

18/4 Two night missions against Portsmouth.

19/4 Two night missions against London.

21:45 22 He 111s to attack London.

01:50 10 He 111s to attack London.

21/4/1941 Night mission to Hull.

22/4 Mission by selected crews against following targets: merchant vessels, supply installations in East-English ports, armament industry around Nottingham and Norwich, night bomber bases with emphasis on aircraft on the ground. The following crews were selected:

Target No.	1. *Staffel*	2. *Staffel*	3. *Staffel*
785	*Lt*. Leske	*Uffz*. Raßloff	*Lt*. Plank v. Bachselten
8234	*Lt*. Meyer	*Fw*. Schaper	*Lt*. von Sieber
2022	*Obfw*. Haug	*Lt*. Lehmann	*Uffz*. Endress
Ships	*Uffz*. Schliemann	*Lt*. Kreuzer	*Uffz*. Strasser

23/4 Attack on industrial targets, shipping, night bomber bases and Portsmouth. *Uffz*. Raßloff's crew successfully attacked Waddington airfield (10236) from a height of 600m. *Uffz*. Endress' crew successfully attacked Stradishall airfield from a height of 750m. 1 hangar collapsed. Because of inadequate cloud cover, 4 aircraft bombed Great Yarmouth after nightfall.

26/4 Night mission against Liverpool.

29/4 Attack on Cardiff.

2/5/1941	Night raid on Liverpool. Noticeable increase in British night-fighter activity.
3/5	Attack on Liverpool by 21 He 111s. 2 aircraft failed to return. As there was no radio contact after the aircraft signed off, it is impossible to say what happened to the crews. It is possible that they were shot down by night-fighters.

Missing crews:	A1+EK A1+LL	
Pilot:	Lt. Baller	Lt. Plank von Bachselten
Observer:	*Uffz.* Palubicki	*Gefr.* Regnat
Radio operator:	*Uffz.* Stolper	*Gefr.* Kauhardt
Flight engineer:	*Gefr.* Donner	*Uffz.* Richter II (Walter)
Gunner:	*Uffz.* Fleischmann	–

4/5/1941	Night raid against Burrow of Furness.
5/5	Night mission against the Clyde Estuary.

Missing crew: A1+CK

Pilot: *Uffz.* Raßloff, observer *Gefr.* Lernbass, radio operator *Uffz.* Simon, flight engineer *Gefr.* Schmidt, gunner *Gefr.* Quittenbaum.

7/5	Large-scale night raid on Liverpool with excellent results.
8/5	Night raid on Sheffield, 22 He 111s took off. Because of 10/10 cloud 19 machines bombed the alternate target Trashcan (Hull) with resounding success. All bombs in the target area, several large fires, plus 3 major explosions. 2 He 111s had to drop their bombs over the sea due to persistent night-fighter attacks on this very bright night.
10/5/1941	
22:44	In reprisal for the English raid on Berlin, the Gruppe conducted a maximum strength raid on London in two waves. 23 He 111s took off to attack London. These aircraft bombed the city in excellent visibility with resounding success. 1 crew failed to return.

Missing crew: A1+CL

Pilot: Lt. von Sieber, observer Fw. Fischer, radio operator Uffz. Schurff, flight engineer Obfw. Meister, gunner Fw. Wylezol.

11/5	Raid on night bomber bases.
12/5	5 He 111s attacked shipping. Attack unsuccessful due to darkness and haze.
14/5/1941	
Vitry	
11:00	*from Geschwader:* I./KG 53 to ready 4 He 111s for solo attacks on specific targets for annihilation.
11:58	3 He 111s took off to attack destroyers and other shipping. 1 He 111 bombed railway workshops.

	Nottingham: results not observed.
	1 He 111 attacked a merchant ship (2,500 – 3,000 GRT). 1 SC 500 scored a direct hit amidships, ship sank within two minutes. 1 He 111 (Lt. Kreuzer and crew) attacked Waddington airfield (10236) from a height of 350 m and scored one direct hit on a hangar. Aircraft parked nearby (4-engined) probably damaged by fragmentation effect.
15:30	1 He 111 took off against same targets. Flight aborted due to fighter attack.
from 16:08	Because of the ideal weather conditions, during the course of the day 11 'He 111s were despatched with the same orders and returned with extraordinary results: 1 He 111 (Oblt. Jacobi and crew) attacked Target 8234 (Nottingham railway shops) with great success from a height of 250 m and returned with photos of Digby airfield and Targets 8234 and 785. 1 He 111 (Obfw. Fern and crew) attacked Target 2022 (Norwich supply dump) from 600m with complete success. Bombs clearly struck aircraft hangars and warehouses. 1 He 111 (Uffz. Endress and crew) attacked the same target from 350 m. Bombs fell amid hangars. 1 He 111 (Fw. Oelker and crew) attacked 1 merchant vessel in grid square 23305 East despite attacks by two Spitfires which made three passes. One Spitfire shot down in flames. Seen to crash into the sea. Effects of bombing on steamer not observed. 1 He 111 dropped bombs on a large factory north of Colchester. 1 He 111 jettisoned its bombs over Felixstowe. Returned on one engine due to flak damage. 1 He 111 attacked a merchant vessel without success. 1 He 111 aborted due to engine trouble.
	4 He 111s aborted mission due to inadequate cloud cover. General der Flieger Loerzer praised the crews and the entire Gruppe for its successful missions that day.
	It was the Gruppe's most successful day since the start of individual attacks against targets in England.
22:00	from the Geschwader: as per order from Geschwader received by telephone, the start of the 14-day training period has been further postponed.
22:30	from the Geschwader: the training period is to commence on 15 May 1941.

A fourteen-day period of training began on 15 May 1941 with emphasis on aerial gunnery, bomb dropping and formation flying. The training plan also included a lecture by General Staff *Oberstleutnant* Dörr (army) concerning the organization of an infantry division at rest, on the move and in combat. It soon became clear that this "training" heralded the unit's next action, the war in the east.

But suddenly, beginning on 27 May, there was a cascade of orders that persisted until the 30th:

27/5/1941
Vitry

09:30   from the *Geschwader*: prepare transfer of 20 crews to Brest. Call-up and further details to follow.

14:50   from the *Geschwader*: transfer order to Dinard near St. Malo. There the *Gruppe* will be placed under *Oberstleutnant* von Chamier. Anticipate attack on the English fleet and support for the Bismarck.

           Mission cancelled by order of the Commander Atlantic, as the English fleet is beyond the range of our machines.

from 20:00   All aircraft returned to Vitry.

28/5/1941
Vitry

05:00   from the *Geschwader*: ready all serviceable aircraft for transfer back to Dinard.

14:00   Move to Dinard called off.

29/5/1941
Vitry

04:00   from the *Geschwader*: ready aircraft again for transfer to Dinard. Move again called off in the afternoon.

30/5/1941
Vitry

07:00   from the Geschwader: keep aircraft ready for move to Dinard for the next few days.

The move to Dinard was cancelled for good in the afternoon. General preparations were begun for transfer of the *Gruppe* by rail in two waves to an unspecified destination. This move with an unknown destination was soon cleared up: direction east.

i) *The Battleship Bismarck*

Alfred Sticht provided the following account concerning the *Bismarck* action:

"At 16:20 on 27 May 1941, we flew in A1+AB, the commanding officer's machine, from Vitry en Artois to Dinard on the French

Atlantic coast. This move took everyone by surprise. No one knew why we were moving to Dinard, but we 'old hands' suspected that something special, something very big, was up. At 17:47 we landed with the commander of the 1st *Gruppe* of KG 53, *Oberstleutnant* Kaufmann, in Dinard. Several aircraft flown by experienced crews had already arrived. Also there were *General der Flieger* Milch, *Geschwaderkommodore* Weitkuß, the commander of the 1st *Gruppe* *Oberstleutnant* Kaufmann and the *Staffelkapitäne* – everyone with rank and status.

Our aircraft were fully fueled and loaded with bombs. All of the command officers were summoned to the command post for a briefing, while the crews, ready for action, waited expectantly. Finally it was over and our commanding officer drove up in a car. From *Oberstleutnant* Kaufmann's face we could tell that something had gone wrong, but what? We learned that our battleship *Bismarck*, the biggest battleship in the world, had sunk the *Hood* in a naval engagement and had itself taken hits in the same battle. The English immediately sent all available ships into the area. After the battle far out in the Atlantic, beyond our radius of action, had taken place, the *Bismarck* tried to get to a point where we could reach her. We would take off as soon as we could reach our battleship, in order to protect it and attack the enemy warships. Anxious hours passed, until finally we received the grim news that the *Bismarck's* rudder had been hit and that it was only able to steam in a circle. Therefore we could not reach our proud battleship.

Thus the fate of the *Bismarck* was settled. It was sunk after an heroic fight against superior British sea forces."

j) Attack on Raynham Airfield on 16 February 1941

By order of the *Geschwader* commander, on 2 June 1941 I./ KG 53 was directly attached to the *2. Fliegerkorps* and subsequently received all mission orders directly from the corps. There followed several missions against Manchester, Hull and Birmingham. On 19 June 1941, however, the *Gruppe* moved by *Staffeln* to Crojec in the *Generalgouvernement* with 23 crews. The following is a description of an attack on West-Raynham by *Leutnant* Meyer and his crew on 16 February 1941, again provided by Alfred Sticht:

"It was 16 February 1941. The 1st *Staffel* of KG 53 was in the Château Corbehem near Douai in France. Our crew: pilot *Lt.* Meyer, observer *Oberfeldwebel* Sticht, radio operator *Feldwebel* Breinlinger, flight engineer *Uffz.* Kriegler, gunner *Uffz.* Lehner.

Our orders were to attack West-Raynham airfield when the weather was favorable. On this day conditions were right. At 13:40 we received the weather report we had been waiting for. Our machine, the He 111 with the code A1+KH, had already been loaded with high-explosive, fragmentation and incendiary bombs. Ammunition was loaded for our cannon and machine-guns. At 14:24 we lifted off the ground, heavily laden. We headed for radio beacon 72a near Ruddervoorde and left the coast on a back bearing from radio beacon 72a, course north. We climbed up to the base of cloud and then entered cloud to check for possible icing. Above the clouds we fixed our position over the North Sea using cross-bearings and checked our speed. At different times we saw small dots moving in the sky. We immediately ducked into cloud so as not to be seen. It interested us not whether they were friend or foe. We had to avoid all contact in order to reach West-Raynham, which was being used by the Anglo-American bombers, unhindered, paste it with bombs and destroy the aircraft and hangars.

We took regular bearings to check our flight path, in which bearings on the Swedish radio station in Kalundborg were helpful.

This was the observer's time. We had set up this part of our attack so that we would wait until fifteen minutes after crossing the English coast before acquiring ground contact. As we crossed the English coast our altimeter showed 2500 meters. We were flying between two cloud layers, with a thin layer of stratus above. The upper boundary of the main cloud layer was at 2450 meters, where would the base of cloud be? These were worrying questions that now moved us. According to the information from our comrades of the weather reconnaissance *Staffeln*, the cloud base should be at about 100 meters with some broken cloud below it. As experienced England flyers, however, we knew that the weather over Great Britain could change rapidly because of the effects of the Gulf Stream. We descended, engines at idle. There was not a sound on the intercom, no throat microphone moved, the bomb doors were open, and the bomb fusing system was switched on, thus the bombs were live. The altimeter now showed 700 meters as we continued our descent. The radio operator's and dorsal gunner's machine-guns and the two cannon operated by the flight engineer and observer were ready to fire, five pairs of eyes strained, directed downwards. Suddenly, at 200 meters above the ground, the cloud deck became darker and darker. Seconds later we obtained ground contact, English soil lay beneath us. I lay on my belly in the nose, the map of England in my hand, and tried feverishly to determine our position. Every member of the crew helped out by drawing my attention to prominent features on the ground. The visibility was very bad. Off to our left I saw railroad tracks running in an east-west direction. I soon figured out our position and said to the pilot through my throat microphone: follow the railway line! He immediately turned, and seconds later we flew over a railway station at a height of fifty meters. The people standing crowded on the platform looked up at us. They may well have got a terrible shock when they saw our black crosses as we flew by. Happily I shouted into the microphone: the defenses haven't identified us as a hostile aircraft yet, otherwise they would have sounded the air raid alarm down there, no doubt about it.

According to my dead reckoning navigation, we should be over the target in one minute. We flew through several patches of broken cloud, the visibility steadily grew worse. Suddenly – to the left, the airfield. Aircraft after aircraft was parked on the field. *Lt.* Meyer immediately made a steep turn. I asked him to gain some altitude, as I couldn't aim my bombs accurately from this banked attitude. We began another pass. The pilot pulled the machine up into the clouds, made a 210-degree instrument turn, and two minutes later we again flew over the airfield at a height of 50 meters. I set the bombs to delayed detonation so that our machine would not be hit by fragments from our own bombs. Below us there were at least 50 to 60 twin- and four-engined bombers. We could see the soldiers walking about among the aircraft and in and out of the aircraft hangars. At the words 'Attention! Bombs gone!' our machine-guns and cannon fell silent to avoid hitting our own bombs and blowing us up with them.

The bombs fell among the parked aircraft, one 250-kg bomb struck a large hangar. All of this took several seconds. Below all hell broke loose! The flight engineer confirmed that all bombs were on target. Only fire and smoke could be seen as we flew away. The anti-aircraft guns blazed away. They were just as surprised as everyone else down there; the flak chased us but didn't hit us. My comrades in the back of the aircraft also fired everything they had, it was about 16:00.

After we had dropped our bombs we immediately climbed into the low cloud. To the east the clouds were lighter, and so we decided to initially continue in a southwesterly direction, first because the cloud cover appeared to be thicker and second to avoid the enemy fighters that had surely been scrambled to intercept us. After ten minutes flying time, however, the clouds broke up and we had blue sky before us. The next few minutes demanded extreme watchfulness from all of us. We headed for the next cloud and for those minutes literally jumped from cloud to cloud. If only everything worked out. It wasn't long before we heard the voice of our radio operator: 'Attention, fighters behind, left and above.' All of our machine-guns and cannon were ready to fire. Four Spitfires closed in. We tried to escape. With the engines at full power in a shallow dive, we tried to reach the nearest cloud before the English fighters got into firing position.

Now began the life and death struggle. Our pilot, an experienced instrument pilot, made the most amazing maneuvers. We fired the first bursts at the onrushing Spitfires just as we reached the next cumulus cloud. Once inside we made a ninety-degree turn. When we emerged from the cloud the enemy fighters were swirling around near the cloud, ready to dive on us immediately. We at once turned back into the cloud and made course changes inside the cumulus, in an effort to shake off our pursuers. It was a 'cat and mouse game' with deadly seriousness. This engagement may have lasted about twenty minutes, for us it was an eternity, until we finally reached a solid cloud layer again and approached the North Sea. We flew 'blind' for a long time, until we were sure that we had left the English fighters behind and reached the area of our own fighter cover. Only then did we report our success, beaming with joy, to our home base in Vitry en Artois. Using the code chart, our radio operator transmitted the coded text: Special target attacked with great success.

The next day we learned from our commanding officer *Oberstleutnant* Kaufmann that our monitoring service (with the codename 'Meier Ostende') had intercepted the following instructions sent by the British ground controller to the fighters in the air: 'Land at alternate airfield. West-Raynham airfield heavily bombed at 16:01.'

A few days later *General* Loerzer came to Vitry and congratulated us for a job well done. He invited the crew to eat in the officer's mess and arranged for us to receive 25 bottles of champagne."

k.) A Wellington Bomber Lands at Our Airfield

When returning from combat missions at night, our crews increasingly found themselves subjected to harassing attacks by lone enemy aircraft over their airfields. A lone English aircraft would position itself behind a German machine on approach and open fire as it prepared to land or in other cases drop bombs.

Such daring led to disaster for the crew of a Wellington bomber. Once again Alfred Sticht:

"Tonight we are to attack London again. The shipyards and docks, the West India Docks and the Victoria Docks are our targets. At first all goes according to plan, just one thing makes me begin to wonder: it takes much longer than usual to reach the English coast. Not that we are yearning for the heavy anti-aircraft fire that usually awaits us on reaching the coast, no, all of my navigational flight preparation has been thrown into disarray. The dead reckoning navigation is no longer accurate.

Radio (bearings) and terrestrial navigation show that our ground speed is much lower than I have calculated. Has the wind picked up that much? In fact there is a gale of 120 kph from the northwest. Finally, far behind schedule, we are over the target and attack. The visibility is good for bombing. Despite furious anti-aircraft fire, we attack our assigned target. The bombs are on target and we set course for home. Our engines drone as we fly over the dark, angry sea. In winter it is freezing cold at altitudes of 5000-6000 meters; the storm-tossed North Sea, fog and clouds make high demands of the crew.

We have left England behind us. Shortly afterwards our searchlights on the French coast flare up like ghost fingers. We fire the recognition signal to identify ourselves and begin our landing approach.

The commanding officer *Oberstleutnant* Kaufmann is waiting for us and we make our report.

We are about to board the bus that will take us to our quarters when we hear another aircraft droning in the dark night sky. *Hptm.* Großholt, our adjutant, immediately orders: 'Airfield lights on, church tower on, flare path on.'

All of the airfield lighting is turned on and we can see an aircraft on approach to land at our airfield. It has its navigation lights on. Our adjutant says, 'Marshal the aircraft past the control tower to the command post immediately. It can only be a German machine whose radio has failed or been shot up, and at daybreak it will surely want to take off again.'

Following our signals, the machine taxis by quite close to us, and we give the sign for it to cut its engines.

We are about to board the bus when a German soldier with rifle and steel helmet, who was assigned to guard our aircraft, comes running up to us excitedly and shouts: 'Come quickly, the aircraft's crew, 6 men, just got out, and when they saw me they quickly climbed back in and are trying to take off again.' But we are faster and fetch six Tommies from the machine, two officers and four sergeants. Only now do we look more closely at the aircraft. It is a Vickers Wellington, a British heavy bomber with a crew of 5 or 6 designed for long-range night attacks. It has three movable machine-gun positions and a cruising speed of 340 kph. On closer examination of the aircraft we find that it still has six bombs in its bomb bay. The crew became lost because of the unexpected storm that night and thought it was landing at a British airfield.

The next day we heard on the radio that last night British bombers had attacked Turin in Italy for the first time."

l) Forced Landing in England by the Hufenreuter Crew

On the night of 10-11 May 1941, *Hauptmann* Hufenreuter and his crew of the 5. *Staffel* were shot down during a night raid on London. The aircraft was on its way home when it was shot down.

The crew consisted of: pilot *Fw.* Richard Furthmann, observer *Hptm.* Albert Hufenreuter, radio operator *Uffz.* Karl Gerhardt, flight engineer *Uffz.* Josef Berzbach, gunner *Gefr.* Karl Beutel and gunner *Uffz.* Egbert Weber.

The crew was able to save itself by making a forced landing in a meadow in 'The Camp' on the outskirts of Kennington, which is located near Ashford, Kent. The English author Richard Collier investigated this incident and described the fate of the crew and its aircraft in detail in his book *The City That Wouldn't Die*.

An author and historian, Collier wrote about many themes concerning the last war. In his writing he strives to point out the human qualities, strengths and weaknesses of both sides based on careful research and interviews. His latest work is *A History of the Berlin Airlift*.

The photo from Collier's book shows the aircraft after its successful belly landing. Loosely translated, the caption accompanying the photo says: "A windbreak hedge of hawthorn bushes saved the Heinkel from crashing into a row of oak trees."

Originally the He 111 had been on its way home, flying south towards Brighton. Then the battle-damaged port engine failed and the coolant temperature rose to 160 degrees. Hufenreuter agreed with pilot Furthmann's suggestion that they not risk flying across the Channel at nearly its widest point. They therefore turned east, staying over the English mainland and heading for the Channel's narrowest point between Dover and Calais. Then fate took its course: by the time they reached Ashford the aircraft could no longer be kept in the air. They were too low to bale out and so all that was left was a belly landing.

The members of the crew sustained injuries of varying severity and they became prisoners of war. Collier: " ... a man walked across the meadow towards the aircraft. Hufenreuter waved and called to him in English: 'Where are we?' Taken aback, the man called back: 'In England!' Then from the area of the aircraft, in modest English but still understandable, came an 'Oh damn!' More in detail: the Heinkel had made a belly landing in a meadow called The Camp above the small town of Kennington near Ashford. A windbreak hedge of sturdy hawthorn bushes had slowed the sliding aircraft and saved it from a destructive collision with a row of mighty oak trees and a group of houses behind it.

The first man to appear on the scene was the ambulance worker Frederick Huckstepp. He lived nearby and thought that a British aircraft had gotten into trouble. He was quickly joined by others ... butcher Edward Ward and his wife Ann, who had feared that the aircraft was going to crash in their back garden ... Charles Peters with his daughters Joan and Joyce. But given the waves of Heinkel bombers overhead, still flying north to bomb London, the people were uncertain how to approach the situation: either to see the Germans as people in distress or to repel them as the unscrupulous enemy. Many however, wearing coats over their pajamas, stared in amazement, as if men from Mars had dropped onto their sleepy village.

But some were more positive. The Peters daughters ran back into the house and fetched blankets and pillows. With difficulty Huckstepp and several others lifted pilot Furthmann from his seat and laid him tenderly on the grass, while Joan Peters wrapped an eiderdown around him. It later turned out that this man had a fractured spine. Others pulled gunner Weber, who had two broken legs, out of his seat. Gerhardt and Berzbach, though only shocked, were both unconscious. Someone phoned for a doctor and an ambulance. As Joan Peters coaxed Furthmann to drink a little water, an artillery captain arrived to take charge, steel helmeted, with a pistol belt strapped over his pajamas. Hufenreuter asked him if he wouldn't mind looking in the cockpit and retrieving his forage cap. The captain obliged without demur.

Now Hufenreuter was lying on the frosty grass with his neck against a cushion. One of the women, kept saying, 'Soon going ambulance', spacing out the words carefully so that he should understand. He felt grateful, but he felt an overwhelming disgust, too they had been within an ace of home and now this.

He understood the woman's English well enough; his father, back in Quedlinburg, was the local schoolmaster. By degrees it dawned on him that he might now have some years to perfect this language."

In 1978 Hufenreuter saw his helpers and eye-witnesses again. Over tea they had long and cordial talks about the past and present.

For the English, from the outset this aerial offensive took on the qualities of a crusade. For them the continued existence of their lives, their nation, the Empire, their culture and their honor hung on its outcome, whether triumph or disaster. The Battle of Britain even inspired one of the most famous lines by Winston Churchill, the wartime prime-minister: "Never in the field of human conflict was so much owed by so many to so few." This helps explain why the English fought so hard, meeting our attacks with a defense which, in concentration and determination, had no equal during the rest of the war.

m) Mission over England by the Headquarters Staffel

As well as flak and fighter defenses, in the London area in particular there were tethered barrage balloons, which caused many of our aircraft to come to grief.

The former *Oberleutnant* Wittmann described one mission by the Headquarters *Staffel* during the Battle of Britain as follows:

"For the *Luftwaffe* there was no rest and no time for recovery following the surrender of France. The Headquarters *Staffel* received new crews, bringing it up to strength, and was directed to conduct reconnaissance over the south of England.

Large formations attacked airfields and ports in the south of England. The bombers formed up over Calais, after which the bomber stream headed for its targets. Our fighter units caught up to us on the way to the target and were supposed to provide fighter cover.

The English fighters attacked us from the front, from above, from below and from behind. Aircraft after aircraft was shot out of our formation. We experienced a new and ghastly air war. Despite heavy losses, no unit deviated from its path to the target. Losses in men and equipment were disastrous.

On 25 September 1940, during a visit by the *Reichsmarschall*, *Oberleutnant* Wittmann was promoted to *Hauptmann* for bravery in the face of the enemy, *Leutnant* Bichowski to *Oberleutnant*, *Feldwebel* Langer and Fiedler to *Oberfeldwebel* and *Unteroffizier* Psdurek to *Feldwebel*.

In all unit operations the *Stabsstaffel* assigned one aircraft to take photos. It flew as one of the outer aircraft in the last *Kette*. This position may also have been the reason why this *Staffel* had such heavy losses. The last *Kette* usually suffered the worst – the devil takes the hindmost.

We also flew reconnaissance missions in bad weather and at night.

Oberleutnant Fink and his crew returned from one such mission and reported having shot down about 20 barrage balloons which were drifting peacefully above a solid layer of cloud in the London area. What must the English have thought when suddenly the wire cables, some up to 3000 meters long, which perhaps had brought down some of our aircraft, came crashing down?

The large-scale missions continued unabated.

Our fighter escort failed to carry out its mission, the range of our fighter aircraft was simply too short. During missions over the London area our fighters had to turn back as soon as they reached the city in order to regain their bases. We bombers were then exposed to fighter attack, usually while flying over the Channel.

The Messerschmitt Me 210 (sic) *Zerstörer* were inferior to the English fighters.

For better self-defense a new machine-gun was installed in our He 111 and another gunner was added to the crew. Not often, but now and then, we had the luck to fight off an enemy fighter attack or perhaps even shoot down one of the determined attackers.

The airfields in the area between Dover and London were destroyed and the enemy fighter arm was forced back, but the bloodletting in the bomber units was out of all proportion to their successes.

To our surprise, in mid-October preparations for the 'Robinson' landing, for which we airmen had made such great sacrifices, were called off.

Only someone who took part in the air battle of England can appreciate the physical and psychological demands it placed on the crews. Crew after crew was lost. Only a few forced to ditch in the sea were picked up, while others who came down in England became prisoners of war and spent the rest of the war in Canada.

In the Headquarters *Staffel* there was still one veteran crew still in action, that of *Staffelkapitän* Wittmann and *Oblt.* Bichowski. All of the others had been killed or were missing. The unit's will to fight remained unbroken, however, and the spirit and comradeship in the *Staffel* were exemplary. I would also like to mention here that, from the beginning until the end of the war, only military targets were assigned in our mission orders. In no theater of war was an order given for the bombing of an open city. Of course during attacks on port facilities in London and Liverpool, Southampton etc., for example, some bombs also fell on residential areas. You should know that with a load of twenty 100-kg bombs with an interval between bombs of 20 meters, the stick strikes the ground in a line 200 meters long.

The deeds of the ground personnel were unimaginable and deserve the highest respect. Working day and night, they had to maintain the aircraft and refuel and arm them before the crew chief could report: 'Aircraft ready for takeoff!'

I have seen such crew chiefs weep when a crew, whose aircraft he had personally maintained, failed to return."

The following account by the former *Obfw.* Georg Geib describes his training and activities from the point of view of a crew chief of the airfield operating company:

"My hobby was glider flying. I joined the gliding group in Kassel-Dörnberg in 1931. I later joined the aviation group at Katterbach airbase.

Following an apprenticeship with an electrical installation company from 1932 to 1936 and completion of my Reich Labor Service (RAD) duty, I volunteered for the air force. I received my basic training from the *Flieger-Ersatz-Abteilung*'s 2nd Company in Quakenbrück. After that I was assigned to the aviation technical school in Jüterbog. In the school complex there I attended lectures by civilian instructors in eighteen theoretical and practical subjects.

From time to time there were midterm exams, and after six months of training there was the big theoretical final exam. An aircraft serviceability report consisted of 52 individual reports. We practiced these often during peacetime.

On fifteen occasions as a maintenance crew chief during five years of war, I waited for my He 111 only to find out that my waiting was in vain. My crews did not return from their combat mission.

How often did I wonder, did you really do everything to your aircraft and forget nothing, are you perhaps partly responsible for your crew's failure to return?

Many young crews came and went over the years. Often I never even learned the names of the crewmembers. The aircraft were kept serviceable with the help of the FBK (airfield operating Company) units. Each crew chief reported the number of maintenance personnel needed to service the aircraft to the aircraft *Oberfeldwebel*. From these FBK units came many up-and-coming crew chiefs as well as many air gunners, radio operators, pilots, armorers and equipment technicians for the *Staffeln*.

Once again my He 111 had failed to return from a combat mission. A young replacement crew had given its life for the Fatherland. I was packing up their things – that was one of my duties as crew chief – when I was advised that a new He 111 was waiting for me at the Heinkel factory in Marienehe near Rostock. Four men were sent in a Bf 108 to collect the aircraft. We took charge of the He 111 on the spot and flew it to Langendiebach near Hanau. I took the aircraft into the maintenance hangar.

At the request of the *Staffel*, I made sure that the aircraft's camera and armament were brought to operational condition.

Finally the aircraft was taken to the compass swing platform.

When everything was in order, I taxied the aircraft to its dispersal. The radio technician then came and checked the radio equipment with the outboard battery starting cart.

An hour passed, then we were ordered to Operational Readiness Level 3: load bombs into the aircraft.

For this purpose I was supposed to taxi the aircraft to the bomb-loading station. This resulted in a collision.

When I looked back inside the fuselage, I saw that half the starter cart was in the aft fuselage. Oh what a shock!

I immediately contacted the maintenance hangar and reported the accident to the officer responsible.

The comradeship between a *Staffel* and FBK now paid off! Twenty mechanics were ready and they worked all that day and night to make the aircraft serviceable.

The following parts were replaced:

Skinning between the fuselage frames, horizontal tail surfaces, tailwheel, sections of the control cable tubes, elevator."

Geib went on to describe an incident at the frontline base in Lille-Nord:

"Regular missions against England. The aircraft are painted black for night operations and washed off again before daylight sorties. Every able-bodied man had to help out. As well, the *Geschwader* was taking heavy losses.

One day was especially costly. Of the five aircraft sent up by the *Stabsstaffel* just one returned to base, and it had 370 bullet holes. Three members of the crew were wounded. The aircraft could not be repaired as the spar in the wing center-section had been shot through. We received new crews and aircraft and in 10 days we returned to action.

That was also a memory of my marriage on 12 August 1940. I went along on a number of combat missions, taking the place of an absent crewmember. Exactly how many I cannot say, as my logbook was lost."

Now back to Wittmann's account:

"After the air battle over England the emphasis switched to bad weather and night missions.

At the mission briefing, which was always held by the *Gruppenkommandeur* or *Staffelkapitän*, the route to and from the target, attack altitude and bomb spacing were discussed with the aid of aerial photographs. If possible, each crew received a target photo reproduced by the Headquarters *Staffel*. Meanwhile orders were issued to the technical officer to bomb up and arm the aircraft. The radio operators set their radio equipment using the frequency of the day, and the observer and pilot established the flight path.

Flying skills, navigation and homing had improved significantly, and locating the target and returning to base posed few problems. The radio beacons from France to Norway simplified things greatly, especially during night flights. The new Lotfe C bombsight was so improved that it was possible to achieve excellent accuracy, even at night.

We flew many of our missions in bad weather, especially those against shipping. A low-level attack on a convoy of up to 60 ships is a very exciting affair, especially when all the ship's light anti-aircraft guns open up with tracer. One is jolly glad to emerge safely from this hail of fire, and especially proud if something was achieved in the attack.

We were caught by a night-fighter during a raid on Liverpool. The radio operator and flight engineer lay wounded in the ventral bath. One engine was shot up and the tail section was damaged. And we still had to cross the brook and get back. We made a wheels-up landing on the beach at Dunkirk. Once again all had gone well.

Oh what is there to tell about missions, and about what had our He 111s endured in the process?

We trusted not only our faithful ground personnel but our machine, which we flew until the end of the war, albeit in improved form.

During mass raids on clear nights, we effectively bombed port installations in London and Liverpool plus industrial sites in Birmingham, Manchester, Glasgow and especially the ammunition and armaments factories in Coventry.

England gradually became a big aircraft carrier, from which the English and Americans sent bomber streams against our cities in 1943-45, inflicting heavy casualties on our civilian population.

What we lacked at the time was a big bomber. Already in 1936 *General* Wever called for a large four-engined bomber with a large payload, great radius of action and heavy armament. It was certainly not a glorious chapter for our aviation industry that, apart from the Ju 88, it failed to produce a usable large bomber during the war.

We had to watch with envy as the English and Americans flew their missions with effective fighter support."

7. RUSSIA – THE WAR IN THE EAST

a) The situation from the German-Soviet non-aggression pact to the attack in the east

The German attack on the Soviet Union was preceded by the following diplomatic events.

On 8 May 1939 the British ambassador approached Soviet foreign minister Molotov with a proposal for an alliance, in which the Soviets would provide assistance in the event of a German attack on Poland and Rumania. For their part, Britain and France would fulfill their obligations.

The Soviets were skeptical, pointing out that there were no guarantees from the British and French in the event that the Soviet Union became involved in a war as a result of abiding by such a treaty.

Despite these ongoing negotiations, the Soviets put out feelers to the German government. In Berlin, Astakhov, the Soviet ambassador, cavalierly told the German undersecretary Dr. Peter Kleist: "A statesman must be capable of changing his spots. Let us decide on a common policy instead of tearing each other's heads off to benefit the interests of a third."

As a result of the British and French support for Poland, the German government found itself in a situation in which the return of Danzig and the establishment of a link to East Prussia through the corridor could not be achieved by peaceful means.

To prevent the Soviet Union from deciding to support Poland, Hitler changed his spots.

On 23 August 1939, after the necessary diplomatic preparations, foreign minister von Ribbentrop flew to Moscow. At the airport the swastika flag flew alongside the red flag with the hammer and sickle.

Negotiations began immediately, and the only assurances the Soviets asked for were the ports of Libau and Windau.

A short time later, in the presence of Stalin, the German-Soviet non-aggression pact was formally signed by Molotov and von Ribbentrop in the Kremlin.

Its essential points:

"Both High Contracting Parties obligate themselves to desist from any act of violence, any aggressive action, and any attack on each other either individually or jointly with other powers.

Should one of the High Contracting Parties become the object of belligerent action by a third power, the other High Contracting Party shall in no manner lend its support to this third power."

There was also a secret protocol in which the two parties agreed that:

"In the event of a territorial and political rearrangement in the areas belonging to the Baltic States (Finland, Estonia, Latvia, Lithuania), the northern boundary of Lithuania shall represent the boundary of the spheres of influence of Germany and the USSR. In this connection the interest of Lithuania in the Vilnius area is recognized by each party. In the event of a territorial and political rearrangement of the areas belonging to the Polish state the spheres of influence of Germany and the USSR shall be bounded approximately by the line of the rivers Narew, Vistula, and San.

The question of whether the interests of both parties make desirable the maintenance of an independent Polish state and how such a state should be bounded can only be definitely determined in the course of further political developments."

Then came the Polish war. Hitler endeavored to draw the Soviet Union into this war.

Stalin waited until he had certainty about a clash with the Japanese in the Manchurian-Mongolian border region. When Japan requested a ceasefire and with the Allies obviously waging a phony war, units of the Red Army crossed the Polish border at dawn on 17 September 1939, "to safeguard the interests of the Soviet Union and the interests of the minorities living in the area."

Astonishingly, neither England nor France declared war on the Soviet Union. Their guarantee to Poland was obviously limited to, or against, Germany.

A German-Soviet border and friendship treaty signed on 28 September 1939 settled the fifth partition of Poland.

The western powers shrank from a conflict with the USSR when Stalin incorporated eastern Poland into the Soviet Union. They also remained silent when he forced the three Baltic States into signing so-called assistance pacts.

Then the picture changed, when Stalin surprised Hitler and the world by suddenly attacking tiny Finland on 30 November 1939, in contravention of the existing non-aggression treaty.

Efforts by Great Britain and France resulted in the Soviet Union's expulsion from the League of Nations as an aggressor. At the same time, member nations of the League were called upon to help Finland. Plans were in fact drawn up, such as the preparation of an allied force, which Stalin of course learned about. Fearing a widening of the war, he brought the Finnish adventure to an end.

With the leap to Scandinavia, Hitler took possession of the Norwegian coast, flanking the Atlantic shipping routes. After the surrender of France on 22 June 1940, he controlled the west coast of Europe from the North Cape to the Bay of Biscay.

The southeast-Asian possessions of Great Britain, France and the Netherlands were largely isolated as a result of the Western

Campaign. For this reason, Japanese leaders in Tokyo decided to begin preparations for a southern expansion of the empire. These preparations included a reduction in tensions between Tokyo and Moscow. By ending its border conflict with the USSR, Japan enabled her to expand in the west.

The Soviet Union had already assimilated the Baltic republics and, contrary to its agreement with Germany, had positioned Russian troops in areas near the border. Stalin had also forced Rumania to cede Bessarabia, Northern Bukovina and the Moldau district of Herta.

With these last two steps Stalin had crossed the demarcation line established on 23 August 1939. The armored forces concentrated in the area of Northern Bukovina were within a day's march of the Rumanian oil fields.

This westward expansion must have been a disturbing factor for Hitler, for it must lead London to speculate about a break between the USSR and Germany. Churchill understood how to exploit this and began efforts to reach an agreement with Stalin.

The rejection of German peace offers by the British prime minister led Hitler to plan military action against Great Britain. The landing in England ("Operation Sea Lion") as well as the leap to the Mediterranean by taking Gibraltar ("Operation Felix") both ran into serious technical difficulties; it was also clear to Hitler that failure to eliminate Great Britain would seriously complicate a confrontation in the east. The heavy losses in the Battle of Britain were warning and example enough.

Stalin's actions had brought movement to the Balkans. Hungary and Bulgaria also demanded the return of territories acquired by Rumania after the First World War. Hitler was able to defuse these tensions through the "Vienna arbitration."

Concluded on 27 September 1940, the Tripartite Pact (Berlin-Rome-Tokyo) was as of little use to Japan as it was to Hitler. The pact was, however, a thorn in Stalin's side, especially Articles 1 and 2, which acknowledged the leadership of the Axis powers and Japan in the establishment of new orders in East Asia and Europe, respectively.

For Russia, which was supposed to join the pact, Persia, Afghanistan and India were left as possible areas for expansion.

Molotov was in Berlin on 12-13 November 1940 to ascertain Hitler's willingness to accept new Soviet demands.

Molotov stated quite plainly that the Soviet Union wanted to tie Finland and the Baltic States closer to itself. The intermittent presence of German troops in Finland, which was permitted by Finland in order to supply German troops in Norway, unsettled Moscow greatly. Hitler declared that he was strongly opposed to a war in the Baltic region, and he was also loathe to provide England with a reason to move into Sweden.

Molotov persisted, however, and Hitler remained evasive. Finally, in a discussion with Foreign Minister von Ribbentrop, Molotov presented the territories in which the USSR was interested: the Black Sea straits, the Baltic straits, the Big Belt, the Little Belt, Öresund, Kattegatt and Skagerrak. Ribbentrop said nothing; these Russian demands were unrealizable.

Hitler made one more attempt to define the spheres of influence together with the three parties to the pact and the Soviet Union as the fourth. But now it was Molotov who was evasive. Not until two weeks later, on 26 November 1940, did the Soviet foreign minister present the German ambassador Count von der Schulenburg with the Soviet conditions for joining a four-power pact:

1. Immediate withdrawal of German troops from Finland (with economic concessions to Germany),

2. Assistance pact with Bulgaria in the "Black Sea – border security zone", creation of a Soviet military base in the district of the Bosporus and the Dardanelles on the basis of a long-term agreement,

3. Focus of the Soviet Union's aspirations in the area south of Batum and Baku in the general direction of the Persian Gulf,

4. Japan to wave its concession rights to coal and naphtha on North Sakhalin.

In other words: Germany was supposed to agree that Finland and Turkey would come under Soviet control and that the British Empire's influence in the Arabian-Indian region would be destroyed. Hitler was not prepared to accept this, he dodged, and relations between Germany and the Soviet Union began to cool.

Hitler's decision to attack the Soviet Union the following spring was now fixed. As Great Britain refused to surrender, Germany came under time constraints.

The United States was beyond the range of German arms, therefore Hitler saw the defeat of the Soviet Union as the only way to avoid a two-front war. The campaign in the east had to be concluded before the combined forces of England and America could land on the European continent.

b) Case Barbarossa

On 18 December 1940 Hitler signed Directive No.21 for "Case Barbarossa" (see facsimile). The start date was 15 May 1941.

When Roosevelt and Churchill received reliable information about Hitler's Barbarossa plan they warned Stalin, accepting that an understanding between Berlin and Moscow might still be possible. As much as Stalin desired it, in order to gain time to rebuild the Red Army and carry out his next attack against Finland, this did not happen.

At dawn on 22 June 1941 German armies crossed the Prut, Bug, Niemen and Memel Rivers to attack the most powerful state in Europe. "Case Barbarossa" had begun.

The five-week delay in the start of the attack caused by the Balkan campaign, the result of actions by Mussolini, was later to prove disastrous with perhaps war-deciding consequences.

Preparations for the attack on Russia had begun in October 1940. From then until spring 1941, *Luftwaffe* construction units worked to repair airfields in occupied Poland, and in March 1941 preparations were accelerated.

At the State Aviation Ministry, *Generaloberst* Rüdel casually asked his boss *Generalfeldmarschall* Milch, who had just returned from leave, if he agreed with the high-level directive which stated that no winter clothing was needed for the new campaign. Milch was completely perplexed, because he had obviously heard nothing about it. His comment: "Completely crazy." Rüdel: "We have orders to prepare a campaign against Russia which is to be completed before the onset of winter." The general staff, especially Quartermaster-General von Seidel, therefore refused to accept responsibility for the procurement of winter clothing. Milch: "I gladly accept responsibility, for it is clear that a war against Russia would last several years and thus several winters."

Milch directed that winter clothing be ordered for one million *Luftwaffe* personnel: four complete sets of underwear and five pairs of woolen socks per man plus felt boots and sheepskin coats. Thus it was that the *Luftwaffe* was the only branch of the armed services that got through the first Russian winter fairly well.

In October 1940 Hitler had ordered the start of high-altitude reconnaissance flights, a novelty in the history of warfare. The then *Oberstleutnant* Rowehl was ordered to set up a strategic reconnaissance unit for the purpose of conducting high-altitude reconnaissance over western Russia. Hitler's exact words to Rowehl: "The altitude must be so exceptional that the Soviets don't notice."

The units began operations at the end of the winter. The *1.* and *2. Staffel* of "*Geschwader Rowehl*" were based in Seerappen and Insterburg in East Prussia. They flew converted He 111s and Do 215 B-2s, which were capable of reaching altitudes of 9000 meters. The *3. Staffel* operated from Bucharest, while the *4. Staffel* flew from Cracow and Budapest. These two *Staffeln* flew converted Ju 88s capable of reaching 12,000 meters, a sensational altitude for that time.

All went well, the Russians noticed nothing. The crews brought back extraordinary photos which showed that all of the airfields in western Russia and the well-camouflaged fighter bases near the frontier were packed with aircraft.

These reconnaissance operations made it possible for the *Luftwaffe* to destroy the bulk of the Soviet air force on the ground at the outset of the campaign. The first strike would thus be of vital importance, as was the timing of the attack, of course.

For the army the attack time was at first light, 03:15. The *Luftwaffe* would begin operations somewhat later, and it thus had to expect that enemy aircraft would be in the air. Air attacks prior to 03:15 would have denied the army the element of surprise.

General von Richthofen, *General* Loerzer, or *Oberst* Mölders, one of them found the solution: like the strategic reconnaissance aircraft, the bombers can sneak in high over unpopulated areas, swamps and forests at such a time as to arrive over their targets when the attack begins.

And that is what happened. Crews with experience in night flying flew in small groups of three to five bombers; each group was assigned a Russian airfield as its target. Almost all located their targets. They couldn't believe their eyes: bombers, fighters and reconnaissance aircraft packed the airfields, lined up as if on parade.

The German bombers dropped tremendous showers of fragmentation bombs, reducing the bulk of the Red Air Force to scrap.

The following is from the Soviet book *History of the Great Patriotic War*: "During the first days of the war, enemy bomber formations launched heavy attacks on 66 frontline airfields … the result of the air attacks and air combats was the loss of 1,200 of our aircraft by noon on 22 June …" Other accounts speak of 1,811 Soviet aircraft destroyed. Göring found these figures so fantastic that he ordered a count of the burnt-out wrecks. The result, more than 2,000 destroyed aircraft.

With the Soviet air Force largely eliminated, the *Luftwaffe* was able to concentrate almost completely on ground support operations.

Generalfeldmarschall von Leeb commanded Army Group North, which was supported by *Luftflotte 1* under *Generaloberst* Keller. Army Group Center under *Feldmarschall* von Bock received air support from *Luftflotte 2* under *Feldmarschall* Kesselring, Army Group South under *Feldmarschall* von Rundstedt from *Luftflotte 4* commanded by *Generaloberst* Löhr.

c) KG 53 Moves East and Operations in the Central Sector

The *III. Gruppe* moved to Silesia on 16 February; the headquarters and 7. *Staffel* went to Lübe, the 8. *Staffel* to Liegnitz and 9. *Staffel* to Freiwaldau.

The *I. Gruppe* in Vitry en Artois and the *II. Gruppe* in Lille-Nord initially stayed where they were, continuing operations over England and receiving supplies as required from the *III. Gruppe*, which was training in Silesia.

On 18 June 1941 the entire *Geschwader* moved to new bases in Poland (Radom, Radzyn, Grojek). Its future area of operations was the central sector, attached to *Luftflotte 2, II. Fliegerkorps* (Loerzer).

"Our new theater of war was Russia, something we hadn't thought possible," described Herbert Wittmann. "We moved from Lille-Nord to Grojek near Radom in Poland. The most fantastic rumors and latrine talk were circulating at that time. Russia was granting free passage to Baku, and the Near East was to be rolled up by way of Turkey, occupied and its oil fields secured. On 20 June 1941 we learned the truth: Germany was declaring war on Russia! Psychologically we were least prepared for this theater of war. Now we were fighting against a merciless enemy. Even today, forty years later, I still remember how every man tried to come to terms with this event by himself or with the help of his comrades or unit. We were flying against a new foe, against Russia, against Soviets. Was this blind obedience or was it trust in the military and political leadership? We were too young and also lacked the necessary insight, we were just soldiers."

What the situation meant to a "people's crew" (airman's slang for a crew with no officers) was described by Arnold Döring, who was later promoted to *Leutnant* on 1 October 1943:

"Apart from me as pilot, our crew, which was attached to the 9th *Staffel*, consisted of observer *Uffz.* Richard Wowarek, gunner *Fw.* Richard Brösing, flight engineer *Fw.* Karl Krupitza, radio operator *Fw.* Toni Grimmer and radio operator Georg Eberhardt.

The entire *Staffel* was assembled at about 16:00 on 21 June 1941. When everyone was there, the *Staffelkapitän*, *Hauptmann* Pockrandt, passed out a number of maps. He was unusually serious. He explained the situation: 'Russia intends – as extensive aerial reconnaissance on our part has revealed – to move against East Prussia and the Generalgouvernement. Extensive measures have also been taken on our side, as we have become well aware in the recent weeks and days. In case it should begin tomorrow, we will attack the following targets: Bielsk-Pilici airfield, south of Bialystok, about 80 km behind the front. The airfield is occupied by fighters. Target assignments: we will attack the ammunition bunker and the landing field, 7th *Staffel* the living quarters and 8th *Staffel* the aircraft parked on the eastern edge. I hope that in these first and subsequent missions the new, young crews will perform well and stand the test like the old ones. Pilots and observers will receive maps and sketches; and here's hoping you bomb well tomorrow!'

Deep silence reigned at first, everyone was too deeply impressed, and then the excitement broke through. After in some cases years of training, the young crews were visibly anxious in anticipation of their first operational sortie and the opportunity to prove themselves.

We gathered again at eleven in the evening. The flying personnel immediately fell in in the long barracks corridor. The *Kapitän* announced the takeoff – it was going to begin tomorrow at 03:30. Then we did everything to get ready for the flight and went to bed: but who could sleep before his first combat mission?!

22 June 1941, first combat mission. We were awakened at 01:30. Several minutes later we rushed to the airfield. In the distance a fire burned, and in the east a pale, narrow light strip announced the approaching day. At the command post the *Gruppenkommandeur* again explained the situation, announced the distribution of targets and then wished us good luck. He himself would be leading the mission.

Each crew was driven to its aircraft. The crew chiefs reported their birds serviceable.

All kinds of thoughts were going through my head. Would we be able to take off successfully from this dog-miserable tiny field, where we had arrived just a few days before?

We climbed into our brave old kites. One last quick check to make sure everything was alright. We could depend 100% on the work of our mechanics. The old man ran up the engines, then raised his hand. It was time. A moment later the first *Kette* began to taxi, bumping over the uneven airfield. Despite their heavy loads, the kites lifted off quite easily. We took off punctually at 03:30.

We climbed out in a wide left turn. The *Gruppe* formed up and set course for the Sielce airfield to pick up out fighter escort. The gentlemen of the fighters didn't show, however. Well, that was alright with us. It wasn't for nothing that we had our guns in the kite.

After a minor course change the formation droned towards the target. We overflew the Bug, the frontier, at 04:15. I calmly scanned my instruments and made no course corrections. I took a look outside. Below it was very hazy, but I could already make out our targets. I was amazed that the defenses hadn't reacted. It was going to be a fine surprise for them.

Then we dropped our eggs. The glow of fires, mushroom clouds of smoke, fountains of earth and mud, mixed with wreckage of all kinds rose steeply. Pity, our stick of bombs fell just to the right of the ammunition bunker. But the rest of the stick fell across the entire airfield and tore up the landing field. The runway took two hits. No fighters would be able to take off for a while, especially as the other *Ketten* of our *Staffel* had bombed the entire landing field. As we turned I could further see that 15 of the parked fighter aircraft were in bright flames, as well as most of the living quarters. Toni shouted 'flak', but I only saw a single shot and it was a kilometer away, for we were already out of range. Then an alarming call on the intercom: 'Fighters from behind!' Our machine-guns began to rattle. The formation closed up. In doing so we offered the Russians a bigger target, but it concentrated our defenses. Tracer from 27 machine-guns sprayed around the Russians' ears, and they immediately dove away and disappeared.

The Bug appeared before us again. Apart from artillery duels we saw nothing.

The airfield came into view and soon the entire formation had landed. We came home without loss. Our success was so great that a second mission planned against that field did not have to be flown.

Toward evening we took off on a second mission. Our target was Bialystok airfield, which had been attacked by other units during the day.

23 June 1941: second combat mission. Attack on tanks and motorized units on the road northeast of Brest-Litovsk through Koboyn to the village of Breceza-Karuska. That was roughly what the mission order said. About ten minutes later the *Gruppe* was in the air, heading towards the target. We flew over Brest-Litovsk at a height of 800 meters. Parts of the city were on fire. The citadel was the scene of fierce fighting. We also met our fighter escort there. Mölders personally led the fighters. Heavy traffic on the road to Koboyn. Below packed with troops everywhere. In some cases our men advanced beside the road. Our advance rolled deeper into the country, with the panzers leading the way. Before them about two kilometers of no-man's-land, but then more enemy columns, en masse. Clumsy tanks of all sizes, motorized columns, horsedrawn vehicles, with artillery wedged in between. Everything was fleeing eastwards in a wild flight. We had reached our target. The *Staffel* descended and we sprayed the road with machine-gun fire. The first bombs fell. We flew down the road one behind the

other and also beside the road. Our bombs fell among tanks, guns, vehicles and Russians fleeing in all directions. Panic had broken out down below and no one was thinking about defense. We only bombed close to the road to preserve it for our advance. The effect of the high-explosive and fragmentation bombs was devastating. Against these targets none of our bombs missed. Tanks were tipped over or left in flames after taking direct hits. Guns with their tractors blocked the road, between them wildly rearing horses increased the panic."

A steady stream of such sorties against troop concentrations and railway lines followed during the rapid German advance. The bombers hunted trains and bombed railway stations, other airfields, columns and villages harboring enemy troops.

With the Soviet air force as good as eliminated, our aviation units could concentrate almost exclusively on supporting the army, and the ground battle proceeded with astonishing speed.

On 29 June Panzer Groups 2 and 3 linked up west of Minsk, and the cities of Brest-Litovsk, Minsk, Smolensk and Kiev fell in rapid succession in a series of further pincer movements. German forces met no resistance as they advanced from Bialystok in the direction of Minsk. The Red Army had already lost 324,000 men and 3,300 tanks.

Smolensk was encircled on 27 July and on 5 August the Soviet forces in the pocket surrendered.

Our *Geschwader* followed the advancing ground forces, moving from base to rapid succession, often as soon as a town with an airfield was taken.

The operations by the *1. Staffel* of the *I. Gruppe* illustrate the pace of operations by KG 53:

Date	Base	Remarks
22/6/41	Grojec	*Gruppe* attack on Wysokie-Mazowieckie airfield
22/6/41	Grojec	2nd attack on Wysokie-Mazowieckie airfield
23/6/41	Grojec	Attacks against troops in the Kobryn-Baranovichi area
23/6/41	Grojec	Attacks against troops in the area south of Slonim
24/6/41	Grojec	Attack on airfields and roads near Slutsk
24/6/41	Grojec	Night attack on railway installations near Gomel
25/6/41	Grojec	Night attack on railway installations near Orsha
26/6/41	Grojec	Night attack on railway installations near Smolensk
28/6/41	Grojec	Attack on Bobruisk airfield
28/6/41	Grojec	Attack aborted due to engine trouble

On 29 June the *Gruppe* moved to Rogoznica, on 2 July to Miedzyrzee, on 3 and 4 July operated from Baranovichi, on 5, 7 and

9 July it operated from Chernovitsi and finally on 9 July it moved to Minsk-Dubinskaya, where it was joined the *Stab* and the other *Gruppen*.

Operations until 2 August were flown from intermediate bases including Dubinskaya:

10/7/41	Minsk-Dubinskaya	Attack against troops on the Orsha-Mogilev road
13/7/41	Minsk-Dubinskaya	Attack against troops near Gomel
14/7/41	Minsk-Dubinskaya	Twilight attack on bridge near Shlobin
16/7/41	Minsk-Dubinskaya	Twilight attack on railway installations at
	Shlobin-Gomel	
18/7/41	Minsk-Dubinskaya	Aborted due to engine trouble
18/7/41	Minsk-Dubinskaya	Low-level attack on rail line and troops
	Spas-Demenskoye-Sukhinichi	
21/7/41	Minsk-Dubinskaya	Large-scale night raid on Moscow (Klara Zetkin)
22/7/41	Minsk-Dubinskaya	Large-scale night raid on Moscow (Klara Zetkin)
23/7/41	Minsk-Dubinskaya	Large-scale night raid on Moscow (Klara Zetkin)
26/7/41	Minsk-Dubinskaya	Troops and tanks on road 100 km E of
	Dorogobuzh	
27/7/41	Minsk-Dubinskaya	Troops and tanks on Spas-Demenskoye-Roslavl road
28/7/41	Minsk-Dubinskaya	Kalinkovichi-Mozyr railway station
28/7/41	Minsk-Dubinskaya	Attack on Kalinkovichi-Mozyr railway station
28/7/41	Minsk-Dubinskaya	Attack on artillery positions W of Rogachev
28/7/41	Minsk-Dubinskaya	Large-scale night raid on Moscow (Klara Zetkin)
29/7/41	Minsk-Dubinskaya	Night attack against railway installations near Briansk
30/7/41	Minsk-Dubinskaya	Daylight attack on railway installations at Rogachev
30/7/41	Minsk-Dubinskaya	Night attack on railway installations near Orel
31/7/41	Minsk-Dubinskaya	Daylight attack on railway installations at Vyazma
1/8/41	Minsk-Dubinskaya	Attack on troops near Roslavl
2/8/41	Minsk-Dubinskaya	Large-scale night raid on Moscow (Klara Zetkin)

On 4 August the *Gruppe* moved to Orsha. The rapid victories were not always easy to secure. The *Luftwaffe*'s method of using all types of bomber for ground support missions also had serious disadvantages.

To our sorrow we discovered that Soviet troops employed every available weapon against enemy aircraft and must inflict serious losses on us in the long run.

Wittmann observed the following about this and the operations being carried out at that time:

"Why did they not send us bombers deep into the enemy rear? Incomprehensible, using us in direct support of the army was wrong. It would have been better tactically to employ all our strength in attacks on railway stations, airfields, depots, industrial facilities, etc., instead of artillery positions, tank concentrations and bridgeheads near the front.

The advance went on. Our new base was Dubinskaya airfield. We were now on Russian soil.

Looking back, one must still be amazed that after this enormous advance by the army, almost 1000 kilometers to the east in a short time, the supply system still functioned. The technical ground personnel were moved forward by transport aircraft, while the rest, including the photo section, followed in trucks.

It was almost a miracle that fuel, bombs, ammunition of all kinds, food and not least our personnel, continued to arrive at our new bases despite the roads, which were bad and overloaded, and the railroad system, most of which had been destroyed.

They also saw to it that the mail – our link to home, our families and our loved ones, so vital to morale – also soon began arriving.

Our signals corps did outstanding work … No sooner did we arrive at a new airfield than the lines of communication were established.

Every soldier simply gave his best, even though in many cases they were forced to work in very primitive and difficult conditions.

Our medical services are deserving of special praise. They were not just responsible for caring for the sick and wounded. The medical officer was also responsible for the overall hygienic conditions. One only has to think about drinking water, quarters, food and also the Russian civilian auxiliaries we employed. The 'Hiwis' were often of great help to us and are deserving of positive mention.

The *Stabsstaffel* returned to the tasks of reconnaissance, target location and aerial photography, at the direction of the *Geschwader*, and was constantly in action.

After the German fighters achieved air superiority in the first days of the campaign, we returned to flying lone daylight sorties. The interpretation of aerial photos was of great importance to the *Geschwader* and the high command.

What we feared most over England were the English fighters. What we feared in Russia was the Russian flak. Its accuracy at all heights was frightening.

Dubinskaya was a Russian forward airfield near Minsk. For the first time we airmen had no permanent buildings for quarters. No matter whether it was the *Staffelkapitän* of ground crew chief, pilot or driver, we all crawled into an unfamiliar tent. We also visited the city of Minsk, which didn't make a bad impression. There were also no complaints about the population, which remained calm in our contacts with them."

The first air raid on Moscow took place on 21 July 1943. Stalin responded by issuing an order of the day. The New Zurich News reported on 23 July 1941:

"On Tuesday Stalin, in his capacity as supreme defense commissar, issued an order of the day concerning the attack on Moscow by the German air force. It read:

'On Tuesday night the German air force carried out its first major raid against Moscow. Thanks to the alertness of our observer corps, despite the darkness the enemy squadrons were located long before they reached the capital and attacked by night-fighters. The defensive batteries in Moscow put up an effective barrage with outstanding support from searchlight battalions. As a result of these defensive measures the German formation, consisting of more than 200 aircraft, was broken up and only a few bombers were able to overfly Moscow. Firefighters quickly extinguished several fires.

The defense commissariat congratulates the civilian population on its calm and discipline. It has been determined with certainty that the Russian night-fighters and defensive batteries shot down a total of 22 German bombers.'"

A report in *Life* magazine in August 1941 was somewhat more cynical:

"Moscow was prepared for war. Nothing illustrates this better than Margret Boruke-White's beautiful and shocking photos of the German air raids on 23 and 26 July. The first air raid took place on 21 July, after one month of war. According to reports, 100 German aircraft took part in the raid on 26 July, of which six were shot down. But the Moscow show sounded bigger. Apparently the Nazis tried to bomb Stalin personally, as shown by the concentration of parachute flares over the Kremlin. The Russians had massed heavy flak defenses around this citadel of communism.

Such photos as these of the bombardment and defense of Moscow were never released by British censors during the Battle of Britain. Doubtless the communist state, though far from its ideals in peacetime, is well suited for war. The fire services worked as well as in London after one night of bombing. The people were even calmer. By day they swim in the Moskva, at night they stay in their air defense posts with sleeves rolled up."

Obfw. Alfred Sticht took part in the first raid on Moscow on 21 July 1941, flying as a member of *Obfw.* Willi Haug's crew:

"It is Sunday afternoon. The crews are lying in their tents. The blazing hot sun shines down on the Russian ground. It is 21 July 1941. Minsk-Dubinskaya is our airfield. None of us dares leave our tent. Heat, thirst and mosquitoes are our constant companions. The mosquito net lies close at hand. Our drivers, *Feldwebel* Panizzi and *Uffz.* Methner, have been at the only water distribution point for three hours, waiting in vain for the precious fluid. We must wait at any cost. Despite everything, there is a solemn stillness in our 'tent city'. In the afternoon the *Gruppenkommandeur, Oberstleutnant* Kaufmann, visits the aircrews and tells us that we will probably be flying another mission today. My crew sits contemplatively in the tent, one or the other thinking about his loved ones at home. The request program playing on the radio represents the binding tie between the front and home. Our youngest crewmember, Martin Lehner, *Unteroffizier* and gunner, is just writing to his mother, telling her that he will soon be coming home on leave, when the duty officer announces Readiness Level III. Now there is a flurry of activity in the tent. The crews get ready, breaking out parachutes, flight suits, flying helmets, maps, navigation equipment, fur-lined boots, oxygen equipment and their belts with pistol. The latter is just in case, especially if one is shot down and has to make his way back through enemy territory in the night and fog. The faces have become more serious. I study the map and prepare our route of flight. Our flight engineer, *Obfw.* Höfler, the 'Man from Fürth', packs the emergency rations as a precaution, and Martin Lehner, the most carefree of us, strikes up a little Viennese song. Our pilot Willi Haug is still cleaning his pistol, and Hannes Dünfelder, our radio operator, is preparing fried potatoes for the crew. He has become our 'fried potato specialist'.

Ten minutes later the duty officer announces Readiness Level II. We now know that it will start in about half an hour.

We have just finished our 'princely meal' when the *Staffelkapitän, Hauptmann* Allmendinger, a fearless Swabian (known as Emil among his comrades), returns from the command post and summons the aircrews for a briefing. The mission order is revealed: large-scale night raid on Moscow ('Klara Zetkin').

Klara Zetkin is the codename for Moscow. Now the airfield is bustling with activity. Our maintenance crew chief, *Uffz*. Retschek, reports the aircraft ready for takeoff.

We have been the *Staffelkapitän*'s crew and a close-knit team since the start of the war (Poland, France, England). Each of us can rely on the others 100%. We are the first machine to taxi out for takeoff. One last look at the clock and we begin our takeoff run. Heavily loaded, our A1+AB races down the runway into the evening twilight. We overfly the radio beacon on the airfield and turn onto an easterly heading. Smolensk is behind us. We fly along the highway that leads to Moscow. We pass Vyazma. Our He 111 drones serenely over vastness of Russia, east towards Moscow. Our target is Moscow's main airport and the nearby aircraft factory.

Our crew – pilot *Obfw*. Willi Haug, observer *Obfw*. Alfred Sticht, radio operator Hans Dünfelder, flight engineer Hans Höfler and *Unteroffizier* Martin Lehner (our youngest, from Vienna) – has stood the test in more than 200 combat missions in various theaters and is one of the veteran crews of *Kampfgeschwader 53*. Our operational experience bestows upon us a certain degree of safeness. Nevertheless, maximum attentiveness, conscientiousness and a large portion of soldier's luck are vital in completing a combat mission.

The sun is just going down. We pass over the front, below us is enemy territory. Our cannon and machine-gun positions are manned, the weapons ready to fire. Five pairs of eyes tensely scan the sky for enemy fighters. The sunset is magnificent. We pass Gzhatsk. Before us, shrouded in darkness, is Moscow. The light from several searchlights strikes our eyes like sharp needles.

The altimeter shows 1200 meters. We are not expecting much in the way of defenses. The first searchlights flash on in the outskirts of Moscow, excitedly probing the dark night. The searchlights haven't touched us yet. More and more come on as we approach Moscow. Below me I see the highway, stretching through the dark countryside towards Moscow. I count 50 to 100 searchlights. Hopefully all will go well. The anti-aircraft guns are still silent. At the flight briefing we were told to expect little in the way of defenses: nevertheless, this mass of searchlights is slowly making us uneasy. As a precaution we slowly gain altitude, climbing at two meters per second. Then – what is that in front of us? An aircraft, harshly illuminated, caught by a searchlight. In a flash several more searchlight beams cone the machine. Through the binoculars I can see that it is a He 111, one of ours. It takes wild evasive action in an attempt to shake the searchlight beams. In vain.

Full power and climb as fast as we can, that is our motto. Five more aircraft are seized by the countless mass of searchlights. By now we have reached 1700 meters and are over the outskirts of Moscow. Every anti-aircraft gun opens up, shells begin bursting at all altitudes.

A searchlight grazes us, loses, us, comes back and has us. We quickly put on our sunglasses and begin to 'corkscrew'. Normal evasive maneuvers are not enough. More than thirty searchlights shine their harsh light on us. The anti-aircraft guns blaze away. Shells burst in front of us, above us, to the left and right. Our aircraft doesn't have the usual dark finish on the underside of the wings and fuselage. We curse our *Gruppe* technical officer, *Hauptmann* Buder, because he didn't procure the black paint for our machines from Jüterbog in time. We will be lucky if we escape this witch's cauldron. We never experienced anti-aircraft fire as heavy as this over London.

A bang, a jet of fire, our machine shakes, we have been hit. I arm the bombs and pull the emergency release. Below us one huge pillar of fire. We turn away to the southwest. The vertical speed indicator shows that we are descending at ten meters per second. The airspeed indicator shows that our speed has risen to 500 kph. The engines are screaming. There is a roaring noise in my ears. Is anyone wounded, I ask through my throat microphone. Everyone checks in, no one has been hit. Meanwhile we have descended to 300 meters in the dive and roar low over the metropolis of the east. The searchlights have lost us, we have left the municipal area of Moscow and are heading south. After five minutes we turn west, towards Minsk. Slowly, our wounded bird flies bravely towards the west. Hardly a word is spoken, and everyone is thinking the same thing: will the engines hold out, will we get home? They are still running well, with no great loss of revolutions. The pilot constantly scans the instrument panel. We breathe a sigh of relief when we reach the front. After almost five hours in the air we land, exhausted but safe, in Minsk-Dubinskaya. Though damaged, our brave He 111 has brought us safely home again, although it was the only 'wounded.' German workmanship."

The impetus of the initial attack carried Army Group Center along the Napoleonic route to Smolensk. The commanders of the army were agreed: Moscow was the primary objective.

But suddenly Leningrad seemed more important to Hitler. Not until Leningrad had fallen would he decide whether the next objective was to be Moscow or the Ukraine. He ordered a regrouping of forces, then finally cancelled it, and on 23 August 1941 he made his decision: the next objective was the Ukraine.

There followed a series of victories that surpassed anything that had gone before: the battles of encirclement at Roslavl, Uman and Kiev. Overwhelmed by these successes, in October, by then too late,

Hitler gave the order for the attack on Moscow – the troops found themselves stuck in the mud with their objective in sight.

By the end of August, however, Hitler had realized that in the east 'lightning fast' brought no lasting results. On 26 August he was forced to admit that the eastern campaign could not be completed in 1941. Stalin was also able to withdraw divisions from Siberia after being informed of Japanese plans by the German spy Dr. Sorge.

On 4 August 1941 the *Geschwader* moved to Orsha. The missions it flew until 28 September reveal the nature of air operations at that time:

4/8/41	Orsha	Large-scale night raid on Moscow (special target)
7/8/41	Orsha	Large-scale night raid on Moscow (special target)
9/8/41	Orsha	Large-scale night raid on Moscow
10/8/41	Orsha	Large-scale night raid on Moscow
11/8/41	Orsha	Twilight attack on Briansk station
12/8/41	Orsha	Twilight attack on Briansk station
12/8/41	Orsha	Night attack on Vyazma station
14/8/41	Orsha	Daylight raid on Zlobin
14/8/41	Orsha	Daylight attack on artillery positions 2 km NE of Zlobin
15/8/41	Orsha	Daylight attack on troops on road north of Gomel
15/8/41	Orsha	Daylight attack on artillery positions north of Yelnya
16/8/41	Orsha	Daylight attack on troops near Uschtscherpje near Klintsy
16/8/41	Orsha	Daylight raid on Novosybykov (70 km E of Gomel)
21/8/41	Orsha	Daylight attack on Gomel – Snovsk rail line and rolling stock
22/8/41	Orsha	Daylight attack on rail line 10 km N of Snovsk and rolling stock
23/8/41	Orsha	Daylight attack on Nyedantshitschi-Cherny rail line
23/8/41	Orsha	Night attack on Chernikov railway station
24/8/41	Orsha	Daylight attack on Krolevets railway station
24/8/41	Orsha	Daylight attack on Chernikov railway station
25/8/41	Orsha	Daylight attack on Konotop-Putivl rail line
25/8/41	Orsha	Daylight attack on Konotop-Krolevets rail line
26/8/41	Orsha	Daylight attack on Kholmechi railway station
28/8/41	Orsha	Daylight attack on Kholmechi railway station and trains
30/8/41	Orsha	Daylight attack on Paliki and North-Briansk railway stations
1/9/41	Orsha	Daylight attack on Komarischi railway station
6/9/41	Orsha	Night attack on supply installations in Briansk
7/9/41	Orsha	Daylight attack on railway station and Klimoska-Sumy rail line
8/9/41	Orsha	Daylight attack on moving trains on the Bakhmach-Konotop line

9/9/41	Orsha	Daylight attack on Romny railway station and rail installations
10/9/41	Orsha	Daylight attack on Piryatin railway station and rail installations
10/9/41	Orsha	Daylight attack on troops and tanks near Jtschija
12/9/41	Orsha	Daylight attack on troop concentrations and tanks near Razmany
13/9/41	Orsha	Daylight attack on troop concentrations and tanks near Chernychi-Piryatin
14/9/41	Orsha	Daylight attack on troops near Priluki
15/9/41	Orsha	Daylight attack on troops and tanks Priluki-Piryatin
16/9/41	Orsha	Daylight attack on moving trains Klinovka-Sumy
17/9/41	Orsha	Daylight attack on Komarichi railway station
19/9/41	Orsha	Daylight attack on Smorodino railway station
20/9/41	Orsha	Daylight attack on moving trains near Kirikovka
24/9/41	Orsha	Daylight attack on Briansk-Orel-Kursk-Lgov rail line
26/9/41	Orsha	Daylight attack on railway crossing 10 km NW of Kaluga
27/9/41	Orsha	Daylight attack on moving trains near Kaluga
28/9/41	Orsha	Daylight attack on moving trains as on 27/9.

"No pause – onwards to the east! We're moving to Orsha", is how Herbert Wittmann, former *Kapitän* of the *Stabsstaffel*, continued his description of the activities of his unit, which was always in the heat of the action.

"This Russian airbase was up to date and had roughly the same installations as our new, comfortable bases in Germany. We lived in permanent quarters again.

The Russians had abandoned Orsha in haste. Technical installations, training aircraft and the like were intact, and the quarters also showed clearly that they couldn't have been evacuated according to a plan.

From Orsha we flew a special, 'top secret' mission. Two crews were each given the job of transporting five Russian agents deep into the rear and dropping them there. It wasn't a very pleasant task. Over the drop zone we opened the hatch in the ventral bath, and any of the Russians who hesitated were forcefully assisted by the flight engineer and gunner. It is said that the mission was of help to the army command.

We also flew missions into the enemy hinterland in bad weather, and in addition to reconnaissance we conducted a type of 'free hunt', attacking and photographing important railway stations and industrial facilities.

Compared to the air war against England, losses were lighter but all the more painful. The foe was merciless. And as we knew, baled-out crews were rarely taken prisoner.

The missions in direct support of the army were disappointing. As previously mentioned, it would have been correct to fly attacks deep in the enemy's rear against railway stations, depots, airfields, industrial complexes, etc.

The Russian front should have been cut off from its supplies. At that time the bomber arm was powerful and entirely capable of penetrating deep into the enemy rear by day. This was not done and so the Russians, who were undoubtedly badly battered at that time, were able to stabilize their situation and in the months that followed even alter the course of the war.

The foolish idea that the Russian front was at the point of collapse in October 1941 was false. I still remember clearly the records of the interrogation of Stalin's son, in which he said something to the effect of: 'Russia will win even if Moscow should fall, the Russian territory is large.'

We flew in the Kursk-Orel-Rzhev-Tula-Kaluga area and at night to Moscow as well. The anti-aircraft fire over Moscow was ineffective at night. The countless searchlights probed the night sky in confused disorder and rarely illuminated us during our attacks. This would soon change, however.

After Japan concluded a non-aggression pact with the Russians, our reconnaissance detected fresh troops arriving from the east. Unfortunately the railway stations packed with troop transport trains were also not attacked.

The performance of the ground personnel at that time is deserving of respect and high praise."

Georg Geib wrote:

"For the Russian campaign the *Stabsstaffel* was assigned its own workshop platoon with inspector. The advance proceeded in the direction of Moscow. Our task was to provide air support for Panzer Group Guderian. Its objectives were Brest-Litovsk, Minsk, Orsha, Smolensk, Tula and Moscow.

Our transfer flight to the east was an ill-starred beginning. One of our He 111s flew into the ground in the Riesen Mountains and eleven men were killed. Among them were the parachute technician, the radio technician, the cook, the stores NCO and a clerk. On arriving in Dubinskaya near Minsk, all we found were drums of fuel in a meadow. To fuel the aircraft, the 200 to 300-liter drums had to be rolled out to the machines. The truck transport columns for bombs, supplies and the like had not arrived yet, and so operations were limited to strafing sorties in support of the army.

During an early mission from Dubinskaya I was surprised when a returning crew informed me that my He 111 GA had just been involved in a midair collision. While being flown by *Hptm.* Wittmann, it had collided with *Fw.* Häußler's He 111 CA. *Hptm.* Wittmann and his crew were able to parachute to safety, but *Fw.* Häußler and four men were killed.

The winter of 1941-42 was extremely difficult for us. On the night of 11 October 1941 the temperature suddenly dropped to minus 22 degrees Celsius.

The engines of our aircraft had not been filled with sufficient anti-freeze, consequently the radiators and coolant pumps froze. We also lacked equipment for winter operations. People lost feet, ears, noses and fingers to freezing. Even answering the call of nature outdoors posed risks. At such temperatures, passing the night without moving could be fatal. Long missions at high altitude were risky, because the internal heating was insufficient for such temperatures. Oxygen equipment froze up, resulting in altitude sickness and frostbite.

Our casualties during that awful winter of 1941-42 were so great that the *Geschwader Staffel* had to be reorganized into a *Geschwader Schwarm*."

This ends Geib's account, now back to Wittmann:

"The servicing of the aircraft, arming as per mission orders, fueling, checking of the camera and radio equipment, in short everything that was part of the *Staffel*'s operational readiness, went on day and night without pause. I also do not want to omit our cooks as well as our supply officer, who worked closely with the *Geschwader* administration. To this day I still wonder how the kitchen conjured up the food. At any rate it had to be prepared under the most primitive conditions.

During a mission against artillery positions near Orel, our port engine and wing were shot up by anti-aircraft fire, whereupon the aircraft began to roll and became uncontrollable. Order to everyone: 'Bale out immediately!' I could tell that this did not need to be practiced. We were all out of the machine in no time, who went first or last I cannot say. We hung beneath our parachutes, wondering what fate awaited us on the ground. When my parachute opened, the sudden jerk caused me to lose both of my flying boots. It was a hot August day and I landed in a cornfield beneath a blazing sun. No sooner did I hit the ground than I was surrounded by a crowd of Russian civilians, young, old, both sexes. I detected no hostility and in my distress I presented my parachute to one of the women and perhaps gained the sympathy of all. One of the Russians also offered to act as my guide. My objective was the military road, which was in German hands. They could also have turned me in, but I don't think the Russians were in agreement among themselves about that. The German army was still advancing. After a ten-hour walk my Russian and I came to a road, where by chance a German VW *Kübelwagen* came by. Looking at me in my flight suit, the soldiers took me for a Russian, until I cleared everything up and they took me with them. I gave my kopeks to the helpful Russian, almost having to force them upon him. Yes, luck is part of the soldier's trade. The other members of the crew also made it back safely.

During a mission against a target in front of Moscow, an aircraft of the *Stabsstaffel* was shot down. *Hauptmann* Küster, our oldest member, escaped by parachute. A Russian farmer concealed him for weeks in a feed bin on his farm. After about six weeks *Hauptmann* Küster, dressed in a Russian sheepskin coat, made his way to the German front with the help of the Russian farmer. We never heard any more about the rest of the crew.

As a result of our rapid advance there was no home leave, and one day a member of the *Staffel* came with a request for a long-distance marriage. As *Staffelkapitän* I was the registrar, two of his comrades were witnesses, and the entire *Staffel* was present. Surely a special event at the front. I can confirm today that the two people married that day were an especially happy couple.

Two crews shot down by Russian flak were buried in the military cemetery in Orsha, where Russian and German soldiers are buried side by side."

An impression of the severity of these missions may be gained from the diary entry of Arnold Döring regarding his flight on 15 August 1941, when he was accompanied by *Hauptmann* Pockrandt, the *Staffelkapitän*:

"15 August 1941. I will always remember this 30th combat mission. The entire *Gruppe* was sent to attack encircled troops near Yelnya. We bombed in *Gruppe* formation from a height of 1200 meters. I was flying with the old man in the lead aircraft in the third *Kette*. Over Yelnya itself we came under heavy anti-aircraft fire. There was a huge number of aircraft of all types in the air. They all dropped their bombs on the Russian divisions squeezed into an area of about 4 to 5 kilometers. Below us it swarmed like an ant's nest. About 300 to 400 bombers of all types circled over the target. Above them were fighters, covering us against attacks by Russian fighters.

The *Gruppe* split up by *Staffel*, and the *Staffeln* increased their intervals so as to cover as much of the area as possible with bombs. The bombs fell one after the other at short intervals. On this day the old man was doing the bombing. Scarcely had he closed the bomb doors when a heavy jolt shook the aircraft. It slowly rolled onto its left side and stalled. The yoke was knocked from my hands and the controls scarcely reacted to movements. I quick glance at the starboard wing revealed that part of it was missing and that the aileron was gone. Great shooting by the Russian flak. Anxious moments passed before I was able to regain control of the aircraft. By then the formation was far above us. We had lost more then 500 meters of altitude.

Cautiously I moved the other aileron. It was difficult to operate. The loss of speed because of the shot-up wing was considerable. The sun also shone through numerous holes in the fuselage. Everyone in back was alright, but we had grown pale for the first few minutes. I was barely able to control the aircraft. I had already trimmed it as much as I could. To regain some balance, I transferred fuel from the right to the left. That was a little better, but I still had to apply full aileron. The slipstream tore huge holes in the ripped skinning. Each time a new piece of the thin metal tore, a jolt when through the aileron. The aircraft continually wanted to roll to the right. It was lucky that the good old He 111 could also be straightened up with the rudder. Our greatest piece of luck was that it was evening, when the air masses were calm. If there had been turbulence I seriously doubt that we would have regained our airfield.

The other two aircraft of the *Kette* flew alongside us. They had also been hit by a few fragments. We flew homewards at low speed. After anxious minutes we finally reached the airfield. The landing cross was lying right in our direction of flight. I increased power and lowered the undercarriage. I scarcely dared use the flaps, as my brave machine was already tilting sharply to the right. I didn't lower them until we were just above the ground. The machine immediately tipped further to the right and touched down starboard wheel first. It then rumbled like a drunken man from one side to the other. The bird stopped just short of the opposite airfield boundary. I slowly taxied to the dispersal. The entire technical staff and all the people from the tent camp were already there, altered by the two red flares fired by the old man. The ambulance was already waiting, but it wasn't needed. I shut down the engines and then climbed onto the wing to examine the damage from above. The old man followed me and was the first to shake my hand, promising a bottle of something good to 'celebrate my birthday'.

The hole was so big that one could easily have dropped through it lengthwise. The skinning was badly torn by shrapnel. Holes could be seen everywhere in the wings, fuselage and tail.

The maintenance crew chief taxied the machine to the maintenance hangar, where it received new wings and patches were riveted over the shrapnel holes. The bird was repaired in two days.

In the evening the old man donated a bottle of red wine and awarded me the Iron Cross, First Class. Another reason to celebrate.

Ivan came during the night. The anti-aircraft guns banged away like mad and we had to take cover against falling fragments. A number of tents were pierced. The bombs fell away from the airfield and caused no damage. One bomb set a barracks on fire. It had been evacuated by Labor Service people just the day before, because it was infested with vermin.

As for a change it was just the one Russian aircraft that paid us a visit, we soon went to sleep."

On 1 October 1941 the *Geschwader* moved to Shatalovka, where on the 15th *Hauptmann* Herbert Wittmann left the unit. Of the *Stabsstaffel* and its subsequent fate, he wrote:

"Once again we moved farther forward – Shatalovka-East was and remained the easternmost airfield for us. It was also an impressive air base.

The pace of operations accelerated. Moscow was the big objective for the supreme command. It was supposed to fall before the onset of winter and decide the war in our favor.

It was there that my time as commander of the *Stabsstaffel* came to an end. My last mission was an attack on the Maloya Roslavets airfield just outside Moscow.

After more than 150 combat missions, on 15 October 1941 I handed my *Staffel* over to *Oberleutnant* von Horn, who in February 1942 would fail to return from a sortie.

In March 1942 the *Staffel* was disbanded. The *Geschwader* was left with only a command flight.

It was proper that a *Geschwader* should be able to conduct its own reconnaissance – target scouting and bombing results. It was utterly wrong, however, to equip the *Staffel* with the cumbersome He 111 for this purpose.

I am qualified to pass judgment on what this *Staffel* accomplished. The air and ground personnel were a unit, a close-knit team. (Percentagewise, the *Stabsstaffel* is best represented at *Geschwader* reunions. Proof of how strong this comradeship remains to this day.)"

Retired *Generalarzt* D. Dr. Ernst Ebeling was a graduate of the army officer's school and joined the *Luftwaffe* as a young *Leutnant* on the first day of the war. He began his flying training at the *Luftwaffe* officer's school in Werder/Havel, where basic (A/B) training lasted until May 1940. He completed his training in October 1940 after attending the advanced (C) flight training school in Neubrandenburg and the instrument flying school in Königsberg-Devau and its satellite airfield in Griesslingen near Hohenstein.

By way of the Central Bomber School in Tutow and the replacement training *Gruppe* in Quedlinburg, in March 1941 he joined the newly-formed *IV. Gruppe* of KG 53. It was the training and supply *Gruppe* for the *Geschwader* and was based at Lille-Nord.

Each of the operational *Gruppen* had an authorized strength of 36-45 crews. After the losses during the rapid advance, each demanded replacements, and the most experienced crews from the *IV. Gruppe* were sent to Russia.

Ernst Ebeling, then a *Leutnant*, recalled:

"At the end of August 1941, *Oberfähnrich* Lorenz and I reported to the commander of the *III. Gruppe*, *Major* Fabian, in Orsha. He was less than enthused to learn that my crew and I had neither dropped bombs nor had any night flying experience. We were disappointed to hear him declare that he couldn't complete his mission with such crews, who would be employed on transport flights in the rear area to begin with, but our spirits picked up again after talking with comrades who had come from the army at the same time – *Gruppenadjutant Leutnant* Gobert, technical officer *Leutnant* Kindt and the fatherly reserve officer Kürten (a *Leutnant* and pilot during the First World War), who had been made *Major beim Stabe*. When our *Staffelkapitän Hauptmann* Pockrandt showed us to the *Staffel* billets and gave us fresh hope by telling us that we would be fine for the current four-hour missions, of which just twenty minutes was spent over enemy territory, the world looked better again. These would allow us to practice formation flying and also quickly learn about bombing in *Staffel* and *Gruppe* formation.

We selected our 'beds' (piles of straw on the floor), were introduced to the other officers in the *Staffel* and the NCO specialists, and after one or two 'spare parts collection flights into the rear' we were assigned to our first combat mission into the Kiev pocket. My formation flying, especially while passing through cloud banks, not only made my hair stand on end at times but also earned me threatening gestures from the *Staffelkapitän*, to whose flight I had been assigned. My performance obviously improved during the two-hour flight to the target, however, for I was not sent home before we crossed the front line and successfully completed the mission.

After ten more missions against roads, rail lines, a railway bridge, columns of trucks and railway stations in the same pocket, I was deemed combat ready. The distance between us and the veteran crews with the Iron Crosses, First and Second Class and Operational Flying Clasps in Bronze, Silver and Gold (20, 60 and 100 combat missions) gave way to a growing comradeship."

The description of the first combat mission by *Leutnant* von Glasow, "Peewee", and his crew by his radio operator, the then *Gefreiter* Rudolf Graf, may provide a vivid picture of these missions, especially as it comes from the point of view of a young radio operator. Graf's account speaks the simple, clear language of the frontline soldier:

"Then it was time!
For *Leutnant* Dieter von Glasow and crew the eastern campaign began on 26 September 1941. The duty officer came into our former bug hut and said, 'E 1 for the Glasow crew.'
'E' was the abbreviation for operational readiness.
When it was 'E 3' we were not permitted to leave the airfield area. When they told us 'E 2' we had to remain in quarters and await further orders.
'E 1' meant flight suit on, parachute over one arm, grab the radio operator's notebook and navigation case, and run down the stairs to the waiting truck that would take us to the flight briefing in the command post. Already standing there were five five-man crews with many decorations on their flight jackets. In their presence we made ourselves small like field mice. To these 'grizzled veterans' we were 'young plugs'!
Gunner Breuer had not been placed on 'E 1' for our first combat mission. His place was taken by war reporter Feikert, who was later supposed to write a combat report for the illustrated air force magazine *Der Adler*. He got his story.
This is my story," continues Graf: "I gloss over nothing and exaggerate nothing. My account of our combat missions that follows contains just one omission: emotionally I can't describe them as we experienced and felt them.
Every day they gave us the opportunity to die. We didn't take it, we ignored it.
The command post, a big room with field telephones and maps of the Eastern Front on the walls, was located on the first floor of a stone house on the airfield. Our *Kommodore*, *Oberst* Weitkus, walked into the

room. 'Our target is in Belev on the Oka. At present it is about 100 km behind the Russian main line of resistance. We are supposed to destroy the railroad bridge over the Oka, across which the Russians are bringing war materiel to the southern front. Your aircraft are each loaded with eight 250-kg bombs. The fuses are to be set to delayed action, which means you will bomb from low level. *Kette* takeoff, form up over the airfield and make for the target at a height of 2000 meters. A thin layer of cloud is reported over Belev at 1000 meters. Little anti-aircraft fire is expected, fighters are possible. Just prior to the target the formation will break up and descend for a maximum low-level attack. Do not lose sight of each other and maintain a sufficient interval with the man ahead, meaning staggered. After the attack reform and head home. A1+ES will transmit bombing results here by short wave. Good luck!'

The ground personnel had readied the aircraft for takeoff. A1+LS had numerous small metal patches on its fuselage and wings. We weren't happy about flying our first combat mission in such a battered old bird. But with each passing mission it became clearer to us that the He 111 could take all the bullet and shrapnel holes without falling from the sky. For our first flight they gave us A1+LS. Every crew that had flown her claimed that she was the *8. Staffel*'s good luck bird – one simply couldn't crash while flying in her. Other aircraft of the *Staffel* were lost or cracked up, A1+LS survived.

It took us fifteen minutes to form up at 2000 meters. The weight of 2000 kilograms of bombs was noticeable. We set course for Belev, with us flying on the right in the second *Kette*.

Visibility was good all around. We flew through huge towering clouds and overflew the main line of resistance. Things became serious. We flew through a massive cloudbank, and when we emerged one aircraft was missing. We later learned that engine trouble had forced it to turn back. There were clear skies all around us, making us a feast for flak and fighters. I had the feeling that it had nothing to do with Christmas. Below us was enemy territory. We searched the sky for enemy aircraft. For half an hour nothing happened. Then everything happened very fast. Köster and Feikert were standing below me in the ventral bath, manning their machine-guns. 'Peewee' turned the kite to the right and the formation broke up as ordered. We dropped a wing and went over to low-level flight. To my right houses came in sight, many houses, and I recognized roads, where men hastily took cover and milled about. Below me in the ventral bath machine-guns began to rattle. I saw tracer smoke trails heading downwards. Then I saw the river, rising fountains of spray. The bombs from the aircraft ahead of us had fallen into the water. Then our He made a jerk upwards:

Walter had dropped the bombs! Then I also saw what the two below me were shooting at, Russian soldiers training and drilling. They ran in all directions, some threw themselves flat on the ground. I loosed off several bursts downwards. Suddenly a tremendous force pressed me into the seat: 'Peewee' had put the kite into a steep climb. Now I could make out the iron girders of the Oka bridge. Black fountains of earth shot up near the entrance, then there were several huge flashes on the bridge, and the rest of the bombs exploded beyond it. The span's iron supports sagged and fell, Walter had hit the target.

We flew through a thin layer of cloud at about 3000 meters. Then there was blue sky above us and we searched for the other four. Nothing. There was also nothing on the radio, but it was only good for a range of about 1000 meters. As soon as we turned onto a westerly heading we saw a Heinkel in front of us. It was flying on just one engine. We caught up. It had taken several hits from rifle fire, one in the ignition system. 'Peewee' throttled back to half power and flew alongside the lame duck. I switched to home base frequency and informed them of our ETA. Then Knoppig requested a bearing from the airfield. I therefore switched to long-wave, the air traffic control frequency. Our DF operator answered and gave me a heading for the airfield. Suddenly three Russian fighters whizzed past. I was so shocked that my recorder dropped from my knee and fell into the ventral bath. I saw the huge red stars on their fuselages. They made a steep turn behind us and moved into firing position.

In no time I switched drums and turned my machine-gun in the direction of the fighters. Our two aircraft were now tucked in close. I was unable to make radio contact with the other radio operator. He was an old hand and, by using sign language, he gave me to understand, 'don't shoot until I shoot.' He had opened his Plexiglas hood all the way and I did the same. The first Russian came in. The range was still 500 meters. There was a cacophony of voices on the intercom: 'Where are they? How many are there?' That made me nervous and I switched off. In the ventral bath Köster and Feikert couldn't see the attackers, but their bullets could have been the first to reach them. Both were standing behind the armor plates that had been installed on the right and left of the fuselage interior. They looked up at me to see which way I would turn the machine-gun ring, to see from which direction the Russians were approaching.

I kept sight of the Russians. They made individual firing passes. We wouldn't have stood a chance against a combined attack. 300 meters – 200 meters – still closer!

I peeked over at my colleague. Why didn't he open fire? But what had our old weapons instructor said: 'if you're frightened, then open fire, even if you aren't in firing position, for that will calm you down …' The other radio operator smiled over at me, as if he was in the Moulin Rouge in Paris. In the situation we were in, he felt superior – that became clear to me later. With his almost monastic smile he wanted to show me how an veteran air fighter should behave, and as if he wanted to give me to understand that he had also felt fear his first time.

Then I saw muzzle flashes from the fighter. For the first time I saw invisible bullets coming towards me. Finally my neighbor's tracer flitted in the direction of the Russian and disappeared into his big radial engine (Rata). The fighter reared up and, leaving a white smoke trail, fell away in a steep turn and disappeared. Hit! My continuous fire disappeared into the air without hitting anything. Then the second came rushing in. I changed drums. Finger bent, continuous fire, all timidity and nervousness gone. There were 150 rounds in a drum. A third Rata moved into attack position, loosed off a few bursts and at 200 meters broke away to set up for another pass.

My machine-gun fell silent, jammed. I opened the breech, removed the jammed shell and resumed firing. The gun fired three more rounds then jammed again. Then I bumped against something hard, the bag that collected the empty shell casings: I had forgotten to empty it. I undid the button fastener and the casings clattered down into the ventral bath. Through a bluish wall of powder smoke I saw the puzzled faces of Köster and Feikert. It must have been a crummy feeling to know and see nothing. We kept on firing. Albert passed up drums of ammunition. The Ivans increased their spacing. Another peeled off trailing white smoke.

I heaved a sigh of relief and boldly decided to let one of them come. The third Rata approached, fired from a good 200 meters, came closer, fired again – I ducked behind my machine-gun sight, then pieces flew from my Plexiglas roller roof. I felt glass splinters between my teeth, blood from my upper lip ran into my mouth, the left earphone was gone from my flying helmet and there were holes in the shoulder of my flight suit. Several bullets had shattered the roller roof of my machine-gun position not five centimeters from my head. That was close, very, very close.

There was another exchange of fire with the Russian. Then he broke away. We had expended almost all of our ammunition. After about ten more minutes we crossed the main line of resistance and the Russian was forced to return to his base. We could stay in the air for up to ten hours, he only 45 minutes! The ventral bath was a mess. To avoid having to repeatedly empty the spent casings bag, I had left it open and the casings had fallen down. The other radio operator must have sent a message to Orsha, for when we flew over the airfield the fire trucks and ambulance were waiting beside the runway. We let the lame duck go first. Then we landed and climbed out of our machine. Walter passed out 'Junos', which his girlfriend in Berlin sent him by the carton. The ground personnel threw up their hands in horror when they examined our Ludwig-Siegfried. The barrel of my machine-gun was burnt out from too much sustained fire, the roller roof was riddled and there were bullet holes in the fuselage and wings.

The *Gruppenkommandeur* congratulated us on our success."

Ebeling continued:

"On 1 October 1941 the *Gruppen* moved from Orsha to Shatalovka-East. In contrast to Orsha, at this more forward airfield there were already beds and other quartering equipment in the barracks. The water lines and heating, like the toilets, weren't working, however, so that latrines had to be set up in the open and warmth remained a rare item in the coming months. Even when cylindrical iron stoves eventually began arriving, heating material remained a scarce commodity.

Our missions from the new airfield were in support of army units advancing on Moscow. We attacked troop and tank assembly areas, railway stations and rail lines in the Sukhinichi area, Kaluga, Kirov, Medyn, Tula, Naroforminsk and finally in Klin and Moscow itself. Winter came, and with it the cold. Snow and low cloud forced us to fly at lower altitudes. When attacking troops and railway stations, we encountered defenses that resulted in casualties among the crews.

At the end of October, for example, the *Staffelkapitäne* of the 7th and 8th *Staffeln*, *Oberleutnant* Gäbler and *Major* Haster, failed to return from the same mission, after the commander of the 7th *Staffel*, *Oberleutnant* Leonhardi, had been shot down over enemy territory about two months earlier. His observer and radio operator, *Feldwebel* Seufert and Schnerr, had managed to parachute from the burning machine, and despite suffering burns they made their way to our lines in a day-long foot march. After a period of sick leave they joined my crew, by which time I had been placed in command of the 7th *Staffel*. *Leutnant* Berkemann took over the 8th *Staffel*."

As an example of what so many crews experienced during that first winter in Russia, and the life of our men during, after and between missions, we once again turn to the diary entries of radio operator Graf:

"A combat mission.

On 2 October 1941 we were placed at 'E 1' at 09:00. It smelled like a 'major battle day'. The command post was buzzing like a beehive. At least twenty crews were standing there with their parachutes, waiting for mission orders. Attack support for our infantry and tanks in the Medyn area. Shoot at any Russian uniform that shows itself. The aircraft have each been loaded with 24 50-kg fragmentation bombs with contact fuses. Safety height 500. Takeoff by *Kette*. The main line of resistance is very near. Expect light flak and fighters after ten minutes flying time. 'Good luck!' said the *Gruppenkommandeur Major* Fabian.

The Eastern Front on 2 October 1941, a lucky day for the crew of Dieter von Glasow.

Our *Kette* leader was *Leutnant* Gade, the right '*Kette* hound' was *Feldwebel* Grave and we were the left. That's how they had assigned us at the command post. Because of the *Kette* takeoff there was awful confusion behind the landing cross. The *Kette* leaders sat there lined up, waiting for their wingmen. We taxied up to the left of one of them, thinking it was Gade. But it wasn't. He was on the other side, consequently when we took off we were on his right. Grave and our 'Peewee' agreed to the change by hand signal. Ultimately it made no difference on which side one flew.

But this time it did make a difference.

The pilots of the 'Emils' applied power as they had been taught. The Heinkels gathered speed, their tails lifted in unison, then they were airborne and began climbing to 1500 meters. Far above there was light cirrus, below us burning villages. We could observe very well the duel between the artillery of both sides.

Then there were several explosions above us. Flickering explosions that ended in small black clouds: 100-mm flak. Another salvo came up – Grave's starboard engine was burning. A long wave of flame billowed out, stopped and then formed anew. That's how gasoline burns when it flows from a tank. The aircraft fell behind, losing altitude. I saw four parachutes billow, then the fifth. The Heinkel went down like a blazing torch and I saw it explode in a mushroom of smoke and flame. And then the five parachutes disappeared behind a forest. If we had taxied properly prior to takeoff, we would now be the ones hanging beneath parachutes over Russian territory.

The Russians didn't fire a single shot upwards while Grave was going down. The buggers must have been watching in fascination. But afterwards they loosed off a tremendous display of fireworks and a hellish inferno enveloped us. The sky was filled with small black clouds. We flew through these 'blotches' and could smell powder inside the aircraft. The explosions sounded like thunder and their shock waves shook the aircraft. The air around us was full of iron. We couldn't see the shell fragments, only assume their presence. A single shard of iron could be fatal. I sat in the dorsal gun position, safety off, and was unable to defend myself. At the bomber schools 'Peewee' had had it beaten into him to fly straight and level while under anti-aircraft fire and vary the revolutions of the two engines. This made it more difficult for the gunner on the ground to aim by means of sound locator. I could see muzzle flashes on the ground. More than anything I wanted to shoot back.

Then it was quiet. We were out of the flak zone. The gap between us and our *Kette* leader had grown larger, and so we moved in closer.

We were approaching the target to the east when two dots appeared behind us and quickly drew nearer.

'Fighters from behind!' I announced over the intercom.

Then the two Ratas were upon us. One flew over our tail, the other attacked our *Kette* leader. I saw the tracer from his radio operator's gun. I swung my machine-gun round and began firing controlled bursts. On target! My tracer disappeared into the Russian's fuselage. He abruptly peeled off and fell away. Below me in the ventral bath, Jakob opened fire. He raked the first Rata, which was flying beneath us. Albert moved to the left, then to the right, standing behind the armor plates. Again he couldn't see what was happening outside.

Then something quite unusual happened. Like a huge colossus the Rata rose up beside us and, in knife-edge flight, passed between the wing and fuselage, just a few meters away. He remained so for seconds – I could see the pilot laughing, I could almost touch him. I shouted, 'Albert look!' He fired a short burst from his side machine-gun, scoring hits on this barn door of a target. Then the Russian, still in knife-edge flight, pulled up over us, his wingtip missing us by no more than two meters. Then he rolled onto his back and dived away. A cool pike that Ivan.

Why hadn't he fired at us?

Our bombs were still in the cells. Knoppig dropped them on a bridge, which immediately collapsed. 'Peewee' turned west for home and climbed to 'Knight's Cross altitude', at least 5000 meters. We entered the flak zone again. This time, however, the Ivans' fire was very inaccurate. Then, suddenly, our port engine began to cough and finally stopped. Large shell fragments had struck the wing and fuselage. *Lt.* Gade's bird looked bad: it had been riddled by hundreds of splinters. It was a minor miracle that no one had been wounded.

Three days later we learned about the fate of the Grave crew from its radio operator. He and the flight engineer were the only ones to make it back, the other three had been taken prisoner. He and the gunner came down in a forest clearing. They rolled up their parachutes, hid them in a large pile of leaves and then crawled into a huge pile of brushwood, about twenty meters apart. No sooner had they done so when Russians with rifles and fixed bayonets appeared from a forest lane. They were already looking for them. The radio operator related that the Ivans were 15 meters from the gunner's hiding place when, probably having lost his nerve, he began shooting with his 08 pistol. Two Russians squatted and then fell to the ground, the others began firing wildly; they still didn't know where the firing was coming from. Soon a truck arrived with reinforcements. The gunner began shooting again, and this time the Russians discovered his hiding place. When they began shooting, he crawled from the pile and raised his hands. Furious, the Russians rained blows upon him. He screamed terribly. They threw him into a truck and drove away. Our radio operator remained still and waited until darkness. Then he began walking west towards the main line of resistance, whose rumble of guns and fireworks could not be missed. He skillfully avoided enemy troops, swam two ice-cold streams and the following night came upon German infantry. After four weeks' special home leave, he returned to Shatalovka and joined the Kunzmann crew. He failed to return from his first mission with it. During a low-level attack their aircraft was hit by the accurate Russian medium anti-aircraft fire and exploded in the air. One of the other aircraft in the flight saw it happen."

Graf described in detail the forced landing behind enemy lines by the Glasow crew and their rescue:

"I ran into Butzer again on 23 November. He had been assigned as our permanent observer. It was his first combat mission. Why he never got along with a crew I do not know. He was a *Gefreiter* like we other three. He was a tall, thin, taciturn ascetic. He joined us in the room in the morning. He didn't know how to play *skat*, only *doppelkopf* and *binoggeln* [*Translator's note: skat, doppelkopf and binoggeln are German card games*]. He was an esthete and was crazy about Wagner's operas and music in general – and roast goose. By way of introduction he gave us three bottles of the best Lithuanian vodka. We allowed ourselves a couple of rounds, more was not permitted. We were at 'E 2', and 'E 1' could come at any time. We had more or less gotten used to flying missions with foggy heads. Knoppig did so too. The flights in the east were more demanding than our training missions in Lille and Bourges.

Was the new man as good a navigator as Walter? The ceiling may have been at 500 meters. We were supposed to attack a large troop movement on a road southwest of Venev. We were flying above cloud towards the target by dead reckoning, and Butzer declared that we could descend in order to gain visual contact for bombing. We dropped out of the gray cloud masses too soon. Below us a peaceful sea of houses: Tula! Our 'Peewee' applied power and pulled back the yoke into his belly, so as to duck back into the 'duty clouds' as quickly as possible. Medium anti-aircraft guns began spitting their shells at us. We finally reached the clouds over the outskirts of the city. A few more glowing shells hissed up after us and exploded with a dull thump in the cotton wool around us. After a while we descended again. Soon the road came into view with Russian columns kilometers long. Butzer dropped the 500-kilo and eight 50-kilo bombs and then it was back into cloud. There were still eight eggs in two cells, and so we descended again, reversed course and began our bombing run. A fantastic quantity of tracer reached out for us and there were two whiplash-like explosions above us. The short antenna mast, two meters in front of me, was blown off. My short wave went dead. Finally Butzer dropped the rest of the bombs In my open dorsal position I heard the sound of shells exploding, then there was a terrific bang in the wing. Pieces flew out of the port engine and whirled to the rear. The engine began to smoke. In the cockpit they closed the fuel cock and the smoke stopped. We lost quite a lot of altitude. Over the intercom I heard that the starboard engine was no longer running properly. We were flying over flat, snow-covered terrain. 'Peewee' cautiously turned the Heinkel onto a westerly heading for home, so as to bypass the flak near Tula. The port engine's propeller was still turning. Both engines were squeaking and rattling, and we were still 100 meters high, 50 kilometers as the crow flies behind the Russian main line of resistance, we must cross it soon. We continued to descend, tail down. I saw the wind from the propellers whipping up snow.

Did we have enough altitude to get home? Hardly, I gave up.

We flew low over a large forest, the engines vibrating and shaking. Beyond the forest a telegraph or power line appeared across our path. 'Peewee' gave the He the spurs again using the elevator. I saw the tailwheel catch the wires and rip them from the poles. Seconds later we were rattling over hard-frozen farmland; the din was terrific and dust and dirt flew. The tail of our Heinkel rose again and it seemed as if it would flip over, but it fell back and everything became eerily still. When the engines stopped, the silence was simply crazy. Below me Köster and Breuer were standing on a heap of mixed snow and earth that had welled into the ventral bath as a result of the belly landing, urging me in subdued voices to get out. I jumped down into the snow. The next to climb out was Breuer. He braced himself against my machine-gun. The safety was off and it wasn't locked down. He probably touched the trigger, whereupon a burst of fire hit the snow beside me. Köster crawled through the passageway between the bomb cells to the cockpit and grabbed the incendiary bomb that was kept there for the purpose of setting the downed machine on fire, as per regulations. He vainly struck it against the fuselage several times in an effort to ignite it, then jumped down from the wing. Breuer had removed a machine-gun, Butzer or 'Peewee' brought several drums of ammunition, and I pulled my Parabellum 08 from my pocket. When we look back on our reflex actions, rash, the whole thing! We were ready to start a small war behind the Russian lines.

I saw a man and a child standing about 200 meters away, looking at us. My pistol drawn, I ran at a crouch towards some reeds 50 meters away. Through the blades I saw two men standing with slung rifles. Bent low, I rushed back to the others.

They were already on their way to the forest we had previously overflown. Breuer was still carrying the machine-gun. Suddenly the two Russians opened fire on us from about 300 – 400 meters. The machine-gun and ammunition drums fell into the snow. We ran for our lives, and the closer the seemingly safe forest edge came, the more the fear grew in me that they were waiting for us there. Then this anxious feeling about the situation came over me again. Perhaps it would be OK. Then I let myself fall into the snow at the edge of the forest.

'Come on, come on!' urged Peewee, 'into the forest, spread out and stay within shouting distance!'

Inside the snow was knee-deep in places. Köster and I reached a huge spruce, whose bottom branches were under the snow. We crawled under. There was no snow, it was quite comfy-cozy.

'Do you have any cigarettes?' I had two Attikah. We smoked and waited for the night.

'Do you think we'll make it back?' 'Don't really know.' 'Peewee has a hand compass.' 'But we're at least 40 kilometers behind the Russian main line of resistance.' 'Perhaps we're sitting in the middle of the Tula Pocket.' 'Then they can give us a ticket to Siberia.' 'Why shouldn't we have good luck this time?'

It may have been 16:00. The approaching twilight bolstered our spirits. We would run home in the darkness. There wouldn't be Russians everywhere. Somewhere there was a gap. We had to move without attracting attention to ourselves. Huge mushrooms of fire now lit up the forest. Russian heavy artillery. Before long the Russians fired another salvo towards the west. We counted, until in the silence we heard the gentle thump of impacting shells. 'It's at least sixty kilometers, where the shells are falling,' declared Albert.

The Russian batteries continued firing. All five of us met in a small clearing. Peewee already had the compass on his wrist, and we set off towards the west. We came to the edge of the forest and in the open terrain we saw figures and lanterns moving about. The Russians were busy with our Heinkel. We had probably walked in a circle. We continued walking through the snow at the edge of the forest and after an hour came to open country. The snow wasn't so deep there and our pace picked up. A figure came towards us from the left. A rider. He stopped about thirty meters away – Butzer pretended to rough us up and shouted in Russian, whereupon the rider turned his horse.

We undid the chin straps of our flying helmets and tied them together at the top. In the darkness we now looked like Russians in their winter caps. The snow made things brighter. We entered a forest. No sooner had we done so when we heard a horse whinny. We ran out again and into a spruce plantation, where we lay down in the snow for a while for a breather. Then we went to the right, down a steep bank, across a frozen river, and up the other side into a birch plantation. We walked along its rows until an earth bunker suddenly appeared in front of us, and we dropped into the snow. The snow had been tramped down in a wide circle around it. We skipped three rows of birches further to the left and crouched behind the leafless trees. Before us there was a great deal of movement. We moved two more rows of trees to the left after a squad of Russians marched past the spot where we had just been lying and disappeared into the bunker. We lay flat beneath the trees. That had been close again, very close. Oh, no! A Russian wearing a peaked cap was standing not fifteen meters away looking at us. Had he recognized us? If he alerted the area, then the war for us five was over. Did he know that the men in front him were Germans? I gripped the handle of my knife more firmly: if he comes it has to go quickly and silently, for we knew what they did to shot-down German airmen.

The Russian disappeared into the darkness. The tension eased. We set off in the other direction. Again we saw figures in front of us. We moved laterally to the left and, when required, to the right and arrived in a treeless area. From somewhere came the rattle of a machine-gun, star shells rose high and went pop. Between them short, sharp explosions, shells from field artillery. Dense streams of tracer passed overhead into the distance. In the glare of star shells, Peewee looked at his compass. We headed south. An endlessly long snow fence set up like a roof to block snow drifts crossed our path. Bent low, we walked beneath it for a while, thinking that we couldn't be seen in the glare of star shells. We trotted on across the absolutely flat snow-covered surface. To the right we could hear the boom and thunder of the front. That's where we had to get through.

At about 20:00 we came to scattered bushes. Further forward we heard noise. It came closer and we took cover under small spruces. We lay flat in the snow beneath them. There must have been a road, not 100 meters in front of us. Two tracked vehicles came from the left and disappeared to the right into the gloom. Fires rose up in the distance, bathing the horizon in pinkish-yellow. The two vehicles came back again. The road now became the scene of hectic activity. Trucks came, panye wagons, light tanks, riders and between them many people on foot, loudly shouting, swearing, coughing, screaming and ranting. After an hour the apparition disappeared to our right. I froze and sweated. Sucked some snow. I was about to roll out of the row of spruces when I saw a figure coming behind me, damned close. In the snow brightness his upper body stood out well against the horizon. On his chest he had a reel of cable, and he reeled in a cable over which we had almost tripped. I lay flat on my back, a terrible position, seized by fear. The Russian stopped two rows away. I slowly felt for my zero-eight. I wasn't going to allow myself to be captured. There were eight shots in it, 16 with the spare clip. I would shoot fifteen of them at the Russians and place the 16th in my own head before allowing myself to be maltreated as the two gunners from the Grave crew had been. Once again the 'L-M-A feeling' (*Translator's note: **Leck mich am Arsch**, literally "kiss my ass."*) seized me again, relaxing my body. The Russian continued on, the Parabellum stayed in my pocket.

Suddenly it was quiet around us. A few more explosions were heard in the distance, then the sector of front fell silent. We began walking, crossed the road and came to open country with gentle rises. This walking in the snow, which wasn't too deep there, in fur-lined boots was awful. My toes hurt. We trudged along single file, now and then exchanging places as front man, again heading west. We began to feel thirst and sucked snow. I also became hungry. Peewee could undoubtedly read my thoughts. We stopped and he divided a bar of Scho-Ko-Kola which, as a non-smoker, he always had in his flight suit [*Translator's note: A German brand of chocolate containing additional caffeine. The chocolate is divided into triangle-shaped pieces held inside a round metal container. Schokakola was a standard component of Luftwaffe emergency rations and survival kits. It is still sold today.*] We moved off again at a slightly wobbly trot, as the snow permitted. Yellow and white star shells rose into the sky and burned up. Ahead of us the front, now much nearer, began to rumble and thunder. The explosions seemed very close, star shells whizzed over our heads and exploded in the distance. Heavy machine-guns could be heard from the right; dense clusters of tracer arced low across the horizon. We crawled once again into a snow fence that appeared before us in our direction of travel. Star shells repeatedly rose up, illuminating the night sky. I was almost beginning to think that they were looking for us five. The snow fence was curiously long. When we emerged from its end, machine-guns began to rattle on the right. We ran back into the fence and headed south. There were fires somewhere, their glow lighting up the horizon. We ran past freshly dug foxholes, and dark giants appeared, tanks! The first was tipped on end, obviously knocked out. It posed no threat to us, and it would have been too late anyway. Then we turned west again. Mechanically, we trudged down hard-packed roads, my concern about possible danger apparently gone. Sometimes I walked with sleep-closed eyes, thirst plagued me, probably the others too. We hadn't spoken a word for hours. Butzer began to limp. We took turns pulling him along by the arm. This nature boy didn't put up with that for long. Reluctant, he shook us off. He also had very good teeth, which were clenched in pain.

Two in the morning. As we trudged down gently sloping terrain, a strung-out village appeared before us. We squatted in the snow and debated what to do. We didn't want to go round it. Peewee wanted to wait until it got light and then see. We four *Gefreite* were against it (!).

If the Russian military was in the village, we argued, it was better to go through at night. By day we would have no chance of escape. Lastly we had Butzer up our sleeve with his few words of Russian, with which we could fool the Russians. In the light of day they would easily recognize us as German airmen. We moved out.

We casually sauntered down the village street. I cannot describe the feeling that came over me. Sure, each of us had sixteen rounds of ammunition hanging on his belt and a folding knife in his flight suit.

'*Stoy!*" None of us had seen the Russian on the right with the rifle to his shoulder. Butzer alertly spoke a few words of Russian and the rest of us walked on down the village street, apparently unimpressed.

I would have preferred a J-61. At least I could have raked that with my MG 15. None of looked around at the Russian. And that was very, very good. His mistrust appeared to have been extinguished. Once again we got away.

We ran down the embankment by the road into an open field and suddenly we were standing in a lane in a huge tent camp – white on white, like snow.

We slowly moved on. A Russian might appear somewhere at any minute. That would undoubtedly have been the end of us. Or were there no Ivans in the tents? Perhaps they contained weapons, ammunition or vehicles, camouflaged to prevent them being seen from the air. The sentry earlier was probably guarding the whole thing. My heart was in my throat. It was the longest 100 meters I have ever walked in my life. We passed the last tents and found ourselves in front of a tall embankment. We crawled up like bugs. There were a few low bushes we could grab onto to keep from sliding back. No sooner had we reached the top when submachine-gun fire came from the area of the tent camp. Panting, we ran onwards, passed through a small wood and out into open country. Then we walked through an uncut oat field, over hundreds of terrified mice. For the first time Butzer complained of severe pain in his ankle. Every ten minutes Peewee looked at the compass.

'We're now going southwest. *General* Guderian intends to go south round Tula and Venev with his tanks. The Russian columns that passed us during the night came from the south and were going north. All of the roads and rail lines here run in a north-south direction. The Ivans have therefore reached safety in the north. Perhaps we will run into our own if we stay more to the south.' That was what our Peewee said and he was right.

Onwards at a gentle trot. Fatigue crept through my limbs. Sleepy, my head fell to my chest. Thirst plagued me. We ate snow, but the hunger returned immediately. Silently we walked one behind the other, passing fresh foxholes, then into an area that had been flattened by armored vehicles. We heard nothing and so carried on. The night seemed to be getting lighter. Far ahead we saw the outline of a large vehicle. It was already five in the morning when we came to a well-used road leading west. Furrows, holes and ruts made the walking difficult. We stopped to rest on a small rise and dropped to the ground.

'Come on, come on, get up!' urged Peewee, 'or else the fatigue will get into your bones and make walking hell.'

Far behind us the flames of war began again. Parachute flares, artillery, tracer, rumbling, thunder, explosions.

Two hours later, with dawn slowly arriving, we came upon a heavy cable. We walked along it until we came to a junction in an open field. We read 'Siemens' and the words 'Beginning, End'.

'Man, we've made it,' said someone. There was no celebrating. Overcome by exhaustion, we dropped into the snow. Even Peewee couldn't stay on his feet. We were lying on our bellies and were almost asleep when Köster roused us. 'Look over there!' We sprang up as if electrified and saw a small building and men and horses moving about. We took cover in an unfinished beet clamp. An old man was fussing with two horses. We moved on. For the first time since 17:00 the day before we looked at one another. Our fur-lined flying boots were completely soaked through and coated with mud, and with our tied-up flying helmets, from which the connecting cables still hung, we looked half Russian. The zippers of our flight suits were open to the belt; our German flying blouses were visible under our flight suits. Somewhat fearfully, it seemed to me, a Russian saw us coming. An elderly *muschik* with a wrinkled face and grey stubble beard was holding a small pony by a halter tether. He had no idea if we were friend or foe. Butzer asked: 'Where Germansky, where Russky?' He pointed to a small village, visible about 500 meters away in the morning sunlight, and repeated 'Germansky' several times. More he would or could not say.

We came to a section of road that led to the village. On the left and right there were large snowbanks in front of the first blockhouses, behind which two figures appeared holding submachine-guns. '*Stoy!*' I stopped and slowly raised my hands. Over! Our trek had been for nothing.

I can't remember who was first to pull down his flight suit, identify himself as a German airman and recognize the two men in front of us as German grenadiers, a *Leutnant* and an *Obergefreiter*. They must have taken us for Russians in our get-ups.

Still mistrustful, they ordered us to approach. We showed them our military identity cards. They showed us into the village. Our legs heavy as lead from exhaustion, we trudged onwards and entered the nearest blockhouse. We were met by two young pigs, many chickens, numerous children and an elderly Russian woman – laughing, squealing, clucking and crying. And an unaccustomed heat, probably generated by a large, white-tiled stove in the background, on which grandpa was lying. We pulled off our flight suits. The Russian woman looked on and cried: 'Ah, swastika, good, very good', when she saw the emblem on our uniforms.

As if she had been waiting for us, she produced a large pot of hot boiled potatoes and dark brown bread. Sitting on the table was a wooden bowl containing coarse salt. Feebly we began peeling the potatoes, sprinkling them with salt and greedily wolfing them down. The bread tasted fantastic. Those present watched us feasting with satisfaction. Only the creatures took no notice of us. Unconcerned, they lolled about on the tramped dirt floor. The Russians had good eyes. There was joy in them because they had been able to render a favor. To them we were just people, not the enemy. It mattered not at all to them what we had been through. Butzer was in no mood to chat. Why should he be?

In a sudden inspiration he picked his flight suit up from the floor, felt around in it, produced a handful of ice candies and laid them on the table.

Make me crazy! We ate snow from the Russian ground for ten hours, and you forgot about these thirst-quenching sweets! He urged the children to take them. As soon as they realized that they were sweet, a tussle broke out over them. A guttural scolding from the stove brought them to reason, and they went obediently to the corner.

And we had dropped bombs on these people and their wretched houses!

It wasn't easy for me to digest such facts with the boiled potatoes.

The food and warmth had loosened our limbs again. We trudged on our way again. A truck picked us up and took us to Borogodisk, where we arrived at eleven in the morning. We had been walking for eighteen hours. In a stone building belonging to Guderian's Panzer Group IV we were given plenty to eat, after which we slept like logs until 20:00. A cook from the kitchen brought goulash.

That night a radio message was received ordering us to march to Orel, where we would be picked up.

Enough of marching! We hitched a ride in a truck to Orel, sixty kilometers away. We suffered terribly from the cold. We had been wearing the same clothes for three days, our whiskers sprouted unchecked, the dirt clung to our bodies.

On 28 November an aircraft of the 8th *Staffel* picked us up in Orel and took us back to Shatalovka.

They welcomed us like prodigal sons. We had aged by years.

Our *Hauptfeldwebel* Schratter had covered a table in our billet. For our birthday party. On it were two roast chickens, biscuits, Schokakola and two bottles of real cognac. Schratter also said we would be getting leave, four weeks.

We cleared the table and dank the cognac. But I became filled with an 'emptiness' for which there are no words. I didn't ask the others if they felt the same.

There was no leave. The *Gruppe* had taken heavy casualties. Every crew was needed.

But dense fog, hoarfrost, occasional snow and fierce cold kept us grounded. The small stove in our billet was incapable of heating it to more than 15 degrees. We sat playing cards wrapped in blankets, with two pairs of wool socks in our lambskin boots. For days our windows had been covered with ice which, though it made it impossible to see outside, formed a perfect seal against cold drafts. Food was more plentiful and tasted better."

The Red Army had been badly weakened in the battles of encirclement at Bialystok-Minsk, Smolensk, Uman and Gomel. Entire army groups were destroyed east of Kiev and at Briansk and Vyazma, and 1.3 million Russians laid down their arms. But the German military had been forced to pay a high price in blood. Out of 3.6 million troops, 767,415 had been killed or captured. These casualties were only partially offset by 450,000 men from the replacement army.

The early arrival of winter and Soviet counterattacks halted the German army at the gates of Moscow. Hitler now realized that the war could not be won, but he still placed some hope in a major blow by the Japanese. The Americans were not distracted by the

Japanese surprise attack on Pearl Harbor on 7 December 1941, however. Roosevelt and Churchill agreed upon a 'Europe first' strategy at their Atlantic Conference.

Generals "Mud" and "Winter" had struck hard. The *Luftwaffe* desperately needed a rest. The extreme, unaccustomed environmental conditions, overexertion during intensive operations and the decimated units had left their marks. There was no time to rest, however, for on 5 December the Russians launched their counteroffensive. The *Luftwaffe* was forced to continue operations in desperate circumstances.

The initial success of the Russian attacks threatened to bring about the collapse of the entire German front. At Demyansk the Soviets succeeded in encircling six German divisions with about 100,000 men. The *Luftwaffe* was ordered to the necessary supplies – 300 tons daily – by air. It was the first airlift, and others were to follow.

On 16 December 1941 Alfred Döring wrote in his diary:

"Supply flights for the infantry are on the schedule. The area is Klin, south of Kalinin. Weather awful. We had to circle round for a long while until we found the drop point. We finally found it. A bunch of tanks and trucks sat clustered together. They desperately needed fuel, so that is where we dropped our load, close to them. The fuel was put in the tanks, each of which then took three or four trucks in tow and pulled back to the winter position. Several burning tanks were destroyed.

Our infantry waved at us in gratitude, we waggled our wings then swept over the encroaching Russians and fired off all our ammunition.

Then we headed for home."

To conclude this chapter on the first year of war in Russia, a contribution from the memory of Fritz Pockrandt, then a *Hauptmann* and commander of the *9. Staffel*:

"Soon the muddy period began. It made things very difficult for us, as water struck the propellers and wings during takeoffs and landings.

We supported Panzer Group Guderian's attack towards Tula and the northern pincer in the direction of Kaluga. Bad weather with 10/10 cloud and ceilings of less than 1000 meters limited our missions to *Kette* strength. Powerful anti-aircraft defenses inflicted casualties on men and machines.

The sudden onset of winter, almost overnight, brought the first foretaste of what was to come. The army suddenly found itself in a miserable situation. The heavy equipment stuck in the mud became frozen there, the attack on the entire central front bogged down, snow fell from the skies in huge quantities, the retreat began. The troops on the ground were totally unprepared. As were we! Cold billets, the technical personnel without the necessary clothing or hangars, were forced to work on the aircraft in temperatures that rapidly fell to minus 15 or 20 degrees and even lower. The army screamed for air support, but against this onset of winter we were almost powerless. We were supposed to fly maximum effort missions, but often we were happy if we got even one aircraft into the air at the specified takeoff time. Vehicles that were supposed to drive the crews to their aircraft refused to start. We were usually soaked to the skin by the time we had walked to the machines. And then we climbed to altitude, where the temperature gauge often bottomed out, meaning about -50 degrees C. Despite fur-lined suits and boots we froze terribly, and the cold came through every crack. The heating system was inadequate to deal with this. Often the entire *Gruppe* only succeeded in putting up single aircraft or flights of three. And this was often in absolute qbi (bad weather conditions in force), as the wind whipped up the dry snow to a height of 20 or even 30 meters over the airfield. Above this there was brilliant sunshine. When we returned we could only identify the airfield by the tall water tower, which stuck out of the cloud of snow. The technical personnel suffered their first cases of frostbite, working selflessly in shifts, even at night, to achieve the highest possible serviceability level. Very, very slowly we began to receive fur-lined clothing and boots, earmuffs and gloves for the men and heating devices for the engines. Every member of the *Staffel* and *Gruppe* performed magnificently during this period. But what of the front? What missions awaited us daily? Support for the army and more support for the army. There had long since ceased to be a continuous front. Some strongpoints held out to the last man in the desert of snow. Frostbite decimated the units, in many cases rations and supplies were almost non-existent. And the Russians attacked with fresh forces from Siberia. They were able to move on skis, sleighs and horses, and their tanks could roll despite the deep snow. Each day we were ordered to attack Russian spearheads and supply lines, but they were difficult to spot in their winter camouflage.

A shipment of fresh infantry forces arrived from France in summer clothing and was partially equipped with toboggans. We were supposed to fly them into the Demyansk pocket. The *Gruppe* and *Geschwader* helped as best they could with winter clothing.

First supply mission into the same pocket with ammunition and food. Foretaste of the suffering of the ground troops. We always returned to our permanent quarters, with their slow cast-iron stoves. Despite our best efforts, serviceability levels remained unsatisfactory. Mice gnawed wires, and it took us a while to find out.

Attacking the advancing Russians remained our first priority. There was no more talk about attacking the enemy rear. With temperatures in the minus 30-35 range, our operational strengths sank more and more."

d) 1942 – The Second Year of the War in Russia

In the autumn of 1942 the soldiers of the army, but especially the German airmen, began to wonder: so many Russian aircraft destroyed on the ground and shot down by fighters, flak and other ground weapons: yet their numbers are not diminishing, instead there are always more.

Most surprised, however, was the German leadership, which in ideological blindness had completely underestimated the potential strength of the Soviet Union. After its air force suffered heavy losses in the first weeks of the war, it drastically stepped up production of warplanes.

In the second half of 1941 the Soviet aviation industry delivered 3,160 fighters, 1,300 close-support aircraft and about 1,900 bombers. This output far surpassed the number of aircraft we received as replacements. The Soviets were also able to conduct flying training beyond the Urals, where it was undisturbed. Until the beginning of the mud and frost period our air force was able to seal off the battlefield through round the clock operations. Roads and railways were kept under surveillance day after day, and moving transport was strafed and bombed.

The Russians developed astonishing abilities in restoring to operation wrecked railway stations. It would have been more effective to conduct carpet bombing raids against marshalling yards and rail junctions, but by the autumn of 1941 the *Luftwaffe* was already no longer strong enough.

With the start of the frost period the operational strengths of the *Gruppen* and *Geschwader* deteriorated rapidly. Instead of 40 aircraft per *Gruppe*, often just three or four were serviceable. At temperatures of minus 20 degrees, up to 80 percent of the *Luftwaffe*'s fleet was immobilized. The relevant manuals had not been written with Russian temperatures in mind.

And so, in the second half of November 1941, only a few long-range reconnaissance aircraft were still active. These reported sighting numerous westbound troop trains east of Moscow. *Generalfeldmarschall* Kesselring, commander of *Luftflotte 2*, to which the reconnaissance units were attached, later wrote that they should have drawn far-reaching conclusions from this discovery. But nothing was done, and in view of the situation the *Luftwaffe* would have been incapable of effectively intervening. Each train brought elite divisions from Siberia. Accustomed to the cold and well-equipped, they stopped the attack on Moscow and immediately went over to the offensive themselves. The Siberian divisions attacked west of Moscow and encircled the entire II Army Corps under *General* Count Bockdorf-Ahlefeld. Hitler ordered the pocket held at all costs and the *Luftwaffe* was forced to fly.

Temperatures dropped to minus 40 degrees. Working in such cold, the fingers of the mechanics froze to their tools and to the aircraft. They had to be thawed out with warm air, but the lives of their comrades in the pocket depended on them.

The already low serviceability levels fell to 25%, but they did it. Supplied by air, the Demyansk Pocket held out for three months until it was relieved.

In that three months the *Luftwaffe* flew 25,000 tons of food, ammunition and weapons into the pocket, plus 15,000 tons of fuel and 15,000 fresh troops. The aircraft, which landed on a packed snow landing strip, flew out 23,000 wounded.

The pocket south of Kholm, in which 3,500 men of the 281st Infantry Division under *Generalmajor* Scherer were encircled, was supplied in a similar manner. Units of the *I. Gruppe* of KG 53 took part in the airlift along with Ju 52 and other He 111 units. As the pocket grew smaller, Ju 87s ultimately made pinpoint drops using supply containers. Battle Group Scherer held Kholm until the beginning of May, when it was relieved by Grenadier Regiment 411.

The cost of the two successful airlift operations at Demyansk and Kholm was high: 265 supply aircraft were lost.

The plan for the winter offensive of 1941 and its collapse are clearly depicted in two maps from the book *Im Wehrmachtsführungsstab* by Bernhard von Lossberg.

The Russian pressure continued until April 1942. Then warmer weather arrived and the mud brought all combat operations by friend and foe to a stop.

In the summer the Germans returned to offensive operations. Their objective was the Caucasian oil fields. A significant part of this campaign was the conquest of the Crimean Peninsula with the fortress of Sevastopol.

VIII. Fliegerkorps under *Generaloberst* von Richthofen with 600 aircraft supported the army. The *Luftwaffe* and the artillery were in continuous operation in the Sevastopol area.

After the Crimea was taken, on 28 June German forces began their breakthrough near Kursk. They reached the Don near Voronezh on 6 July and then drove farther to the southeast. With outstanding support from the *Luftwaffe*, by 10 August the panzer columns were already deep in the Caucasus, while on the eastern flank German advance guards reached the outskirts of Stalingrad.

Perhaps the armies of two great nations would not have concentrated so doggedly on Stalingrad if the city, previously called Tsaritsyn, had not been renamed in 1925. After the denunciation of Stalin, in 1961 the city was renamed again, this time becoming Volgograd.

The strategic importance of the city was not proportional to the gigantic struggle that took place there. Hitler and Stalin began massing forces there in August 1942 and by November more than a million troops of both sides faced each other.

Then the Russians struck back. On 19 November troops of the Red Army crossed a line north and south of the city, at a spot where they faced relatively weak forces. That afternoon the two Soviet spearheads linked up and encircled 22 German divisions with about 330,000 men in the pocket. The Russians of course still had to deploy their forces, and there is not doubt that the German forces trapped in the pocket could have broken out.

Hitler asked Göring if the *Luftwaffe* could supply the pocket from the air as it had done at Demyansk the previous December. Göring, who could never admit that anything was beyond his capabilities, irresponsibly said that he could do the job.

Believing Göring, Hitler than ordered the commander-in-chief of the encircled army, *Generaloberst* Paulus, to hold on and wait for the *Luftwaffe* to fly in supplies.

A total of 500 aircraft was committed to the airlift, but from the very start the operation went badly. Instead of 500 tons of supplies per day, just 100 tons were flown into the pocket per day on average. The cold of the Russian winter, the terrible flying weather, the long flights over enemy territory to and from the pocket, the constant bombardment of the airfields in the pocket – all of these rigors prevented the delivery of adequate quantities of supplies.

The Russians continued to press, and the pocket became smaller. The vital airfield at Pitomnik was lost on 16 January 1943 and the remaining airfield at Gumrak was completely inadequate. The only remaining option was to airdrop the supplies. That was the beginning of the end. Weakened by hunger, the soldiers were often incapable of recovering the supply containers from the snow.

A comparison with the quantities of supplies sent by the Americans to the Soviets in the second year of the war is enlightening:

7,000 tanks

15,000 vehicles

430,000 Jeeps and trucks

710 warships and other vessels, etc., etc.

The fate of Stalingrad was fulfilled on 2 February 1943. At 05:15 a final radio message was sent from Stalingrad to *Führer* Headquarters: "True to its oath of allegiance, for Germany the 6th Army has held its position to the last man and the last round of ammunition. Signed Paulus."

Of the 120,000 men who surrendered, by cautious estimate fewer than 6,000 survived. The *Luftwaffe* lost 488 aircraft, 165 of them He 111s, which had not been designed for use as transport aircraft.

General Paul Deichmann described Göring's behavior during this catastrophe: "On the evening of 21 December 1942, when I visited the Führer's *Wolfsschanze* headquarters near Rastenburg in East Prussia, I reported to Göring in the *Führer* bunker. I knocked on the door to the room that had been assigned to Göring. *General* Bodenschatz opened it and asked what I wanted. Behind him I saw Göring at his desk, head down and crying loudly. Göring asked me to come in and, ignoring me, continued to indulge in his pain. Then he asked me several questions, repeatedly interrupted by crying fits, and dismissed me in order to continue devoting himself to his desperation."

The aircraft losses ate up the *Luftwaffe*'s assets, but far worse were the losses in crews, especially as training of crews by the schools had already been cut back because of a shortage of aircraft and instructors.

At the beginning of 1943, KG 53 detached its *II. Gruppe* to take part in the Stalingrad airlift. The next chapter contains an account of its part in the airlift by Gilbert Geisendorfer.

e) Operations by KG 53 in the Year 1942

At the start of the year, the *Geschwaderstab* and the *II. Gruppe* continued operating in the central sector. The *I. Gruppe* took part in the airlifts to the Demyansk, Kholm and Volkhov pockets as well as anti-submarine and anti-shipping operations in the Gulf of Finland. The *III. Gruppe* was temporarily stationed in the west at the airfield in Chartres, from where it carried out day and night raids against industrial targets in England.

In August the entire *Geschwader* was reunited on the Eastern Front, where it flew missions in support of the army on the northern front, attacked targets in Leningrad, railroads, and mined the sea canal west of Leningrad. Finally, at the end of the year, the *Geschwaderstab* and the *I.* and *III. Gruppe* concentrated on supplying Velikiye-Luki, while the *II. Gruppe* was withdrawn and prepared for supply operations at Stalingrad.

In January 1943 the *III. Gruppe* was sent back to Ansbach to rest and reequip. This meant leave for all the crews after a year of extremely difficult operations.

Fritz O. Pockrandt wrote:

"By order of the *Geschwader*, on 11 April 1942 I assumed command of the *II. Gruppe* after its previous *Kommandeur*, *Major* Wienholtz, was killed over the Volkhov pocket on 30 March 1942. But first to *Luftflotte 1* (Keller) on the northern front.

The muddy period. Riga, the only airport far and wide with paved runways, was completely overfilled. Ju 52s, He 111s, Do 17s – almost every type of aircraft was represented. My *Staffelkapitäne* were *Hptm.* Rauer, *Hptm.* Lehmann and *Hptm.* Grözinger, adjutant *Oblt.* Fuchs.

The *Gruppe*'s assignment: supply the Demyansk pocket and Fortress Kholm. While the large pocket at Demyansk could be supplied without major difficulties, the 'Kholm' mission was one of the most difficult tasks given the aircrews, who knew what it was like in the fortress. They understood that 'fortress' meant a small Russian city that had to be held by the garrison at all costs. Our daily bread consisted of low-altitude flights in bad weather, delivering supply containers of all kinds by day and night. There was a steady flow of casualties, though not always total as respects the crews. The machines, however, often sustained damage from flak and small arms fire. At least the *Gruppe* and surely all of the other units involved had the satisfaction of seeing Kholm relieved in the end. After fierce fighting the pocket at Demyansk was opened from the west, making it possible to for the airlift to be concluded.

After the muddy period we were relocated to Korovye-Selo south of Pskov – a nice airfield without taxiways but with corduroy roads over which all traffic moved.

The *Gruppe*'s mission continued to be support of the army units keeping open the corridor to the Demyansk pocket, attacks against Russian troops on the pocket's flanks, strikes against the Vlasov army encircled in the Volkhov pocket until its surrender, raids on Leningrad, support for the army in its breakthrough to Lake Ladoga, raids on Volkhovstroy and against oil storage sites on Lake Ladoga supplying Leningrad.

In June we moved to an airfield west of the Leningrad pocket. Our mission was to prevent Russian submarines from breaking out to the Baltic Sea. It was a crazy assignment for the *Gruppe* given the time constraints. We flew by day. Certain sectors west of Kronstadt were off limits on account of our minefields. We were not allowed to fly at night because of our navy's activities. The alternate target was a Russian airfield on the island of Lavaasari, where fighters were based. Most of our missions were flown by flights of two or three bombers. For weeks we had no success and always dropped our bombs on Lavaasari. Curiously, as I recall we had few encounters with Russian fighter aircraft. Were they perhaps just mock-ups? One day I finally came upon a ship, probably a torpedo boat or minesweeper. We immediately went into a steep dive and began our attack, but before we could drop our bombs we flew into a storm of anti-aircraft fire. And that at just 200 meters. The cockpit was wrecked, the aircraft was on fire and both engines quit almost simultaneously. The radio operator jettisoned his hood and extinguished the fire. In no time the fireball disappeared out the back of the aircraft. As we later learned, however, the flames had singed both me and my pilot. With both engines out we landed in the water just offshore and our momentum carried us to the beach. Thank God we had landed on the Finnish side. We received excellent medical care and five or six days later we arrived back in Korovye-Selo by way of Helsinki. By then this Lapp operation had finally been called off and the *Gruppe* had returned to its 'home base'. Who could have conceived such an operation? Instead of a fully operational *Kampfgruppe*, a few reconnaissance aircraft would surely have sufficed to monitor the maritime area under these circumstances.

The *I. Gruppe* of KG 53 was surely urgently needed elsewhere at that time.

After this episode we returned to missions in support of the army in all parts of the northern front: Leningrad, Lake Ladoga, Volkhov, Lake Ilmen, and the Demyansk Pocket until it was relieved. Attacks on marshalling yards with the emphasis on Ostashkov and Bologoye. Ostashkov was supposed to be eradicated (Keller). Some attacks very successful, but rail traffic soon resumed each time. A joker painted a large caricature on the wall of the *Gruppe* command post showing Keller in the sky above a railway station with a huge eraser. It was supposed to remind us every day. Even the *Generaloberst* couldn't help but laugh when he saw the drawing up close one day. Finally we were again flying combat missions that were more to our liking. Happily, losses were kept within limits despite heavy anti-aircraft fire and on occasion fighters. Thanks to the outstanding cover provided by the Trautloft *Jagdgeschwader* we suffered no losses to Russian fighters for weeks. The Russians opened the siege ring around Leningrad from the east, south of Lake Ladoga. We moved to the forward airfield in Gostkino in order to increase the number of sorties we could fly daily. Increasingly our targets were in support of the army, especially in the area of the Russian breakthrough.

The Russians began their second winter battle by focusing on the Valdai Heights. They also broke through near Velikiye-Luki and encircled the German forces there. It was declared a fortress, with all the now familiar consequences. Once again all our forces were committed to supply the pocket in all kinds of weather, which did not differ significantly from the first winter of the war. Only now we were better prepared. The low-altitude flights once again resulted in casualties in equipment and personnel. The units assigned to the airlift were placed under the command of *Oberst* Wilke, who was named *Gefechtsverbandsführer* Velikiye-Luki. His account, which appears later, provides a detailed description of the airlift. Despite a maximum effort, the Russians continued to reduce the pocket, which was ultimately split into two parts, the railway station and the citadel. Transport gliders were flown into the pocket, a self-sacrificial act by the pilots. The army tried to relieve the pocket from the southwest but failed. The relief force got to within a few kilometers of the encircled troops before lack of fuel halted their advance. We were ordered to rest, because the relief attempt had allegedly succeeded, but then in the middle of the night we received mission orders. We had already begun celebrating the liberation of the surrounded troops, and now got the cold shower that quickly revived us. Velikiye fell after heroic resistance. The mood of the *Gruppe* was worse than depressed. The question was asked: 'Who was responsible for this failure? Contrary to the daily reports, what was the real situation of the frontline troops?' There were no answers."

The actions of the *II. Gruppe* from May 1942 were described by Gilbert Geisendorfer, then a *Leutnant* and pilot, who initially flew with the *6. Staffel* and later the *4. Staffel*:

"In May 1942 I was transferred from the *IV. Gruppe* in Lille to II./ KG 53 at the front in Russia, along with a number of other young officer crews like *Lt.* Kornblum, *Lt.* Dreher, *Lt.* Lucherig, *Lt.* Blieweis, *Lt.* Boresch and *Lt.* Klinkel. We arrived at Shatalovka, a forward airfield in the central sector south of Smolensk. Soon afterwards, however, the unit was transferred to Korovye-Selo, south of Pskov in the northern sector, and was attached to *Luftflotte 1*. The *Gruppe's* commanding officer was *Oberstleutnant* Schulz. The commanders of the *4.*, *5.* and

6. Staffel were *Hptm.* Klein, *Hptm.* Köhler and *Hptm.* Thierig. I was assigned to the *6. Staffel* but later moved to the *4. Staffel*. My crew included observer *Fw.* Sepp Schmauz, radio operator *Uffz.* Robel, *Uffz.* Alfons Dürrnagel, *Uffz.* Wunderlich, *Uffz.* Fürbeth, flight engineer *Uffz.* Hermann Kern and gunner Gerhard Stubbe.

There we would receive our baptism of fire, for which, because of our training, we had waited so long. In our idealism and enthusiasm, which in those days motivated most young men, we were worried that we would not get a chance to take part in the serious fighting. But now we were part of the fighting front and would soon learn how fiercely this battle had to be fought, even under extreme conditions.

While, in the north, the front between Lake Ladoga-Lake Ilmen-the Demyansk Pocket-Velikiye Luki had again stabilized, our forces were still under heavy Soviet pressure. South of Lake Ladoga the Russians attempted to break through and relieve encircled Leningrad, and north of Lake Ilmen German forces succeeded in pinching off and encircling a Russian breakthrough across the Volkhov River. That was our area of operations with the objective of taking the pressure off German troops by bombing Russian assembly areas and encircled units.

In good weather we usually flew in close formation, covered by German fighters of the Green Heart *Geschwader* under *Major* Trautloft, but we also carried out many individual low-altitude sorties when the situation at the front required it, even in bad weather.

Dense forests covered the Volkhov swamp. There in the pocket the Russians had laid down their corduroy roads. One could see them plainly when flying over them during low-level attacks. I still remember well the forest lanes called Erika and Friedrich. We had to dive out of the clouds for quick attacks, for at the very start accurate rifle and machine-gun fire brought down two of our aircraft.

My aircraft was also hit, once in the cockpit and on another occasion in a coolant line. I was able to shut down the damaged engine and return to base. One mission from that time is still fresh in my mind. The entire *Gruppe* made a formation attack on a railway station in the city of Volkhovstroy south of Lake Ladoga. It was my 40th combat mission and as yet I had not experienced any particularly exciting situations. We new crews had still not been assigned a regular aircraft. As machines were in short supply we had to fly whatever was available. On that day I was given an especially lame kite and had difficulty keeping formation. Even worse was the fact that I had to engage the superchargers at 3000 meters. The engines simply couldn't do it and I fell farther and farther behind. The formation initially flew a northeast heading, passing east of Volkhovstroy, in order to then reverse course and head for the target. Near the target numerous anti-aircraft guns opened up. They concentrated on the formation flying ahead of me and at first left me alone. Our fighter escort held enemy fighters at bay.

Because of my predicament, I wanted to beat my formation to the attack. Abeam the city I turned left in order to approach the target from east to west. I flew over the power station and the Volkhov dam, coming under anti-aircraft fire, but finally reached the target at the same time as the main body of our formation, which was above me and dropped its bombs at the same time as I. Each aircraft released sixteen 50-kg bombs. We – my crew and I – were initially frozen in fear, involuntarily ducking our heads, as if that could save us, but nothing happened.

Shortly after the tension had eased, there was suddenly a loud crash and the instruments for the starboard engine stopped working. We must have taken a hit. I immediately feathered the propeller in order to shut down the engine and used the rudder trim tab to take pressure off the rudder, a procedure I had gone through in my mind so many times. Everything worked. But the aircraft, whose performance had been poor from the outset, was unable to stay aloft on one engine. We steadily lost height and, accompanied by a German fighter, set course for Krasnogvardeysk, a fighter base east of Leningrad, where we landed safely.

From the outside the engine showed no evidence of damage. Only on close examination did we find a small tear in the supercharger intake scoop caused by a shell fragment. It had pierced the supercharger, wrecked the turbine and thus damaged the engine. A lucky hit that had a big effect.

Immediately after our emergency landing, another aircraft from our formation appeared, roared quite low over the hangars and made a belly landing. It was badly damaged and had one dead and one wounded on board. I can no longer remember which crew. On 10 June 1942 there was a ceremony at the Korovye-Selo airfield in which *General* Keller, the commander of *Luftflotte 1*, awarded the Knight's Cross to *Fw.* Teige. He was the first member of II./KG 53 to win the Knight's Cross and the third in the *Geschwader* after the *Kommodore*, *Oberstleutnant* Weitkus, and *Hptm.* Wittmann, commander of the *Stabsstaffel*. On that occasion we junior *Staffel* officers were also awarded the Iron Cross, Second Class by *General* Keller.

On 5 August 1942 II./KG 53 moved to Smolensk-North and soon afterwards to Sechinskaya, a large airfield between Smolensk and Briansk, where other *Kampfgeschwader* were also stationed.

At first our area of operations was centered on Rzhev, a railway and road junction approximately 200 km northwest of Moscow, where large numbers of Russian troops were massed for an offensive that had already begun. We bombed the Rzhev railway station, tank concentrations east of Rzhev, troop and artillery concentrations near Staritsa northeast of Rzhev, and various villages reconnaissance aircraft had identified as supply centers. What now became our area of operations was a vast area: beginning in Kalinin, approximately 200 kilometers northwest of Moscow, it extended in an arc around Moscow through Rzhev, Vyazma and Sukhinichi to the area north of Orel.

The situation demanded that we often fly three or four missions per day. In order to interdict Russian supplies, we flew armed reconnaissance over the Sukhinichi-Kaluga rail line and attacked trains with bombs and guns. The railway stations in Pogoreloye and Volokolansk were bombed. At night we successfully attacked the Kalinin and Serpuhkov airfields, located on the Oka about 100 kilometers south of Moscow (confirmed by fires and aerial reconnaissance).

It was a tough struggle, and the Russian defenses were powerful and dangerous, for we often had to approach our targets at low altitude. We began to take casualties. *Lt.* Klinke and his crew were among those that failed to return. While attacking positions near Novogryn, I came under heavy fire from light anti-aircraft guns. My starboard wing was hit, damaging the aileron, and the fuselage was holed above the ventral bath. My radio operator *Uffz.* Dürrnagel and gunner *Uffz.* Stubbe were wounded.

We also did not escape the attentions of the Russian airmen. We had a day off and were enjoying an open-air *Gruppe* party with a band and everything that went with it. Suddenly bombs went off, the anti-aircraft guns opened fire and the ground shook. We ran to covered slit trenches. An inferno broke loose which lasted three hours. We were certain that we would find nothing left of our aircraft and hangars, but it wasn't so bad. Only a few machines had been damaged or were burning. The Russian airmen always attacked individually and most were driven off by the anti-aircraft guns, which fired without letup.

One clear, moonlit night however, there was another alarm. The attack on our dispersal was brief and the explosions not all that powerful, nothing burned. When daylight came, however, we found a lovely mess. The enemy had scattered fragmentation bombs over a wide area. Almost all of our aircraft had been damaged by countless fragments and were no longer flyable. My aircraft, which had just gone into the maintenance hangar, suffered no damage. At that time our supply system was still functioning. That same day the crews were loaded into a Ju 52 and flown to the Heinkel factory in Rostock, where they picked up new aircraft. Several days later we were back at full strength.

Then we went back to *Luftflotte 1* in the northern sector. On 9 September we moved to Korovye Selo, where we had been based earlier. From there we took off on missions over the front in the Leningrad area, sometimes from the forward airfield at Gostkino, situated on a lake near Luga. For a week we attacked positions, vehicle columns and troop concentrations southeast of Schlisselburg. Russian units made repeated attempts there to reach the siege ring around Leningrad south of Lake Ladoga.

During one of these missions, on 3 October 1942, we lost our Knight's Cross wearer *Obfw.* Teige. His badly-shot-up machine just made it to German territory. The crew baled out, but Teige became hung up on the tail surfaces. We buried him in the military cemetery in Pskov.

We flew from Korovye Selo and the larger Pskov airport several kilometers farther northwest until December 1942, ranging deep over enemy territory in the northern sector. Our principal task was to interdict the Russian supply lines, and so we attacked the railway stations of Tikhvin in the north and Firovo and Ostashkov in the south of our sector of front. Ostashkov in particular was repeatedly bombed. The station was always full of transport trains and defended by railway anti-aircraft guns. We attacked in close formation at daybreak, using 1000-kg bombs, and achieved complete success. We thus fulfilled the demand made by *General* Keller in our command post, that 'the Ostashkov railway station must be destroyed'.

At home.

In December 1942 our II./KG 53, which had been reduced to a handful of crews, was withdrawn from combat and sent home to rest and reequip. The flying personnel were sent to Greifswald air base and given leave over Christmas.

Led by *Oblt.* Wolf, our technical officer, the technical personnel were sent to Insterburg air base in East Prussia. In the maintenance hangar there our personnel outfitted brand-new He 111s for operational service, which meant installing bombsights and the newly-developed MG 131 machine-gun. Part of my crew and I were attached to *Oblt.* Wolf, who used us to fetch spare parts. Work in the maintenance hangar proceeded apace, even on holidays.

I had an unusual flying experience when, soon after New Year, I was sent to the air park in Sagan in the Niederlausitz to pick up parts. During the return flight, I ran into a thick, solid cloud layer over Posen. As I was flying without an observer and had only the flight engineer and radio operator with me, I was all on my own and also had to do the dead-reckoning navigation myself.

I flew towards Insterburg air base using a DF station bearing. When we signaled our intention to land, however, we were advised QBI, QGO, which meant we could not land because of bad weather and should proceed to our alternate in Allenstein. Knowing how badly the spare parts were needed, I continued my approach to the airfield. The DF operator advised me 'airfield overflown', whereupon I had the radio operator switch on the automatic direction finder and began an ILS (instrument landing system) approach.

I had not had any opportunities to practice this procedure since instrument flying school, for at the front it was important to minimize the intervals between aircraft landing in bad weather. Usually we made a formation descent through cloud and landed visually when the ceiling was low. So I was initially somewhat skeptical, especially as there was heavy fog at the airfield. But I had to attempt it and my very first approach was a success. The radio guide beam, outer marker, middle marker by radio signal, and instrument readings gave me confidence that it would work. We approached the field with landing gear and flaps lowered. I nevertheless placed the flight engineer in the nose and tried, my gaze pointing downwards, to pierce the fog. Suddenly the asphalt runway appeared just beneath us. I closed the throttles and we touched down, happy and relieved.

We taxied to the airfield building and were proud. But what did we meet? A furious, frowning *Major* with clenched fists, the airfield commander. When I climbed out all I heard was the words, 'I'm going to have you court-martialed'. Then he was gone.

My instructions had been to land in Allenstein, but the technical officer straightened things out, telephoning the commander in Brunswick and explaining the urgency of my mission. In the end I received a commendation. How important this was would soon be seen."

In January 1942 the *III. Gruppe* was withdrawn to rest and reequip and was sent to the *I. Gruppe*'s peacetime base in Ansbach. There was some reorganization of personnel there and tests were carried out with the new Lotfe D 7 bombsight. Overall, the *III. Gruppe* was operational again by June 1942. It was not immediately sent back to Russia to join the other *Gruppen*, however, being transferred instead to France for operations against England. In mid-August the *Gruppe* returned to the Eastern Front."

Ernst Ebeling, whose following account also includes Rudolf Graf's story of how then *Leutnant* von Glasow's crew was shot down, ditched in the Channel and became POWs, continues:

"Our losses in men and machines climbed steadily in the course of our missions, most of which were flown at low altitude and in bad weather. Our quarters were poorly heated and our food supplies inadequate. Personal items and mail were scarce or non-existent. We were given no respite, not even at Christmas and New Years. Further costly missions over Tula, Kaluga, Naroforminsk, Medyn, Yukhnov and Rzhev – we were now on the retreat – further decimated the unit's complement of aircraft and crews, and in the last days of January 1942 the *Gruppe* was moved to Ansbach, the peacetime base of the *Geschwader*'s *I. Gruppe*.

Operational aircraft and young crews were transferred to the two remaining *Gruppen*, which continued operations. All that was left in each *Staffel* was the commander's crew plus two others, all with the Iron Cross, First Class and at least the Silver Operational Flying Clasp, to serve as cadres for the new crews, which were supposed to join the unit in Ansbach along with new equipment. Deliveries took longer than anticipated, however. After everyone returned from leave – some men had had none for two years – aircraft and crews were slow in arriving. The He 111 was retrofitted with the new and improved Lotfe 7D bombsight, which produced astonishingly good results from altitudes between 4000 and 7000 meters. Practice bombing with this sight was conducted by single aircraft and formations in Anklam in Pomerania from May to July. This intensive theoretical and practical training welded the new *Gruppe* together.

We were initially told that more senior, experienced officers would be coming to fill the *Staffelkapitän* positions in the 7. and 8. *Staffel*, but then there was a complete shakeup in the leadership positions. *Major* Fabian, the *Gruppenkommandeur*, was transferred to the Central Bombing School in Tutow in order to pass on his experience. *Hauptmann* Pockrandt, *Kapitän* of the 9. *Staffel* since 1 September 1940, became *Gruppenkommandeur* of the *I. Gruppe* in April 1942. His successor as *Kapitän* of the 9. *Staffel* was *Oberleutnant* Kindt, former *Gruppe* technical officer. *Oberleutnant* Eicke, known to many from his time with an instructor crew in the *IV. Gruppe* and with experience over France and England, was named *Kapitän* of the 8. *Staffel*. *Oberleutnant* Ebeling ultimately became *Kapitän* of the 7. *Staffel*.

While these personnel changes were taking place, in July the *Gruppe* was unexpectedly transferred to Chartres, France. The high command feared an invasion of France from England. With all available forces in action in the east, we were supposed to conclude our training of new crews and act as a reserve. At the end of July, however, a moonlight period brought favorable weather for operations against England. These were still being carried out by weak forces in order to unsettle the English mainland. In addition to instructors from training units, our old crews were also suddenly called to take part. Against the powerful defenses – anti-aircraft fire and especially coordinated operations between searchlights and night-fighters – we calculated that our average life expectancy was 5 to 10 missions flying the He 111, which was much too slow for use in the west. In just a few night missions between 25 July and 15 August the *Gruppe* lost its new commander, *Major* Brautkuhl, who had just arrived, and the two cadre crews from all three *Staffeln*, though the three new *Staffelkapitäne* survived.

The night missions lasted six to seven hours and were carried out under radio silence. We took off from Chartres and flew at extreme low altitude around the Scilly Isles at the southwest corner of England to the St. George Canal. There we climbed to 4000-5000 meters, after which we flew to the target – Birmingham, Swansea, etc. – in a shallow dive, which we maintained until the English east coast. We crossed the North Sea at low level and landed in Holland (Gilze-Rijen or Tilburg). After breakfast and refueling we flew back to Chartres.

After getting a little sleep, the *Staffelkapitäne* had to write letters to the families of the missing crews and by evening they were at readiness for the next mission. The survivors had also encountered night-fighters, especially in the area of the St. George Canal, and had only escaped through luck and hard work.

The new crews also flew their first combat missions, daylight sorties with cloud cover: approach in cloud over the Channel, drop out of cloud over the English coast short of the target, bomb run, release bombs and return to base in the cloud. If the cloud cover dispersed over the Channel the mission was called off, as the He 111 was no match for the English day fighters in speed, maneuverability or armament.

On 8 August 1942 all of the crews aborted their missions because of clear skies over the Channel. Only *Unteroffizier* Menzel, who was on his first combat mission, was missing. Not until one or two hours later did he land in Chartres, his aircraft riddled by machine-gun bullets and other calibers. Confronted as to why he hadn't followed the abort order, he declared that as a Rhinelander he could not understand that nothing was being done while German cities were repeatedly attacked by the English.

He had therefore risked it.

He was given a dressing-down and told that it was madness to spend two years training a crew just to send it to almost certain death on its very first mission. This, together with his experiences with flak and enemy fighters, caused him to realize that he had blundered. The young airmen were sweat-soaked, pale and exhausted. We were all happy that luck and daring had allowed them to return to us. Unfortunately the crew did not last long in subsequent operations in Russia and was lost in action. Even the new crews learned very quickly just how harshly demanding this war was.

III./KG 53 received a visit from the chief-of-staff of the air fleet to which we were attached. After inspection the men gathered round him in a semicircle. His skill in motivating the men for the coming missions against England was impressive. The officer who knew how to speak to the soldiers was General Staff *Oberst* Herhuth von Rhoden.

Before the scene again shifts to Russia, I would like to speak about radio operator Graf once more. Under its commander *Lt.* von Glasow, since October 1941 this crew had experienced and survived almost everything that a bomber crew could encounter on the Eastern Front: light, medium and heavy anti-aircraft fire in all its grades and effectiveness, Russian fighters, members of the crew killed and wounded, single-engine flight after battle damage by day and night, an emergency landing in enemy territory with successful return. And now, during operations over England, they were shot down over the St. George Canal. Two comrades died in the water, the other three were rescued by the English and were sent to POW camps in England and later Canada. This description from Graf's diary shows what many other crews – we all – experienced in our lives as bomber crewmen:

'Forced landing in enemy territory on 4 August 1942.'

From 22:00 we thirty men waited at the command post for orders to take off. They brought us canteens of hot, strong brewed coffee, Schokakola and ship's biscuit.

I wasn't feeling well.

Tonight's mission could definitely be our last. Was I afraid?

I wasn't sure. Was the frog afraid when the viper cornered him? For us thirty, too, there was no escape. And we still had a weak flicker of belief in the final victory. The 'Racial Observer' spoke of confidence, hope and the unbroken spirit of the German soldier on every front, which also included those operating against the island.

23:30. With dimmed landing lights we taxied towards the green takeoff lamp. Red warning lights shone from Chartres cathedral, then a small row of white takeoff lights. Cleared for takeoff, we began to roll, lifted off and the lights went out until the next aircraft took off.

We climbed on three comma three (??) and a direct course over Exeter. The Channel was clearly visible. Then came land. Down below muzzle flashes, flak. It was terribly inaccurate, because we could only just hear the shells exploding. Then water again, the Bristol Channel.

The port of Swansea should be coming up. I starred, searching for night-fighters. Over the intercom I heard them searching for the target. With the certainty of a sleepwalker Knoppig had found the target again. He made numerous course corrections on the run-in to the target, then he released his clusters of incendiaries.

Seconds later Rudi Breuer screamed over the intercom: 'Night-fighter below us!' Peewee instinctively put the Heinkel into a steep left turn, of course with some loss of altitude, and then returned to straight and level flight. I was wide awake and staring behind us. Like a massive lift, a twin-engined machine rose up behind us, not twenty meters away, and oscillated behind our tail. I called: 'Fighter from behind!' Peewee put the He into a criminal right turn; I was unable to move because of the centrifugal force. Then we leveled out again, and the English night-fighter came from the left. I thought, he can't see me in the darkness, nothing of the sort! I fired a long burst, Peewee applied rudder, my opponent some elevator and began to fire. Reddish-yellow flames spurted from his nose, and the muzzle flashes from his cannon and machine-guns colored the leading edges of his wings yellow-green. Tremendous firepower! I had experienced plenty on the Eastern Front, but faced with this hail of bullets coming towards us in the darkness, I was ready to give up. With my measly MG 15 I felt betrayed. The Ju 88 already had the MG 42 in a twin mount.

I got goose bumps. Two seconds can be an eternity. I began to fire. Drum on, drop the empty one, continuous fire, bursts. Smoothly the Tommy tried to get behind our tail again. Up front Peewee knew what his radio operator behind him was doing and forced the tail to the left and right to give me a clear field of fire. As a result the Beaufighter couldn't get a clear shot. Suddenly Peewee closed both throttles, the He dropped like a stone. Then the two Jumos roared again, and Glasow put the ham into a steep climb. Only an expert like our Dieter could fly the fantastic He 111 like that. During his evasive maneuvers I stuck to my seat like a postage stamp.

The nasty, fire-spitting fighter had disappeared. Below I saw water glinting in the moonlight. My altimeter showed 3000 meters. But that didn't mean that the altitude was correct. To determine that I had to call an English ground station and ask for the local barometric pressure. I had forgotten the Q-code for that.

Over the intercom I heard Glasow and Knoppig discussing the course for home. Either over Exeter and the Channel Islands or the Scilly Isles over Brest into Brittany and Chartres. The route over Brest would be fighter and flak free.

The 'elevator' rose again, not ten meters behind us. I fired immediately. My tracer disappeared into its cockpit, bounced off of the probably armored parts of its fuselage like glowworms and whizzed into the darkness. Peewee immediately let the He drop. We were barely still flying, but the fighter stayed behind us. We fell to 2000 meters, the Beaufighter sticking to us like a burdock. We faced each other: I, *Gefreiter* Rudi Graf of KG 'Legion Condor' 53, resident of Upper Bavaria, armed with a MG 15. And you, who are you? A pilot of the Royal Air Force? Are you married? Do you love a young woman? Do you hate me? They gave you four cannon and six machine-guns with which to destroy me. Will you shoot? We began firing at one another. An unequal combat! The Englishman won.

Aiming at the Beaufighter's engines, I held the trigger down and saw strikes. Then, for a second, its cockpit lit up. There was a great flash and pieces flew from our port engine. I smelled gasoline. The Englishman moved closer, held his fire, bobbing up and down behind our tail. Out of ammunition, I let my machine-gun slip from my hands and I waited for the enemy's burst of fire. As far as I was concerned, that was it. The end.

It didn't come. Either his guns had jammed, or he was out of ammunition, or I had hit his radio operator, compelling him to head home. Like a shadow, he dropped away and disappeared behind us.

By closing the fuel cock, Glasow extinguished the fire. The propeller stood still. Not even the airstream moved it.

I installed a fresh magazine on my machine-gun, unwilling to believe that the Tommy had flown home. At least he couldn't confirm our destruction. We maintained our course after he broke away. But he could still guide another Beaufighter to us. I stared into the gloomy darkness. Breuer and Birkmeier lurked below me at their machine-guns. Over the intercom I heard Walter searching for a reference point. My altimeter showed 1500 meters. Beneath us sparkled a large expanse of water. The altimeter needle continued to vibrate downwards. The intact engine was running at full power. Twice in Russia we had reached our own line this way.

Knoppig marked a lighthouse on his map and without further ado was now in a position to navigate our lame sled home.

The indicator needle stood at the number 500. Peewee's voice came over the intercom: 'OK, listen up. We have to go down. At best on the water. Over land we'll break our necks on the smallest obstacle. Leave via the ventral bath. Don't jump. I will try to fly as close to land as possible.' On the Eastern Front we walked home, but below us here was water. It was night, 02:00 on 5 August 1942. Like a flash the thought went through my head: Out? That means I won't be coming home! Mama, Papa, my sisters Hedi and Mia, will I ever see you again? Helene, surely there was a letter from her in Chartres. The surface of the water came nearer, much more quickly than Peewee wanted, the needle had been at zero for some time. I stretched both my legs up beneath the FuGe 42, my hands on the machine-gun ring, hold on!

A tremendous jolt shook our A1+AS when it skimmed the first Atlantic wave. Then a crashing, thundering, hissing and snapping, followed by an eerie stillness. I felt as if I was dead. My mouth was full of water. It tasted like salt and gasoline. I spat, cautiously moved my limbs and discovered that I was still alive. The belly landings on frozen ground in Russia had been very much softer than this one on water. The impact had squeezed the opening of my dorsal position into an oval, the fuselage had fractured at the break point, the empennage rocked on the waves and the fuselage stump rose up slowly.

Below me, Breuer roused me from my musings. 'Let's go, out! Jakob, push up the dinghy!' I called down. A terrible cry came from there: 'My foot, my leg! Help me!' It was Birkmeier. The night-fighter couldn't have hit him, otherwise Hans would have said something before we ditched. I suspected that he had been standing too deep in the ventral bath when we touched down, and that a spar or frame had pinned his leg below the knee.

I was already outside, holding onto my machine-gun with my left arm and pulling on Birkmeier's parachute strap with my right, while Breuer pushed him out through the dorsal position. He slid along the fuselage onto the wing. Goose flesh covered my body when I saw the flying boot swinging loosely on his flight suit.

'Hold tight while we break out the dinghy!' The water rose higher on me, or more accurately the aircraft sank slowly into the Atlantic. Breuer already had the packed dinghy in the dorsal position. I pulled on it but couldn't get it out. It must have become hooked on something. The stump of the He 111's fuselage was already pointing vertically into the air. Breuer was still inside. A wave washed over my head and I let myself fall backwards. Around me it became dark. My kapok life vest, which each of us wore, brought me to the surface. A pale moon lit the scene. Of the Heinkel there was nothing more to be seen. I only saw the empennage briefly, bobbing on the waves. I danced like a seahorse in the moving sea, using swimming motions to keep myself vertical and closing my mouth whenever a wave covered me. But where were the other four? A body appeared from the deep a few meters away. The yellow of its life vest shone. I heard a gurgling cough, followed by a scream. It was Breuer. I couldn't understand what he was screaming. Jakob was a non-swimmer. I was about to find out just how dangerous one such can be, especially one with great physical strength. I was just wondering how he might have gotten out of the sinking aircraft, when he grabbed me and forced me under the water.

176

Like any drowning man, he was trying to stay on the surface. I went under and came back up, and he reached after me from behind. Arms extended, I reached for his vest and turned up his kapok collar. Close your mouth when the water comes. You can't drown, the vest will keep you afloat! He became calmer. Across the surface of the water I heard a crowing: 'Hey! Rudi, Jakob, where are you? I'm here!' So Walter was still alive. But where was Birkmeier? Peewee checked in: 'Do you have the dinghy?' 'No, it's gone. Damn!' Then cries of pain that must have been heard as far as the English mainland. 'Help, my foot. Come help me !' I thought of the effect that this oily-salty water must be having on his wound.

For seconds I saw a dark flat something bobbing on the waves. That must be a fuel tank! It was pure luck that it drifted towards me within a minute. Given the sea state, my efforts to swim towards it were pointless. I was still holding the unopened dinghy packet in my arms. Excitedly I shouted about my find across the water. I thought back to our dinghy practice from the diving platform in the indoor pool in Lille. Racy French mermaids had swum about, distracting us. My brain had retained just one fact: one had to twist the top of a small compressed air bottle and the dinghy automatically filled with air.

But where was it? I had clamped the package between my legs so that it couldn't float away, and I fumbled with the packing straps that encased it. I wanted to undo them, remove them, grasped a fastener and pulled on it like crazy, and then Breuer once again forced me under the water. I swallowed a mouthful of Atlantic brew then struggled desperately to the surface – the packet had slipped away from me. With all my strength I pushed against Breuer's face with the flat of my hand and forced him away. My waterlogged flying boots hung on my legs like lumps of lead. Peewee appeared beside us; a wave must have carried him over.

'Where is the boat?' There was nothing I could say. But, even then, luck did not abandon Dieter von Glasow's crew.

Not far from the three of us something dark shot from the water, our dinghy. It slowly filled with air. Had I got hold of the bottle after all? I really don't know.

Breuer clung to the bulging side. The dinghy immediately flipped over and covered him. We righted it again. Peewee held the dinghy and I pushed Breuer in from the other side. Then Peewee and I tried to climb in. Repeatedly I tried to kick my waterlogged boots back from beneath the dinghy. Peewee simply pulled his off and was in in no time. Then he helped me in.

That Breuer and the boat were even still there is still a mystery to us today.

I ran into Breuer twice after the war and asked him about his impressions. 'I don't know, it was black around me. I can't even say that I was frightened, that I felt pain. I must have been in some weird semi-conscious state.'

We heard Birkmeier shouting and Knoppig calling. It must have been three in the morning. We opened the three soldered metal containers in the boat and inside found brandy, ship's biscuit, schokakola, bandages, several flare pistols and ammunition. I inserted the first flare and fired it. A garish light illuminated the surface of the water, and before it slowly went out we saw the two yellow life vests of Knoppig and Birkmeier bobbing on the waves. We couldn't tell how far away they were, but Peewee and I began paddling with the two oars in the dinghy. I fired another flare. This time it was green, then red, then a whistling shell, then another white, and so on. We paddled like crazy, the waves lifting us up and down. Wind came up, dawn began, and we fixed the sail. The wind threatened to crush us – we paddled on, how long I can no longer say. Then my oar slipped away from me. There was 20 cm of water in the dinghy. The sides of the dinghy felt spongy. Air had escaped. Peewee broke out the bellows and pumped air through the valve. The water in the boat was ice-cold, outside it was warm. Breuer's face was snow-white, I poked him and he grunted and began coughing up water. I had feared that I was sitting next to a corpse. We ate Schoka and drank brandy. Jakob didn't want any. That was understandable, given how much water he had swallowed.

'Birkmeier, Rudi, do you still hear Birkmeier?' The *Leutnant* always addressed his *Gefreiter* radio operator using 'Rudi' and the familiar '*Du*'.

In fact Hans Birkmeier from Ansbach was silent forever. Numbness relieved him of all his pain and let him go under.

We kept paddling, which was pointless as we couldn't see anything. The two yellow life vests had disappeared. Peewee insisted that he could still hear Knoppig calling.

It might have been about four when the crack of a German Parabellum 08/15 9 mm reached us. It was the last we heard from our observer Walter Knoppig, the Berliner. We all felt left alone and frozen in the endless solitude of the water around us and the breath of the mystical touched us. We were going to have to understand and accept the inevitability of our fate. Walter hadn't deserved this kind of death. Why had he made up such nonsense? In his own head for good measure? He with his nerve and his calmness!

English crab fishermen found the two on the west coast of England near Ifracombe. I read that later in a POW newspaper in Scotland. Wanting to know more, I went to the English camp commander and discovered the whole truth. Knoppig had a bullet hole in his head and Birkmeier a completely shattered knee. Their mothers were informed that they were dead, but not told how they had died. Both mothers wrote repeatedly to my parents, trying to learn more. In my letters I gave only vague hints, which revealed nothing however. The English censor blotted out the relevant sentences.

Six in the morning, freshening wind. The waves blew the three of us towards the west, up and down, into the rising sun. I scooped water out of the boat, Peewee pumped in more air, and the wet cold finally revived Breuer's spirits. I was freezing. Like ice, the wind blew through our completely wet things.

We said nothing. What now? Peewee told us how we should behave if we were taken prisoner. I didn't believe it, thinking that the wind might blow us onto the French coast. Breuer enjoyed the last sips of brandy, became responsive again and sucked on the hard ship's biscuit. For the first time I saw seagulls. Stupid birds. Sparrows and finches were nicer. The land they flew over too.

Peewee saw it first.

'There's a lighthouse over there. We're drifting towards land. That's still England. It's over boys, for us the war is over. Fire off the last flares so they'll find us.'

I fired all the smoke and noise shells into the air.

The English had begun looking for us at 03:00, when I fired the first flare. I learned this many years later.

At 09:00 we sighted a small cutter. 'Here they come!' We zipped up our flight suits, unhooked our belts and tossed them, with our pistols, into the water: *fini la guerre*. The cutter came nearer, circled us, our boat danced on the waves. The white life preserver came nearer. Then we could grasp it. Someone pulled us out – into captivity.

A slender civilian stood at the railing of the English rescue boat, pointing a rifle at us. (In 1975 I had the opportunity to shake hands with him.) Our Peewee spoke a little English. He told the man that we were unarmed and that he could put his gun away. With practiced grips powerful hands pulled us on board. We crawled out of our wet flight suits and hung them over our shoulders to dry. One of the men tried in vain to start the engine, until suddenly thick clouds of smoke rose from the engine room and three of the crew raised a sail. It may have been nine o'clock by then. A stiff breeze brought the cutter up to brisk speed. Peewee told him that two of us were still in the water somewhere and that they should look for them. They thereupon steered towards land, which appeared on our right. We could see a house, from which two men emerged. One of the crew called something through his megaphone. Then we turned away, and with no wind the sail hung from the mast. The boat rocked on the spot. One of the men brought us hot grog and a package of excellent shortbread biscuits. We thawed out. Even Breuer became cheerful.

A large motorboat came alongside. None of us three had seen it coming. English airmen of the Royal Air Force stood at the railing and stared at us. They took our boat in tow, and at about 14:00 we sailed into a small bay.

On a high quay wall of large square stones stood a throng of people, vacationers and beachgoers, based on their clothing. They all looked down at us. So these were Englishmen. The quiet up there irritated me. They must have recognized us as German airmen, who bombed their cities. Surely someone in their town had said that a *damned German plane* had been shot down that night and that they were now bringing the *German krauts* ashore. No howls of outrage greeted us. Only a silence, like that for a dead man being carried to the grave.

The crowd slowly approached the slipway onto which our boat now ran aground. I jumped down into captivity.

A tall Bobby with a black helmet placed his hand on my shoulder and said something. They did the same to Glasow and Breuer. They took us through a narrow alley of the picturesque village (Clovelly) to a small stone building on the quay wall, the first we had noticed when we sailed in. A sergeant in the khaki of the British Army took charge of us. He had a well-trimmed beard á la Kaiser Wilhelm. It was a glossy brick red, such as I never saw again. In broken German he asked us if we would like cocoa, coffee or tea. We ordered cocoa.

The moustache went back into the hut and began telephoning wildly, all the while keeping an eye on us.

Peewee: Take a look to see if you have any other papers apart from your identity cards, anything that might reveal from where we took off. If they interrogate you, simply say I don't know or can't say.

The red beard sat down beside us. He didn't like our conversation. He acted as if he understood German, but this was limited to 'have tea or coffee?' I pulled a sick chit from a dentist in Chartres from my flight jacket, crumpled it into a ball and let it drop over the quay wall into the sea. Much later I was served the five photos in my inner pocket.

The Englishman came out of a stone hut with a massive oak stick with a ball end, like the one Danielo twirls elegantly in the air in the Merry Widow, and ordered the three of us in the direction of three black limousines that had pulled up about 100 meters away. There they separated us. I got in. A civilian dressed in dark clothing chatted to me in perfect German. How was I and did I have any complaints? 'Did they treat you badly?' 'No.' 'Cigarette?' 'Thanks.' I took it reluctantly and made the acquaintance of Players Navy Cut, whose aroma could make one addicted. I was becoming increasingly tired from the previous night's trials. The events of the past hours unwound in my mind like a fast-playing film: takeoff – flight - bombs gone – the night-fighter – combat – belly landing in the water – Knoppig, Birkmeier dead? – the dinghy disaster – and now I was smoking an English cigarette on English soil!

The limousine pulled away, thus began my path into 4½ years of captivity.

I was a prisoner of war and was given the number 20 7 21."

Ebeling wrote further about the *III. Gruppe*:

"Back to Russia. After an operation-free evening we unexpectedly received the transfer order for the next morning, directing us to fly to Hildesheim to refuel before continuing to Warsaw-Okeczie and the next day carrying on to Smolensk-North.

Our new *Gruppenkommandeur* was *Hauptmann* Waldforst, an officer with combat experience serving as a *Staffelkapitän* in the *IV. Gruppe*. From Smolensk he would lead his *Gruppe* in formation attacks against enemy troops during the Battle of Rzhev, Vyazma and Zubtsov, sometimes flying as many as four sorties per day. The unit also carried out supply missions and attacks on railway stations.

The depressing losses during the few missions against England had not failed to leave their mark on the remaining crews. The *Kommandeur* and the *Staffelkapitäne* managed to bolster the men's self-confidence through the success of our *Staffel-* and *Gruppe*-strength raids, in which we achieved outstanding accuracy with the new bombsights. This was especially so because the defenses there could not be compared with those in England and losses were initially low.

But after the transfer to Gostkino at the end of August and the subsequent missions in support of army units in the defensive battle south of Lake Ladoga, the wind again blew harder. The Russian anti-aircraft fire on the Volkhov front, at the Mga, Shum and other railway stations, was massed and even the medium four-barreled weapons were effective to more than 4000 meters. As a result the aircraft often returned with battle damage, some crewmen were wounded and occasionally there were total losses caused by flak or fighters.

Nevertheless the crews took the poor quarters, lack of support facilities, inadequate supplies of rations and the resulting poor quality of the food with good humor, probably feeling that there they were being properly employed with good effect as horizontal bombers, though mostly against troops near the front, but occasionally against railway stations, bridges, depots and other supply installations, proper targets for bombers. The accurate bombing of the Mga, Shum and Volkhov railway stations, the Shum – Volkhov rail line, the crossings over the Neva at Putilovo and Dubrovka, and the oil depots on the Kobona peninsula impacted the Russian supply system in the Leningrad area and, together with the numerous strikes against enemy troop concentration areas, artillery positions and the armored train near Poliano, relieved and supported the army.

Along with other crews, these missions also cost the *Gruppe* its new commander, *Major* Waldforst, who was shot down with his crew near Leningrad and failed to return. *Oberleutnant* Eicke had to take over the *Gruppe* in an acting capacity.

Despite the predicament of our troops in this area, who had failed to take Leningrad and were now involved in difficult defensive fighting, the even more serious situation at the Demyansk land bridge made it necessary to transfer the *Gruppe* to Dno. From there, beginning on 20 October, attacks were made in the area south and southeast of Leningrad, concentrating on troop concentrations southeast of Staraya Russa, the Ostashkov railway station and rail lines leading from there to Firovo and Belokoye. Missions followed against oil refineries in Leningrad, the Volkhov railway station and the Kobona Peninsula itself. In scale and accuracy, the anti-aircraft fire over Leningrad surpassed anything yet encountered. We were often amazed to return home with no or only a few hits from fragments, even though 80- and 100-mm shells exploded around us in spades. Probably these shells didn't burst into sufficient small pieces. Nevertheless, there were wounded and forced landings. Given the proximity of the targets to the front, however, the crews usually managed to reach fighter bases near the front, even after the loss of an engine, or at least make a forced landing in our territory.

Shortly before the new crisis and the encirclement of Velikiye Luki, where once again orders from the highest level prevented a timely evacuation, the *Gruppe* received its new commander, *Major* Mönch. While we initially continued our attacks against enemy troops west of Velikiye Luki, after a short Christmas party on Christmas Eve, from the first holiday until 5 January we flew several transport flights per day in support of the German troops encircled in Velikiye Luki. In order to put the supply containers on target we usually approached the encircled fortress at low level, often from several different directions at once. Under fire from guns positioned around the town, we had to climb to 200 meters to drop the containers, allowing for wind, and then quickly descend to low level again. Despite heavy losses during these missions, the *Gruppe*'s crews again gave their best at Velikiye Luki, even though the best they could do was mitigate the shortages of ammunition, food and fuel inside the pocket. Many containers were blown off course by the wind and could not be recovered. An attempt to relieve the fortress on the ground was not a success."

Two diary entries by Ernst August Lorenz, observer in the crew of pilot Georg Juditzke, may typify the 300 sorties flown by the *1. Staffel*:

"16 Aug. 1942, Sechinskaya, 06:40-08:20, train-hunting mission on the Koselsk-Tula line.
We took off from Sechinskaya at 06:40 carrying eight SC 250s, weather in the target area 7-8/10 cumulus, ceiling 1600-1700m. After takeoff we climbed to 2000 meters and flew on instruments to the target area. Just short of it we let down to acquire visual contact. Far ahead a transport train heading west, switches to bomb preselect on the RAB 14, short interval 20 m. We dropped lower on account of the visibility, approached from directly ahead. Target steady in the crosshairs. About 10 seconds before the bombs were dropped, light anti-aircraft guns at the end of the train began putting up heavy fire, damned close. But the bombs fell. Bomb doors closed, power on and up into the clouds. Three minutes straight ahead, 180° instrument turn to the left, cautious descent after about 2½ minutes. On gaining visual contact, an approximately 500-meter-high mushroom cloud of smoke to our left, beneath it 7-8 overturned cars, some burning, anti-aircraft fire stopped. We landed in Sechinskaya undamaged at 08:20."

Second report:

"27 Dec. 1942, Korovye Selo, 12:15 – 14:00. Mission: attack on enemy rocket firing positions at the south end of Velikiye Luki. Snow falling, ceiling 100 m, bomb load SD 2s in bomb dispensers. Takeoff at 12:15. We flew towards a navigational aid point southwest of Velikiye Luki, visual low-level flight, from there on instruments in the direction of the target at a height of about 200 meters, after appropriate flying time of just under 4 minutes we let down, gaining partial visual contact with the ground at about 100 meters. Very heavy defenses. Flak hit in cockpit made continuation of the bomb run impossible. Jettisoned bombs. Landed at 14:00. After treatment by Dr. Mehlhorn, I was evacuated to hospital in Pskov with a bullet in my thigh."

Two mission reports by the *I. Gruppe* concerning attacks in the Demyansk area and the Ostashkov railway station show in bare numbers the sequence of such missions.

"**Mission report No.22** of 1/10/1942, air commander, I./KG 53, 15 He 111 H-6, takeoff time: 09:35 – 10:00, landing time: 11:15 – 11:45, attack time: 10:10 – 11:00, attack height: 200 – 2200 m. Mission: armed reconnaissance in the area south of the land bridge.

Results: 1. Kette: Grid square 581 b-c 3 and 4, 117 f 4 on 3-4 trucks, effects not observed.

2. Rotte: Grid square 581 a-c 3, b-c 4

3. Kette: Gris square 581 a, b, c 4 and 5, 117 f 4 – 118 a 5 on 4-5 vehicles on road, near misses on vehicles, hit on bridgehead with SD 250.

4. Rotte: Grid square 591 b-c 4-5

5. Kette, 6. Rotte: Grid square 581 b c 3 4, d e 3. Effects not observed.

Alternate target: – aborted: – bombs: 15 SD 250, 112 SD 50, 64 SC 50, 64 SBe 50, ammunition 46 magazines MG, 1 magazine MG/FF on target area, victories: – losses: – defenses: light anti-aircraft fire, inaccurate, from target area. Other: two Me 109s over target. Weather: no clouds over target, hazy, visibility 10 km. Reconnaissance: 4 positions in grid square 579 d-f 4. In grid square 579 finished bridge near Lipno. 4-5 tanks in grid square 173 b 6 – 117 f 1. Westbound crossing traffic in grid square 559 c 4 d. White swastika at edge of forest in grid square 574 e 6 c. Positions on the Lovat in grid square 572 d 5 and 6. Light truck traffic in entire target area."

"**Mission report No.32** of 4/10/1942, air commander, I./KG 53, 14 He 111 H-6, takeoff time: 14:10 – 14:15, landing time: 16:20 – 16:30, attack time: 15:15, attack altitude 3800 – 4000 m, mission: Ostashkov. Results: bombs blanketed entire station area. In station itself about 5 trains blown apart. 1 train heading west, anti-aircraft train in track system NW of station. Several hits on stationary trains, tracks and sheds. 1 train left on fire. 1 explosion and much smoke after direct hit on sheds. After leaving target area 3 fires with heavy smoke observed. Alternate target – 1 He 111 aborted due to engine trouble, bombs 112 SC 50, 112 SD 50, 14 SC 250. Defenses: heavy flak from Medvodovo area, heavy flak from target (flak train). Fighter escort 4 Me 109. Weather: good visibility approximately 1400-2300m, 1/10 – 5/10."

f) Battle at Velikiye Luki

In December the *II. Gruppe* went to Greifswald to rest and reequip, while at the same the *I. Gruppe* began bombing and supply sorties to

Velikiye Luki. The *III. Gruppe* had begun similar operations at the end of November. These would continue until 19 January 1943, when the pocket was surrendered. Retired *Generalmajor* K.E. Wilke, then an *Oberst* and commander of KG 53 and also battle unit commander of Velikiye Luki, has written about the events surrounding this battle. His first-hand memories provide an impressive and disturbing picture of combat operations there:

"The battle near and in Velikiye Luki on the northern wing of Army Group Center lasted from 24 November 1942 until 19 January 1943. It is for good reason that historians write and speak of the events there as a little Stalingrad. I experienced this winter fighting at my command post on Big Ivan Lake approximately 11 km west of Velikiye Luki as battle unit commander while retaining command of the *Geschwader*. The *I. Gruppe* (Pockrandt) and the *III. Gruppe* (Mönch) were committed either as supply or bomber groups against targets in and around Velikiye Luki almost every day, while the *II. Gruppe* (Schulz-Müllensiefen) temporarily left the *Geschwader* command to serve as a transport unit during the final phase at Stalingrad. At that time the *IV. Gruppe* (Grözinger) was in Orleans-Bricy in the west.

The situation on the ground and in the air will be described in detail here. It will be shown that while the hard-pressed ground forces desperately needed our help, the results achieved could not be compared with the losses in personnel and aircraft for a role that had never been intended and can only be seen as the result of the desperate situation that then existed on the Eastern Front.

We remember the major airlift at Stalingrad, but also the successful supply operations at Kholm, Demyansk, the Kuban Bridgehead, during the evacuation of the Crimea and the air-dropping of supplies to the 1st Panzer Army.

The Battle of Velikiye Luki from 24 November 1942 until 19 January 1943 (according to the combat report by *Luftwaffe* Command East of 26/3/1943): development of the situation on the ground: the enemy's strategic plan was to launch an attack from the Toropets area with powerful ground and air forces, break through the left wing of Army Group Center (9th Army) and advance far to the west in the direction of Vitebsk, and tie up German forces desperately needed on the Don and in and near Stalingrad. In order to accomplish this goal, the city and fortress of Velikiye Luki, whose origins go back to the 17th Century, had to be taken. Under the command of *Oberstleutnant* Sass, Velikiye Luki was fortified with a system of strongpoints and field emplacements on both sides of the city. The centerpiece of the strongpoint was the old citadel above the city.

The Russian plan was to attack when winter set in, employing heavy artillery to soften up and reduce the strongpoint. After capturing the field emplacements on both sides of Velikiye Luki, the Soviet 3rd Shock Army attacked the city and the well-fortified citadel, which was held by almost 8,000 German troops. As they withdrew from their field emplacements, grenadiers, artillerymen, pioneers, and train and medical units of the 83rd Infantry Division entered the 'fortress'. Also there were: construction troops, rocket launcher units, a security battalion, a light observation battalion, an Estonian volunteer battalion, army and air force anti-aircraft guns in battery strength, and elements of the 183rd and 70th Regiments.

Supplying the fortress created difficulties from the outset. Because of heavy losses in weapons and equipment, the increasingly serious situation near Velikiye Luki required immediate relief through constant artillery and mortar fire. The ammunition situation was critical.

Army group and the army did what they could to relieve Velikiye Luki. But – as we saw so often – the forces were inadequate. While the encircled troops fought off every enemy attack until mid-December, the troops of the relief force had to temporarily halt the relief attack. This was due to the absence of reserves and the complete exhaustion of the troops, worn out by severe cold and deep snow. The strength of the defenders also began a steady decline.

Enemy situation in the air – enemy flying activity: despite periods of bad weather, the enemy was extremely active in the air throughout the battle of Velikiye Luki. Due to insufficient defensive weapons and inadequate deliveries of ammunition, the Russians were able to conduct most of their operations at low altitude. Massed attacks on our offensive spearheads hindered their advance.

Here is an example of the ferocity and stubbornness of the fighting, but also of the political attitude of the Soviet people. In December 1942 a Russian two-seat reconnaissance aircraft was forced down near my command post. When our troops, including me as battle unit commander, approached the aircraft to capture the crew, the two Russians shot themselves. The aircraft was undamaged and yielded documents concerning the crew's mission.

Air defenses: in contrast to earlier experience, the enemy fighters carried out their attacks with great determination and were difficult to shake off. The enemy formed a defensive strongpoint around Velikiye Luki in the form of defense lanes, which, given the low supply drop altitudes, led to heavy losses and battle damage and seriously complicated the airlift.

Own situation in the air: the battle unit command became responsible for the conduct of the defensive effort on 25 November

1942. Looking ahead, *Luftwaffe* Command East had prepared the Izocha, Idritsa and Derrun airfields for winter operations. As well, the Big Ivan Lake was also an ideal takeoff and landing place for our He 111s.

Attached units: 25/11/42 – KG 53 with *I.* and *III. Gruppe*, 16/12/42 – III./StG 1, 8/1/43 – 9./StG 77, 4/1/43 – JG 51 with *I.* and elements of *III. Gruppe*, 6/1/43 – II./JG 54, 2/1/43 – 2. *Störkampfstaffel*; temporarily attached: II./KG 4, III./KG 4, Verb.Kdo.(S)V.

Bomber units: unfavorable weather conditions halted operations on 11 days and permitted armed reconnaissance only on 7 days. On the remaining 37 days and nights of the 55-day struggle, the tireless efforts of the units produced good success and brought relief to the ground forces. The combat report of the *Luftwaffe* Command East states that, 'the crews were equal to the highest demands while displaying tireless dedication'.

At Velikiye Luki the Ju 87 Stuka was used for the first time with supply bombs. The steadily shrinking drop zone forced the adoption of this measure with good results.

Our fighter units were able to hold their own against powerful enemy fighter forces. Flying free chase missions, they largely retained air superiority over the Velikiye Luki area. On 6 January 1943 alone, approximately thirty enemy aircraft were shot down over our attack spearheads. Supply missions by the bomber units: whenever the weather permitted, supply containers were dropped by day and night over the city and later onto the citadel and the area of the east railway station. The containers held desperately needed supplies such as weapons, ammunition, medical supplies and food. Not all of the goods reached their targets. Many were lost or captured by the Russians. Losses rose after the Russians set up of defense lanes and employed every caliber of weapon up to automatic rifles, while small and medium searchlights created uncertainty, blinding the bomber crews. Nevertheless, the *Luftwaffe* Command East's combat report declared: all of the bomber and Stuka crews engaged in the dropping of supplies made unique achievements by carrying out their missions in the face of intense ground fire.

Two reports in facsimile by the *I. Gruppe* dated 31 December 1942 and one dated 1 January 1943 may deepen the impression of the airlift.

It turned out that dropping containers on small-area targets such as the citadel (250x150m) in horizontal flight was an impossible task. Every possibility, such as exploiting low cloud cover until the run-up to the target with pull-up short of the target, twilight and night drops (the snow made it easier to find the base) was exhausted.

The *Gruppenkommandeur* of I./KG 53 at that time, *Major* Pockrandt, wrote:

'After the Russian discovered that during our final approach to the target we had to orientate ourselves by means of a fire signal in the Velikiye Luki base, he himself began lighting an increasing number of fires in the vicinity of the citadel and the east station, so that locating the target became almost impossible. Our accomplishments paled against the suffering of the encircled ground forces. I remember the last mission. We were on standby. Suddenly, towards evening, came the order 'rest', because Battle Group Wöhler had relieved the garrison. We were as happy as children and every unit celebrated the news. I cannot but confess that we were all tipsy when the mission order came. Apart from a few vehicles and tanks that had broken through, Battle Group Wöhler had been halted just short of its objective. That was terrible news and there was great disappointment. The mission was flown but was not a success, because the only thing still moving down below was Russians. Thank God we suffered no losses on our last mission.'

Glider operations (directly attached to *Luftwaffe* East): for the sake of completeness – from the historical point of view – this action, in which gliders successfully landed on Fair Street in Velikiye Luki, must be mentioned. Not for nothing does the *Luftwaffe* Command East's combat report state 'that, in a daring operation, 17 transport gliders succeeded in flying in anti-tank guns with crews, assault teams, machine-gun ammunition, flamethrowers, food, medical supplies and (important enough) mail. The heroic actions of the glider pilots, all volunteers, brought material and moral support to the fighting units on the ground, enabling to continue their stubborn defense.'

The airlift by bomber, transport and glider units, conducted with daring and dedication, enabled the garrison of Velikiye Luki to hold out for as long as it did. Without this brilliant commitment, the ability of the defenders to hold on would have come to a standstill much sooner. The Velikiye Luki strongpoint was a successful breakwater, preventing the enemy from attaining his objective of a large-scale breakthrough.

Missions: In the period from 25 November 1943 to 19 January 1943 the following operational sorties were flown: 298 by reconnaissance aircraft, 1,393 by bombers, 46 by nuisance raiders, 403 by dive bombers and 1,554 by fighters. Supply sorties: 310 by bombers, 94 by Stukas, 25 by gliders, 1 by Ju 52. Total aircraft sorties 4,124.

Results (from the air): 232 enemy aircraft shot down, 2 armored trains hit, 9 trains hit, 2 locomotives damaged, 9 tanks destroyed, 3 tanks damaged, 5 anti-tank guns destroyed, 25 guns silenced, 1 four-barrel machine-gun destroyed, 49 vehicles destroyed, 61 horse-drawn vehicles destroyed. Flak artillery also claimed 49 aircraft shot down, 14 tanks destroyed, 26 machine-gun and mortars captured by flak.

Material losses (flying units only): Total losses 1 Ju 87, 1 Ju 52, 6 Bf 109, 1 Fw 190, 17 He 111, 4 Fw 189, 6 DFS 230 gliders, 11 Go 242 gliders – total 47 aircraft. Crashes: 60-100% - 2 Ju 87, 2 Bf 109, 3 He 111, 1 Hs 126; under 60% - 3 Ju 87, 19 He 111, 3 Bf 109, 1 DFS 230, total aircraft losses 81.

Personnel losses:

Aircrew:	a) Officers killed	4
	wounded	2
	missing	11 = 17
	b) NCOs killed 11	
	wounded	23
	missing	59 = 93
	c) Enlisted men killed	3
	wounded	3
	missing	34 = 40

Summary: the weeks-long defense of Velikiye Luki frustrated the enemy's intention of breaking through the army group's left wing towards the west. Even though relief – with the exception of 80 men who broke out – was not possible with the forces available, the Russians suffered heavy losses in men and materiel and were denied their planned operational success. The *Luftwaffe* units played a decisive role in what, on the whole, was a defensive success.

After the fall of the Velikiye Luki strongpoint the Russians took fanatical revenge. On 29 January 1946, a total of twelve German veterans of the Velikiye Luki fighting, one of each rank from general down to rifleman, was publicly hanged in the city marketplace. Only eleven of the German soldiers captured at Velikiye Luki survived Russian captivity and retuned to Germany between 1953 and 1955.

That was the winter battle at the critical point of Velikiye Luki – only overshadowed by what took place in and around Stalingrad at about the same time.

Supply flights to Velikiye Luki: In order to see for myself the growing difficulties and problems in the airlift to the small area of the citadel, on 2 January 1943 I took off from Izocha for Korovye Selo, I./KG 53's airfield. This field was 1000x1000 meters in size, had no hangars, only makeshift billets, no runway, poor access roads, but had an unobstructed landing and takeoff area. It was about 30 km SSW of Pskov and in addition to I./KG 53 the *Geschwader* headquarters was located not far from the airfield.

After thorough pre-flight preparations using the mission order from the same day, He 111 A1+AA took off on a supply flight with veteran pilot *Unteroffizier* Schüpstuhl at the controls. Instead of the usual bomb load, the bomb cells contained supply containers with badly needed goods such as food, medical supplies, ammunition and small arms.

In the midst of winter the temperature was about minus 10 degrees. It was basically an ideal winter day, no snow flurries, no clouds, little wind and good visibility. Schüpstuhl knew the route from many previous flights. He and his men were veteran flyers. The He 111 was as steady as a board at 1000 meters. Here and there a village peeked out from the white winter landscape, otherwise all we could see was scattered woods and one or another rail line. From the mission order, we knew that nine more He 111s were behind us, heading for the same target.

We arrived over the target after about 70 minutes flying time. The city and citadel, surrounded by fires, could just be made out in the snow-covered landscape. I tried to keep the target in sight, and Schüpstuhl had already started his descent in order to arrive over the courtyard of the citadel at about 200 meters. We were also over the northwest to southeast flight corridor, which provided a clear path for dropping the containers. Furious defensive fire accompanied the He 111 for the last 1200 meters. All we could see was the paths of the tracers. The citadel courtyard approached quickly. A press of a button and the supply containers were released. Schüpstuhl flew a zigzag course and, relieved of its load, the machine responded like the student to the teacher. I had been an infantryman in the First World War. I knew land warfare with all its horrors and the many different sounds a major battle brings. Here in the air it is all different. It is not the ear that governs the scenery, but the eyes and senses alone. Only near misses exploding close to the machine can be heard, or direct hits, which we were spared. Otherwise the eye only sees the flash of exploding shells, which blossom like bursting fireworks around the He 111. The whole thing lasts only seconds. If one makes it through the valley of death, it means that one has completed his mission, the chest breathes easier, and a benevolent stillness surrounds us as we fly towards the night. Only the sonorous, comforting noise of the two powerful engines surrounds us. Questions move us: was the drop a success? Were our comrades below able to recover the supply containers? Where are the other aircraft? Did they reach the target?

At about 20:00, after 2½ hours of flight, we land safely in Korovye Selo, where the He 111 is immediately examined for hits. As aircraft commander, Schüpstuhl makes his report and we soon learn that two of the He 111s that took off are overdue. There is also no news from neighboring airfields. We begin to worry. We know what it means to have to force-land behind the front in darkness, should it come to that. That was not the case with the He 111 with the crew whose name I have forgotten. The aircraft must have been shot down while on its run-in to the target. The crew is reported missing, and we know that missing can be worse than being reported killed in action.

After two anxious days, during which we received no news about the two missing aircraft, the crew of *Hauptmann* and *Staffelkapitän* Lehmann call from the command post on Big Ivan Lake after a 40-kilometer trek. The crew covered half of the distance, through partisan country, in a requisitioned panye wagon. Unfortunately a dead comrade had to be left behind, while the rest of the crew escaped with less serious wounds. The stresses of the night forced landing and foot march can be seen in the young faces. Our comrades were very lucky. They came down in a place where the lines were thinly manned, making it possible for them to get through. Their fur-lined boots, winter flight suits, emergency rations, packet dressings and compass proved to be knights in shining armor. But without the firm resolution to get home, none of that would have mattered. Overjoyed, we welcome our comrades home. The good news is passed on by telephone and they learn that soon they will be going home on leave. The same feelings of happiness are absent on 19 January 1943, when we – the battle unit – receive the first five of the approximately 180 men from the Velikiye Luki strongpoint (including wounded from all branches) who, two days earlier, were ordered to break out to meet the spearhead of the relief force four kilometers away. Of course all of them are wounded. It is impossible to understand what these men have endured in the past weeks. Without sleep, without the least personal hygiene, lousy, filthy, hungry and always cold, they fought on – hoping for relief. About 3,000 shells fell on the citadel and the grounds of the east station every day. Among the accumulating rubble lay numerous wounded who had received only makeshift care. I confess that I have never seen such miserable-looking young men in my life. They were unresponsive. The horrors of what they had been through could only be seen in their eyes, and they were all deeply exhausted. We did what we could. Medical care, washing, fresh clothes and the only food available – stew made from horse flesh – several times a day, that was all that we could do for them at first. Sleep, sleep and the sense of being free was all that mattered to these Velikiye Luki fighters. After two days ambulances arrived to collect those who had returned to the living. When they waved goodbye to us – still dead tired – there was a new gleam in their eyes. They were taken away in the direction of Nevel. We don't know what became of them."

The order of the day issued by *General* von Greim, commanding general and Commander-in-Chief of *Luftwaffe* Command East, on 22 January 1943, has survived. In it he acknowledged the severity of the fighting.

In conclusion three result reports from the war diary, dated 16/12/1942, 25/12/1942 and 11/1/1943, which may be seen as representative of many missions over Velikiye Luki:

"Result Report No.131 of 16/12/1942 Lfl.Kdo. 1, I./KG 53, 11 He 111 H-6. Takeoff: 10:10 – 10:20, landing 11:35 – 11:50, attack time: 10:55 – 11:15, attack height 1450 – 3000 m, mission a) attack on northwest part of Velikiye Luki, b) attack artillery positions west of Velikiye Luki. Results a) 5 He 111 attacked the northwest part of Velikiye Luki. All bombs fell in the designated target area. No special results were observed. B) 4 He 111 bombed recognized artillery positions. Positions: at southwest edge of Patyanino, in village of Melenka, Niteleva, Gritskovo and west of Polkhova. The positions were identified by gun flashes, most of the bombs fell on the positions, no special results were observed. 2 He 111s aborted due to engine trouble. Ammunition: bombs 2 SD 500, 1 SC 500, 5 SD 250, 64 SD 50, 32 SC 50, 64 AB 23, 22 drums of machine-gun ammunition at fighters and targets. No enemy aircraft shot down, accurate medium flak from target area, approximately 8 MiG-3s, occasional fighter cover from two Bf 109s. Weather clear, visibility 40 km, reconnaissance none, photographs: 5 aircraft. I.A. *Leutnant* (signature)."

"Result report of 25/12/1942 Lfl.Kdo. 1, I./KG 53, 12 He 111 (11 H-6, 1 H-14). Takeoff: 11:58 – 12:10, landing 13:21 – 13:50, time over target: 12:35 – 12:55, altitude: approach at low level, bombing height 200-250m, mission supply of Velikiye Luki. Results: 61 containers dropped (55 artillery ammunition, 4 infantry ammunition, 2 illumination ammunition). 55 containers landed without problem. The parachutes of two containers opened just before the containers struck the ground, 1 container fell near a burning house, the parachutes of four containers did not open, 1 container exploded on impact. Position of containers on main road (drop target), due west and about 200 meters SE of it. Alternate target – aborted –. Containers: 61 containers, ammunition: 152 drums MG 15, 44 MG FF fired at anti-aircraft guns, troops and fighters. 1 enemy aircraft shot down (1 attacking LaGG-3) seen to crash and explode due north of Velikiye Luki. Losses: 7 aircraft hit by fighters and ground fire, 1 aircraft belly landing at airfield, 1 aircraft smooth forced landing in grid square 9762 or 3. Defenses: 3 fighters, several of which attacked (LaGG-3), south of target accurate light flak, artillery and small arms fire. Weather: hazy patches, 10/10 QBB 150-500, visibility 2-8 km, target QBB about 800-1000 m, hazy, cloud patches. Reconnaissance: strongly manned enemy positions all around Velikiye Luki. Heavy traffic on roads south of target, lone tanks in grid square 07594, also heavy battery on the move. Larger troop camps in grid squares 8 AR 87 and 88. One tank attacking from SE towards position in the track loop S of Velikiye Luki. I.A. *Leutnant* (signature)."

"Result report of 11/1/1943 Lfl.Kdo. 1, I./KG 53, number 8, takeoff 12:00, landing 13:30 – 14:50, attack time 12:40 – 13:15, height 200-400 4 He 111, 1300-3100 m 4 He 111, mission attack recognized concentration areas and artillery positions in area NW of Velikiye Luki, focal points Maslova, Kamenka. Results: 4 He 111 bombed identified positions in and around village of Maslova, no special effects observed. Bombs of 1 He 111 fell among positions NE of Kamenka, 1 He 111 attacked positions at eastern exit from village of Zaryanina. Four small fires observed during approach. 1 He 111 dropped its bombs on positions identified due east of village of Ilino. Alternate target – aborted 1 He 111 due to hits by anti-aircraft fire in wings and machine-gun hit in fuel tank. Bombs: 12 SD 250, 80 SD 50, 6 SD 500, ammunition: 14 drums of machine-gun ammunition on positions in target area. Enemy aircraft shot down – losses: 5 He 111 hit in wings and fuselage by flak and machine-gun fire. Defenses: heavy machine-gun and light anti-aircraft fire, fighter escort two Bf 109. Weather 6/10, high fog at 200 m, top of layer at 350 m, visibility 10-20 km. reconnaissance: 1 He 111 (which aborted) jettisoned bombs blind NE of the airfield approx. 2 km N of Staroselye-Ussi grid square 88541. Photographs – A.B. *Leutnant* and adjutant."

g) Stalingrad

On 25 November 1942 the 6th Army was encircled in Stalingrad. An airlift was begun immediately from Tatsinskaya airfield, 240 kilometers from Stalingrad, under Airlift Commander *Oberst* Otto-Lutz Förster using Ju 52s. All He 111 units stationed in Morozovskaya, 200 kilometers away, were placed under the command of *Oberst* Ernst Kühl, who was named "Air Transport Commander Morozovskaya." In the beginning the units under his command were III./KG 4 under *Major* Werner Klosinski, I./KG 100 under *Hptm.* Hansgeorg Bätcher, KG 27 under *Oberstleutnant* von Beust, and KG 55, his own *Geschwader*. Known to every Eastern Front airman simply as Moro, Morozovskaya was situated in the midst of the steppe. In those November days rainstorms and low cloud raced over the steppe. The ground became softened and there were no runways.

The wet weather soon turned to snow flurries and falling temperatures, however. It was a miracle that the black men were able to keep the He 111s serviceable at all. Loaded down with ammunition, food and fuel containers, the He 111s struggled into the air on their flights to Stalingrad.

None of those who lived through it will ever forget Christmas Eve 1942. All orders were received by radio. Russian tanks were at the gates of the airfield. *Oberst* Kühl received orders for a combat mission, supply flights were out of the question. Now he was fighting for his own survival against the Russian forces.

He succeeded in holding on until 2 January 1943, but was then forced to evacuate the airfield. In bad weather, total qbi, the aircraft took off from Moro for Novocherkassk on the Don. The new base was 350 kilometers from Stalingrad and 50 kilometers from Rostov.

At the same time the airfield at Tatsinskaya, occupied by Ju 52 units, was under tank and artillery fire. The first Soviet tanks were already rolling through the town. At the last second, at the urging of his chief-of-staff *Oberstleutnant* Lothar von Heinemann, *General* Pflugbeil ordered the aircraft to also take off for Novocherkassk. Under enemy fire and low cloud, the aircraft took off "in two rows, one after the other, into fog that made a mockery of controlled flight operations … a feat of flying!" There were collisions and crashes, but of 180 aircraft 124 Ju 52s and Ju 86s were saved.

On 12 January 1943, during the final phase of the merciless battle for Stalingrad, the *II. Gruppe* of KG 53 was sent east to take part in the Stalingrad airlift after resting and reequipping in Greifswald. Here Gilbert Geisendorfer resumes his account of operations by the *II. Gruppe* and his own crew during the Stalingrad airlift and subsequent operations in the southern sector until March 1943:

"After a short Christmas leave we returned to Greifswald, where we soon noticed that there was something special in the air. We soon got our answer, when *Oberstleutnant* Schultz, the *Kommandeur*, advised us that we had been given an important job and would be returning to the front in the coming days.

On 12 January 1943 my crew and I took the night express train to Insterburg, took charge of a combat-ready He 111 and took off for Cracow. The *Gruppe* assembled there and listened as a mission order from *Reichsmarschall* Göring was read aloud. Now we knew – Stalingrad had been declared a fortress and was to be supplied from the air until the siege ring could be broken.

The order stated in part: 'You, my transport flyers, have proven yourselves on every front, and I know that you will also do your duty here. Stalingrad must be supplied until relief from outside comes. The *Führer* has prepared the highest decorations for you.'

But what did the airlift look like: every unit that could be spared, whether battered like us or fully operational, was assembled in the Kirovograd-Stalino-Voroshilov area. Our base was Voroshilovgrad, a well-equipped airfield with concrete runways and large apartment blocks for billets. As airmen we found them modest – small rooms for four to five men, straw mattresses with blankets, a small pot-bellied stove. Outside temperatures minus 20 degrees Celsius. We slept in our uniforms or simply kept on our warm flight suits.

In these extreme conditions, keeping the aircraft serviceable and repairing damaged machines was a big problem. Our technical personnel were on their way by train with the airfield operating company and all their equipment, and would be arriving in about ten days. The local facilities were overtaxed. And so, on average, we had only two or three serviceable aircraft per day and two to three days off between missions, a break we could well use given the physical and psychological stresses we faced. The same experienced crews did most of the flying, nevertheless losses were high on a percentage basis. We lost five crews in the first ten days of operations. We did our best, but our resources were simply inadequate.

On 16 January 1943, with the situation became increasingly critical and threatening, *Feldmarschall* Milch arrived in Taganrog with special powers given him by Hitler to reorganize the airlift.

Court officers were employed to interrogate every crew after it had flown a mission to Stalingrad. The minutes were sent to Milch's headquarters. It was embarrassing for us airmen, as if we had not completely done our duty.

My first flight into the Stalingrad pocket took place on 15 January 1943. The day before, the crew of *Uffz.* Dürenbach with *Lt.* Dragesitz as observer had failed to return. The flight to Pitomnik airfield in the pocket and back required us to fly more than 300 km over enemy territory. German fighters accompanied us for a short distance, but then we were on our own. Below us was a vast white wintry landscape, the Don Bend, and beyond it the smoking rubble of the city of Stalingrad. The flight was relatively uneventful until we approached the siege ring at a height of about 4000 meters. There we encountered heavy anti-aircraft fire. The airfield was clearly visible. We descended in a steep spiral and despite the many fresh bomb craters we made a good landing.

Military police marshaled us to a parking spot, where there were already several other aircraft. Our cargo was unloaded and a number of wounded were put aboard. It was an orderly scene, but as we later discovered this changed from hour to hour.

We joined the queue, but when we shut down the engines and climbed out, we were struck by the entire weight of this murderous struggle. The din of battle surrounded us. There were frequent explosions, fires here and there. Russian artillery was bombarding the airfield, and exploding shells tossed clumps of black earth and the white snow cover into the air and made the frozen ground tremble. Work parties scurried about, quickly filling shell holes. Wrecked aircraft lay about and among them fallen soldiers, including airmen in their one-piece flight suits, frozen like wax figures in the snow and ice. The air was filled with the droning of aircraft, whether friend or foe it was impossible to say. In any case our fighters and Stukas tried to clear the airspace around the airfield.

Our wounded soldiers waiting to be evacuated made a distressing picture. Their faces were haggard and expressionless. Yet others with flickering eyes, desperate, but with a spark of hope on account of the aircraft that had just landed. They had temporary dressings on their wounds, and pus and blood seeped through the bandages. In their inadequate uniforms they shivered in the icy cold. Others, with no boots, moved about on their knees, their feet wrapped in rags. At the edge of the airfield we saw a dressing station, from where the seriously wounded were taken straight to the aircraft.

At first this inferno seemed so unreal to us, like a play in which we were only peripheral players. Perhaps that's how it was for us airmen, for, provided we got back, we could always flee this hell.

Meanwhile our aircraft had been unloaded and fifteen wounded had been put aboard. After some fuel had been siphoned from our tanks we were ready to go. We only retained enough fuel for the return flight. With our cargo of wounded we couldn't bring ourselves to put on our parachutes. If we were hit we wouldn't stand a chance either.

We had just started the engines when we again heard crashes and explosions around us. We couldn't tell of it was bombs or shells, and after we had survived intact it was time to get out of there. Flying with me in the *Kette* was *Lt.* Klunker and his crew, who failed to return two days later. *Uffz.* Meier and his crew did not return from this mission.

On the evening of the same day (15 January), I took off again for the pocket, destination Pitomnik. It was already dark when I began my approach to land. But the airfield had become a battle zone. The Russians were dropping pyrotechnic bombs which, though they revealed every detail on the ground, also made us an easy target for the enemy's light flak. Bombs dropped, shells fell, there were fires everywhere. After an hour we gave up our attempt to land. By the morning of the next day (16 January) Pitomnik airfield was in Russian hands. The enemy seized the radio beacon and the airfield lighting and set up a decoy installation. In the days that followed they fooled several aircraft into landing at Pitomnik.

That's what must have happened to *Lt.* Klunker and his crew. A radio transmission was heard: 'After landing, taxi back to the landing cross.'

On the night of 18 January, the crew of *Uffz.* Staib, with observer *Uffz.* Probst, also landed at Pitomnik but realized their mistake and immediately took off again.

At 14:00 on that 18th of January I also took off again for a third flight into the pocket. The weather was extremely bad. My crew and the crew of *Lt.* Lucherig were actually supposed to take off in the morning, but on account of the bad weather our *Kommandeur, Oberstleutnant* Schulz, left it up to us to decide whether to take off.

A motorcyclist with sidecar brought my friend Lucherig and me from our billet to the airfield. There we found low cloud and a snowstorm that almost blew us off our feet. We could surely take off, but how to land again? We declined the responsibility.

In the afternoon the meteorologists reported good weather in the pocket and so we were ordered to take off. We departed at half-hour intervals. First *Lt.* Lucherig, then me, then *Uffz.* Staib. We were supposed to land at Gumrak, just twelve kilometers from Pitomnik airfield, now in Russian hands. It was already dark by the time we reached the pocket. We had flown in cloud until we reached the area of the encircling front, where we encountered clear conditions. At first we oriented ourselves using the Volga and the city of Stalingrad and requested a bearing from Gumrak, which we promptly received. We flew on the stated heading and descended to 500 meters. Lights came on, revealing a large airfield. That couldn't be Gumrak! A comparison with the map made us more suspicious, as the railroad track next to Gumrak wasn't there. We now knew for sure that it was Pitomnik, and from there we found our way to Gumrak. We received a call from the Pitomnik DF station asking why we weren't landing.

We flew quite low, and despite the darkness had no difficulty making out the airfield. There were countless black shell holes in the vast field of white. We fired our recognition flares, they answered from the ground and turned on two lights. As we flew over at 200 meters we saw wrecked aircraft and because of the uncertain conditions decided not to risk a landing. We dropped our supply containers by parachute.

We still had a long flight home ahead of us. To the west the weather grew increasingly worse, the clouds sank ever lower, and as we didn't like flying at low level at night, we had to switch to instrument flight. We first tried to acquire ground contact in order to orientate ourselves visually, but all we could see were dark shadows flitting past, and as hard as my observer *Fw.* Schmauz and I tried to pierce the darkness, we were unable to make out any prominent features.

There was supposed to be a light beacon near the airfield, but only darkness surrounded us. The radio operator tried to get a bearing from Voroshilovgrad but all that could be heard on the frequency was hissing, cracking and squeaking, which was not unexpected on account of the atmospheric interference.

We had already passed Voroshilovgrad and were navigating by dead reckoning towards Stalino, which was further west and, as an air traffic control center, had a more powerful DF station. But we were unable to establish contact with it either.

And so we headed northwest – in the direction of Kharkov – and requested a bearing from Kharkov-North. We transmitted PAN-QDM, which meant we were declaring an emergency and urgently needed a bearing. The situation was slowly becoming critical and our low fuel warning lights came on, indicating enough fuel remaining for just twenty minutes flying time. Then the Kharkov DF station checked in. They gave us a bearing but advised that the weather was below landing limits – then radio contact was lost.

We now had to decide whether to bale out or make an emergency landing.

I cautiously descended, broke into the clear at about 100 meters and saw a city below. We fired flares, but nothing moved. I began circling the city and inwardly began making preparations for a forced landing in the vicinity. My radio operator Dürnagel continued his efforts to obtain a bearing. Suddenly he received an answer and a heading to fly. This was a relief at first, but we didn't know how far away we were or if we would still reach the airfield.

Then, suddenly, airfield lights came on below us, there was a flare path. We took no more risks and landed across the flare path on our approach heading, literally on our last drops of fuel. Only when our feet were on the ground were we really relieved.

The tower controllers told us that it had only been chance that they were testing the airfield lighting. We had landed at Kharkov-Rogan, We had been talking to Kharkov-North, whose DF operator had telephoned to enquire about an aircraft with which he had lost radio contact.

Lt. Lucherig and his crew failed to return from this mission. *Uffz.* Staib and his crew landed at Kharkov-North. With somewhat better luck they had flown straight to the airfield and thus saved half an hour flying time.

On 20 January my crew and I took off on another supply mission with the destination of Gumrak. It was a daylight mission. A low cloudbank favored our plan, in that it enabled us to evade the enemy defenses at first. We flew above the clouds and tried to obtain a bearing, but without success.

And so in the area of the pocket, based on our dead-reckoning estimate, we descended through the cloud. We established ground contact at 800 meters but could not locate any prominent orientation features. There was no ground fire, therefore we must have overshot our target. Then Russian fighters appeared in front of us, forcing us to duck back into cloud again before we could orientate ourselves.

We made another attempt, but no sooner had we emerged from cloud at 500 meters than we were greeted by light anti-aircraft fire. Tracer whizzed past us from all sides, so we were forced to begin the cat and mouse game all over again. Our third attempt was successful. We were right over the pocket and could see the city of Stalingrad with its smoking rubble and ruins. We located the rail line to Gumrak, followed it to the airfield and landed.

The airfield looked rather small, there was just one east-west runway, and the many aircraft wrecks limited its width to about 80 meters.

Apart from us there were no other supply aircraft there. They waved us in and immediately began the unloading and draining of fuel. Wounded were brought out and put aboard the aircraft under the watchful eye of military police. Everything had to be done quickly. I urged them to hurry as the Russian artillery had begun using us for target practice.

The bursting shells came ever closer, crashing and banging surrounded us. We were already sitting in the aircraft with the engines running, when a shell exploded nearby, shaking the machine. The explosion even drowned out the engine noise. I applied power, taxied for takeoff and turned into the wind. Then I heard the voice of my radio operator Dürnagel over the intercom. '*Herr Leutnant*, don't take off, the fuselage is bent!' he shouted excitedly. I looked back and saw that the aft fuselage had been badly damaged, probably by the last impacting shell. The effects were only visible when we turned, and luckily the radio operator had noticed it from his vantage point.

I taxied the machine off the runway and the wounded were unloaded again. Many had lost the concept of time and asked where we had landed.

When the realized what was happening they looked at me with a desperate look and several began to sob. They had felt as if they had been saved, and now there was this hopelessness and horror surrounded them again. We went with them into an earth bunker near the takeoff and landing cross. We passed around our emergency rations and cigarettes. They became quiet and stared apathetically. Only the badly wounded groaned. The semi-darkness made the situation even more depressing and nightmarish. As airmen, we too felt the menace of the power of fate, which now also included us in this hopelessness.

The Russian artillery fired without letup. When the shells landed nearby the ground shook, one could sense the taste and smell of earth. I couldn't take being confined any longer and had to go outside for a look around.

The clouds were still low, and a sharp, cold wind swept over the airfield. Then an aircraft, a He 111, emerged from the clouds, looking for the airfield. I ran to my aircraft and got the flare pistol with the recognition signal and fired the flare into the sky. The aircraft approached the airfield again but Russian fighters appeared and attacked.

Suddenly several supply containers appeared, hanging beneath parachutes. Our aircraft disappeared into the clouds.

After a long wait we again heard the drone of aircraft engines, another He 111. It landed. My crew was fetched from the bunker and, together with those wounded who could walk, we made our way across the open to the aircraft. Other wounded were already waiting there. A fight for spaces began. There was no sign of the military police. We made contact with the crew, climbed over the wing into the cockpit. I was the last to enter, after having tried to make the desperate soldiers see reason. Men were clinging to the undercarriage and the tail surfaces. The hatch in the ventral bath couldn't be closed because men were also holding on there. Some were pulled out by the legs while we were still taxiing.

The takeoff and subsequent landing in Voroshilovgrad were successful. One day later the landing field in Gumrak was in Russian hands and there was nowhere for our aircraft to land inside the Stalingrad pocket. The tragic fate of our encircled men began to fulfill itself in tragic fashion.

On 21 January we had to move back to Konstantinovka, because the Russians were already nearing Voroshilovgrad. From there we continued flying missions with supply bombs, which we dropped on marked places in metropolitan Stalingrad. During one such mission my *Staffelkapitän Hptm.* Klein and his crew crashed after a night takeoff. Their blind flying equipment had iced up.

The observer, *Uffz.* Leitmannstätter, was the only survivor. He baled out from 150 meters and escaped with a broken leg. The others were buried with military honors one day later.

I flew another night mission into the pocket on 27-28 January 1943. The only fighting was in the urban area, which extended along the Volga from north to south like a long tube. On 25 January the Soviets had succeeded in splitting the city into two halves.

All of my missions were to the northern pocket. Signal fires had been laid out in a large square there, and we dropped our supply bombs between them from an altitude of 200 meters. Then we had to drop ten sacks filled with bread and other food from the ventral bath. This required several passes at a height of 30 to 50 meters.

We witnessed an unparalleled spectacle. A sea of light in a tiny area, fires, explosions. The flash of artillery pieces, searchlights that pierced the night and tried to seize us, streams of tracer from light anti-aircraft guns, which put up barrage fire through which we had to fly on every pass. When we overflew the drop point star shells rose up, lighting up the ground and revealing every detail, even the soldiers. Everything looked so ghostly to us, like a final flashing and flaring up before a dark curtain. We could only imagine the true, harsh reality faced by the soldiers on the ground with all the immeasurable suffering, deprivation and sacrifices.

On 30 January I flew my last mission over the fortress. The weather was bad and I, as element leader, was accompanied by *Uffz.* Staib and his crew. Soon after taking off we were attacked by eight Russian fighters. The Staib crew was shot down but managed to make a forced landing in enemy territory. They made their way back on foot, returning on 4 February. I reached the pocket and after dropping my supply bombs returned safely.

On that day Paulus was promoted to *Generalfeldmarschall.* He surrendered the southern pocket on 31 January 1943. The northern pocket surrendered on 2 February 1943. Thus the tragedy came to an end. Our *Gruppe* was again entrusted with new tasks.

We didn't have much time to come to terms with this event and these experiences."

A hand drawing of the Stalingrad pocket and a map showing the airfields in the pocket provide a graphic depiction of the situation.

The *II. Gruppe* remained in the southern sector of the Eastern Front until the beginning of March 1943, and Geisendorfer continued:

"After the fall of Stalingrad our II./KG 53 was badly decimated. There were only ten crews available for further operations. Together with the crews of *Lt.* Kornblum and *Lt.* Dreher, my crew and I were among the veterans. We three crews each had logged almost 200 combat missions.

The remnants of the *Gruppe* moved to Stalino on 6 February 1943. All forces were needed to prevent a breakthrough by Russian forces near Stalingrad and establish new defense lines. It was particularly important to frustrate the Russian plan of cutting off the German front in the Caucasus and keep open an avenue of retreat for our forces.

The Russians attacked on a broad front, striking all of our forces between Voronezh and the Caucasus. In January 1943 Russian units began attacking along the Don, advancing to the mouth of the Donets and farther down the Lower Don towards Rostov. Our missions were varied. We bombed troop concentrations in the Russian front line, tank concentrations, supply centers, railway stations, traffic junctions and port facilities on the Black Sea.

In bad weather we flew individual sorties, so-called armed reconnaissance, which included train-busting missions in certain sectors of the front. These were very dangerous, for they included strafing attacks against Russian troops in our heavy machines, which exposed us to heavy ground fire. On such missions our Plexiglas noses were often pierced by rifle bullets.

We were very flexible in our attack strategy. Between 7 and 15 February 1943, for example, we flew from Stalino, attacking troop concentrations, traffic junctions and railway stations to the north. A raid against a fuel dump in Krasnodar on the Kuban River was particularly impressive.

From 15 to 24 February 1943 we operated from the Dnepropetrovsk airfield. The main German railway center for the east and much industry were located there.

A no-fly zone had been extended around the city. We had to use specified approach corridors. Outside these corridors our flak engaged every aircraft, but in the event of navigation errors we could identify ourselves by firing the recognition signal. This was the undoing of one of our replacement crews. They were already overdue from a night mission, and we stood on the airfield and waited. After an hour an aircraft appeared. It was immediately caught by the searchlight and was about 3000 meters high. We waited nervously, but at first nothing happened, no recognition signal. Then the anti-aircraft guns opened fire and after a few salvoes a hit. The machine went down like a blazing torch. It was our crew.

We took off from Dnepropetrovsk to attack Poltava and villages with troop and tank concentrations in the Pavlograd-Novomoskovsk-Petropavlovka area to the east. After a mission into the Pavlograd-

Novomoskovsk area, as was our habit we had the radio operator tune in the military radio station, which played music. By chance it was broadcasting Goebbel's famous speech about total war from the Berlin Sports Palace. It was 18 February 1943. And any of our combat airmen who had failed to realize how serious the situation now was after Stalingrad was instructed in the facts by this speech, which was delivered with all the tricks of dialectics and rhetoric.

From 24 February until 8 March 1943 we flew missions from the Kirovograd airfield into the Kharkov area in support of our army units.

The Russian offensive was finally halted in this area and our army units launched a counter-offensive with the support of SS panzer units. On 8 March 1943 we moved to Dnepropetrovsk again.

We had succeeded in retaking Kharkov and holding the newly-established defense front.

On 3 March 1943 we moved back to *Luftflotte 1* in Pskov.

All of these missions after the fall of Stalingrad were tough. The Russian air defenses were powerful and dangerous, not just at strategically important locations but also in their front lines and offensive formations.

Between 7 February and 18 March 1943 we lost the crews of *Fw.* Beguhn, *Uffz.* Laun, *Uffz.* Komm and *Oblt.* Fink.

Personally, I was lucky again. Twice I had an engine shot out and twice I came home with a holed fuel tank, and both times I landed safely. A particularly noteworthy incident from that period is the adventure of *Lt.* Dreher and his crew.

During a mission in the area south of Rostov their aircraft was badly shot up by light anti-aircraft fire and the crew was forced to bale out. They must have done so very quickly, for the crew remained together and came down in enemy territory near a collective farm. They hid behind a shed. When a Russian soldier rode up on a horse, they greeted him with accurate pistol fire and fled into a nearby wood. The crew was aided by the onset of darkness. After walking for days in the cold and snow, they made it to our lines on the Don and returned to the *Gruppe* eight days after being shot down."

h) The Situation after the Fall of Stalingrad

The Battle of Stalingrad had been lost. The German front there collapsed on a width of 350 kilometers. Skillful maneuvers by Manstein halted the enemy and at the beginning of 1943 Hitler was already planning another attack. There was no hiding the worst defeat suffered by Germany in her history, however. Three of her allies had been sucked into the catastrophe. When, on 13 May 1943, approximately 250,000 German and Italian troops also surrendered in Tunisia, Rumania's head of government approached Mussolini with the idea of initiating negotiations with the Allies by the small Tripartite Pact nations. Italy, Finland, Hungary and Rumania had sacrificed entire armies in the struggle against the Soviets. These states now either collapsed or got out. Their efforts were complicated by the demand for unconditional surrender made by Churchill and Roosevelt in Casablanca, but events superseded them. Hitler, who had planned to bring down the Soviet Union before an invasion in the west, tried to fill the gaps through the mass conscription of former Red Army soldiers and other segments of the European population. By the time two Russian volunteer divisions were formed under former Soviet General Andrey Andreyevich Vlasov in autumn 1944, there were already 600,000 Russian and Ukrainian auxiliaries serving in the *Wehrmacht*. It was all for naught. The German Army suffered a heavy defeat in its last major offensive in the east at Kursk.

The *Luftwaffe* was seriously overtaxed from the spring of 1943. It was under constant pressure in Russia as well as in the west and the Mediterranean. The *Luftwaffe* had been conceived for lightning campaigns, but now the situation had changed radically. It faced a long campaign for which it was in no way prepared, in particular on account of the collapse of the training program and its shortage of modern equipment. We began to fall behind the enemy, not just numerically but qualitatively as well.

Strength at the beginning of 1943:

Eastern Front	1,530 aircraft
Western Front and home defense	1,445 aircraft
Mediterranean	855 aircraft

Generalfeldmarschall Milch, who was responsible for the production of aircraft, had made progress since taking over the position in 1941, but the numbers problem remained. Proven but aging types like the Bf 109, Bf 110, Ju 87, Ju 88 and He 111 still made up the bulk of production.

The loss of Africa was a serious setback for the Axis powers, but the decisive battle had to come in Russia. Hitler's first move was to order an offensive with a double pincer movement in the center of the front in the critical area around the city of Kursk, the objective being to pinch off the Russian salient there.

This operation also had prestige reasons for Hitler. It was to give the army the chance to regain the self-confidence it had lost in Stalingrad. It was dubbed "Operation Citadel."

In an order of the day issued to the troops on 15 April 1943, Hitler declared:

"This attack is of decisive importance. It must be carried out quickly and with complete success. It must give us the initiative for this spring and summer. All preparations must therefore be made with the utmost care and energy. The best troops, the best weapons, the best unit commanders and largest quantities of ammunition must therefore be committed on the front of the main assault. Every troop commander and every soldier must be convinced of the decisive importance of this attack. Victory at Kursk will send a message to the world!"

The German Army's commanders concentrated an army group with 900,000 men, 10,000 guns and 2,700 tanks in a 180-kilometer width of front. Göring assembled 1,800 combat aircraft. *General* Otto Deßloch's *Luftflotte 4* with 1,100 combat aircraft would support the southern attack force, while *Generalmajor* Paul Deichmann, commander of the *1. Fliegerdivision*, had 700 combat aircraft with which to support the northern attack force.

Of course the Russians were not kept in the dark about this concentration of forces. They massed units that were at least as strong or stronger on the same front. The stage was set for the biggest clash of armored forces in the Second World War. This time the Russians could not expect any help from Generals 'Mud' and 'Winter'. The Battle of Kursk began on the morning of 5 July 1943. From the beginning the *Luftwaffe* made a maximum effort. In tactics proven in many battles, close-support bomber units operated over the battlefield, directly supporting the armored spearheads.

Despite the most powerful air support, however, the German armored spearheads gained little ground and suffered heavy casualties at the hands of Russian 'Stalin Organs'. The Russian air force was also far from eliminated. Stronger than ever before, in many cases it was able to attack troop concentrations and targets in the German rear. The German pincers became bogged down and the Soviets launched a counter-offensive. In the central sector the front had taken on the shape of a large 'S', with the German salient to the east near Orel and the Russian salient to the west at Kursk. On 11 July powerful Russian armored forces struck at Orel and gained ground. *Luftflotte 6* intervened massively at Orel in the hope of yet stopping the Russians. The latter were screened by dense forests, however, where German aircraft could not reach them. But then the Soviet armor reached open country and quickly gained ground to the west. With few German troops standing in their way, the only hope was German bombers and close-support aircraft. In a battle that lasted all day, waves of aircraft successfully bombed and strafed the Russians, slowing their spearheads and giving German forces time to prepare defensive positions. However this maximum effort took a toll on experienced crews, aircraft and dwindling fuel supplies. Many requests for air support could not be met.

The Russians faced no such limitations. By exerting heavy pressure on the Orel salient, they forced the German units back. By 23 July, three weeks after the start of the offensive, it was plain to see that the entire operation had been a catastrophic failure. It was to be the last major German offensive operation in the east.

At almost the same time in the Mediterranean, on 3 July 1943 the Allies began large-scale attacks on targets in Sicily in preparation for a landing, which took place one week later.

Hellmuth Günther Dahms wrote in Issue 65 of the magazine "The Third Reich": "The last major offensive in the east ("Operation Citadel") had to be called off, especially because Allied forces had set foot on Sicily and the Italian army offered little resistance." Then on 25 July 1943 the King of Italy dismissed Mussolini. At the same time his successor was directed to negotiate a ceasefire with the western powers. Hitler learned of this and had the Italian Army disarmed. The king fled and Italy became a theater of war.

Meanwhile Stalin had been constantly pressing the Allies for a second front in Western Europe. Roosevelt favored a so-called "Operation Overlord" (the Allied landing on the coast of Normandy), while Churchill preferred an advance through the Balkans into Central Europe. Roosevelt ultimately gained the upper hand, and at a meeting with Stalin in Teheran in late November 1943 it was decided that they would continue the campaign in Italy as far as Rome and then turn to 'Overlord'.

i) 1943 – The Northern Sector – "Operation Citadel" – Airlifts to Pockets in the Ukraine

At the beginning of 1943, the *Geschwaderstab*, the *I. Gruppe* and *III. Gruppe* continued operations in support of the northern front in the area of Velikiye Luki, Demyansk, Volkhov and Leningrad, anti-shipping operations on Lake Ladoga, attacks on the Volkhov bridges and attacks designed to deny supplies to the encircled city of

Leningrad. In the early summer the entire *Geschwader* was committed in support of "Operation Citadel", the battle for Kursk and Orel. At year's end it returned to operations in support of German pockets, this time in the Ukraine.

Major Pockrandt took over the *Geschwader* on 14 April 1943. In his report for the year 1943 he continued:

"In January 1943 the *II. Gruppe* was assigned to take part in the Stalingrad airlift, followed by several weeks in the southern sector. In March 1943 the *I. Gruppe* was sent to Gablingen to rest and reequip, which was absolutely necessary. It was good to be home again. Contrary to orders, our wives joined us. Who can blame us! I closed both eyes.

14 April 1943: recalled to Korovye-Selo to take over the *Geschwader*. Transfer of command by Wilke in headquarters. I was honored by the trust shown in me, but the fact itself was a complete surprise. Major changes among the *Gruppe* commanders.

Hptm. Rauer took over the *I. Gruppe.*

II. Gruppe – Schulz-Müllensiefen left, Wittmann was requested from the RLM.

III. Gruppe – Major Mönch stayed on as *Kommandeur.*

IV. Gruppe – Hptm. Grözinger in Orleans-Bricy.

Bases: I. Gruppe to Gablingen, *II. Gruppe* Pskov, then to Gablingen to be brought back up to strength, *III. Gruppe* Pskov, *IV. Gruppe* Orleans-Bricy, *Geschwaderstab* Korovye-Selo. Composition of the *Geschwaderstab*: *Kommodore* Pockrandt, adjutant *Hptm.* Thierig, *Major beim Stab Hptm.* d.R. Sattler, operations and navigation officer *Hptm.* Bake, signals officer and signals company commander *Hptm.* Siebel, technical officer *Oblt.* Pfister, meteorologist Reg.Rat. Müldner, Reg. R. a. Kr. Meinz, IV a. Mission: continued support of the army on the entire northern front, attacks on the Volkhov bridges in close formation. Bridges were damaged several times but were soon repaired. Oil tank farms Lake Ladoga, shipping on Lake Ladoga in cooperation with Siebel ferries. Attacks on railway stations in the rear area and the tank works in Gorki.

Kommandeur of the III., *Major* Mönch, shot down over Lake Ladoga-Volkhov. Successor is Allmendinger. The bright nights are making things difficult for us. Russian night-fighters.

Summer 43: Move by the *Geschwader* to the central sector of the Eastern Front. Airfields Olsufyevo, Sechinskaya, Briansk. Army support, double battle at Orel-Kursk, several missions per day, some in formation. After battle lost, transfer back to Bobruisk, Pukhovichi,

Gomel-Pribitki. Continued support for the army, especially attacks on sometimes large Russian readiness positions with more than 1,000 tubes of all calibers, especially Stalin Organs. Successes consisted mainly in hitting the assigned targets. Reports from the army acknowledging the actual results were rare. As I recall, this series of retreats ended in Brest-Litovsk and Pinsk, supply of the moving Hube Pocket, supply of the Cherkassy Pocket.

Attached to *IV. Fliegerkorps* under *General* Meister. Transfer of *Geschwaderstab* and *I. Gruppe* to Kauen, *II.* and *III. Gruppe* to Schaulen. *Gruppen* brought up to strength and trained for night raids against strategic targets. Attached to the corps in addition to us were KG 4 (pathfinder *Geschwader*), KG 27 and KG 55. An assignment that gave hope that we could be finding our way back to our true purpose. But these missions should have come much sooner. As always, the entire front in the east was now ablaze. At that time four *Geschwader* were simultaneously taken out of action, more or less for a certain time. More than once training was interrupted by transfers to airfields in the Ukraine and Bessarabia-Golta-Permovaysk to support the army."

Reference has already been made several times to errors made by the supreme command in failing to conduct massed, continuous bombing raids against the Russian railroads far in the rear.

Obviously impressed by successful attacks on armaments factories in Gorki and Yaroslavl, the Commander-in-Chief of the *Luftwaffe* once again decided to make preparations for strategic bombing operations in the east, issuing the following order on 26 November 1943: "I intend to concentrate the bulk of the bomber units in the east, bolstered by special precision-bombing units, under the command of *IV. Fliegerkorps* to conduct a bombing campaign against the Russian armaments industry. The mission of these units will be to conduct destructive attacks against the Russian armaments industry in order to deprive the Russian masses of tanks, guns and aircraft before they reach the front, thus taking more pressure off the hard-fighting eastern army then by actions on the battlefield alone."

On 9 November 1943, however, the *Luftwaffe* staff could only make the appraisal that, seen realistically, Göring had already missed the time for this measure. The evacuation of the Russian armaments industry and action against the Russian railroads deep in the rear should have begun in the autumn of 1941 after the destruction of the Soviet air force and the reaching of the Dniepr River line. The increase in strength and ultimate numerical superiority of the Russian air force and the distancing of the major enemy armaments targets because of our retreat had changed the situation.

The *III. Gruppe* transferred to Dno in February. It was a satellite airfield of Pskov, where the *Geschwaderstab* and *I. Gruppe* were already stationed. Ernst Ebeling described the missions flown from these two airfields:

"After the Velikiye-Luki missions, the *III. Gruppe* under *Major* Mönch conducted 'road hunts' after columns and troops in the Kholm-Volkhov and Kholm-Ostashkov areas and in the area around Demyansk. Here, too, we could not avoid losses to enemy small arms and machine-gun fire.

Pskov-South, like Dno, was a well-equipped airfield by Russian standards both with respect to the billets as well as technical and other installations. The men were able to enjoy some entertainment and relaxation by occasionally visiting the service club in Pskov, although, in addition to occasional showings of films, good *Wehrmacht* entertainment groups with well-known artists also performed in Gostkino and Dno. In Pskov we also experienced the celebration of the *Geschwader*'s 30,000th combat mission. It was attended by the fighter commander *Oberst* Trautloft, highly respected by us bomber crews on account of the excellent fighter cover we received, the commanders of other neighboring units, and our air commander, *General* Rieckhoff. This, along with visits by *Generaloberst* Keller and *Generalfeldmarschall* Kesselring, were rare rays of hope for the entire *Gruppe* and also especially for the officer corps and its tight cohesion resulting from its common mission.

The defensive fighting by the army during the evacuation of the area around Demyansk and the defensive battle south of Lake Ladoga made it necessary for the *Gruppe* to carry out attacks on troop assembly areas, moving transport in the form of road and rail hunts with bombs and guns against railway stations like Toropets, Zhikharevo, Bologoye, Tikhvin, Volkhov and Shum, the Russian airfields of Yedrovo and Yam Shatilovo and once again targets in Leningrad. After *Major* Pockrandt, the *Kommandeur* of the *I. Gruppe* and former *Staffelkapitän* of our *9. Staffel*, became *Geschwaderkommodore* on 14 April, on 20 April 1943 there was a *Gruppe* parade by III./53 in which the three *Staffelkapitäne*, all with far in excess of 200 combat missions and the Honor Goblet for Distinguished Achievements in the Air War and other decorations including the German Cross in Gold, were promoted to *Hauptmann*. *Major* Mönch, who by then had become 'our *Gruppenkommandeur*', did this in an especially ceremonial manner which pleased us all.

In addition to attacks on Cape Morye, Cape Kobona and Cape Ossinovich on Lake Ladoga, in May 1943 the *Gruppe* was directed to cooperate with flak-armed Siebel ferries in night anti-shipping missions over Lake Ladoga, in order to disrupt supply traffic to and from Leningrad. The effective and well-respected Leningrad fighter pilots – allegedly a French squadron – who occasionally rammed our aircraft when they were unable to bring us down with their guns, also achieved some success in the bright northern sky there.

Major Mönch went missing on one of these missions. None of the crews saw an aerial combat or a fire on the ground. Not until 1955 did we learn from his observer, *Hauptmann* von Volxem, a reserve officer and a licensed captain, that their aircraft had been set on fire by fighters. *Major* Mönch, who did not want to be captured by the Russians, refused to bale out but gave his crew permission to do so. Only Volxem succeeded in baling out. Soon after his parachute opened he saw the aircraft crash and explode. Moving by night, he tried to reach our lines, but he was discovered by Russian soldiers in the main line of resistance. He endured many hardships in captivity until 1955. His wife and their five children lived in uncertainty until then, even surviving the Russian occupation of Halle.

While *Major* Fabian had been *Staffelkapitän* of the *8. Staffel* in 1939-40 and knew the *Gruppe* through and through, *Major* Brautkuhl went missing after a few days as *Gruppenkommandeur*. The same thing happened to *Major* Waldforst, who was known by many of the newer crews from his days as a *Staffelkapitän* in the training *Gruppe* (IV./53). And so in *Major* Mönch the *III. Gruppe* received its fourth *Gruppenkommandeur* in 1942. Like Brautkuhl and Waldforst, he had been decorated with the Iron Cross, First Class in the first year of the war. After serving on the ceasefire committee in Casablanca, he left the warmth of North Africa for the winter cold of Dno and there experienced the difficult and costly missions at Velikiye Luki.

Like *Major* Fabian, the last *Kommandeur* of III./KG 53 was also able to exercise his post for almost two years. After serving for two years at the Central Bomber School in Greifswald, where as an instructor and course director he passed on his operational experience to new crews, and his transfer to Bourges in June 1943, *Hauptmann* Allmendinger, who has been mentioned in this book several times as *Staffelkapitän* of the *1. Staffel*, became the new and last *Kommandeur* of III./KG 53. Allmendinger had been one of the first soldiers to be decorated with the German Cross in Gold.

Two special operations of six to seven hours duration took place during the first days in his new command, namely the massed bombing raids on the rubber combine in Yaroslavl (9 June 1943) and the tank and engine works in Gorki (10 June 1943). Also successful were the combined attacks by horizontal and dive-bombers in the days before and after these raids. The German bombers struck targets on the

Kobona Peninsula, in particular the oil storage tanks on Cape Morye, the Volkhov railway station and Lavansari airfield and especially the various bridges over the Volkhov, where the *Jagdgeschwader* under Trautloft once again provided effective fighter cover for us all.

In the early days of July the army again found itself in trouble, requiring the transfer of the *Gruppe* to Osulfyevo. From there operations centered on Russian troop concentrations and artillery positions around Olkhovalka, Molotshchtchi, Salovka and Staritsa. These were followed by attacks on the Sukhinichi and Ostashkov railway stations and the Yedrovo airfield.

After a year of difficult operations the *Gruppe* was again so bled dry, the aircraft park so decimated, that it had to be sent home again to rest and reequip. On 19 July 1943 it moved to Gablingen near Augsburg. Once again, crews not eligible for leave and intact aircraft were given to the other two *Gruppen*.

During the following six months three *Staffelkapitäne*, all of whom had flown 300 or more combat missions, were transferred out to other positions. Prior to this *Oberleutnant* Gobert, longtime *Gruppenadjutant*, was transferred to the *I. Gruppe* where he became a *Staffelkapitän* and then, after the awarding of the Knight's Cross, left to begin general staff training. He was replaced by *Oberleutnant* von Ehren, who came from the former *Stabsstaffel*. Gobert completed general staff training but then volunteered for service in the Defense of the Reich; he was killed in one of his first attacks on the Flying Fortresses. He was the brother of Boy Gobert, who is now a well-known actor and director.

Hauptmann Eicke left his *8. Staffel* while it was still in Pskov and was replaced by *Hauptmann* Pfister, the *Geschwaderstab*'s technical officer. Ecke didn't stay long with the *IV. Gruppe*. He volunteered for night-fighters and saw action on the He 219 and Me 262 until the end of the war. *Hauptmann* Bichowski, one of the few veterans of the Spanish Civil War still in the *Geschwader*, took over the *9. Staffel*. In January 1944 *Hauptmann* Ebeling was also transferred to the *Geschwader* as operations officer. His *7. Staffel* was taken over by *Oberleutnant* Jessen, whose marriage in Pinneberg in July 1943 was attended by a number of comrades. On his wedding night Jessen was forced to watch as Allied bombers pounded Hamburg.

But back to Gablingen. After leave and the arrival of new crews and aircraft, the *Gruppe* began a period of intensive formation flying and bombing training.

Even in the homeland we were not spared difficult experiences. During a *Gruppe* formation flight, German fighters took the opportunity to carry out mock attacks. In addition to passes from behind, above, below and the side, they also made head-on passes, a requirement for them, whizzing through our echeloned *Ketten*, making our hair stand on end. It was an unpleasant and frightening experience. And then it happened. One of the fighters collided head-on with a He 111. Apart from a cloud of smoke we saw no wreckage floating down. Tragically, the wife of the observer in that aircraft was waiting on the airfield in Gablingen. They had planned to celebrate their daughter's first birthday after he went off duty. During one of the following *Gruppe* formation flights, two aircraft collided over the airfield as the formation broke up and spun down. There were ten dead. One of the crews was *Leutnant* Lewitzki's. At about the same time the *Gruppe* lost another aircraft during a flight to the maintenance facility in Orleans to return an overhauled machine. The aircraft, flown by Knight's Cross wearer *Oberleutnant* Großendorfer, who had been transferred to the *I. Gruppe*, went down in bad weather. On board the aircraft were several NCOs of the 7. *Staffel* who were being treated to a one-day visit to France to buy gifts for their wives as a reward for their faithful service. Good intentions sometimes lead to strokes of fate.

In terms of weather, the transfer flight to Russia was cursed. Low cloud and snowstorms grounded the *Gruppe* in Deblin-Irena for several days. During the subsequent flight to our assigned airfield in Pukhovichi, not far from Minsk, *Unteroffizier* Bayer and his crew were lost in a snowstorm. While the Headquarters and the 8. and 9. *Staffel* reached the airfield on 5 December 1943, the last *Staffel* to take off had to land in Bobruisk and did not reach Pukhovichi until 8 December. The extraordinarily deep snow frequently prevented takeoffs during those weeks. But whenever a runway and several small taxiways were cleared, even if it meant that the aircrew had to pitch in, we were in the air, attacking enemy troop assembly areas in the Gorodok area and supply movements on the Vitebsk-Smolensk highway to take the pressure off the army."

Uffz. Lorenzen, observer in the Juditzki crew of the *1. Staffel*, sheds a ray of light on a mission flown on New Year's Eve 1943:

"31 December 1943 Golta, 12:00 – 14:20. We were about to begin preparations for our New Year's Eve party when we and four other crews were ordered to the command post. Mission: train hunting with a 100-meter ceiling and snow. Each crew was assigned a section of track east of Kiev. Ours was between Kiev and Nezhin. Brief preflight preparations. Takeoff 12:00, visual flight to the Dniepr at low level. Then instrument flight to a prominent navigation point in the vicinity of the target area. We descended based on our dead reckoning estimate. We had some orientation problems because of the poor visibility and crossed the rail line diagonally. Then we saw a signal from a marshal.

We were at the very eastern end of our section of track. We made a left turn and flew next to the high railway embankment. The bomb doors were open, interval preselected, cannon ready. After a few minutes a shadow appeared before us. 'Judas' (Juditzki) turned the machine over the embankment and had to climb slightly to pass several hundred meters over the train. We saw the Russians in the anti-aircraft car with their collars turned up. Then the bombs fell, eight 250-kg. We closed the bomb doors and made a turn to the right. Several seconds later we saw bright flashes on the horizon behind us, caused by our bombs exploding. We ducked into the clouds, course 210 degrees. Landing in Golta at 14:20."

This ends Lorenzen's account.

At the beginning of the year the *II. Gruppe* was still in the southern sector, but its days there were numbered. In mid-March this *Gruppe* also moved to Pskov and the entire *Geschwader* was reunited again. The then *Oberleutnant* Geisendorfer continues his account:

"After the situation in the southern sector had solidified again, and our troops had succeeded in parrying the Russian thrust from the Stalingrad area and establishing a new defensive line, our *Gruppe* was able to return to its former area of operations in the north. It was 19 March 1943.

There was a big farewell party in our mess in Dnepropetrovsk, attended by some German girls from the railroad center there.

For us young officers, such parties were not held because of a need to anesthetize ourselves or suppress memories of often disturbing experiences. As young men, we simply needed to be happy, and where better to do this than within the circle of one's friends and comrades. The spirit of comradeship, which often deepened into friendship, outweighed everything else. This comradeship and chumminess also existed within the crews, without regard to rank. In the machine we were a tight-knit team. Questions of discipline and readiness for duty resolved themselves.

After a farewell from our *General* Pflugbeil, we took off and headed north – direction Pskov, our base of operations south of Lake Peipus.

We landed after dark, and soon afterwards – even before we got to our billets – there was a Russian air raid on the airfield. A member of our airfield operating company was killed in the attack.

A few things had changed in our old combat zone while we were in the southern sector. The Russians had broken through south of Lake Ladoga and had restored links with the encircled city of Leningrad. The area around Demyansk had been abandoned in order to straighten the front.

We were reunited with the *I.* and *III. Gruppe* of our *Geschwader* and initially flew night missions against strategic targets which were heavily defended by anti-aircraft guns. Several of the selected targets were the Bologoye airfield and railway station, the Tikhvin railway station, the Volkhovstroy aluminum works, the Rybinsk dam and the Shum railway station. For a time we only attacked targets in Leningrad, factories and power plants on the Neva River.

The Russian anti-aircraft defenses were always very strong, but in the Leningrad area they were unsurpassed. It was said that there were 120 super-heavy flak batteries, with eight guns to a battery as a rule.

One time the entire *Geschwader* was committed, the aircraft taking off singly at brief intervals. Even *Oberst* Wilke, the *Geschwader* commander, was there. According to calculations by our aviation weather service, we should have reached our target at dusk, but it was still light when we arrived. The concentrated fire from the defenses was particularly impressive. Smoke clouds from bursting shells literally darkened the previously clear sky. '7/10ths cloud cover' one would say in airman's parlance.

My observer Schmauz and I looked at each other. I must have had a rather worried expression, for he said: '*Herr Leutnant*, it's better if you just look at the instruments!' What is meant well is not always the right thing, however. During later lone night sorties to Leningrad one had to keep an eye on the flak bursts. Our attack altitude varied between 6000 and 8000 meters, as high as we could go with our heavy bomb loads. Because of the intervals between the individual machines, each aircraft attracted the attention of a number of flak batteries. The attacks were supposed to last the entire night, and each crew flew two missions in succession. Once again it was an impressive spectacle. Searchlights flashed on, clusters of them trying to cone us, which they usually did, followed by exploding anti-aircraft shells whose shock waves sometimes shook the aircraft. Using every evasive trick in the book, we felt our way to the target. We navigated using a 1: 25,000 map. The many twists and turns of the Neva River were clearly depicted and a great aid in finding the target. But what to do when flak bursts came ever nearer, when suddenly a black cloud the size of the aircraft appeared just in front of the cockpit and one flew through it with the feeling that the next salvo must inevitably hit? Better then to risk another bombing run.

The bombing run itself was the critical phase. The aircraft had to be kept absolutely steady. No deviation in altitude, course or speed, exposed to the rangefinders in the flak batteries. Who is faster, we with our bombing run, or the flak until it finds the range?

How much everything depends on a good bomb aimer, and how I came to value the skill and calm of my observer Schmauz in such situations. A glance and a nod were all that was needed for us to understand each other.

But what about when one was flying over Leningrad at night and, as pilot, one was overcome by a human requirement and the pressure became ever greater and finally unbearable? To be sure we had a large bag for that purpose, which we never used because the whole procedure was too uncomfortable, indeed impossible to manage. Just think about the uniform, and over it the flight suit, plus the straps of the parachute harness.

The rest of the crew had an easier time dealing with this problem. They simply made their way to the bomb cells. This to the annoyance of the aircraft mechanics, who often wondered when there was a short circuit in the electrical system.

While we took off from Pskov night after night on our missions to Leningrad, the Russians in turn again attacked our base with bombs. Each crew alternated one day of flying with one day of rest. If one 'stayed home' it was to get some night rest.

We lived in log houses, at ground level. I always stayed in bed when there was an air raid warning. The anti-aircraft guns began firing and there were bangs as the bombs went off. Usually they didn't cause much damage. Things only got hairy once, when the blast wave blew out the entire window frame in my room.

If we returned from a combat sortie in the middle of one of these nuisance raids, we were sent to Lake Peipus to wait until recalled.

In Pskov *Oblt.* Spellig, who had come from the *IV. Gruppe*, succeeded *Hptm.* Klein (killed at Stalingrad) in the *6. Staffel*, where I was the only *Staffel* officer. It wasn't long before *Oblt.* Spellig also failed to return. It was in the early evening. I waited in our officers club with our adjutant *Oblt. Oblt.* Zabel, *Lt.* Dreher and *Lt.* Kornblum. We were all extremely depressed, as our casualties had been very heavy in recent weeks and we had lost so many comrades and friends.

We recalled difficult missions, spoke about critical situations and the inevitability and unpredictability of fate. And nevertheless we simply didn't want to believe that Spellig wasn't coming back.

The telephone exchange had instructions to inform us, in case any news was received. Then at three in the morning the phone rang. It was an infantry command post calling. The Spellig crew had turned up there after making a forced landing.

Now we thought about sleep less than ever. The tension was past and a large aluminum commissary jug of red wine ensured that we relaxed further. We finally 'crashed and burned' and we awoke the next morning in the mess with heavy heads. I returned to the *Staffel* with my flight suit and parachute just as the senior NCO was conducting morning roll call.

It was also during our time in Pskov that *Oberst* Wilcke handed the *Geschwader* over to *Oberstleutnant* Pockrandt, the commander of the *I. Gruppe*.

There was also a change in our *Gruppe*. *Oberstleutnant* Schulz was transferred home to command a flying school. He left us soon afterwards and *Hptm*. Maubach took over as acting *Kommandeur*.

By then our entire *Gruppe* was in need of a rest. On April 1943 we moved to Gablingen air base near Augsburg, where on 25 May *Major* Wittmann, the *Geschwader's* first winner of the Knight's Cross, took over the *II. Gruppe. Oblt*. Zöllner arrived from the *IV. Gruppe* and took over the *6. Staffel*.

New crews joined us and new aircraft were assigned. As the senior airmen in the *Gruppe*, *Lt*. Kornblum, *Lt*. Dreher and I received the German Cross in Gold and were promoted to *Oberleutnant*. The new crews began a period of intensive training – formation flying, formation bombing over the Ammersee with cement bombs, flights over the Alps, night flying, etc. Despite everything it was a restful period.

Then on 15 July 1943 it was time. We moved back to the front with a full fighting complement of forty-five aircraft and a similar number of crews. Our new base was Olsufyevo, a large airfield with stone barracks-like buildings, situated near Briansk in the central sector of the Eastern Front.

The front there had come to life again. On the German side "Operation Citadel" had begun with the objective of cutting off an encircling the Russian forces in the Kursk area by attacking from the south and north. To prevent this, the Russians launched their own attack from the Orel area north of Kursk. Their powerful tank and infantry forces achieved a breakthrough.

We airmen were assigned to support our infantry by attacking frontline targets, especially tank and troop concentrations. We flew two or three missions per day regardless of the weather. The Russian ground defenses were powerful and dangerous. They moved heavy flak batteries into the front lines. These were accurate and inflicted heavy losses on us in the very first days.

On 31 July we took off in close formation, led by *Major* Wittmann, to attack Staroye. The weather was good, and we approached our target at 4000 meters. The heavy flak fired like crazy and tried to drive us off, but we continued unflinchingly towards our target. My bomb aimer Schmauz had already opened the bomb doors and armed the bombs and was just giving me the final course corrections when, suddenly, there was a bang. My control column fell forward and no longer reacted. We had been hit in the tail section. The bomb aimer immediately released the bombs. The aircraft was still flying, initially staying straight and level.

Our intercom had been knocked out. I cautiously tried to reverse course and succeeded. I was able to control the rudder using the autopilot and dared not disengage it. I was able to correct height using the elevator trim.

My flight engineer came forward and said that we had a big hole in the tail, the result of a direct hit. I said: 'We'll try a landing with the aid of the trim tab.' But he shook his head no, remarking: 'There are still three 50-kg bombs in the cells. They are armed and hanging half out of the bomb cells.'

The bomb doors had been torn away and the bomb cells had probably been bent by the force of the explosion.

We were going to have to bale out. I headed for Krachev, a frontline airfield that was on our flight path. The famous *Oberst* Rudel and his Stuka *Geschwader* were based there. We wanted to bale out right over the airfield, for the area was heavily infested with partisans, who had their strongpoints in the surrounding forests.

We were still 200 meters high. The radio operator and dorsal gunner left through the aircraft's ventral hatch. But then my flight engineer Kern came forward. He smiled impishly. Our mascot, a little sailor dangling from the control column, couldn't stay behind. He was a souvenir from a party in Insterburg. I stuffed him into my flight suit.

Our bale-out maneuver was delayed as a result. Gunner Kern and observer Schmauz waved to me and disappeared through the hatch. Now it was my turn.

Fearing that the machine might begin to spin when I left the controls and went aft, I decided to climb through the sliding window above my seat and bale out over the wing.

At first the cable of my flying helmet became caught, then I stood up in the seat and swung my right leg out over the side. But the aircraft immediately put its nose down and gained speed. I was pressed against the machine, my gaze toward the tail, and could not get loose.

No feelings of fear overcame me, however. I couldn't imagine that this was the end. I even thought that I would only be thrown clear when we crashed and escape uninjured, but that was probably just wishful thinking.

The pressure from the airflow became ever greater. My groin hurt, making it difficult for me to remain in that position. I was straddling the fuselage side. I had to do something now. Instinctively I grabbed my left leg, which was still inside the machine, with my left hand and slowly lifted it. With my heel just sticking out of the cockpit, the wind caught my leg and pulled it out. I was free, whirling through the air. A feeling of peace and liberation enveloped me. My arms and legs flapped about. I kept my yes closed, waited a bit, grasped the release handle to open the parachute, and felt the auxiliary parachute fluttering out, which dragged the main chute with it.

There was suddenly a jerk in the straps, I swung and above me saw the open canopy. How wonderful! It was as if I had rediscovered the world. I enjoyed the view of the forests and fields. Finding myself drifting towards several ponds, I tried to steer my parachute and succeeded. Then the earth rushed towards me, I hit the ground, immediately stood up again and looked around.

About fifty meters in front of me was a field in which Russian women were working. They laughed. A truck appeared from a village about 300 meters away and headed towards me. Men in civilian clothes holding rifles walked towards me. Were they partisans? Then the driver, an O.T. man (*Organisation Todt*), got out. He recognized me as a German, walked over and congratulated me. It was my 254th combat mission.

We drove to the village, where an O.T. unit was stationed and was building fall-back positions. I felt awful. First the O.T. man told me that I had a head wound; the blood had already dried. A glass of schnapps did nothing to improve my condition. On the contrary, it came back up.

My aircraft had crashed in a forest nearby. Some O.T. men headed there on horseback, were shot at by partisans and returned.

I used the O.T. unit's field telephone to contact my *Gruppe*. My crew was already using the exchange and so I was able to talk to my men and we knew that we had all gotten down safely.

In the evening I was taken to an Armenian field battalion led by German officers. *Lt.* Eicke, a brother of *Oblt.* Eicke of our *Geschwader*, was there. We celebrated my fortunate rescue in the officer's mess.

Finally I was given a bed in a farmer's cottage. The Russian women were sleeping behind the stove, but their snoring didn't bother me. I was dead tired.

The next day they took me to the Briansk airfield, where one of the *Gruppe*'s liaison aircraft picked me up.

Back at my unit I learned that an aircraft had been shot down over the target during the attack and that the crew had baled out over enemy territory. Another machine had taken a flak hit in the cockpit, blowing off one of the pilot's legs. He died in the aircraft. The observer, who had a basic pilot rating, was able to land the aircraft safely. Two days later I was in action again, but I began having headaches and dizzy spells. Then I developed a fever as well, and the medical officer ordered me to rest.

Then my deployment at the front was interrupted, and my crew and I were transferred to the *IV. Gruppe*."

Mention was made of the *Kampfgeschwader 53*'s 30,000th combat mission. It was flown in May 1943 by *Lt.* Otto Engel and his crew of the *5. Staffel* and stories about it appeared in the frontline newspapers 'The Airman' and 'Airman, Radio Operator, Gunner'. While serving as a pilot, *Lt.* Engel was awarded the Knight's Cross on 28 February 1945.

Retired *Oberst* Herbert Wittmann, born in Döllnitz, Upper Franconia in 1914, was awarded the Knight's Cross as a *Hauptmann* and *Staffelkapitän* on 23 November 1943, and the Oak Leaves as *Kommandeur* of II./KG 53 on 1 February 1945. He returned to *Kampfgeschwader 53* after a year at the air force officer school in Fürstenfeldbruck and took over the *II. Gruppe*. He described this and the *II. Gruppe*'s subsequent operations in 1943:

"After a year in the homeland as chief inspector of the Fürstenfeldbruck officer school, I was back at the front. In February 43 the adjutant of KG Legion Condor 53, *Hauptmann* Thierig, visited me in Fürstenfeldbruck and asked if I was interested in a position as a *Gruppenkommandeur* in the *Geschwader*. There was no need to think it over, for me returning to my *Geschwader* was a matter of honor.

And so on 25 May 1943, I took over II./KG Legion Condor 53, succeeding *Oberstleutnant* Schulz. The handover took place in Gablingen, where the *Gruppe* was stationed while it received replacement personnel and aircraft.

On 15 July 1943 the *Gruppe* returned to the Eastern Front, to Osulfyevo near Briansk. In the very first days I quickly realized that conditions at the front had changed dramatically.

The Russian air defenses had improved considerably and the Russian fighter arm, equipped with maneuverable and well-armed aircraft types, also made our life difficult.

As far as Osulfyevo, it was a rather large airfield with permanent quarters, but within a kilometer of the airfield the countryside was controlled by the Russian partisans. The air base group had a hard time keeping the supply routes open. Almost every night Russian aircraft came to drop supplies to the partisans and to bomb our airfield as well.

German air superiority was beginning to fade and daylight missions required fighter escort. Here I would like to highlight the, in my experience, reliable fighter escort provided by the Spanish air force.

Things did not look good on the army's entire front. The big offensive in the Kursk area had achieved little success and had to be called off. Aerial reconnaissance revealed clearly that the Russian was assembling powerful forces in the central sector, especially in front of Moscow, indicating that an offensive in that area was imminent.

And so it came. At the end of August the Russian attacked both from the south, from the direction of Kursk, and the north, from Rzhev, and tried to take our army in a pincer movement.

We flew constantly in all kinds of weather, by day and night. Depending on the weather situation we flew missions individually, in flights of three or in *Staffel* strength. The reliability of the improved Lotfe 7 D bombsight came as a surprise to me. Accuracy depended on acquiring the target early, meaning the higher the approach and the better the visibility, the better the bombing.

In my experience the best bombing altitude was 5000 meters, although this was also where the Russian flak made things most difficult for us. The Russian partisans shot at us as we were taking off and landing at Osulfyevo. On one occasion partisans shot out my port engine while I was taking off and I had to make a forced landing with the bombs still on board. At first all went well. We removed the machine-gun and began heading towards a supply road, but then partisans opened fire. My radio operator was fatally wounded, but the other four of us were able to make it to a strongpoint. With the help of the strongpoint commander, we recovered our dead comrade and buried him in Osulfyevo.

The Russians succeeded in breaking through the German front north of Orel. The army withdrew accordingly on the entire front in that sector.

So on 10 September we were forced to fall back from Osulfyevo to Gomel-South and on the 24th to Bobruisk. Calls for air support came in from every sector. Depending on the target, the aircraft were loaded with high-explosive or fragmentation bombs of various calibers. As soon as mission orders were received from the *Geschwader* by telephone or telex, orders went to the technical units to arm the machines. Referring to the situation map, the *Gruppenkommandeur* discussed the operation with his pilots and observers, briefing them on the target, route and altitude to the target, payload, bomb interval and, if necessary, the alternate target. Immediately after landing each crew handed in a report on the mission. These and all other available information were passed on to the *Geschwader*.

The ground personnel worked round the clock. Mechanics, bomb technicians, armorers, radio technicians – all were constantly in action, keeping the aircraft serviceable and maintaining the *Gruppe*'s high level of readiness. From Bobruisk we attacked targets in the areas around Kiev and Zhitomir. Getting used to other sectors was difficult for the flying personnel, for every airfield has its own character.

On 24 October 1943 II./KG53 moved to Rotmistrovka in the Ukraine. Another new sector. From there we flew missions in support of the army during the evacuation of the Kuban Bridgehead. We bombed targets in the Nikolayev and Dnepropetrovsk areas and on 22 November moved to Kirovograd.

The supply missions to the Cherkassy Pocket deserve special mention. I believe that we provided significant support and help for the encircled army units and made a decisive contribution to the success of the breakout. By day and night in all sorts of weather we attacked targets and dropped supplies, mainly from low level. The *Gruppe* was in constant radio contact with the encircled army units, which played a major role in the success. The Russian light and heavy guns put up a storm of anti-aircraft fire, resulting in heavy losses, and we never heard again from any of the crews we lost.

II./KG 53 remained under *General* Richthofen's *Luftflotte 4* and received its operational orders from there. We then moved from Kirovograd to Vinnitsa and continued flying supply missions to Cherkassy. The Russians pushed our front further back and on 5 December 1943 we were forced to abandon Vinnitsa and fall back to Rauchovka.

There was a very special wartime experience there. Rauchovka was a small town located on the Bug River north of Odessa, but we were surprised to discover that the place was 'German'. Swabians and Alsatians had emigrated there about 200 years earlier and had retained their German, and even more so, their Swabian or Alsatian way of life. The *Gruppe*'s personnel were assigned private billets with the German-Ukrainian farmers, and with this our 'goulash cannon' was put out of action. What the population did for us was more than hospitality, it was a sacrifice in every respect. Teacher, minister, miller and tailor, blacksmith and farmers, like in a German village, went out of their way to make us welcome. As well there was the delicious Ukrainian wine and peach brandy. All of the meals were also prepared using plenty of sunflower oil. My *Gruppe* medical officer was less than pleased about this, for many of our men weren't able to tolerate the freshly slaughtered pork and the parties very well.

The population provided unimaginable support during our missions, in the great hope that the German troops on the Bug would stabilize the front once again. I should mention that these villages were evacuated in the spring of 1944. The inhabitants were moved to the Warthe District, where they later suffered an awful fate at the hands of the invading Russians."

j) 1944 – Retreat

During a staff conference in *Luftwaffe* headquarters in Kalinovka in July 1942, *Generaloberst* Jeschonnek, the head of the *Luftwaffe* General Staff, declared: "Every four-engined bomber the western allies build makes me happy ... we will shoot them down just like the twin-engined ones."

On the night of 31 May 1943, one-thousand Stirling and Halifax four-engined bombers attacked Cologne and set the city on fire. Enemy losses were trifling (4%). The horror reached its temporary climax in "Operation Gomorrah." Hamburg was attacked repeatedly between 24 July and 3 August 1943 and 40,000 people died in the firestorm. Even Jeschonnek was appalled by the destruction of Hamburg. Hitler ordered retribution, resulting in the operational use of the V 1, which had been developed in Peenemünde. On 17 August 1943 the Messerschmitt factories in southern Germany were bombed by the American 1st Air Division, and on the same day 229 American heavy bombers struck the ball bearing factories in Schweinfurt. The next night 579 British bombers dropped many tons of bombs on Peenemünde. The attack on Peenemünde affected Jeschonnek deeply. While his staff was waiting for him at breakfast and his secretary, *Frau* Kersten, informed her chief about a situation briefing, Jeschonnek made his decision. He put the receiver down and reached for his pistol. He ended his life at the age of 44. He left behind a note: two of his adversaries were not to attend his funeral. He wrote: "I can no longer work with the *Reichsmarschall*, long live the *Führer*!"

Two years earlier, on 17 November 1941, Ernst Udet, Minister of Air Armaments, had taken his own life as a result of quarrels with Göring, who had cast him off. *General der Jagdflieger* Werner Mölders, who in 1940 had become *Kommodore* of a *Jagdgeschwader* at the age of 27, was killed in a crash near Breslau on 22 November 1941 while on his way to the state funeral.

To understand the situation at the turn of the year 1943-44, a brief look back is necessary: in the late autumn of 1943 the Red Army had launched an offensive in the southern sector of the Eastern Front on a broad front. The Russians again took Kharkov, Taganrog fell on 29 August and on 25 September Russian armored spearheads reached the Dniepr between Zaphorozhye and Dnepropetrovsk. After heavy fighting, the Kuban bridgehead was lost. In the central sector Smolensk and Roslavl had to be abandoned under heavy Soviet pressure on 24 September 1943. Only in the north was it relatively quiet.

In October 1943 the Red Army attacked again in the south, breaking through near Melitopol on 23 October and driving the

German forces back across the Dniepr. Kiev fell on 6 November 1943. The German front was totally shattered and Russian tanks rolled west almost unhindered. A desperate German drive into the Russians' southern flank finally brought the advance to a temporary halt on 11 November.

Nevertheless the German units, often in contact with the enemy day and night, were forced to steadily fall back. Having battled a five- to eight-fold enemy superiority for years, they were exhausted. They could no longer cope with the human masses and the overwhelming materiel sent by the USA. More and more towns and sectors were lost.

During the autumn fighting in the south in 1943, German units were still beyond the Dniepr east of Nikopol, through Krivoy Rog near Cherkassy east of Brusilov, east of Radomysl and Korosten.

In the 1943 Christmas season was able to break through west of Kiev near Radomysl, and on 1 January 1944 the Russians were at the gates of Zhitomir. Far and wide there was no one who could have resisted this breakthrough. In the days that followed, the Red Army troops crossed the old Polish border. The continued to march westwards, meeting almost no resistance.

All through January 1944 the Soviets attacked on the Eastern Front, forcing the German troops to retreat.

In often confused fighting, German units and positions were overrun and encircled. Staraya Russa had to be abandoned on 18 February 1944, Kholm on 21 February and one day later Krivoy Rog fell.

In March 1944 the 1st Ukrainian Front under Marshall Zhukov and the 2nd Ukrainian Front under Marshall Konev continued their mass attacks. Uman fell on 10 March, followed shortly by Vinnitsa. The Russians crossed the Dnestr near Soroki and Mogilev on 20 March. Armored spearheads reached Czernowitz on the 21st. Ternopol, which was defended by its German garrison to the last round, fell on 15 April. The Russians took Sevastopol on 7 September 1944.

Stalin, tired of the Soviet Union having to bear the main burden of this war, increased his pressure on the western allies to take up the struggle with Germany in the west. American deliveries of war materiel to the Soviet Union had already reached the astronomical sum of $9,477,666,000 and included commodities and luxury items, food and uniforms, weapons, military equipment of all kinds and even heavy water, uranium and cobalt, everything the USA had. Roosevelt: "Stalin is working with me for a world of peace and democracy." In June 1942 Harry Hopkins, Roosevelt's intimate, waxed enthusiastic about America's Bolshevik allies: "We are determined to allow nothing to stand in the way of our sharing everything we have with you!" America even informed the Bolsheviks about their atomic research.

k) Final Operations in the East

At the turn of the year 1943-44, the *Geschwader* was attached to the *"Auffrischungsstab Ost"*, joining *Kampfgeschwader 4, 27* and *55*. There the units were brought up to strength in equipment and personnel and the crews were trained for new tasks. The training period ended at about the end of March 1944 and on 31 March 1944 the *Auffrischungsstab Ost* was renamed Headquarters, *IV. Fliegerkorps* under the command of *Generalleutnant* Rudolf Meister.

The *IV. Fliegerkorps* was supposed to conduct a strategic air war against targets in the hinterland of the central and southern sectors, however these plans did not come to fruition. The attacks flown by units of the *IV. Fliegerkorps* between the end of March and mid-August 1944 were directed exclusively against transportation targets and not the Russian armaments industry.

One major success was achieved during these operations, however, namely the destruction of an American heavy bomber unit that landed in Poltava in June 1944. Operations in the east then came to an end, due in large part to shortages of fuel and supplies.

The invasion of France, which had begun on 6 June 1944, brought an end to the grueling missions against German cities by the Allied bomber fleets. They could now concentrate on the critical area of the German war economy, the fuel production system. The synthetic fuel plants, which were spread all over Germany – in Brüx, Böhlen, Leuna, Lützendorf, Zwickau, Magdeburg, Ruhland, Zeitz and Politz – sustained heavy damage.

The Allied bomber formations now came with their own fighter escort. The effects of these day and night attacks on the German refineries were devastating. From May to September 1944 the production of fuel fell from 195,000 to just 7000 metric tons. As monthly consumption was 150,000 metric tons, the consequences were obvious to anyone who knew about it.

The flight training schools were closed. Pilots and other aircrew went to the front as infantry. The next step was the disbandment of the bomber units and a reduction in reconnaissance flights. Only home defense fighter operations could continue as before. The only aircraft not affected by the critical fuel situation were jet fighters and bombers, which used simple, low-grade fuel.

In August 1944 KG 53 moved to the Western Front, to the Verdun-Sedan area to supply encircled units in Normandy.

In August-September 1944 the crews began training in Germany in the firing of V 1 rockets from aircraft. *Oberstleutnant* Pockrandt, then the *Kommodore*, continues his account:

"On 17 April 1944 we moved to Lithuania for further training, and on 29 April we moved to the Generalgouvernement. The *Geschwaderstab* and the *I.* and *III. Gruppe* went to Radom, the *II. Gruppe* to Radzyn-Jedlanka. The same airfields, therefore, from which we had begun the great crusade. What a long road now lay behind us! The entire *Geschwader* flew night missions against important supply stations, some of which were very successful. Cooperation with the Graubner *Gruppe* of KG 4 was outstanding, and we were often able to congratulate each other. Losses were minimal despite heavy flak defenses over the targets and now and again night-fighters. Our most important mission and also greatest success was against a division of American heavy bombers on the Poltava airfield, which had landed there after attacking targets in Germany. Reconnaissance showed that about 200 aircraft had landed at a total of three airfields. Our target was Poltava, which we bombed after flying through an extended storm front. The majority of the American aircraft at Poltava were destroyed or damaged. The airfield was a sea of flame. During the return flight and refueling stop in Pinsk all of the crews were in high spirits and almost beside themselves with joy. The Ami had taken it on the chin for once. It did us good. As not all three airfields had been hit, we were supposed to repeat the operation the following night, but reconnaissance revealed that the Amis had left and so we could no longer reach them. This mission was the topic of discussion in the *Geschwader* for days afterwards.

Our attachment to the *IV. Corps* ended at the end of July 1944. We moved to East Prussia, the *Geschwaderstab* and *II. Gruppe* to Jesau, *I. Gruppe* to Heiligenbeil and *III. Gruppe* to Insterburg, Gerdauen and Seerappen. From there we carried out nuisance raids against troop concentrations, targets near the front and bridges over the Vistula."

The following description may provide an overview of the attack on the American heavy bombers that landed at Poltava and Mirgorod on 21 June 1944:

"On 21 June 1944, 114 American B-17 Flying Fortress heavy bombers, escorted by 70 P-51 Mustang long-range fighters of the USAAF, attacked the Ruhland hydrogenation plant approximately 120 kilometers south of Berlin. Instead of returning to their bases in England, they continued east to the Soviet air bases in Poltava,

Mirgorod and Piryatin, which were 2400 kilometers from their home airfields. But our air force was still functioning. It reported to the command post of the *IV. Fliegerkorps* in Brest-Litovsk: approx. 140 B-17s landed at Poltava, about 56 P-51s at Mirgorod.

The attack order from the air corps arrived at 15:00: '... the Poltava and Mirgorod airfields are to be attacked tonight.'

Kampfgeschwader 53 'Legion Condor' took off from its bases in Radom and Radzyn, KG 55 from the Deblin, Ulez and Podlodovka airfields, and KG 4 as pathfinder unit from Baranovice. KG 27 did not take part.

Next order: 'Prepare to move! New target! Load bombs at the staging airfields, SC 50 bombs with no delay, fragmentation bombs, 10% incendiaries. Bomber stream attack. Probably attack time 00:00. Target for KG 27 and KG 53 Poltava, for KG 55 Mirgorod. Distribute pathfinders accordingly, attack leaders to be designated. Aerial photos are en route.'

IV. Fliegerkorps announced target distribution and flight routes at about 16:00. KG 53 and KG 27, with II./KG 4 as pathfinders, would attack Poltava, KG 55 with III./KG 4 as pathfinders Mirgorod. 'Attack Leader Poltava' *Oberstleutnant* Pockrandt, *Kommodore* of KG 53, 'Attack Leader Mirgorod' *Oberstleutnant* Antrup, *Kommodore* of KG 55.

The attack on Poltava was scheduled to begin at 24:00 so that the participating aircraft could regain the front by 02:00. The attack on Mirgorod was scheduled ten minutes earlier. The route segment over enemy territory alone required 3½ hours flying time.

The weather forecast promised good conditions, 8-10/10 cloud at 2000 meters, breaking up, clear over the target, later a rising full moon.

A sudden heavy cloudburst so soaked KG 27's airfield that a timely loading of bombs was impossible. The *Geschwader* never got off the ground. The decision was quickly made to attack each target with one *Geschwader*. The focal point of the attack was placed in question.

Takeoffs began at 20:30: first the pathfinders from Baranovice, then KG 53 and KG 55 from the Radom-Deblin area.

Shortly after taking off, all aircraft entered cloud and soon found themselves in a heavy thunderstorm. Lightning flashed, the propeller discs lit up in a bright light, the entire outline of the wings and tail was surrounded by a glowing light, St. Elmo's fire. The air was electrically charged, which of course affected radio navigation.

The pathfinders nevertheless found their targets. At 23:43, *Leutnant* Raudenbusch of KG 4 dropped his first illumination bombs directly over Poltava airfield. The night was still pitch-black.

Raudenbusch was in fact ten minutes early, but the target marker had identified the target and did not want to lose it again.

Just two minutes later, at 23:45, *Oberstleutnant* Pockrandt, the attack leader of KG 53, the strike force, reported in by radio. His voice could be heard clearly. Then, at 23:55, five minutes before the start of the attack, the pilot gave the command 'Torchlight Procession'. Within seconds light bombs lit up the airfield bright as day. Then followed target marking and target identification, for example: 'Green bonbon marks the aiming point.' *Oberstleutnant* Pockrandt then gave the order to begin bombing. The small high-explosive and tiny 1- and 2-kg fragmentation bombs began falling on the airfield, interspersed with the explosions of heavy bombs. Stick after stick of bombs fell, as well as fresh target markers. *Major* Graubner, the lead pilot and *Kommandeur* of II./KG 4, wondered: 'How is that possible, it's just one target marker.' The mystery was explained later. When, at 00:20, the strike leader asked if there were any attack crews still over the target and received no answer, he transmitted the command 'Closing Time.'

During the return flight the *Kommandeur* of II./KG 4 was surprised to see no sign of the attack on Mirgorod.

Everything was explained later. Because of the illumination bombs dropped prematurely over Poltava, part of the other pathfinder *Gruppe* had become uncertain and flew there, assuming it was Mirgorod. When the leader of the Mirgorod strike force realized this and decided that there were not enough target illuminators left for Mirgorod, he ordered his crews to also bomb Poltava. The fact that the pathfinders assigned to Mirgorod went to Poltava because of the heavy storm may also have played a role in this decision.

The Commander-in-Chief of the *Luftwaffe* wrote a letter praising the operation. The commanding general of the *IV. Fliegerkorps* also sent a letter with the following contents:

"At about 15:00 on 21 June 1944, a North American heavy bomber unit from England landed at Soviet airfields. Although the units – KG 4, KG 53 and KG 55– which had been at rest since morning, were not alerted until about 15:00, these *Geschwader* succeeded in coming to flight readiness at short notice in masterly fashion. That night, despite difficult weather conditions, they succeeded in making their way to these targets, in some cases more than 1000 kilometers, and in exemplary cooperation with the route markers, target finders, target markers and target illuminators were able to deliver a destructive blow against the North American units.

Photo evaluation revealed:

Photo evaluation revealed:

73 Fortress II
3 Liberator III
4 Lightning
4 Douglas
13 single-engine, type unknown

at Poltava

41 Fortress II
1 Lightning
3 Douglas
2 single-engine, type unknown and
12 fuel dumps were destroyed.

An additional number of bomber aircraft, which could not be determined from aerial photos, were probably also damaged.

To the *Geschwader*, I express my gratitude and special appreciation for once again demonstrating their readiness for action and for the bravado of the crews. This applies, in particular, to the attack leaders

Oberstleutnant Pockenrandt (sic), *Kommodore* KG 53
Oberstleutnant Antrup, *Kommodore* KG 55,
and the lead pilots
Major Graubner, *Kommandeur* II./KG 4
Hptm. Luckau, St.-Kptn. 7./KG 4
Signed Meister, *Generalleutnant*."

On 26 June 1944, 71 B-17s and 55 Mustangs were able to take off for Italy (Foggia).

Because of the attack on Poltava, the United States has abandoned the idea of establishing a bomber base in Russia for shuttle missions against Germany until adequate protection by night-fighters, flak and radar is available."

Former *Hauptmann* Ernst Ebeling continues his account, describing the supply missions to pockets by the *III. Gruppe* and operations with the *IV. Fliegerkorps*:

"At the beginning of January 1944 the *Geschwaderkommodore*, *Oberstleutnant* Pockrandt, came to visit the *III. Gruppe*. On this occasion I learned of my planned transfer to the *Geschwader* as operations officer on 15 January 1944. It wasn't easy to leave the 7. *Staffel* after more than two years, but the *Staffel* was in good hands with my successor *Oberleutnant* Jessen.

At that time the *Gruppe* was not attached to the *Geschwader*. Instead it was attached to another division for night operations. In the course of approximately twelve missions, the division reported that we had achieved good results and provided effective relief. In particular we succeeded in destroying an entire tank division, including its headquarters, in the assembly area near Gorodok.

After these missions in the Vitebsk area, the *Gruppe* returned to the *Geschwader* unit. It first moved to Kovno on 25 January 1944 and on to Schaulen on 31 January. It had scarcely begun training as part of the *IV. Fliegerkorps*, then in the process of being created, when on 9 February it was transferred to Uman in the southern sector of the Eastern Front to supply the pocket near Cherkassy. There it was placed under *General* Seidemann's command. The *Gruppe* worked with the *Transportgruppe Ju 52* – *Major* Baumann, *Oberleutnant* von Ehren, *Hauptmann* Klüter – which expertly organized the planned airlift, which was always difficult in 'pocket situations'. All of the European SS volunteer units under Leon Degrelle had been encircled in the pocket. It was surely for this reason that very tough operational demands were made despite awful weather and rough terrain. The *Staffelkapitäne* and the crews did an excellent job and dropped their supply containers into the pocket from a height of 200 meters, day and night, usually under heavy anti-aircraft fire. They also bombed Russian troops to help take pressure off the encircled forces. On the critical night of 15-16 February 1944 the crews flew as many as seven sorties into the pocket despite fierce defensive fire. The *Kommandeur*'s crew of *Obfw.* Haug and Reidelshofer and the crew of *Leutnant* Rutte, in particular, distinguished themselves. *General* Seidemann praised the outstanding command of *Hptm.* Allmendinger and the brave actions of the crews in writing and saw to it that they received special allowances.

On 21 February the *Gruppe* returned to Schaulen from Uman via Proskurov, Lvov, Lublin and Bialystok. There the crews practiced long-range day and night flying for the planned concentration of bomber forces within the *IV. Fliegerkorps* and also received instruction in navigation techniques. It was hoped that by bombing armaments factories, airfields and especially railway stations in the rear, the German forces might yet be able to halt the Russian steamroller.

But on 30 March the *Gruppe* was ordered to support a new pocket near Kamenets-Podolsk. It flew via Minsk and Mashulishche, where supply containers were loaded, to Mielek. From there and Lvov followed very costly supply missions, hindered by bad weather and strong defenses, into the Kamenets-Podolsk pocket and attacks on recognized flak positions in the Soviet ring around Ternopol. Among the losses during these 12-15 missions was the crew of *Hauptmann* Pfister, which collided with a Ju 52 at night. Several members of the crew were able to bale out. *Feldwebel* Kramer, the pilot, managed to make his way back to the *Gruppe*. Sent by the *Kommandeur*, with the support of an SS patrol *Leutnant* Miedrich was able to recover the mangled body of *Hauptmann* Pfister. The deserving *Kapitän* of the 8. *Staffel*, who was revered by his men, thus received an honorable soldier's grave.

Under *Major* Allmendinger as *Kommandeur* and its new *Staffelkapitäne*, the *III. Gruppe* had once again become a tight-knit unit and, despite heavy losses, it maintained a high and universally acknowledged level of performance. The promotion of its successful *Kommandeur* was an outward sign of this recognition and was gratefully noted by the members of the *Gruppe*. *Oberleutnant* Dengg, a veteran of many years of service, took over the 8. *Staffel*. On 30 April 1944 the *Gruppe* returned to the *Geschwader* unit and from Radom successfully took part in the 'bomber stream missions' by the concentrated bomber forces in the east as part of *IV. Fliegerkorps* under *General* Meister.

From the beginning of May until the end of July, the units of the *IV. Fliegerkorps* bombed targets that had been illuminated and marked by specially trained pathfinders. The targets of these three- to five-hour night raids included the Sarny, Kiev-Derniza, Proskurov, Bakhmach, Rovno, Shepetovka, Smerinka, Fastov and Novosybykov railway stations. The bombers used mainly 250-, 500- and 1000-kg bombs.

As previously mentioned, on the night of 21-22 June the *Kommodore* of KG 53 led the attack force that bombed the Americans in Poltava, destroying more than 70 aircraft on the ground. The aircraft had taken off from England and dropped their bombs on Berlin. As they had done in the past, they were supposed to fly over Germany to Italy – where we couldn't have caught them because of bad weather – and from there over Germany again to England. After the war an American captain told the author that just a single bomber could be made flyable again some days later in Poltava. The crews returned by rail by way of Turkey.

After this outstanding success – which like all of these big raids was of course lauded in the *Wehrmacht* communiqué – the Gorodishche airfield was bombed as well as railway stations like Briansk, Unecha east of Gomel, Smolensk, Rokitno northwest of Kiev, Michalishki east of Vilna, Sarny, Novosokolniki, Molodechno, Orsha and Vilna itself.

Over the larger railway stations the units encountered concentrated flak defenses and increasingly also night-fighters, especially during repeated attacks. By 9 July it was already becoming apparent that these air attacks could not stop the Russian advance. And so costly supply flights in support of German troops encircled in Vilna and German tanks near Minsk were inserted between these proper bombing missions. The front was moving inexorably closer to Reich territory. The *Gruppe* moved to Grojek and again raided the railway stations in Rokitno, Orsha, Vilna and three times Molodechno.

After the destruction of the German synthetic oil plants, aviation fuel was becoming scarce. After the move to Jesau, in July and early August missions were flown from airfields where there was still fuel, like Insterburg, Gerdauen and Seerappen. These were largely directed at the bridge over the Niemen at Prienai and the bridges over the Vistula south of Warsaw, which were finally destroyed on the third attempt."

On 16 January 1944 the *II. Gruppe* also moved to Schaulen.

"As a farewell," recalled Herbert Wittmann, "the German village of Rauchovka gave us half a zoo of pigs, calves, sheep and chickens, some of which accompanied the airfield operating company on the train. This resulted in a considerable improvement in our rations in Schaulen. On 12 February 1944 we loved again, to Proskurov, with the special task of supplying the Ternopol Pocket. A German NCO school had been trapped there and, as I recall, it was able to break through to our lines thanks to air support. We returned to Schaulen on 20 February. Finally Schaulen was also abandoned and in May Jesau near Königsberg became our new base of operations. Retreats were depressing, and yet our operational readiness didn't suffer. Everyone tried in his way to stop the advancing Russians. With the *IV. Fliegerkorps* under *General* Meister, the entire *Geschwader* took part in big raids, mainly against railway junctions. These were probably the most impressive and also effective big missions we bomber crews experienced. As soon as the target markers had located and illuminated the target, the bombers came at brief intervals and dropped their payloads. But these very successful missions had to be suspended, at least by the *II. Gruppe*, as additional air support was demanded in the west because of the invasion."

a) *Invasion*

There were almost three million Allied soldiers, more than half of them American, were standing ready in the British Isles, with orders from Roosevelt to invade the European mainland and (logically) achieve victory over Germany in combination with the other allies.

General Eisenhower, camped in a trailer in the forest near Southwick House, was waiting for favorable meteorological conditions for a landing, like low tides and a late rising moon. The invasion was scheduled for the 6th of June 1944.

The first troop transports carrying men of the American 82nd and 101st Airborne Divisions took off. At 01:00 on 6 June they began landing on the coast by glider and parachute. In the beginning, however, those German commands not directly affected reacted absolutely passively, refusing to believe that the invasion had started.

At the headquarters of Rommel's Army Group B, the staff was in good spirits on the night of 5-6 June. *Generaloberst* Speidel, the Chief-of-Staff, had invited the author Ernst Jünger, who read to the officers from a twenty-page manuscript a plan to eliminate Hitler and bring about peace. (Rommel himself was at home in Germany.) A carefree mood also reigned in the other headquarters. Hitler was at the *Berghof*. His adjutant *Generalmajor* Schmundt woke him after Swiss, Swedish and Spanish radio reported on the Allied landing.

Then, finally, they became convinced of the seriousness of the landing. At 15:40 two panzer divisions, the *Panzer-Lehr Division* and the *Waffen-SS* Panzer Division *"Hitlerjugend"*, both elite units being held in reserve for such an eventuality, were released.

But the Allied landing was a success and steadily gained ground, especially in Normandy. The fortunes of war had decided against Germany.

Generalfeldmarschall Rommel was wounded on 17 July and *Generalfeldmarschall* von Kluge, who relieved *Generalfeldmarschall* von Rundstedt as Commander-in-Chief West, also took over Army Group B. *Generaloberst der Waffen-SS* Paul Hausser commanded the 7th Army. Against the superior strength of the Allies, every counterattack failed.

On the night of 31 July – 1 August 1944 the Americans achieved a breakthrough near Avranches, and their tanks began pouring into open country. Attacks by German armored units on 7 and 8 August were halted with heavy losses in materiel. The Americans reached Le Mans on 10 August. German troops were encircled in Brest, Lorient and St. Nazaire. St. Malo fell after bitter resistance to the end.

On 15 August the Allies landed west of Toulon, which fell on 21 August, followed shortly by Marseille.

South of Falaise powerful forces of the 7th Army and Panzer Group Eberbach fought almost without supplies, almost completely encircled. At the last minute, during the night of 21 August, they broke out of Falaise to the northeast.

In the west the Allies pushed on. There was fierce fighting near Aachen on 4 September 1944, on the 13th Allied forces penetrated the *Westwall* south of Aachen, Kornelimünster fell on the 15th and on 21 October Aachen was lost.

On 17 August 1944 KG 53 was withdrawn from the east and transferred west to take part in the defensive battle against the invasion. While this commitment lasted just several weeks, it was almost the end of the *Geschwader*. Though badly battered, KG 53 was once again able to withdraw and the crews were not employed as ground troops. A special assignment was waiting for them. *Kommodore* Pockrandt continued:

"After the successful invasion by the enemy, on 17 August 1944 we flew by night to eastern France. We flew over Brunswick, which had just been bombed and was ablaze. Our bases were Nancy, Sedan and Toul, where the *Geschwaderstab* and one *Gruppe* were stationed. Mission: supply encircled troops in Normandy, Avranches, Falaise, etc. At twilight, when the last enemy fighters had left the sky, we moved forward to Le Bourget. Our aircraft were loaded, we flew to our drop points and then back to our bases. After more than three years of operations in the east, we learned what it meant to operate in an area where the enemy had complete control of the air. There were air raid alarms all day, from morning to dusk. Thank God the enemy didn't get up too early, for during quiet hours and at night we were at least able to work on the aircraft. Because of the night-fighters, however, this too had to be carried out in darkness. The condition of the retreating troops was depressing, a fact we had never before seen up close. One had the feeling that there would be no more stopping. The rear echelon was more or less in disintegration, and it was more or less: 'Every man for himself'. Was the fighting front supposed to look like this? Heavy losses. Shortly before the withdrawal order was received, all three airfields were attacked from the air. Scarcely a machine survived in Nancy. We took off at dawn, and even though we flew low over the Eifel and the Hunsrück we suffered heavy losses to enemy fighters. [*Translator's note: The Eifel and Hunsrück are two low mountain ranges in western Germany.*] Battered and exhausted, we found ourselves at the Laachen-Speyerdorf and Nidda airfields. Our stay there lasted just a few days, then we continued on to Silesia and Brandenburg. The *Geschwaderstab* and *III. Gruppe* went to Freiwaldau, the *I. Gruppe* to Neuhardenberg near Freienwalde, and the *II. Gruppe* to Rappen. The *I. Gruppe* was disbanded. Most of the crews remained with the *Geschwader* except for those that were transferred to the Defense of the Reich. The remaining personnel were sent to every kind of unit imaginable, including the paratroopers and flak. *Major* Rauer became commander of an airbase in Holland."

Major Wittmann, *Kommandeur* of the *II. Gruppe*, described the unit's operations in greater detail:

"After the *IV. Fliegerkorps* was not committed for some days, probably because of lack of fuel, and was finally disbanded, KG 53 moved to the Metz-Verdun-Nancy area of western France. The *III. Gruppe* went to Toul to fly supply missions in support of German troops cut off in the Falaise-Argentan area. There we felt the full effect of the Allies' air superiority. Shortly after the *I. Gruppe* landed in Nancy, enemy fighters attacked, destroying almost all of its aircraft before they had taxied into the blast pens scattered about the airfield perimeter.

As it would have been senseless to employ the old and slow He 111 by day, and as the supply containers were stored in Creil and especially in Le Bourget, at dusk the crews flew there. The aircraft were loaded, after which they took off with instructions to drop the containers into a triangle marked by three fires. As there were fires everywhere, this first mission on 19 August 1944 achieved little.

Not until the following night, when a *Luftwaffe* radio team parachuted into the pocket with red and green signal beacons, could the two remaining *Gruppen* drop their supply containers at the desired place. It was spooky to see fighting going in Paris while the aircraft were being loaded at Le Bourget airport, which had already been partially destroyed, and in the area to the west of it to the German border *Wehrmacht* personnel leaving France, in some cases in panic."

In a letter to Ebeling in 1980, *General der Panzertruppen* Eberbach wrote of the dropping of fuel to the troops encircled at Falaise: "At Falaise I cleared a narrow corridor to the pocket with the II SS Panzer Corps (meaning what was left of it). Our advance was halted by a hail of bombs and artillery three kilometers short of the pocket, but fuel flown in by the *Luftwaffe* enabled about forty tanks inside the pocket to be made mobile and these fought their way towards me. Thus about 80,000 men escaped the pocket. The catastrophe was bad enough, but without the *Luftwaffe* there would have been no breakout."

b) Operations with the V 1 and Disbandment

The German leadership placed great hopes in the V 1, which had been developed in Peenemünde on the Baltic Sea, as a "revenge weapon." On the night of 12 June 1944, six months later than originally planned, the first Fi 103 (V 1) flying bomb struck London. A total of ten missiles was launched that night, of which only four reached England and just one the capital city. The bombardment grew in intensity until, by the end of the month, 120 to 190 missiles were being launched daily. The opening phase of the operation ended on 1 August 1944. By then 8,564 V 1s had been fired at London. With the capture of the firing bases by the Allies, the *Luftwaffe* began using the He 111 as a 'flying launch ramp' for the V 1.

KG 53 was given this special assignment and about 100 aircraft were used for this purpose. The V 1 was slung beneath the starboard wing of the He 111, between the engine and fuselage. In order to stand any chance against the powerful British defenses, the missions had to be flown at night, at low altitude beneath the British radar chain, and on cloudy nights. The approach was made over the sea at low altitude. At about 70 kilometers from the target, the aircraft climbed to 500 meters and then launched the flying bomb. The launch aircraft then returned to base at low level. Under these conditions the attacks were, of course, irregular. The last V 1 was launched from the air on 14 January 1945 and exploded near Hornsey.

Major Wittmann picks up the story again. About the *II. Gruppe*'s final operations he wrote:

"Babenhausen was just a stopover. At the Reppen airfield near Frankfurt on the Oder we experienced our first short break in operations since July 1943.

Awaiting the *Geschwader* was a new assignment, something never tried before. The launching ramps for the V 1 in northern France, Belgium and Holland had been lost as a result of the Allied advance, and now the V 1 was to be launched from aircraft against England.

In August the crews received practical training for the new mission in Peenemünde, and the ground personnel, plus a special unit, were instructed in servicing, mounting, fueling, etc.

II./KG 53's last great sacrifice began in October 1944.

Because of the heavy enemy air raids on all our airfields, we moved by *Staffel* to Bad Zwischenahn, with quarters in Westerstede in Ammerland, to Wittmundhaven and to Jever. The aircraft were dispersed all over these airfields, further complicating the work of our ground personnel.

We began operations against England with the V 1 in October. By Hitler's special order we were to strike the London area.

As the operations by I., II. and III./KG 53 were similar, I will not repeat myself here.

To what extent our operations were successful we did not know, but the sacrifices we made on these missions from August 1944 to January 1945 were simply catastrophic. The British had deployed anti-aircraft ships all over the North Sea and even more night-fighters. The latter pursued us until we landed, and many crews were shot down over their own airfields while on approach to land.

Compounding this was the fact that our young crews had little experience in low-level flying, especially over water. This concludes my account of the history of my II./KG 53. During the time from July 1943 until disbandment in March 1945, I was constantly at the front with my men.

Having taken this look back from memory after forty years, there must inevitably be gaps. What has stayed is and remains the comradeship and an inextinguishable memory of our dead and missing."

In the conclusion of his account, Ebeling also gives an impression of the V 1 operations and, finally, the bitter end:

"With the front drawing nearer, on 27 August the *Geschwader* was moved to the Pfalz, the *III. Gruppe* to Laachen-Speyerdorf, not without further losses to day- and night-fighters. We were quartered in private billets and received a warm welcome from the winegrowers and the rest of the population. There we learned of the decision to move our *Geschwader* to Silesia to reequip for operations with the V 1 which, after the loss of northern France, could no longer reach England. Afterwards we were to be deployed to the Baltic coast of Schleswig-Holstein and Lower Saxony for operations against the British Isles with V 1s carried beneath the fuselage.

On 6 September the *III. Gruppe* arrived in Nieder-Seyfersdorf near Grottkau in Silesia and the men were billeted with local farmers. In Oschatz the aircraft were hastily modified for the new mission and the crews were retrained in Peenemünde/Karlshagen. They dropped their first practice V 1s over the Baltic Sea. At the end of October the *III. Gruppe*'s headquarters and *8. Staffel* moved to Schleswig, the *7.* and *9. Staffel* to Eggebeck and Leck. V 1 operations against London, and once against Manchester on 24 December 44, began from there in early November 44 as well as from the airfields in Zwischenahn, Jever and Wittmund (*II. Gruppe*) and Ahlhorn and Varelbusch (*I. Gruppe*). The *Geschwaderstab* was based in Zwischenahn. After several missions by all available aircraft resulted in considerable losses, operations were restricted to moonless nights with bad weather to avoid the powerful night-fighter defenses, and a maximum of twenty-five aircraft per night due to lack of fuel.

The British night-fighters were often over our airfields when we took off, but especially during landing, and consequently maximum cooperation and concentration was demanded from every member of the crew from engine startup to shut-down after landing. We weren't supposed to fly higher than fifty meters while flying over the sea, so as to avoid detection by night-fighters and land-based radar. I am certain that, in addition to being shot down while en route to and returning from the target, some young crews in particular were lost as a result of flying into the water. This was particularly so because the V 1 was mounted off-center beneath the fuselage of the slow He 111, aft of the center of gravity, making it even slower and clumsier. Anyone who has flown for long periods at low level over water by day can judge what it means at night and in bad weather, especially while wearing a bulky cold-weather suit with life vest.

The *III. Gruppe*'s flights took it over Helgoland-Zuider Zee to the coast-out point, the Den Helder radio beacon on the island of Texel (this was used by all aircraft of the *Geschwader*) to the varying V 1 release point about seventy kilometers from London. On overflying the coast-out point, the pilot switched on a 'countdown timer' on his control column, a sort of kilometer counter that ran backwards. Its countdown number for the segment from Den Helder to the drop point was precisely calculated and set on the ground, taking into account wind strength and direction, the aircraft's climb to 500 meters prior to release, the turn onto the V 1's heading for the target, and the segment from the starting of the V 1's pitot tube (countdown timer number 10) to the launch (countdown timer number 0). There was an identical countdown timer in the V 1, whose setting was calculated and set from the launch point to the target. On reaching countdown timer number 0, the V 1 extended dive brakes and dove into the target area. If the wind information we were given was correct, the missile was supposed to be accurate to within a radius of twenty-five kilometers.

After launch the V 1 initially lost height, but then picked up speed, climbed to 1500 meters and then flew to the target at about 600 kph, provided it was not shot down by night-fighters or flak.

Depending on the base, the crews had to make a three- to five-hour flight wearing the uncomfortable sea emergency equipment (immersion suit and life vest) under the greatest tension, had to climb slowly to 500 meters off the English coast, hang in the sky brightly illuminated after launch, then peel off so as to get to low altitude as quickly as possible for the flight home. In addition to other good comrades, the *Gruppe* lost *Oberleutnant* Werner, a veteran with many years of experience, over the drop point, and *Hauptmann* Jessen, the *Staffelkapitän* of the 7. *Staffel*, shot down by an enemy night-fighter while on approach to land at Schleswig.

After the lone mission against Manchester on Christmas Eve (up there, where no German aircraft had been for a long time, the ships sailed brightly lit), there was just one more mission, the last one against London on 5 January 1945. The *Geschwader* remained at readiness. The remaining fuel was probably more urgently needed elsewhere than for operations that could no longer have any decisive impact.

What next? It was said that the *Geschwader* would be disbanded. After several officers took part in a tank-killing course, we began training for a ground role. The Fatherland's situation was becoming increasingly alarming. After the Ardennes offensive, which had begun with hopeful words but ultimately failed, no one saw a way out any more. Rumors that the western powers would join us in the fight against the east quickly lost their believability. Our side was completely ready to do it!

While *Geschwader*, with the *I.* and *II. Gruppe*, was held in waiting position, on 17 February 1945 the *II. Gruppe* moved via Wittstock to Greifswald. It was envisaged as a 'target illuminator' unit for 'piggyback missions' by *Oberst* Baumbach's operational group (Ju 88s with explosives, flown by a Bf 109 or Fw 190 mounted on top), but for reasons unknown to us it saw no action in that role.

After receiving the Knight's Cross at the end of March, while serving as *Geschwader* operations officer I visited my old *Gruppe*, with which I had flown most of my missions, in Greifswald.

Despite the serious war situation, we airmen had our usual big parties within our circle of comrades, which have received rather too little space in this account. The *III. Gruppe* had three Knight's Cross wearers in its ranks: *Hauptmann* Gobert, like me awarded the decoration after leaving the *Gruppe*, *Oberleutnant* Großendorfer and *Leutnant* Juditzki.

Before March 1945 was over, the 7. *Staffel* was transferred to Alt-Lönnewitz, from where it was used to supply the Glogau pocket and Breslau. Like the rest of the *Geschwader*, the *III. Gruppe* was disbanded in April 1945. Most of the aircrew went to southern Germany and a large part of the *Gruppe*, especially the ground personnel, was sent to Berlin to defend the Reich capital."

Kommodore Oberstleutnant Pockrandt recalled the final operations with the V 1 the period until the disbandment of the *Geschwader*:

"The remaining front-line *Gruppen* were brought up to strength by the *IV. Gruppe* and we prepared for operations with the V 1. We were attached to Training Command Graudenz in Karlshagen-Peenemünde. There all of the crews were retrained for our new role. III./KG 3 under *Major* Vetter was attached to the *Geschwader* as the new I./KG 53. This *Gruppe* was stationed at three airfields in southern Oldenburg and northern Westphalia and had been in action with the V 1 for several weeks.

At the end of September the entire *Geschwader* was moved to six other bases, from Eggebeck in the north to Bad Zwischenahn in the northwest. Thus one base for each *Staffel*. The *Geschwader* was bolstered by a larger weather section, its own wireless connection, V 1 supply and ammunition column, special V 1 airfield operating company, V 1 supply staff, inland tanker for V 1 fuel on the coastal canal near Edewecht, and 1 tanker on the Schlei near Schleswig [*Translator's note: The Schlei is a narrow inlet on the Baltic Sea in Schleswig-Holstein in northern Germany*].

Operationally the *Geschwader* was directly subordinate to *Führer* Headquarters, otherwise to the *14.* or *15. Fliegerdivision* located in the Altenkirchen/Westerwald area.

Mission: bombard London with V 1s by night and also by day in bad weather.

The first mission by all three *Gruppen* against London took place at the beginning of October. Our drop zone was off the Thames Estuary. For most of the crews this was their first combat mission over the sea at low level, and that at night. An added radio altimeter was installed in each aircraft, but experience was simply lacking in every respect. A typical operational flight looked like this: takeoff, low-level flight over land on account of enemy radar detection and long-range fighters, coast-out over the Den Helder radio beacon, course to the drop point over the sea at low altitude. This point had to be precisely calculated by the navigation officer in close cooperation with the meteorologists due to wind direction and strength and passed on to the *Gruppen*. The drop zone was a sector of approximately 30 degrees, within which variations could be made. At the previously calculated time the aircraft climbed to approximately 500 meters. Carrying the V 1, the aircraft's rate of climb was just 1½ meters per second. It then leveled off and the Walter tube (pulsating athodyd, or pulsejet) was started. At that moment each aircraft was a brightly illuminated flying bus, although for just a few seconds, then release. The fact that there was almost no air-sea rescue service over the North Sea was a great psychological burden to the crews. The first mission was completed without loss. Apparently the enemy was surprised to a certain degree by the large number of attacking aircraft. The defense consisted of anti-aircraft fire from picket boats in the Thames Estuary.

Every night thereafter, and also by day only when the weather was very bad, we attacked London. Daylight raids were only made when the meteorologists could forecast solid cloud at low altitude. These forecasts themselves were more or less a sleight of hand, for apart from us almost no one flew towards the west and weather reports were therefore scarce. I can no longer even say where they came from. But every successful launch of a V 1 depended on accurate information on wind direction and strength from the start, for correcting the drop point during flight was not possible.

The defenses in the drop area were strengthened very quickly, especially by night-fighters. The weather in November was also not exactly the best. Losses over the sea rose, and the strain on the crews became ever greater. Long-range night-fighters over our bases also caused serious problems during takeoff and landing. Word had gotten round among the enemy as to where the attacking aircraft were coming from. They hadn't selected an experienced maritime *Geschwader* for this last action. No, it had to be a *Geschwader* that hadn't flown over the sea to England since the start of the Russian campaign.

Experienced crews with hundreds of combat missions were lost. Casualties mounted. My repeated requests to my superiors – submitted along with the success reports – for permission to attack other major cities in England – we could have brought unrest and burdened the defenses in almost all of England – with reference to rising casualties, were always rejected with the terse sentence: 'Hitler demands that London and London alone be fired on.' It was exasperating. A single mission against Manchester was authorized on 24 December 1944. It was carried out and for the *Geschwader* it was a complete success in that not a single machine was lost. My hope that our concept would prevail proved false. The word from above remained London.

Our ranks continued to thin, and a growing number of aircraft were shot down by night-fighters while landing. The landing lights could only be switched on for a few seconds, giving the crews at least a brief glimpse of the runway. Despite Lichtenstein rearwards-looking radar installed in every He 111, it was difficult to escape the night-fighters during the flights to and from the drop point. Unfortunately we repeatedly heard about the fatal crashes of former KG 53ers who had been transferred to the day- or night-fighters. Then there was the overall situation, which did little to improve our spirits. Our last V 1 mission was a night raid against London on 5 January 1945. Afterwards the big rest. We remained operationally ready, but had to conduct infantry training, including the use of the *Panzerfaust*.

The disbandment of the *Geschwader* began in mid-March 1945. Aircraft were sent to every possible field in the rear, some of which were brimming with machines of every kind. The crews were disbanded and, like the technical and general personnel, were subsequently used in every possible role: flak, parachute troops, ground action at the Elbe River and even to Berlin. During this period our bases were subjected to heavy fighter-bomber attack, causing serious damage to aircraft and installations. By the beginning of April the disbandment was practically concluded with the exception of cleanup detachments at the bases, which had to concern themselves with the disarming of the V 1s. No base commander wanted to keep them, nor would they allow them to be blown up. In some places, such as Bad Zwischenahn, they were sunk in bogs. What became of the stocks held by the ammunition columns, the dumps and the tankers escapes my memory.

On 8 April 1945, after another heavy raid on Zwischenahn, *Hptm.* Kindt, the technical officer, and I took off in the twilight and developing fog for Stade, where I had been ordered to report. East of the Weser we were forced down when we lost visual orientation and landed safely in a field next to a marsh farm. We were given a very warm reception and were well fed. We may also have had a schnapps. In the morning we took off again for Stade. I reported to the division there, after which I drove via Stendal to Torgau in the sidecar of a motorcycle driven by one of our old *Geschwader* drivers. There I reported to LP chief *General* Meister. The place was already in general disarray as the Amis were at the gates. Meister assured me in all seriousness that I had been put on ice for the time being and that I would be given the first four-jet bomber *Geschwader*. It probably only existed on the drawing board. I felt light-headed and asked myself if there was anyone there who would still see clearly.

What followed isn't worth remembering. They were sad weeks until I was taken prisoner by the English in the Lübeck area, to where I had come after a true odyssey. I was overcome by loneliness. Where were all of the comrades of every rank who had been part of my daily life from 1940 until the end? Only then did I realize that I had lost my home, a community of men who belonged to me, but to whom I had belonged just as much. My firm roots with this *Geschwader* were simply too strong. I am still grateful for this today. This *Geschwader* carried out more than 40,000 combat sorties against the enemy, achieved many successes, was forced to pay a high toll in blood, and fought bravely on every front. And now it had ceased to exist. In my thoughts I was always with it and with all those who had loyally stood by my side in the years past and helped me carry out my duty. Even if some memories have faded, my time in the *Geschwader* can never be extinguished from my life.

I remember all those who gave the best that they had – their life or their health – in the fulfillment of their duty."

In conclusion, *Hauptmann* Brandt, then the *Kapitän* of the 3. *Staffel*, recalls the final days of the war. His account typifies the experiences of all those who were forced to leave the air force to fight as infantrymen at the end of the struggle:

"Now it has become fact. For the unforeseeable future we must leave our faithful birds and return to what we were at the very beginning: infantrymen! For the time being the order merely says that we are a reserve of personnel for the flak. But what lies behind these dry words already overshadows the coming events like a threatening storm.

I need only cast a glance at the situation map hung in the flight briefing room. It will be a major accomplishment if all our people reach their assigned units. Most of the pilots have been transferred to a ferry *Geschwader* in Hildesheim, but the Tommies are just 30 kilometers from the city. If we wait a few more days we will be caught in the big Schleswig-Holstein sack. When I think about the last days and weeks, then God knows one must summon all his optimism to be able to still believe. Everything has been going downhill too quickly since Easter. Two days ago the *Kommandeur* was transferred to the officer reserve.

I have now said goodbye to the second part of my brave *Staffel*. Yesterday it was the gunners, today it is the real core of the *Staffel*, the pilots. I found few words, after all what is there left to say? There is nothing more anyone can tell us, we all see our path and probable end the same way. A short time later, when the big airbase bus leaves the yard, there are tears in my eyes. Those leaving our unit, our *Staffel*, have been more than our comrades. Without exception they are men who have flown through hundreds of dangers, who have defied death hundreds of times. They are Germany's last reserve. And they are exchanging the joystick for a gun, for a machine-gun, in the firm belief that they will return to our arm, with the belief in a turn for the better in their hearts. Do you know how valuable they are, you at whose disposal this last reserve is being placed?"

Brandt remembers the infantry actions, which because of the overall situation no longer form a clear picture, before concluding his recollections with the words:

"Thoughts assail me, rush in rapid succession through my head. It is as if it has gone out in me. The fire that gave me the strength to live, to endure the recent days and months, has burned out.

What followed can be said in a few words. A quick awakening, a notification of what has happened, a final order. I disband the company to avoid anything that might lead to the loss of even one of my men. Each shall try to reach his home, his family. All of the weapons are rendered useless and thrown into a nearby brook. I can't watch anymore, turn away, and only after I report that the destruction of the weapons has been completed do I assemble my men for the last time. One last military report, one last time a soldier.

I can't say anything, simply can't find any words that can come close to expressing what I am feeling.

I will never forget a few hundred staring eyes, tears streaming down the face of *Lt.* Dietrich as we said goodbye, I will probably see it before me forever. I myself shed no tears. Where would they come from, everything in me was dead."

IV. The Croatian Staffel

Yugoslavia joined the Tripartite Pact on 25 March 1941. Soon afterwards, however, early on 27 March, a group of pro-English Serbian officers and politicians, backers of the young Serbian King Peter II, overthrew the pro-German government of Cvetkovic. King Peter II installed General Simovic as head of government. The former minister was arrested and anti-German students demonstrated, marching through Belgrade waving Yugoslavian and British flags. Hailed by Churchill, King Peter II ordered mobilization on 5 April. Then British troops landed on Crete and in Greece. Germany reacted immediately to this attempted encirclement. German troops began entering Yugoslavia.

German troops received a joyous welcome from Slovenians, Croats and the ethnic Germans, and even before the Yugoslavian army saw action it was completely splintered and in disarray. On 17 April the Yugoslavian Army surrendered unconditionally.

On 11 April 1941 the Croatian general Sladko Kvaternik had announced the founding of the independent state of Croatia under the leadership of Dr. Ante Pawelic.

The war in the east against Bolshevism alarmed the anti-communists in every country in Europe. Soon men from almost every European country were volunteering to serve in the German army, navy and air force. National combat units were formed from Norwegian, Finnish, Swedish, Estonian, Latvian, Lithuanian, Danish, Dutch, Flemish, Wallonian, Swiss, Spanish and French volunteers. Spain sent its volunteers with the "Blue Division" and they fought in German units alongside Finns, Slovaks, Croats, Rumanians and Hungarians.

Volunteer airmen from Croatia were initially used to form the *15. (kroat.) Staffel* of KG 53, which was later supplemented by a second *Staffel*. As a result of this action, the German liaison detachment was expanded into a *Gruppe* headquarters.

Retired *Oberst* Gerhard Joachim, then a *Major*, was commander of the Croatian *Fliegergruppe*. Here is a brief summary of his recollections:

"15. (kroat.) KG 53 was a bomber *Staffel* consisting of Croatian volunteer crews, including the *Staffelkapitän*, and a German liaison detachment. It saw action on the Eastern Front until November 1942. At the request of the Croatian government, in December 1942 the *Staffel* was moved from the Eastern Front to Croatia in order to combat the armed communist partisans operating there under the later Yugoslavian head of state Tito.

Following the move to Croatia, a second Croatian *Staffel* was formed and the German liaison detachment was converted into a *Gruppe* headquarters. This *Gruppe* headquarters was made up of German personnel. A Croatian liaison officer was assigned to it. Operationally this Croatian unit was subordinate to the German Air Commander Croatia. The *Gruppe* headquarters received its mission and transfer orders from there.

The unit was equipped with the Do 17. In addition to weather and reconnaissance flights it mainly conducted attacks against ground targets (partisan concentrations, supply dumps and barracks camps) in the area of Bosnia and Montenegro. Occasionally it also conducted armed reconnaissance over the Adriatic. 15. (kroat.) KG 53 also demonstrated its effectiveness in land warfare. Powerful partisan units attacked it at Agram-Gorica airfield in 1942. The attack was beaten off. The unit did, however, suffer moderate losses in personnel and parked aircraft.

Beginning in May 1944 there were increasing indications of softening among the Croatian crews. The German military command drew its conclusions and disbanded the unit in the summer of 1944. A few volunteers were transferred back to the Eastern Front with the remaining serviceable aircraft."

V. The IV. Gruppe

Many of the accounts in this book make mention of a transfer to the IV. *Gruppe*. What was this unit about?

When the *Luftwaffe* was formed, thought was obviously given to the organization for providing the operational units with replacement personnel. After specific aircrew training at the flight training, air signals, air armaments and instrument flying schools, there was specialized training at the reconnaissance, fighter and bomber schools. It was there that the crews were put together prior to assignment to frontline units. Until that time the men were under the *Chef AW* (head of training).

This solution soon proved to be less than ideal, however. In particular, crews created in this way lacked unit-specific experience. And so, beginning in 1941, the *Geschwader*, most of which had three operational *Gruppen*, added a *IV. Gruppe*. These units occupied airfields vacated by operational units, for example after the campaign in France, and thus to some extent reduced the need for occupation troops.

Crews could now be formed within the *Geschwader*, taking into account their special requirements. Men who had survived the loss of their crews were combined to form new crews. As well, individuals, such as permanent flying personnel from the schools, could now be detached to the *Geschwader*. The chronicler himself was trained as a radio operator at the marine air signals school in Dievenow and subsequently earned the advanced radio operator's certificate at Instrument Flight School 7 in Gardemon near Oslo. Then he went to the flight training schools as a member of the permanent flying personnel, where, apart from radio and navigation flights with trainee crews, radio and DF training was given to flight cadets, and flight instructors underwent regular radio and DF flight checks. At his own request, in 1943 he was transferred to an operational unit and was assigned to the *IV. Gruppe* of KG 53. After his crew was assembled he saw action on the Eastern Front as a radio operator, later taking part in V 1 operations until KG 53 was disbanded. During the final phase of the war he was transferred to KG 4 in Königsgrätz, which flew supply missions to the Breslau Pocket.

Dr. Joachim Brammer, then an *Oberleutnant*, came to the *12. Staffel* of the *IV. Gruppe* as an observer in June 1941. He went on to earn his wings, saw action and in December 1943 returned to the *IV. Gruppe* as adjutant. Here are his recollections:

"There was no *IV. Gruppe* before the war. It was a child of the war, born out of necessity.

In peacetime the flying personnel of the *Luftwaffe*'s bomber units were assigned to the *Geschwader* after their school training. In their *Staffeln* the pilots, bomb aimers, radio operators, flight engineers and gunners achieved the desired efficiency as crews in practical operations. An attempt was made to bring all of the crews to a roughly similar level of performance.

As one can imagine, providing this obviously necessary further training to new personnel placed considerable demands on the *Staffeln*. In wartime it quickly became apparent that, because of their combat missions, the crews in the *Staffeln* increasingly had neither the time nor the resources to also conduct training. Crew losses, especially during operations against England, reduced the training potential of the *Staffeln*. On the other hand the number of personnel requiring training grew as more replacements arrived to fill the gaps. As well, in addition to passing on flying experience, the units had to share the lessons learned on operations with the new arrivals. It also became apparent that, overall, the training deficit of the new flying personnel had become greater.

A new path had to be taken and this resulted in the formation of fourth *Gruppen* to serve as operational training units. As a rule these consisted of three *Staffeln* plus an airfield operating company, although KG 53 had four (*10., 11., 12.* and *13. Staffel*). Crews qualified to instruct, with operational experience, were transferred to the *IV. Gruppe* from the operational *Staffeln* to serve as instructor crews. At certain intervals these exchanged places with other instructor crews and returned to their old *Gruppen*. They trained the personnel coming from the schools into operationally capable crews. In this they were assisted by other experienced personnel returning to their units via the Quedlinburg Processing Center for the Reassignment of Aircrew after having been out of action due to wounds or other causes. After completing their training the crews were assigned to the *Geschwader*'s operational *Gruppen*.

Our *Geschwader*'s *IV. Gruppe* was formed on 21 March 1941. Its first commander was *Major* Wienholtz, who was later posted missing while serving as *Kommandeur* of the *I. Gruppe* in Russia. He was followed at the end of 1941 by *Major* Zahn. The unit's first airfield was Vembrechis, north of Roubaix, near Lille. In 1943 the *Gruppe* was moved to Bricy near Orléans. Some of the billets were almost castle-like buildings on the Lille to Roubaix road. The *Gruppenkommandeur* then was *Major* Grözinger, wearer of the Knight's Cross and former *Staffelkapitän* in the *I. Gruppe*. Because of the air situation over France, in early 1944 the *Gruppe* was transferred to Szolnok on the Theiss River in Hungary, where it remained until its disbandment. Training in the *IV. Gruppe* was comprehensive: intensive theoretical instruction, practical exercises on technical devices, bomb sights and aircraft weapons, wide-ranging use of simulators (flight trainer, DF trainer, 'Reschke carpet' for target approach and bomb dropping), bombing and firing at ground and towed targets from aircraft, day and night flying, takeoffs, landings, cross-country and formation flights."

Retired *Leutnant* Max Parr came to Flight Training School C8 in Wiener-Neustadt as a *Kapitän* and *Fl.Obernautiker*, serving as head of the navigation group. He had earned almost all every aircrew rating (navigation instructor, observer, pilot (A/B), radio operator (I) and air gunner), received his military training and been named *Feldwebel KOA*. Now he wanted to see action at the front. On 7 June 1943 he joined the *13. Staffel* of KG 53's *IV. Gruppe* in Orléans-Bricy, where he was assigned to the crew of pilot *Obfw.* Schade as observer. His logbook lists the training flights that were required prior to joining an operational unit, completed by 27 October 1943. Several of these flights may provide a clear picture:

Date	Purpose of Flight	Departure/Time	Arrival/Time	Flight Duration
9/6/43	Local familiarization	Bricy 13:26	Bricy 14:30	104 min.
9/6/43	Local familiarization	Bricy 14:34	Bricy 16:00	125 min.
4/8/43	Local familiarization	Bricy 15:22	Bricy 17:15	153 min.
5/8/43	Local familiarization	Bricy 09:57	Bricy 12:34	237 min.
5/8/43	Instrument flight	Bricy 14:15	Bricy 15:38	123 min.
6/8/43	Instrument flight	Bricy 08:40	Bricy 09:55	115 min.
9/8/43	Local familiarization	Bricy 09:24	Bricy 12:45	321 min.

And so it continued with navigation flights, low-level flying, formation flying, target approach practice, descent practice flights, night circuits, air gunnery, bomb dropping, sixty flights altogether during this period.

Those personnel not flying were assigned duties as per the duty roster, of which the following is a typical example:

10. Staffel Duty Roster for Friday, 4 April 1941

Weekly Duty Officer (??)

Duty Officer

Duty Private

07:00	Reveille	Duty officer
08:00	Breakfast	Mess hall
08:30	Muster	Senior NCO
12:00	Lunch	Mess hall
13:45	Muster	Senior NCO
18:00	Dinner	Mess hall

Technical Personnel and Gunners

08:45	Depart for airfield
09:00 – 11:30	Technical duties
13:45	Depart for airfield
14:00 – 17:00	Technical duties

Aircrew

09:30 – 11:30	Technical exercises: pilots
09:30 – 11:30	Taking bearings: bomb aimers and radio operators
14:00 – 14:50	Radio use: pilots and bomb aimers
15:00 – 16:00	Use of code charts: pilots, bomb aimers and radio operators
16:15 – 17:00	Sports: pilots, bomb aimers and radio operators

The instructor crews found plenty of scope for passing on their flying and operational experience. Many, however, especially pilots, were occasionally unable to log sufficient hours in the air, something they had found so abundantly in the operational unit. *Oblt.* Gilbert Geisendorfer, a pilot, described his time with the *IV. Gruppe*, which was then under *Major* Grözinger in Orléans and later moved to Szolnok:

"Leaving the front was difficult, as I had to take leave of my comrades and friends, who were in the midst heavy action to boot. I simply couldn't grasp the point of this transfer, but I was about to take on a new role with an instructor crew. I was assigned to flight training in the *12. Staffel*, but unfortunately I wasn't worked to capacity. Only occasionally was I personally able to take part in flying operations, be it accompanying individual crews or leading the *Staffel* formation. In this way I was able to pass my flying and operational experience on to the junior crews.

Unfortunately, however, flying experience, especially for pilots, can only be acquired in practice. Serious shortcomings in the training given by the schools often revealed themselves, and many pilots were unable to meet the standards set by the *IV. Gruppe*. This wider education often involved casualties or accidents.

I remember one pilot, a young *Leutnant* from Nuremberg, who with his crew flew into a mountain near Clermont-Ferrand while on a night cross-country. I had the sad duty of delivering his things to his parents.

Another time I was on standby in Orléans when aircraft were carrying out night cross-country flights. Just one aircraft was still airborne. Then 'Myo', the code for threat from enemy aircraft, was issued, which required all aircraft to land immediately. Soon afterwards we sighted our aircraft. It was approaching the field, but opposite to the landing direction. The pilot had misread the airfield lighting, descended into the extended centerline lights and touched down. We heard a muffled crash, nothing more.

I immediately headed for the scene in an automobile. I came upon the crew. They had been lucky. The aircraft had clipped a power pylon, which took off half the wing. Immediately afterwards the undercarriage sheared off on a railway embankment and the aircraft came down on its belly just beyond it. Nothing happened to the crew.

During a subsequent day flight, this pilot demonstrated that he completely lost his head in critical situations. After being responsible for seriously damaging another aircraft he was washed out and transferred.

The flying conditions in France became increasingly difficult at the beginning of 1944. Enemy incursions by day and night, plus attacks on airfields, made training activities, as the *IV. Gruppe* was supposed to conduct, almost impossible. The *Gruppe* was ordered to move to Szolnok.

At about noon on 5 February 1944, the day before our departure, I happened to be on the airfield when the sirens began to howl: air raid! I left the airfield by car, drove several kilometers in the direction of Orléans city and stopped on the road. Seconds later a flight of English bombers appeared. The formation flew through our anti-aircraft fire undeterred towards our airfield. I saw the bombs falling, felt the explosions. The enemy aircraft turned for home. It all lasted just a few minutes.

I drove back to the airfield and from a distance saw the destruction. At the entrance to the air base the sentry lay dead beside his sentry box. A large bomb fragment had pierced the middle of his concrete shelter. Then I came to the buildings and found them all damaged or destroyed, however there were no fires. Between the buildings were the covered shelters. But the hail of bombs had fallen over them. Some of the entrances and exits were buried. I heard desperate screaming. Soldiers were there trying to dig out the shelters, but it was a dangerous business. Again and again bombs with time-delay fuses exploded and three of our comrades were dead by the time we got to them. On the airfield itself none of our aircraft had been damaged.

We were supposed to depart the next day. I was already sitting in the aircraft when the air raid alarm was again sounded. I and several others took off, just to get away. We landed safely in Wiener-Neustadt.

We were kept there for about two weeks. Szolnok airfield had been flooded and could not be used. The rest of the *Gruppe*, which took off later, made a stop in Landsberg/Lech. I stayed in Wiener-Neustadt, continued training with the crews and waited. But Szolnok remained closed. And so I, too, was ordered to Landsberg/Lech for the time being.

There we resumed our flying activities. And once again there were casualties. A crew with a *Leutnant* from Munich as pilot crashed during a (low level) training flight in the Altmühl Valley. All aboard were killed.

Another crew inbound from France, crashed while attempting to land at Landsberg/Lech in bad weather. We were on the airfield, over which there was low cloud, and heard the sound of engines. We fired the so-called 'radishes', a pyrotechnic made of flares, as an orientation aid. But the approach was apparently not made exactly according to the instrument landing procedure. We heard the aircraft crash near the airfield.

After a funeral at the airbase the coffins of our comrades were conveyed to their home towns."

But life, and also war, often brings only sweat and tears.

During one of air raids on the Orléans airfield previously described by Geisendorfer, a building caught fire by whatever means. It was the town hall of a small town at the edge of the airfield that had been requisitioned by the airbase. In the building there were stores. The local French fire brigade sprayed and sprayed. As they worked, it became noticeable that brave men were becoming increasingly boisterous. The secret was soon revealed. In the *Gruppe*'s storerooms there was a large quantity of exquisite champagne in the usual containers. In the heat of the fire an inadequately secured cork popped now and then. This music in their ears prompted the firemen to come to the rescue and appropriate as their reward as much of the – not well-tempered – champagne as they could.

The *Gruppe*'s last base was in Szolnok, a picturesque medium-size city on the Theiss. When the *Gruppe* arrived there in February 1944 Hungary was an ally, not an occupied country.

We were surprised to discover that we could by 200 packs of Memphis cigarettes from the local tobacconists. The weekly market over flowed with the fruits of the local agriculture. Skilled cooks created some surprising dishes from these raw materials.

When Hungary was occupied on 19 March 1944, to ensure that it remained on our side, the first thing to suddenly disappear from the market was the cigarettes.

On 21 March 1944 the *IV. Gruppe* was still training at full capacity and could look back on three years in existence. The end came quickly. Just five months later, on 20 August 1944, it was disbanded. The war, personnel and material situation did not permit a continuation. The Red Army stood poised to enter Hungary.

The crews and other personnel needed by the *Geschwader* were transferred, the rest scattered to the four winds. Three days later Rumania left the alliance. The Red Army's way into Hungary was open.

VI. The Geschwader's Losses

In the Second World War, *Kampfgeschwader Legion Condor 53* lost at least 1,493 men:

approximately   146 officers

891 non-commissioned officers

456 enlisted men

The casualties listed here are those until about the end of January 1945. The list surely contains errors. Correcting these is only possible with the assistance of the reader.

Explanation of abbreviations:

Target/Country	Loss through	Position	Fate
G = Germany	C = Crash	PT = Pilot	† = Killed
E = England	EE = Enemy action	OV = Observer	M = Missing
F = France	FT = Fighters	RO = Radio operator	
R = Russia	FL = Flak	FE = Flight engineer	
P = Poland	U = not known,	GN = Gunner	
X = Weather	accident or		

Reconnaissance, bombing raid transfer flight, other

The term "crash" cannot be precisely defined, as most crashes were the result of enemy action.

Stabsstaffel

23/11/39	*Uffz.*	Bormann		F	C	†
23/11/39	*Uffz.*	Wagner		F	C	†
11/3/40	*Oblt.*	Dr. Neef		F	C	†
11/3/40	*Uffz.*	Neumann		F	C	†
11/3/40	*Uffz.*	Werner		F	C	†
11/5/40	*Oblt.*	Schmitz		F	EA	†
11/5/40	*Obfw.*	Beine		F	C	†
11/5/40	*Fw.*	Zeep		F	EA	†
11/5/40	*Uffz.*	Jeschke		F	EA	†
15/6/40	*Hfw.*	Otto Knitsch		G	C	†
15/6/40	*Fw.*	Werner Nest		G	C	†
15/6/40	*Fw.*	Josef Guttenberger		G	C	†
15/6/40	*Uffz.*	Olaf Leßmann		G	C	†
15/6/40	*Gefr.*	Gerhard Görner		G	C	†
15/9/40	*Uffz.*	Heinrich Meyer		E	C	†
15/9/40	*Fw.*	Alois Schweiger		E	C	†
15/9/40	*Fw.*	Arnold Benz		E	C	†
15/9/40	*Uffz.*	Georg Geiger		E	C	†
17/6/41	*Fw.*	Hans Abe			C	†
17/6/41	*Fw.*	Adolf Schorrmann			C	†
17/6/41	*Uffz.*	Peter Janissen			C	†
17/6/41	*Uffz.*	Fritz Schumacher			C	†
13/7/41	*Oblt.*	Franz Wilhelm Franke		R	EA	†
26/7/41	*Fw.*	Herbert Häusler		R	C	†
26/7/41	*Obgefr.*	Josef Robold		R	C	†
26/7/41	*Gefr.*	Hans-Georg Schmitz		R	C	†
26/7/41	*Gefr.*	Walter Bresart		R	C	†
26/7/41	*Gefr.*	Hans Tittel		R	C	†
2/8/41	*Lt.*	Hermann Fust		R	C	†
2/8/41	*Gefr.*	Josef Kriegerl		R	C	†
8/10/41	*Lt.*	Günter Felix		R	C	M
8/10/41	*Fw.*	Alfred Herrmann		R	C	M
8/10/41	*Uffz.*	Georg Eiersebner		R	C	M
30/1/42	*Oblt.*	Jürgen von Horn	OV & St.Kap.	R	C	M
30/1/42	*Obfw.*	Robert Mayer	PT	R	C	M
30/1/42	*Obfw.*	Hans Ott FE		R	C	M
30/1/42	*Fw.*	Kurt Flade	RO	R	C	M
30/1/42	*Uffz.*	Heinz Seidel	GN	R	C	M
28/3/42	*Oblt.*	Helmut Lorenz	PT	R	C	M
28/3/42	*Uffz.*	Fritz Pust RO		R	C	M
28/3/42	*Uffz.*	Friedrich Sefert	GN	R	C	M

28/3/42	*Gefr.*	Heinz Großmann	FE		R	C	M
28/3/42	*Uffz.*	Heinrich Ehlers	OV		R	C	M
9/12/42	*Hptm.*	Helmut Elder von	OV		R	EA	M
10/2/43	*Uffz.*	Jakob Baum			R	EA	†
10/2/43	*Uffz.*	Louis Beck			R	EA	†
10/2/43	*Uffz.*	Andreas Dinkel			R	EA	†
14/7/43	*Obfw.*	Johannes Beneken	PT		R	C	M
14/7/43	*Uffz.*	Walter Hirche	OV		R	C	M
14/7/43	*Uffz.*	Hans Günther	RO		R	C	M
14/7/43	*Obgefr.*	Anton Plodeck	GN		R	C	M
14/7/43	*Uffz.*	Herbert Mansfeld	GN		R	C	M
5/8/43	*Fw.*	Helmut Thiele	RO		R	C	†
5/8/43	*Uffz.*	Kurt Eikmeier	FE		R	C	†
5/8/43	*Hptm. d. Res.*	Fritz Sattler	GN		R	C	†
26/6/44	*Uffz.*	Paul Schlesier			R	EA	M
26/6/44	Stgefr.	Johannes Baggendorf			R	EA	M
21/8/44	*Obfw.*	Willi Rein	PT		F	C	M
21/8/44	*Obfw.*	Heinrich Prestel	OV		F	C	M
21/8/44	*Obfw.*	Georg Schmeling	RO		F	C	M
21/8/44	*Fw.*	Erich Stephan	GN		F	C	M
21/8/44	*Obfw.*	Kurt Schrang	FE		F	C	M

I. Gruppe

2/9/39	*Uffz.*	Georg Adam	RO	2.	P	FL	†
5/12/39	*Reg.Rt. Weather Service*	Wilhelm Endres	–	2.	X	C	†
9/5/40	*Fw.*	Otto Siebold	FE	3.	X	C	†
11/5/40	*Oblt.*	Max Pröbst	OV	1.	F	C	†
11/5/40	*Fw.*	Erwin Bühler	GN	3.	F	C	†
11/5/40	*Gefr.*	Erwin Plätschke	GN	2.	F	C	†
11/5/40	*Gefr.*	Heinz Ahrendt	RO	2.	F	C	†
11/5/40	*Flg.*	Karl Gilber	GN	2.	F	C	†
11/5/40	*Flg.*	Hubert Hiersemann	GN	2.	F	C	†
12/5/40	*Uffz.*	Werner Kortas	RO	2.	F	C	†
12/5/40	*Lt.*	Eduard von Satzenhofen-Fuchsberg	PT	3.	F	C	†
12/5/40	*Fw.*	Georg Stadler	FE	3.	F	C	†
12/5/40	*Gefr.*	Siegfried Holbein	RO	3.	F	C	†
14/5/40	*Oblt.*	Walter Kögl	PT	2.	F	C	†
14/5/40	*Obfw.*	Willi Schmidt	RO	2.	F	C	†
14/5/40	*Fw.*	Kurt Acker	FE	2.	F	C	†
14/5/40	*Uffz.*	Eustach Benkert	OV	2.	F	C	†

14/5/40	*Fw.*	Walter Völter	FE	2.	F	C	†
14/5/40	*Flg.*	Erhardt Rottger	GN	2.	F	C	†
20/5/40	*Uffz.*	Albert Schweighardt	RO	1.	F	C	†
20/5/40	*Fw.*	Alfred Bogdanski	PT	2.	F	C	M
20/5/40	*Gefr.*	Herbert Berner	GN	2.	F	C	M
20/5/40	*Uffz.*	Rudolf Bruckner	RO	2.	F	C	M
20/5/40	*Uffz.*	Georg Wild	FE	2.	F	C	M
20/5/40	*Flg.*	Eduard Damböck	GN	2.	F	C	M
20/5/40	*Fw.*	Herbert Querl	PT	2.	F	C	M
20/5/40	*Uffz.*	Alfons Truskowski	RO	2.	F	C	M
20/5/40	*Uffz.*	Georg Wißmeier	FE	2.	F	C	†
20/5/40	*Flg.*	Oskar Dorer	GN	2.	F	C	†
26/5/40	*Lt.*	Serge von Goertz	OV	2.	F	C	†
27/5/40	*Gefr.*	Herbert Hampel	GN	1.	F	C	†
27/5/40	*Oblt.*	Hans Niklas	OV	1.	F	C	†
27/5/40	*Gefr.*	Ernst Tscherne	GN	1.	F	C	†
15/6/40	*Hptm.*	Bernhard Schwarz St.Kpt.		3.	F	C	†
15/6/40	*Lt.*	Karl Schoeppler	OV	3.	F	C	†
15/6/40	*Obfw.*	Fritz Weidenhammer	RO	3.	F	C	†
15/6/40	*Fw.*	Albert Burger	PT	3.	F	C	†
15/6/40	*Uffz.*	Kurt Berninger	FE	3.	F	C	†
15/6/40	*Uffz.*	Karl Berrang	RO	3.	F	C	†
15/6/40	*Uffz.*	Otto Haas	FE	3.	F	C	†
9/7/40	*Oblt.*	Willi Kollmer	PT	3.	E	C	†
9/7/40	*Oblt.*	Eduard Fritz	OV	3.	E	C	†
9/7/40	*Uffz.*	Franz Huber	RO	3.	E	C	†
9/7/40	*Uffz.*	Ernst Neuburger	FE	3.	E	C	M
9/7/40	*Gefr.*	Walter Stiller	GN	3.	E	C	†
29/7/40	*Lt.*	Otto Kliffgen	PT	2.	E	C	†
29/7/40	*Fw.*	Erhard Knobloch	OV	2.	E	C	†
29/7/40	*Gefr.*	Heinz Fricke	RO	2.	E	C	M
29/7/40	*Fw.*	Martin Eiblmeier	FE	2.	E	C	M
29/7/40	*Gefr.*	Herbert Keil	GN	2.	E	C	†
29/7/40	*Uffz.*	Alexander Angermeier	PT	3.	E	C	†
29/7/40	*Fw.*	Friedrich Prütting	OV	3.	E	C	†
29/7/40	*Lt.*	Wilhelm Schatka	OV	3.	E	C	†
29/7/40	*Uffz.*	Ernst Jendricke	RO	3.	E	C	†
29/7/40	*Uffz.*	Richard Kotz	FE	3.	E	C	†
28/8/40	*Obfw.*	Heinrich Wolter	PT	3.	E	C	†
28/8/40	*Obfw.*	Heinrich Walther	OV	3.	E	C	†
28/8/40	*Uffz.*	Anton Steurer	RO	3.	E	C	†
28/8/40	*Uffz.*	Helmut Heinze	PT	3.	E	C	†
28/8/40	*Hgefr.*	Waltert Beerbohm	FE	3.	E	C	†

29/8/40	*Uffz.*	Leo Bolz	RO	1.	E	C	†
29/8/40	*Uffz.*	August Staudt	FE	1.	E	C	†
30/8/40	*Fw.*	Ernst-Erhard von Kuenheim	RO	3.	E	C	†
30/8/40	*Fw.*	Adolf Saam	FE	3.	E	C	†
30/8/40	*Obgefr.*	Otto Fischer	GN	3.	E	C	†
7/9/40	*Obfw.*	Gerhard Müller	RO	1.	E	C	†
7/9/40	*Flg.*	Hans Hönig	GN	1.	E	C	†
15/9/40	*Fw.*	Friedrich Grotzki	FE	3.	E	C	†
15/9/40	*Uffz.*	Alois Lehner	PT	3.	E	C	†
15/9/40	*Uffz.*	Kurt Röthig	RO	3.	E	C	†
22/10/40	*Oblt.*	Karl Müller		2.	E	C	†
22/10/40	*Obfw.*	Gerhard Leibersberger		2.	E	C	†
22/10/40	*Obfw.*	Karl Zeller		2.	E	C	†
22/10/40	*Uffz.*	Albert Jedelhauser		2.	E	C	†
26/10/40	*Lt.*	Günther Hanau	PT	2.	E	C	M
26/10/40	*Lt.*	Hans Cichy	OV	2.	E	C	M
26/10/40	*Fw.*	Erich Brandt	RO	2.	E	C	M
26/10/40	*Uffz.*	Alfred Schuhbauer	GN	2.	E	C	M
26/10/40	*Gefr.*	Helmut Heuft	GN	2.	E	C	M
9/11/40	*Uffz.*	Rudolf Tinz	FE	3.		U	†
23/11/40	*Lt.*	Joachim von Warzewski	PT	3.	E	C	†
23/11/40	*Gefr.*	August Lorenz	OV	3.	E	C	†
23/11/40	*Fw.*	Hubert Schopf	FE	3.	E	C	†
6/12/40	*Fw.*	Wilhelm Pabst	PT	1.	E	C	†
6/12/40	*Uffz.*	Heinrich Rettig	OV	1.	E	C	†
6/12/40	*Obfw.*	Karl Helber	RO	1.	E	C	†
6/12/40	*Obfw.*	Walter Marbach	FE	1.	E	C	†
16/1/41	*Uffz.*	Hubert Graf	RO	2.	E	C	†
31/1/41	*Lt.*	Wolf Helm	PT	2.	E	C	†
31/1/41	*Gefr.*	Gerhard Hensel	OV	2.	E	C	†
31/1/41	*Fw.*	Reinhard Tässler	RO	2.	E	C	†
31/1/41	*Gefr.*	Willy Wagner	GN	2.	E	C	†
31/1/41	*Uffz.*	Heinrich Schäfer	GN	2.	E	C	†
27/2/41	*Obfw.*	Hans Michalzik	PT	3.	E	C	M
27/2/41	*Oblt.*	Hans-Georg Ziegler	OV	3.	E	C	M
27/2/41	*Fw.*	Karl Ziegler	RO	3.	E	C	†
27/2/41	*Uffz.*	Georg Helgert	FE	3.	E	C	M
27/2/41	*Uffz.*	Heinrich Menetzke	GN	3.	E	C	M
4/5/41	*Lt.*	Karl Baller	PT	2.	E	C	†
4/5/41	*Uffz.*	Leo Palubicki	OV	2.	E	C	†
4/5/41	*Uffz.*	Gerhard Stolper	RO	2.	E	C	†
4/5/41	*Gefr.*	Erwin Donner	FE	2.	E	C	†

4/5/41	*Uffz.*	Karl Fleischmann	GN	2.	E	C	†
4/5/41	*Gefr.*	Blasius Regnat	OV	2.	E	C	M
4/5/41	*Gefr.*	Bruno Kauhardt	RO	2.	E	C	†
11/5/41	*Obfw.*	Max Zieringer	FE	1.	E		†
11/5/41	*Gefr.*	Franz Werner	GN	2.	E		†
11/5/41	*Uffz.*	Adolf Schurff	RO	3.	E	C	†
11/5/41	*Obfw.*	Helmut Meister	FE	3.	E		†
11/5/41	*Fw.*	Edmund Wylezol	GN	3.	E	C	†
23/6/41	*Hptm.*	Othmar Hirschauer	St.Kap.	3.	R	C	M
23/6/41	*Fw.*	Wilhelm Endress	PT	3.	R	C	M
23/6/41	*Fw.*	Heinrich Funke	OV	3.	R	C	M
23/6/41	*Fw.*	Josef Hertle	RO	3.	R	C	M
23/6/41	*Obfw.*	Ernst Bott	FE	3.	R	C	M
28/6/41	*Obfw.*	Albert Becker	FE	1.	R	U	†
31/7/41	*Oblt.*	Adolf Kempe	PT	1.	R	C	†
31/7/41	*Gefr.*	Hans Haase	OV	1.	R	C	M
31/7/41	*Uffz.*	Fritz Gaede	RO	1.	R	C	M
31/7/41	*Uffz.*	Hans Rößler	FE	1.	R	C	†
31/7/41	*Gefr.*	Hermann Betz	GN	1.	R	C	†
31/7/41	*Gefr.*	Kurt Jeschke	PT	2.	R	C	†
31/7/41	*Obgefr.*	Alfred Engler	OV	2.	R	C	†
31/7/41	*Gefr.*	Lothar Hüper	RO	2.	R	C	†
31/7/41	*Fw.*	Hermann Kleeth	FE	2.	R	C	†
31/7/41	*Gefr.*	Andreas Schröffel	GN	2.	R	C	†
2/8/41	*Fw.*	Max Brunzel	PT	2.	R	C	†
2/8/41	*Obgefr.*	Heinz Berkenbaum	OV	2.	R	C	†
2/8/41	*Gefr.*	Gerhard Band	RO	2.	R	C	†
2/8/41	*Gefr.*	Alfred Greulich	GN	2.	R	C	†
2/8/41	*Gefr.*	Rudolf Meier	GN	2.	R	C	†
4/8/41	*Uffz.*	Franz Zieger	Mechanic 1st	R	EA	†
			Airfield Op. Comp.				
9/8/41	*Uffz.*	Oswald Schliemann	PT	1.	R	C	M
9/8/41	*Uffz.*	Amandus Otruba	OV	1.	R	C	M
9/8/41	*Uffz.*	Albert Wetzel	RO	1.	R	C	M
9/8/41	*Uffz.*	Wilhelm Gieselmann	FE	1.	R	C	M
9/8/41	*Uffz.*	Walter Kranich	GN	1.	R	C	M
22/8/41	*Gefr.*	Franz Ruschka	PT	3.	R	C	M
22/8/41	*Uffz.*	Johann Schmid	OV	3.	R	C	M
22/8/41	*Gefr.*	Nikolaus Wand	RO	3.	R	C	M
22/8/41	*Uffz.*	Ludwig Puggel	FE	3.	R	C	M
22/8/41	*Uffz.*	Friedrich Schmidtmann	GN	3.	R	C	M
9/9/41	*Gefr.*	Hans Schröder	FE	3.	R	EA	†
9/9/41	*Gefr.*	Karl Danielmeyer	GN	3.	R	EA	†

27/9/41	*Gefr.*	Horst Hopt	OV	3.	R	C	†
27/9/41	*Uffz.*	Erwin Schmidt	RO	3.	R	C	†
27/9/41	*Gefr.*	Leopold Trappl	–	2nd	R	C	†
	Airfield Op.Comp.						
5/10/41	*Fw.*	August Wicke	PT	1.	R	C	M
5/10/41	*Obfw.*	Ortwin Schwach	OV	1.	R	C	M
5/10/41	*Obgefr.*	Ernst Scheel	RO	1.	R	C	M
5/10/41	*Uffz.*	Franz Prager	FE	1.	R	C	M
5/10/41	*Gefr.*	Josef Grimm	GN	1.	R	C	M
16/2/42	*Lt.*	Heinrich Leske	OV	1.	R	C	M
16/2/42	*Obfw.*	Willi Thoma	PT	1.	R	C	M
16/2/42	*Fw.*	Erich Schmidt	RO	1.	R	C	M
16/2/42	*Obgefr.*	Fridolin Sztmanek	FE	1.	R	C	M
16/2/42	*Fw.*	Peter Jäger	GN	1.	R	C	M
9/3/42	*Uffz.*	Friedrich Schöntag	FE	3.	R	EA	M
18/3/42	*Uffz.*	Franz Ruatti	OV	3.	R	EA	†
22/3/42	*Obfw.*	Rudi Goethel	PT	1.	R	EA	†
25/3/42	*Fw.*	Günter Högel	OV	3.	R	EA	†
30/3/42	*Obstlt.*	Joachim Wienholtz	Gr.Kdr.	I.	R	C	M
30/3/42	*Oblt.*	Siegfried Meyer	PT	I.	R	C	M
30/3/42	*Obfw.*	Karl Saunus	OV	I.	R	C	M
30/3/42	*Uffz.*	Eckhard Pook	RO	I.	R	C	M
30/3/42	*Uffz.*	Karl Kriegler	FE	I.	R	C	M
30/3/42	*Uffz.*	Martin Lehner	GN	I.	R	C	M
6/4/42	*Uffz.*	Fritz Reichhardt	OV	1.	R	EA	†
9/4/42	*Uffz.*	Walter Köller	PT	1.	R	U	M
9/4/42	*Obgefr.*	Franz Hieß	OV	1.	R	U	M
9/4/42	*Obgefr.*	Friedrich Schwerdtfeger	RO	1.	R	U	M
9/4/42	*Obgefr.*	Rudolf Dörfler	FE	1.	R	U	M
9/4/42	*Gefr.*	Harry Teichmann	GN	1.	R	U	M
4/5/42	*Fw.*	Alfred Schön	PT	1.	R	C	M
4/5/42	*Fw.*	Heinz Trenkler	OV	1.	R	C	M
4/5/42	*Obgefr.*	Karl-Heinz Ritter	RO	1.	R	C	M
4/5/42	*Fw.*	Georg Rieger	FE	1.	R	C	M
4/5/42	*Obgefr.*	Albert Pletzki	GN	1.	R	C	M
9/5/42	*Lt.*	Volkmar Diersch	PT	3.	R	C	M
9/5/42	*Lt.*	Volkmar Diersch	PT	3.	R	C	M
9/5/42	*Uffz.*	Jakob Glück	OV	3.	R	C	M
9/5/42	*Obgefr.*	Josef Fürschnaller	RO	3.	R	C	M
9/5/42	*Uffz.*	Josef Grätz	FE	3.	R	C	M
9/5/42	*Uffz.*	Heinz Thiele	GN	3.	R	C	M
2/6/42	*Obfw.*	Erwin Hanft	FE	3.	R	EA	†
9/6/42	*Lt.*	Albert Backhaus	FF	1.	R	C	M

9/6/42	*Obgefr.*	Heinrich Bock	OV	1.	R	C	M
9/6/42	*Uffz.*	Josef Braun	RO	1.	R	C	M
9/6/42	*Uffz.*	Ernst Michalski	FE	1.	R	C	M
9/6/42	*Uffz.*	Ruppert Frank	GN	1.	R	C	M
12/6/42	*Fw.*	Siegfried Bethge	PT	3.	R	C	M
12/6/42	*Fw.*	Herbert Kirchner	OV	3.	R	C	M
12/6/42	*Uffz.*	Walter Malle	RO	3.	R	C	M
12/6/42	*Uffz.*	Alfons Ganserer	FE	3.	R	C	M
12/6/42	*Uffz.*	Rudolf Anibas	GN	3.	R	C	M
12/6/42	*Uffz.*	Herbert Reinert	PT	3.	R	C	M
12/6/42	*Fw.*	Bernhard Krug	OV	3.	R	C	M
12/6/42	*Fw.*	Jonny Rudolph	FE	3.	R	C	M
12/6/42	*Obgefr.*	Herbert Grünzweig	GN	3.	R	C	M
15/6/42	*Uffz.*	Erwin Maier	PT	3.	R	C	M
15/6/42	*Uffz.*	Herbert Grunwald	RO	3.	R	C	M
15/6/42	*Uffz.*	Ludwig Scheungrab	FE	3.	R	C	M
15/6/42	*Obgefr.*	Karl Schwind	GN	3.	R	C	M
26/6/42	*Uffz.*	Gerhard Jirowetz	GN	1.	R	EA	†
11/8/42	*Lt.*	Horst Krüger	PT	3.	R	EA	†
14/8/42	*Gefr.*	Erich Berger	Driver	1st	R	U	†
	Airfield Op.Comp.						
16/8/42	*Fw.*	Karl-H. Lang	PT	3.	R	C	M
16/8/42	*Gefr.*	Werner Fahlbusch	OV	3.	R	C	M
16/8/42	*Uffz.*	Alfons Zinke	RO	3.	R	C	M
16/8/42	*Uffz.*	Eugen Simmendinger	FE	3.	R	C	M
16/8/42	*Obgefr.*	Reinhard Eckert	GN	3.	R	C	M
25/9/42	*Uffz.*	Willi Liebermann	OV	2.	R	C	†
25/9/42	*Uffz.*	Gottfried Kollenz	RO	2.	R	C	†
25/9/42	*Uffz.*	Georg Rentsch	GN	2.	R	C	M
25/9/42	*Uffz.*	Albert Baranowski	GN	2.	R	C	†
9/10/42	*Oblt.*	Lienh. Fuchs	PT	I.	R	C	M
9/10/42	*Obfw.*	Josef Kurz	OV	I.	R	C	M
9/10/42	*Fw.*	Rudolf Schneider	RO	I.	R	C	M
9/10/42	*Uffz.*	Johann Hempen	FE	I.	R	C	M
9/10/42	*Flg.*	Hermann Jürries	GN	I.	R	C	M
16/10/42	*Fw.*	Max Schaff	PT	2.	R	C	M
16/10/42	*Fw.*	Fritz Rink	OV	2.	R	C	M
16/10/42	*Uffz.*	Heinz Laurentsch	RO	2.	R	C	M
16/10/42	*Fw.*	Friedrich Wolz	FE	2.	R	C	M
16/10/42	*Uffz.*	Heinrich Engelbarts	GN	2.	R	C	M
8/11/42	*Gefr.*	Wilhelm Müller	GN	1.	R	U	M
9/11/42	*Fw.*	Ernst Rauth	PT	2.	R	C	†
9/11/42	*Uffz.*	Otto Leipe	OV	2.	R	C	†

9/11/42	Obgefr.	Georg Maschke	RO	2.	R	C	†
9/11/42	Gefr.	Heinrich Jasper	FE	2.	R	C	†
9/11/42	Gefr.	Walter Kassuba	GN	2.	R	C	†
3/12/42	Uffz.	Hans-Joachim Geyer	OV	1.	R	C	†
3/12/42	Uffz.	Johann Blome	RO	1.	R	C	†
3/12/42	Obgefr.	Willi Rautenberg	FE	1.	R	C	†
3/12/42	Gefr.	Karl Blaha	GN	1.	R	C	†
25/12/42	Fw.	Heinrich Wehrmann	FE	2.	R	U	†
28/12/42	Obfw.	Heinrich Buchholz	PT	1.	R	C	M
28/12/42	Hptm.	Ernst Gehrke	OV	1.	R	C	M
28/12/42	Fw.	Arno Groß	OV	1.	R	C	M
28/12/42	Obfw.	Georg Geltinger	FE	1.	R	C	M
28/12/42	Obgefr.	Alfred Bergmann	GN	1.	R	C	M
30/12/42	Fw.	Willi Strunk	PT	2.	R	C	†
30/12/42	Oblt.	Siegfried Rehle	OV	2.	R	C	†
30/12/42	Uffz.	Siegfried John	RO	2.	R	C	†
30/12/42	Fw.	Georg Urban	FE	2.	R	C	†
30/12/42	Uffz.	Werner Linde	GN	2.	R	C	†
1/1/43	Lt.	Jürgen Schalke	PT	2.	R	C	M
1/1/43	Obfw.	Walter Bachler	OV	2.	R	C	M
1/1/43	Uffz.	Heinz Pahlke	GN	2.	R	C	M
1/1/43	Uffz.	Wolfgang Mayer	FE	2.	R	C	M
1/1/43	Uffz.	Heinz Menzel	GN	2.	R	C	M
1/1/43	Obfw.	Xaver Donhauser	PT	3.	R	C	M
1/1/43	Uffz.	Fritz Maaß	OV	3.	R	C	M
1/1/43	Uffz.	Karl Schmidt	RO	3.	R	C	M
1/1/43	Obgefr.	Rudolf Wicher	FE	3.	R	C	M
1/1/43	Gefr.	Hermann Günther	GN	3.	R	C	M
2/1/43	Lt.	Ernst König	PT	2.	R	C	†
2/1/43	Uffz.	Erwin Wiczorek	OV	2.	R	C	†
2/1/43	Uffz.	Heinz Müller	FE	2.	R	C	†
2/1/43	Uffz.	Alfred Abel	GN	2.	R	C	†
5/4/43	Uffz.	Rudolf Bick	PT	3.	G	U	†
5/4/43	Uffz.	Otto Dimter	OV	3.	G	U	†
5/4/43	Uffz.	Fritz Koehler	RO	3.	G	U	†
5/4/43	Obgefr.	Norbert Wolniczak	FE	3.	G	U	†
5/4/43	Gefr.	Albert Hilger	GN	3.	G	U	†
27/5/43	Uffz.	Karl Kestel	PT	2.	R	C	M
27/5/43	Uffz.	Hans Gegner	OV	2.	R	C	M
27/5/43	Gefr.	Günther Brandstätter	RO	2.	R	C	M
27/5/43	Obgefr.	Wilhelm Otto	FE	2.	R	C	M
27/5/43	Gefr.	Hermann Krafft	GN	2.	R	C	M
30/5/43	Obfw.	Willi Pflüger	PT	1.	R	C	M

30/5/43	Uffz.	Erich Zellner	OV	1.	R	C	M
30/5/43	Obgefr.	Rudolf Braunschuh	RO	1.	R	C	M
30/5/43	Obgefr.	Otto Maak	GN	1.	R	C	M
30/5/43	Obgefr.	Walter Müller	GN	1.	R	C	M
5/6/43	Lt.	Karl-Heinz Andresen	PT	1.	R	C	†
5/6/43	Uffz.	Werner Zöllner	OV	1.	R	C	†
5/6/43	Fw.	Werner Zorn	RO	1.	R	C	†
5/6/43	Obgefr.	Paul Zilinka	FE	1.	R	C	†
5/6/43	Gefr.	Eugen Danielowski	GN	1.	R	C	†
7/7/43	Uffz.	Ernst Tiersch	PT	2.	R	C	M
7/7/43	Uffz.	Eberhard Speck	OV	2.	R	C	M
7/7/43	Uffz.	Ferdinand Heinzl	RO	2.	R	C	M
7/7/43	Uffz.	Karl Paul	FE	2.	R	C	M
7/7/43	Obgefr.	Karl Jostmeier	GN	2.	R	C	M
8/7/43	Uffz.	Heinz Bernhard	RO	1.	R	EA	†
10/7/43	Lt.	Werner Schäfer	PT	2.	R	C	M
10/7/43	Uffz.	Karl Wehrum	OV	2.	R	C	M
10/7/43	Uffz.	Rudolf Steinkogler	RO	2.	R	C	M
10/7/43	Obfw.	Hans Schilling	FE	2.	R	C	M
10/7/43	Gefr.	Gerhard Pajonk	GN	2.	R	C	M
14/7/43	Uffz.	Otto Riehl	PT	2.	R	C	†
14/7/43	Fw.	Wilhelm Sprenger	OV	2.	R	C	†
14/7/43	Uffz.	Oswald Jäckel	FE	2.	R	C	†
14/7/43	Uffz.	Hubert Mayer	GN	2.	R	C	†
14/7/43	Uffz.	Johann Mayer	PT	3.	R	FT	M
14/7/43	Fw.	Rudi Weißach	OV	3.	R	FT	M
14/7/43	Uffz.	Gerhard Härtl	RO	3.	R	FT	†
28/7/43	Obfw.	Eberhard Burmeister	PT	3.	R	C	M
28/7/43	Gefr.	Werner Kühne	OV	3.	R	C	M
28/7/43	Uffz.	Paul Wolff	RO	3.	R	C	M
28/7/43	Obgefr.	Richard Köhler	AM	3.	R	C	M
28/7/43	Uffz.	Fridolin Domig	GN	3.	R	C	M
3/8/43	Uffz.	Josef Eppich	FE	3.	R	EA	†
9/8/43	Lt.	Albrecht Schneidewind	PT	2.	X	C	†
9/8/43	Uffz.	Rudolf Reimold	OV	2.	X	C	†
9/8/43	Uffz.	Oskar Kruta	RO	2.	X	C	†
9/8/43	Uffz.	Rudolf Geissler	FE	2.	X	C	†
9/8/43	Obgefr.	Heinrich Zube	GN	2.	X	C	†
9/8/43	Fw.	Erwin Obuch	PT	2.	X	C	†
9/8/43	Obgefr.	Hans Wenzel	OV	2.	X	C	†
9/8/43	Uffz.	Hartwig Engelmann	RO	2.	X	C	†
9/8/43	Uffz.	Heinrich Pudzich	MCC	2.	X	C	†
9/8/43	Uffz.	Rudolf Werner	AM	2.	X	C	†

9/8/43	*Uffz.*	Franz Wolf	MCC	2.	X	C	†
9/8/43	*Uffz.*	Franz Dominik	AM	2.	X	C	†
29/8/43	*Uffz.*	Karl-Heinz Koch	FE	3.	R	EA	†
12/9/43	*Flg.*	Karl Fischer	AOC	1.	R	U	†
18/9/43	*Uffz.*	Waldemar Lauhoff	PT	2.	R	C	†
18/9/43	*Gefr.*	Walter Eberle	FE	2.	R	C	†
22/12/43	*Lt.*	August Warter	PT	1.	R	C	†
31/12/43	*Obfw.*	Herbert Engel	PT	2.	R	C	M
31/12/43	*Uffz.*	Josef Wagner	OV	2.	R	C	M
31/12/43	*Uffz.*	Franz Burggraf	RO	2.	R	C	M
31/12/43	*Uffz.*	Peter Büttner	FE	2.	R	C	M
31/12/43	*Uffz.*	Herbert Reimann	GN	2.	R	C	M
31/12/43	*Obfw.*	Arnold Stork	PT	3.	R	C	M
31/12/43	*Uffz.*	Gerhard Adler	OV	3.	R	C	M
31/12/43	*Fw.*	Heinrich Gesenhues	RO	3.	R	C	M
31/12/43	*Uffz.*	Heinrich Roß	FE	3.	R	C	M
31/12/43	*Uffz.*	Fritz Unterweger	GN	3.	R	C	M
29/1/44	*Lt.*	Heinz Neumann	PT	1.	X	C	†
29/1/44	*Gefr.*	Wilhelm Dragon	OV	1.	X	C	†
29/1/44	*Uffz.*	Johann Mühlbacher	RO	1.	X	C	†
29/1/44	*Uffz.*	Kurt David	FE	1.	X	C	†
29/1/44	*Uffz.*	Erich Werner	GN	1.	X	C	†
9/2/44	*Lt.*	Wilhelm Kamp	PT	2.	R	C	M
9/2/44	*Obgefr.*	Hardi Fortuniak	OV	2.	R	C	M
9/2/44	*Uffz.*	Werner Speer	RO	2.	R	C	M
9/2/44	*Obgefr.*	Walter Strotz	FE	2.	R	C	M
9/2/44	*Obgefr.*	Hubert Spohr	GN	2.	R	C	M
14/2/44	*Uffz.*	Hans-Dieter Junker	PT	3.	R	C	M
14/2/44	*Uffz.*	Otto Zapf	OV	3.	R	C	M
14/2/44	*Uffz.*	Karl Böttcher	RO	3.	R	C	M
14/2/44	*Uffz.*	Walter Schikore	FE	3.	R	C	M
14/2/44	*Gefr.*	Werner Gassewitz	PT	3.	R	C	M
21/2/44	*Obgefr.*	Hans Willim	AOC	1.	R	U	†
3/3/44	*Fj.Fw.*	Paul Zoelzer		3.	R	U	†
8/4/44	*Obgefr.*	Artur Kausch	GN	2.	R	EA	†
9/4/44	*Uffz.*	Robert Wahn	GN	1.	R	C	†
9/4/44	*Uffz.*	Kurt Bregel	FE	1.	R	C	†
29/4/44	*Uffz.*	Franz Lichtenauer	RO	1.	R	C	†
29/4/44	*Uffz.*	Josef Vocht	GN	1.	X	A	†
29/4/44	*Obgefr.*	Heinz Jordan	GN	1.	X	A	†
29/4/44	*Gefr.*	Hans Neumerkel	GN	1.	X	A	†
4/6/44	*Obgefr.*	Horst Geisendorf	GN	1.	X	A	†
26/6/44	*Obgefr.*	Günther Weniger	PT	3.	R	C	M

26/6/44	*Uffz.*	Georg Birkhahn	OV	3.	R	C	M
26/6/44	*Uffz.*	Gustav Hammer	RO	3.	R	C	M
26/6/44	*Uffz.*	Rolf Ramm	FE	3.	R	C	M
26/6/44	*Fw.*	Hermann Löwenberg	AM	3.	R	C	M
27/6/44	*Lt.*	Wilhelm Walker	PT	1.	R	C	M
27/6/44	*Uffz.*	Gerhard Bülow	RO	1.	R	C	M
27/6/44	*Uffz.*	Wilhelm Hoffmann	AM	1.	R	C	M
27/6/44	*Uffz.*	Johann Czech	AM	1.	R	C	M
9/7/44	*Uffz.*	Rolf Niemann	PT	2.	R	C	M
9/7/44	*Obgefr.*	Horst Matschke	OV	2.	R	C	M
9/7/44	*Fw.*	Otto Bührer	RO	2.	R	C	M
9/7/44	*Fw.*	Benno Bastian	FE	2.	R	C	M
9/7/44	*Gefr.*	Herbert Wilke	GN	2.	R	C	M
10/7/44	*Uffz.*	Alfred Herr	PT	3.	R	C	M
10/7/44	*Obgefr.*	Robert Hatzfeld	OV	3.	R	C	M
10/7/44	*Uffz.*	Rudolf Potuzak	RO	3.	R	C	M
10/7/44	*Obgefr.*	Hans-Gerd Kind	FE	3.	R	C	M
10/7/44	*Uffz.*	Karl Daniel	GN	3.	R	C	M
10/7/44	*Uffz.*	Günther Geheb	RO	2.	R	EA	M
10/7/44	*Uffz.*	Otto Schneider	FE	3.	R	EA	M
10/7/44	*Uffz.*	Leopold Kandera	GN	3.	R	EA	M
22/7/44	*Obfw.*	Heinz-Jürgen Fritz	PT	3.	R	C	M
22/7/44	*Fw.*	Max Geiger	OV	3.	R	C	M
26/7/44	*Uffz.*	Ernst Uhl	PT	3.	R	C	M
26/7/44	*Obgefr.*	Johann Wagner	OV	3.	R	C	M
26/7/44	*Obgefr.*	Joachim Nadler	FE	3.	R	C	M
18/8/44	*Fw.*	Friedrich Kropp	PT	1.	R	C	M
18/8/44	*Uffz.*	Fritz Josties	OV	1.	R	C	M
18/8/44	*Uffz.*	Julius Endress	RO	1.	R	C	M
18/8/44	*Obgefr.*	Heinrich Göhry	FE	1.	R	C	M
18/8/44	*Uffz.*	Hans Kohn	GN	1.	R	C	M
30/8/44	*Uffz.*	Adolf Wägner	DR	1.	G	U	†
5/9/44	*Obgefr.*	Werner Amende	MCC	3.	G	U	†
21/10/44	*Uffz.*	Albert Fleischmann	PT	3.	E	C	†
21/10/44	*Uffz.*	Eduard Rothe-Oswald	OV	3.	E	C	†
21/10/44	*Fw.*	Alfred Urban	RO	3.	E	C	†
23/10/44	*Obgefr.*	Walter Hasler	GN	1.	E	EA	†
25/10/44	*Fw.*	Karl Proksch	RO	3.	E	EA	†
25/10/44	*Obfw.*	Othmar Hämmerle	PT	2.	E	C	M
25/10/44	*Obfw.*	Georg Stolp	OV	2.	E	C	M
25/10/44	*Fw.*	Werner Jakobs	RO	2.	E	C	M
25/10/44	*Uffz.*	Kurt Gütlein	GN	2.	E	C	M
25/10/44	*Obgefr.*	Werner Oberbeck	GN	2.	E	C	M

10/11/44	*Obfhr.*	Wilhelm Jansen	PT	3.	E	C	M
10/11/44	*Fhr.*	Rudolf Großmann	OV	3.	E	C	M
10/11/44	*Uffz.*	Artur Sterzing	RO	3.	E	C	M
10/11/44	*Obgefr.*	Erich Krüger	GN	3.	E	C	M
10/11/44	*Obgefr.*	Walter Rydzy	FE	3.	E	C	M
10/12/44	*Uffz.*	Günter Lis	PT	1.	E	C	M
10/12/44	*Fhr.*	Kurt Ternier	OV	1.	E	C	M
10/12/44	*Uffz.*	Fritz Brugger	RO	1.	E	C	M
10/12/44	*Uffz.*	Waldemar Vahle	GN	1.	E	C	M
10/12/44	*Fw.*	Fritz Knep	GN	1.	E	C	M
3/1/45	*Fw.*	Heinz Kowalski	PT	2.	E	C	†
3/1/45	*Obgefr.*	Hans Olm	OV	2.	D	C	†
3/1/45	*Obfw.*	Gerhard Täschner	RO	2.	E	C	†
3/1/45	*Gefr.*	Wilhelm Kirchhoff	GN	2.	D	C	†
3/1/45	*Flg.*	Herbert Rose	FE	2.	E	C	†

II. Gruppe

11/5/40	*Uffz.*	Karl Kramer	PT	4.	F	U	M
11/5/40	*Uffz.*	Ernst Hermann	FE	4.	F	U	M
11/5/40	*Uffz.*	Paul Volz PT		4.	F	C	†
11/5/40	*Uffz.*	Leonhard Bierfelder	OV	4.	F	C	†
11/5/40	*Uffz.*	Richard Lyschik	RO	4.	F	C	†
11/5/40	*Uffz.*	Max Dudzinski	FE	4.	F	C	†
11/5/40	*Gefr.*	Ernst Stäudner	GN	4.	F	C	†
12/5/40	*Fw.*	Manfred Siegle	OV	4.	F	U	†
12/5/40	*Uffz.*	Paul Andreae	RO	4.	F	U	†
12/5/40	*Uffz.*	Heinrich Moosbrugger	FE	4.	F	U	†
12/5/40	*Uffz.*	Hermann Schien	GN	4.	F	U	†
26/5/40	*Fw.*	Martin Unold	PT	6.	F	C	†
26/5/40	*Uffz.*	Reinhold Berner	OV	6.	F	C	†
26/5/40	*Fw.*	Walter Hardecker	RO	6.	F	C	†
26/5/40	*Fw.*	Georg Spatscheck	FE	6.	F	C	†
26/5/40	*Gefr.*	Hermann Guhl	PT	6.	F	C	†
1/6/40	*Fw.*	Artur Nöss	PT	4.	F	FT	†
1/6/40	*Fw.*	Hans Kaltenbach	OV	4.	F	FT	†
1/6/40	*Gefr.*	Otto Müller	RO	4.	F	FT	†
1/6/40	*Uffz.*	Erich Heilmann	FE	4.	F	FT	†
1/6/40	*Gefr.*	Engelbert Plötz	GN	4.	F	FT	†
12/7/40	*Fw.*	Georg Freitag	OV	4.	F	U	†
12/7/40	*Uffz.*	Albert Dombrowski	RO	4.	F	U	†
12/7/40	*Fw.*	Paul Krink	FE	4.	F	U	†
12/7/40	*Gefr.*	Wilhelm Ledl	GN	4.	F	U	†
27/7/40	*Fw.*	Willy Herrberger	PT	4.	F	U	M

27/7/40	*Uffz.*	Richard Wolfhard	OV	4.	F	U	M
27/7/40	*Fw.*	Paul Kurz	RO	4.	F	U	M
27/7/40	*Gefr.*	Rolf Schewitzer	FE	4.	F	U	M
27/7/40	*Uffz.*	Josef Schorpp	GN	4.	F	U	M
30/7/40	*Gefr.*	Anton Brucher	AOC	4.	F	U	M
15/8/40	*Fw.*	Karl Ranft	FE	6.	E	C	†
15/8/40	*Gefr.*	Walter Holzwarth	GN	6.	E	C	†
18/8/40	*Major*	Reinhold Tamm	Kdr.	II.	E	C	†
18/8/40	*Obfw.*	Kurt Heine	PT	II.	E	C	M
18/8/40	*Lt.*	Walter Ludmann	OV	II.	E	C	†
18/8/40	*Obfw.*	Alois Rusch	RO	II.	E	C	M
18/8/40	*Fw.*	Erhardt Rasche	FE	II.	E	C	†
18/8/40	*Gefr.*	Klemens Kahl	GN	II.	E	C	M
28/8/40	*Lt.*	Hans Simon	PT	4.	E	C	†
28/8/40	*Fw.*	Gerhard Maaß	OV	4.	E	C	†
28/8/40	*Uffz.*	Johann Horn	RO	4.	E	C	†
28/8/40	*Uffz.*	Hermann Ries	GN	4.	E	C	†
28/8/40	*Flg.*	Hans Palkowski	GN	4.	E	C	†
28/8/40	*Hptm.*	Harry Neumann	OV	5.	E	C	†
28/8/40	*Uffz.*	Gustav Schlotterbeck	FE	5.	E	C	†
28/8/40	*Gefr.*	Wilhelm Kreckel	GN	5.	E	C	†
28/8/40	*Uffz.*	Theodor Schütze	PT	6.	E	C	†
28/8/40	*Uffz.*	Theodor Schütze	PT	6.	E	C	†
28/8/40	*Uffz.*	Eduard Kreupl	OV	6.	E	C	†
28/8/40	*Gefr.*	Horst Niebuhr	RO	6.	E	C	†
28/8/40	*Uffz.*	Alois Strohmenger	FE	6.	E	C	†
28/8/40	*Gefr.*	Nikolaus Viertler	GN	6.	E	C	†
30/8/40	*Obfw.*	Thomas Dietrich	OV	II.	E	C	†
30/8/40	*Fw.*	Hans Beffart	PT	II.	E	C	M
30/8/40	*Obfw.*	Walter Ostertag	OV	II.	E	C	†
30/8/40	*Uffz.*	Ludwig Brock	RO	II.	E	C	†
30/8/40	*Uffz.*	Hans Frank	FE	II.	E	C	†
30/8/40	*Gefr.*	Karl Schmiedl	GN	II.	E	C	M
30/8/40	*Fw.*	Fritz Eckert	PT	II.	E	C	†
7/9/40	*Obgefr.*	Peter Neumann	RO	5.	E	U	†
15/9/40	*Fw.*	Andreas Graßl	GN	6.	E	C	†
15/9/40	*Uffz.*	Herbert Lange	RO	6.	E	C	†
15/9/40	*Gefr.*	Erich Sailler	GN	6.	E	C	†
15/9/40	*Fw.*	Ottmar Meier	FE	6.	E	C	†
15/9/40	*Fw.*	Edgar Rinderhagen	OV	6.	E	C	†
15/9/40	*Gefr.*	Alfred Hoffmann	GN	6.	E	C	†
1/10/40	*Uffz.*	Wilhelm Wagner	PT	5.	E	U	M
1/10/40	*Gefr.*	Karl Möhlenhoff	OV	5.	E	U	M

1/10/40	Gefr.	Erwin Günther	RO	5.	E	U	M
1/10/40	Uffz.	Hans König	FE	5.	E	U	M
1/10/40	Gefr.	Thomas Petroll	GN	5.	E	U	M
4/10/40	Fw.	Karl Streller	FE	5.	G	U	†
5/11/40	Oblt.	Helmut Bannert	PT	4.	E	C	†
5/11/40	Gefr.	Georg Werder	OV	4.	E	C	†
5/11/40	Uffz.	Eduard Zahn	RO	4.	E	C	†
5/11/40	Uffz.	Willi Göhring	FE	4.	E	C	†
5/11/40	Gefr.	Herbert Schmitz	GN	4.	E	C	†
10/11/40	Lt.	Hubert Janta	PT	6.	E	C	†
10/11/40	Uffz.	Manfred Schlossbauer	OV	6.	E	C	†
10/11/40	Gefr.	Jürgen Meyer	RO	6.	E	C	†
10/11/40	Fw.	Gerhard Ritter	FE	6.	E	C	†
15/11/40	Lt.	Karl Swata	PT	5.	E	C	M
15/11/40	Uffz.	Josef Mutzl	RO	5.	E	C	†
15/11/40	Fw.	Heinrich Engelken	FE	5.	E	C	M
21/11/40	Gefr.	Artur Hagspiel	PT	4.	E	C	M
21/11/40	Gefr.	Wilhelm Stieger	OV	4.	E	C	M
21/11/40	Obgefr.	Bruno Volkmann	PT	4.	E	C	M
21/11/40	Gefr.	Rudolf Deutsch	RO	4.	E	C	M
21/11/40	Obgefr.	Hugo Löffler	GN	4.	E	C	†
21/11/40	Lt.	Hugo Seefried	PT	6.	E	C	†
21/11/40	Gefr.	Franz Schumacher	OV	6.	E	C	M
21/11/40	Obgefr.	Karl Burner	RO	6.	E	C	M
21/11/40	Uffz.	Gerhard Bürger	FE	6.	E	C	M
21/11/40	Hptm.	Franz Schiffer	GN	6.	E	C	M
6/12/40	Fw.	Alfred Weiss	PT	5.	D	C	†
29/12/40	Oblt.	Rudolf Weber	PT	5.	E	C	†
29/12/40	Lt.	Walter Mahle	OV	5.	E	C	†
29/12/40	Uffz.	Franz Lehmann	RO	5.	E	C	†
29/12/40	Uffz.	Karl Weiss	FE	5.	E	C	†
21/1/41	Fw.	Heinrich Sticht	PT	4.	E	U	M
21/1/41	Gefr.	Franz Ahrer	OV	4.	E	U	†
21/1/41	Uffz.	Hans-Joachim Schwarz	RO	4.	E	U	M
21/1/41	Uffz.	Bernhard Lang	FE	4.	E	U	M
21/1/41	Uffz.	Helmut Schenk	GN	4.	E	U	M
3/2/41	Lt.	Max Petry	PT	6.	E	C	†
3/2/41	Gefr.	Robert Massarsch	OV	6.	E	C	M
3/2/41	Uffz.	Herbert Wordelmann	RO	6.	E	C	M
3/2/41	Fw.	Hermann Bock	FE	6.	E	C	M
3/2/41	Gefr.	Eugen Kaiser	GN	6.	E	C	†
23/2/41	Lt.	Peter Ficker	PT	5.	E	C	†
23/2/41	Gefr.	Erich Kowalewski	OV	5.	E	C	†

23/2/41	*Uffz.*	Otto Müller	RO	5.	E	C	†
23/2/41	*Gefr.*	Kurt Himmel	GN	5.	E	C	†
18/4/41	*Uffz.*	Leo Kubla		6.	F	U	†
20/4/41	*Lt.*	Wilhelm Bönisch	PT	5.	E	C	†
20/4/41	*Gefr.*	Rudolf Eickmeier	OV	5.	E	C	†
20/4/41	*Uffz.*	Rudolf Bornstedt	RO	5.	E	C	†
26/4/41	*Lt.*	Josef Buchtmeier	PT	4.	E	C	†
26/4/41	*Uffz.*	Siegfried Kaufmann	OV	4.	E	C	†
26/4/41	*Fw.*	Gerhard Knöbel	FE	4.	E	C	†
9/5/41	*Fw.*	Werner Scheer	PT	9.	E	U	M
9/5/41	*Uffz.*	Ruppert Lackner	OV	9.	E	U	M
9/5/41	*Obgefr.*	Herbert Sohnert	RO	9.	E	U	†
9/5/41	*Fw.*	Oskar Schneider	FE	9.	E	U	M
9/5/41	*Gefr.*	Heinz Kurth	GN	9.	E	U	†
9/5/41	*Gefr.*	Willi London	OV	6.	E	U	†
9/5/41	*Gefr.*	Johannes Kaminski	RO	6.	E	U	†
9/5/41	*Gefr.*	Hans Stieglitz	FE	6.	E	U	†
9/5/41	*Gefr.*	Hermann Decker	GN	6.	E	U	†
9/5/41	*Uffz.*	Günter Reinelt	PT	4.	E	U	†
9/5/41	*Uffz.*	Jakob Kalle	RO	4.	E	U	†
9/5/41	*Obgefr.*	Rudolf Lorenz	FE	4.	E	U	†
9/5/41	*Gefr.*	Heinrich Wulf	GN	4.	E	U	†
24/6/41	*Gefr.*	Fritz Huschke	RO	4.	R	EA	†
29/6/41	*Uffz.*	Franz Paisdzior	PT	6.	R	U	M
29/6/41	*Gefr.*	Theophil Wind	GN	6.	R	U	M
29/6/41	*Gefr.*	Heinz Obst	GN	6.	R	U	M
1/7/41	*Gefr.*	Karl Löffler	GN	5.	R	U	M
1/7/41	*Uffz.*	Heinrich Fleckner	PT	5.	R	C	M
1/7/41	*Lt.*	Georg-Wilhelm Mayer	OV	5.	R	C	M
1/7/41	*Gefr.*	Willi Dümer	RO	5.	R	C	M
1/7/41	*Gefr.*	Johann Papez	FE	5.	R	C	M
1/7/41	*Obgefr.*	Bernhard Thihatmer	GN	5.	R	C	M
1/7/41	*Gefr.*	Hans Vowinkel	WR	5.	R	C	M
1/7/41	*Uffz.*	Ernst Bochmann	GN	5.	R	C	†
2/7/41	*Obgefr.*	Heinz Rüssmann	GN	5.	R	C	†
24/7/41	*Uffz.*	Ludwig Baron	PT	4.	R	C	†
24/7/41	*Lt.*	Kurt Sachse	OV	4.	R	C	†
24/7/41	*Gefr.*	Horst Bührle	RO	4.	R	C	†
24/7/41	*Uffz.*	Karl Schmelzle	GN	4.	R	C	†
12/10/41	*Lt.*	Hans Obernhübner	PT	6.	R	C	M
12/10/41	*Uffz.*	Hermann Stark	OV	6.	R	C	M
12/10/41	*Gefr.*	Johannes Rogoll	RO	6.	R	C	M
12/10/41	*Uffz.*	Willi Kraus	GN	6.	R	C	M

14/10/41	Obgefr.	Kurt Hoppe	GN	6.	R	C	M
14/10/41	Fw.	Heinz Bendrian	OV	4.	R	C	†
18/10/41	Fw.	Willi Manske	AOC	4.	R	U	†
23/10/41	Uffz.	Heinz Wittkamp	PT	6.	R	C	†
23/10/41	Fw.	Max Ziselsberger	GN	6.	R	C	†
23/10/41	Uffz.	Xaver Böck	RO	6.	R	C	†
23/10/41	Gefr.	Klaus Petasch	GN	6.	R	C	†
23/10/41	Gefr.	Helmut Häusler	GN	6.	R	C	†
29/10/41	Lt.	Dietrich Thüme	PT	II.	R	C	†
29/10/41	Gefr.	Helmut Handlos	OV	II.	R	C	†
29/10/41	Gefr.	Herbert Siering	RO	II.	R	C	†
29/10/41	Fw.	Wilhelm Kuhfeld	FE	II.	R	C	†
29/10/41	Gefr.	Alfred Neumann	GN	II.	R	C	†
22/11/41	Obfw.	Richard Blomenhofer	PT	4.	R	C	M
22/11/41	Uffz.	Walter Wilhelm	OV	4.	R	C	M
22/11/41	Uffz.	Alfred Hahn	RO	4.	R	C	M
22/11/41	Fw.	Friedrich Maier	FE	4.	R	C	M
22/11/41	Uffz.	Friedrich Vogt	GN	4.	R	C	M
26/11/41	Obfw.	Bernhard Menke	PT	5.	R	C	†
26/11/41	Hptm.	Willi Peters	OV	5.	R	C	M
26/11/41	Obfw.	Erich Hahn	RO	5.	R	C	†
26/11/41	Obfw.	Reinhold Rüther	FE	5.	R	C	†
26/11/41	Fw.	Gerhard Hentschel	FE	5.	R	C	†
19/12/41	Oblt.	Harl Bonfeld	PT	5.	R	C	M
19/12/41	Uffz.	Martin Donat	OV	5.	R	C	M
19/12/41	Uffz.	Wilhelm Berndt	RO	5.	R	C	M
19/12/41	Uffz.	Ferdinand Schwabe	FE	5.	R	C	M
19/12/41	Gefr.	Herbert Wolf	GN	5.	R	C	M
30/12/41	Lt.	Paul Tewes	PT	5.	R	U	M
30/12/41	Uffz.	Wilhelm Mattke	GN	5.	R	U	M
30/12/41	Obgefr.	Jakob Witte	RO	5.	R	U	M
30/12/41	Uffz.	Helmut Schuh	FE	5.	R	U	M
30/12/41		Anton Dietz	SF	5.	R	U	M
30/12/41	Uffz.	Johann Schuml	GN	4.	R	C	†
30/12/41	Gefr.	Erich Aussenegg	FE	4.	R	C	†
30/12/41	Uffz.	Paul Paruschke	GN	4.	R	C	†
17/1/42	Uffz.	Eugen Kircher	AOC	4.	R	EA	M
17/1/42	Uffz.	Johann Freitag	AOC	4.	R	EA	M
21/1/42	Uffz.	Hans Blunck	FE	5.	R	EA	†
22/1/42	Uffz.	Felix Fuchs	AOC	5.	R	U	†
27/1/42	Fw.	Herbert Oerke		II.	R	EA	†
7/2/42	Uffz.	Otto Zieger	PT	6.	R	C	M
7/2/42	Uffz.	Karl Zilcher	OV	6.	R	C	M

7/2/42	*Uffz.*	Klaus Schüffler	RO	6.	R	C	M
7/2/42	*Uffz.*	Hans Ebert	FE	6.	R	C	M
7/2/42	*Uffz.*	Robert Müller	GN	6.	R	C	M
27/2/42	*Uffz.*	Max Neuberger	AOC	5.	R	U	†
17/3/42	*Uffz.*	Max Thiele	GN	4.	R	EA	†
18/3/42	*Gefr.*	Walter Sternberg		5.	R	EA	†
18/3/42	*Gefr.*	Franz Ronkartz		5.	R	EA	†
25/3/42	*Lt.*	Arno Diehl	PT	6.	R	C	†
25/3/42	*Gefr.*	Hans-Joachim Schneider	OV	6.	R	C	†
25/3/42	*Uffz.*	Wilhelm Daliber	RO	6.	R	C	†
25/3/42	*Uffz.*	Eduard Deiss	FE	6.	R	C	†
25/3/42	*Gefr.*	Paul Marx	GN	6.	R	C	†
30/3/42	*Hptm.*	Justus Trüber	PT	6.	R	C	†
30/3/42	*Fw.*	Heinrich Zeiss	OV	6.	R	C	†
30/3/42	*Fw.*	Erwin Schober	RO	6.	R	C	†
30/3/42	*Obfw.*	Christian Kühnemund	FE	6.	R	C	†
30/3/42	*Uffz.*	Anton Reithner	GN	6.	R	C	†
23/4/42	*Obfw.*	Karl Beutel	FE	5.	R	EA	†
30/5/42	*Uffz.*	Heinrich Haar	AOC	II.	R	EA	†
22/6/42	*Lt.*	Armin Lohsen	PT	4.	R	C	M
22/6/42	*Uffz.*	Arnold Krosta	GN	4.	R	C	M
22/6/42	*Uffz.*	Kurt Rosanowski	RO	4.	R	C	M
22/6/42	*Uffz.*	Johann Reinfelder	FE	4.	R	C	M
22/6/42	*Gefr.*	Innozenz Merschroth	GN	4.	R	C	M
7/8/42	*Obfw.*	Fritz Fern	PT	5.	R	C	†
7/8/42	*Uffz.*	Leopold Widenski	RO	5.	R	C	†
7/8/42	*Obgefr.*	Eugen Heimer	GN	5.	R	C	†
29/9/42	*Lt.*	Helmut Winkler	PT	5.	R	C	M
29/9/42	*Gefr.*	Georg Glossner	OV	5.	R	C	M
29/9/42	*Uffz.*	Hermann Muchow	RO	5.	R	C	M
29/9/42	*Uffz.*	Karl Müller	FE	5.	R	C	M
29/9/42	*Gefr.*	Edmund Bieda	GN	5.	R	C	M
3/10/42	*Obfw.*	Waldemar Teige	PT	6.	R	C	†
29/10/42	*Uffz.*	Karl-Heinz Depmeier	PT	4.	R	C	†
29/10/42	*Gefr.*	Fritz Rudolph	OV	4.	R	C	†
29/10/42	*Gefr.*	Heinz Neumann	RO	4.	R	C	†
29/10/42	*Gefr.*	Willi Hübers	FE	4.	R	C	†
29/10/42	*Gefr.*	Walter Fontius	GN	4.	R	C	†
30/10/42	*Uffz.*	Hans Seifen	OV	5.	R	C	M
30/10/42	*Uffz.*	Herbert Rücker	RO	5.	R	C	†
30/10/42	*Obgefr.*	Josef Trost	FE	5.	R	C	†
30/10/42	*Gefr.*	Alfred Schneider	GN	5.	R	C	†
21/11/42	*Lt.*	Franz Klinkel	PT	5.	R	C	M

21/11/42	*Uffz.*	Herbert Mergner	RO	5.	R	C	M
21/11/42	*Uffz.*	Walter Näder	FE	5.	R	C	M
21/11/42	*Uffz.*	Herbert Mergner	RO	5.	R	C	M
21/11/42	*Fw.*	Vinzenz Wallerich	GN	5.	R	C	M
29/11/42	*Obfw.*	Wilhelm Baumgarten	PT	4.	R	C	†
29/11/42	*Uffz.*	Johannes Goldammer	OV	4.	R	C	†
29/11/42	*Fw.*	Josef Köberle	RO	4.	R	C	†
29/11/42	*Uffz.*	Gerhard Anders	GN	4.	R	C	†
14/1/43	*Uffz.*	Heinz Duvenbeck	PT	5.	R	C	M
14/1/43	*Uffz.*	Friedrich Pross	RO	5.	R	C	M
14/1/43	*Uffz.*	Johann Stock	FE	5.	R	C	M
14/1/43	*Uffz.*	Otto Heindl	GN	5.	R	C	M
15/1/43	*Fw.*	Robert Meyer	PT	5.	R	C	M
15/1/43	*Gefr.*	Herbert Horster	OV	5.	R	C	M
15/1/43	*Uffz.*	Max Hermann	RO	5.	R	C	M
15/1/43	*Obgefr.*	Josef Wittmann	GN	5.	R	C	M
15/1/43	*Uffz.*	Karl Rühl	GN	5.	R	C	M
16/1/43	*Lt.*	Karl Klunker		6.	R	C	M
16/1/43	*Gefr.*	Aloys Schlarb		6.	R	C	M
16/1/43	*Uffz.*	Hans Kelker		6.	R	C	M
16/1/43	*Gefr.*	Walter Bremann		6.	R	C	M
16/1/43	*Gefr.*	Wolfgang Grimmer		6.	R	C	M
18/1/43	*Lt.*	Franz Luchesig		6.	R	C	M
18/1/43	*Uffz.*	Franz Lorrain		6.	R	C	M
18/1/43	*Uffz.*	Walter Pfeiffer		6.	R	C	M
18/1/43	*Uffz.*	Hans Osten		6.	R	C	M
27/2/43	*Oblt.*	Walter Fink	PT	4.	R	C	†
27/2/43	*Obfw.*	Artur Lindig	OV	4.	R	C	†
27/2/43	*Fw.*	Horst Bielaczek	RO	4.	R	C	†
27/2/43	*Fw.*	Karl Moeckel	FE	4.	R	C	†
27/2/43	*Gefr.*	Eduard Berg	GN	4.	R	C	†
26/1/43	*Hptm.*	Richard Klein	PT	4.	R	C	†
26/1/43	*Uffz.*	Mathes Egle	RO	4.	R	C	†
26/1/43	*Uffz.*	Heinz Tiede	FE	4.	R	C	†
26/1/43	*Uffz.*	Fritz Reissner	GN	4.	R	C	M
11/2/43	*Fw.*	Ernst Boguhn	PT	4.	R	C	M
11/2/43	*Uffz.*	Wilhelm Seng	OV	4.	R	C	M
11/2/43	*Uffz.*	Ernst Ferber	RO	4.	R	C	M
11/2/43	*Uffz.*	Anton Hülzer	FE	4.	R	C	M
11/2/43	*Uffz.*	Hans-Werner Kühn	GN	4.	R	C	M
25/2/43	*Uffz.*	Herbert Laun	PT	5.	R	C	†
25/2/43	*Obgefr.*	Ernst Kapeller	OV	5.	R	C	†
25/2/43	*Uffz.*	*Rudolf Kraus*	RO	5.	R	C	M

25/2/43	Gefr.	Rudolf Tille	FE	5.	R	C	†
25/2/43	Gefr.	Werner Jursch	GN	5.	R	C	†
3/3/43	Fw.	Heinz Kraft	PT	4.	R	EA	†
3/3/43	Uffz.	Gerhard Komm	PT	5.	R	C	†
3/3/43	Obgefr.	Gerhard Wackerbarth	OV	5.	R	C	†
3/3/43	Uffz.	Gerd Holnthoner	RO	5.	R	C	†
3/3/43	Gefr.	Theodor Ziaja	FE	5.	R	C	†
3/3/43	Uffz.	Eugen Wirsching	GN	5.	R	C	†
19/3/43	Uffz.	Heinz Bielefeld		6.	R	EA	†
28/6/43	Uffz.	Fritz Klemp	RO	4.	D	C	†
28/6/43	Obgefr.	Eckhard Schmitt	FE	4.	D	C	†
28/6/43	Lt.	Siegfried Germann	PT	4.	D	C	†
28/6/43	Uffz.	Kurt Höhnel	OV	4.	D	C	†
28/6/43	Obgefr.	Willi Koch	RO	4.	D	C	†
28/6/43	Obgefr.	Fritz Danielowski	FE	4.	D	C	†
28/6/43	Obgefr.	Reinhold Buttschereit	GN	4.	D	C	†
28/6/43	Lt.	Karl Wolf	PT	6.	D	C	†
28/6/43	Obgefr.	Gerhard Kalinowski	OV	6.	D	C	†
28/6/43	Obgefr.	Heinrich Fiedler		6.	D	C	†
28/6/43	Oblt.	Karl Novy	PT	5.	D	C	†
28/6/43	Uffz.	Adolf Zechner	OV	5.	D	C	†
28/6/43	Uffz.	Josef Schomaker	RO	5.	D	C	†
28/6/43	Uffz.	Heinrich Clausius	FE	5.	D	C	†
28/6/43	Obgefr.	Alois Priesner	PT	5.	D	C	†
28/6/43	Uffz.	Joseph Kümpel	OV	5.	D	C	†
28/6/43	Gefr.	Norbert Wingender	RO	5.	D	C	†
28/6/43	Obgefr.	Alfred Feickert	FE	5.	D	C	†
26/7/43	Uffz.	Helmut Dondera	RO	II.	R	C	†
31/7/43	Uffz.	Heinz Noweck	PT	5.	R	C	†
31/7/43	Lt.	Hans von Borries	PT	5.	R	C	†
31/7/43	Fw.	Werner Priebe	OV	5.	R	C	†
31/7/43	Uffz.	Franz Podobinski	RO	5.	R	C	†
31/7/43	Uffz.	August Höllwerth	FE	5.	R	C	†
31/7/43	Obgefr.	Gerhard Grossklass	GN	5.	R	C	†
31/7/43	Uffz.	Alfred Wagner	PT	5.	R	C	†
7/9/43	Uffz.	Herbert Godlinski		4.	R	U	†
15/9/43	Uffz.	Herbert Daun	PT	4.	R	C	M
15/9/43	Uffz.	Bruno Preuss	OV	4.	R	C	M
15/9/43	Obfw.	Wolf Leibrand	RO	4.	R	C	M
15/9/43	Uffz.	Franz Hütter	FE	4.	R	C	M
15/9/43	Uffz.	Edmund Göbel	GN	4.	R	C	M
20/9/43	Uffz.	Rudolf Martin	PT	5.	R	C	†
20/9/43	Lt.	Günter Betten	OV	5.	R	C	†

20/9/43	*Uffz.*	Gerhard Romeike	RO	5.	R	C	†
20/9/43	*Obgefr.*	Erich Marks	FE	5.	R	C	†
20/9/43	*Fw.*	Kurt Krusch	GN	5.	R	C	†
20/9/43	*Uffz.*	Wilhelm Schmerzbeck	RO	5.	R	C	†
20/9/43	*Obgefr..*	Alfons Issing	FE	5.	R	C	†
20/9/43	*Gefr.*	Theodor Steinhauer	GN	5.	R	C	†
3/10/43	*Lt.*	Herbert Dulkies	PT	5.	R	C	M
3/10/43	*Gefr.*	August Menke	OV	5.	R	C	M
3/10/43	*Fw.*	Heinz Wurster	RO	5.	R	C	†
3/10/43	*Obgefr.*	Karl-Friedrich Dose	FE	5.	R	C	M
3/10/43	*Gefr.*	Johann Unterburger	GN	5.	R	C	†
7/10/43	*Lt.*	Günter Rheingans	OV	6.	R	C	†
7/10/43	*Obgefr.*	Paul Klinkner	RO	6.	R	C	†
7/10/43	*Uffz.*	Georg Doletschek	FE	6.	R	C	†
7/10/43	*Obgefr.*	Jürgen Nissen	GN	6.	R	C	†
10/10/43	*Oblt.*	Gottfried Kössl	PT	4.	R	C	M
26/11/43	*Uffz.*	Eduard Cichas	PT	4.	R	C	M
26/11/43	*Fw.*	Heinz Below	OV	4.	R	C	M
26/11/43	*Uffz.*	Werner Brüsewitz	RO	4.	R	C	M
26/11/43	*Obgefr.*	Willi Schönhoff	FE	4.	R	C	M
26/11/43	*Uffz.*	Hans Strässer	GN	4.	R	C	M
30/10/43	*Uffz.*	Gerhard Vogt	PT	II.	R	C	†
30/10/43	*Obfw.*	Emil Riffel	FE	II.	R	C	†
30/11/43	*Uffz.*	Jakob Wagner	OV	II.	R	C	M
30/11/43	*Uffz.*	Herbert Reiker	RO	II.	R	C	M
22/12/43	*Uffz.*	Albert Meissner		II.	R	C	†
31/12/43	*Lt.*	Herbert Wiedenhöft	PT	4.	R	C	M
31/12/43	*Uffz.*	Alfred Büchker	OV	4.	R	C	M
31/12/43	*Uffz.*	Erwin Pötz	RO	4.	R	C	M
31/12/43	*Obgefr.*	Gottfried Opp	FE	4.	R	C	M
31/12/43	*Uffz.*	Gottfried Hintenaus	GN	4.	R	C	M
8/1/44	*Uffz.*	Herbert Finger	PT	4.	R	C	M
8/1/44	*Lt.*	Robert Loewenich	OV	4.	R	C	M
8/1/44	*Fw.*	Alfred Erbe	RO	4.	R	C	M
8/1/44	*Obgefr.*	Hans Pedrotti	FE	4.	R	C	M
8/1/44	*Uffz.*	Bruno Cattoi	GN	4.	R	C	M
25/1/44	*Uffz.*	Hermann Morgenthal	PT	5.	R	C	M
25/1/44	*Lt.*	Max Albertsen	OV	5.	R	C	M
25/1/44	*Uffz.*	Robert Litschen	RO	5.	R	C	M
25/1/44	*Obgefr.*	Berthold Narzi	FE	5.	R	C	M
25/1/44	*Obgefr.*	Karl Möbius	GN	5.	R	C	M
25/1/44	*Lt.*	Ludwig Dietz	PT	4.	R	C	M
25/1/44	*Obgefr.*	Mathias Bauer	OV	4.	R	C	M

25/1/44	*Uffz.*	Karl Hess	RO	4.	R	C	M
25/1/44	*Obgefr.*	Wilhelm Domscheid	FE	4.	R	C	M
25/1/44	*Gefr.*	Wolfgang Behm	GN	4.	R	C	M
14/2/44	*Obgefr.*	Friedrich Hoedel	GN	5.	R	EA	†
31/3/44	*Uffz.*	Eduard Kirchhofer	OV	4.	R	EA	†
10/4/44	*Uffz.*	Karl Stummer	PT	4.	R	C	M
10/4/44	*Uffz.*	Otto Langer	OV	4.	R	C	M
10/4/44	*Uffz.*	Helmut Striegel	RO	4.	R	C	M
10/4/44	*Uffz.*	Willi Schuba	FE	4.	R	C	M
10/4/44	*Uffz.*	Mathias Imberi	GN	4.	R	C	M
1/6/44	*Fw.*	Gerhard Auerswald	PT	6.	R	C	M
1/6/44	*Lt.*	Rudolf Hill	OV	6.	R	C	M
1/6/44	*Uffz.*	Göttfried Bröderecker	RO	6.	R	C	M
1/6/44	*Fw.*	Erich Kalisch	GN	6.	R	C	M
11/6/44	*Gefr.*	Josef Henn	PT	4.	R	C	M
11/6/44	*Obgefr.*	Günther Sparschuh	FE	4.	R	C	M
11/6/44	*Gefr.*	Georg Diss	GN	4.	R	C	M
21/6/44	*Uffz.*	Otto Schneider	FE	4.	R	C	M
5/7/44	*Fw.*	Herbert Schulz	PT	6.	R	C	M
5/7/44	*Gefr.*	Josef Salvenmoser	OV	6.	R	C	M
5/7/44	*Gefr.*	Friedrich Meyer	RO	6.	R	C	M
5/7/44	*Uffz.*	Julius Gaukler	FE	6.	R	C	M
7/7/44	*Uffz.*	Alfred Speer	GN	6.	R	C	M
10/7/44	*Oblt.*	Werner Schulze	PT	6.	R	C	M
10/7/44	*Obgefr.*	Kurt Brodmerkel	OV	6.	R	C	M
10/7/44	*Obgefr.*	Rudolf Wörmann	RO	6.	R	C	M
10/7/44	*Obgefr.*	Herbert Funke	FE	6.	R	C	M
10/7/44	*Flg.*	Ernst Lind	CN	6.	R	C	M
21/7/44	*Fw.*	Hans Fremgen	PT	5.	R	C	M
21/7/44	*Fhj.Uffz.*	Robert Haas	OV	5.	R	C	M
21/7/44	*Obgefr.*	Ernst Wilkinghoff	RO	5.	R	C	M
21/7/44	*Uffz.*	Fritz Weber	FE	5.	R	C	M
21/7/44	*Uffz.*	August Werner Böttel	GN	5.	R	C	M
20/8/44	*Obfw.*	Erhard Klein	PT	5.	X	C	†
20/8/44	*Obgefr.*	Willi Tennagels	OV	5.	X	C	†
20/8/44	*Obgefr.*	Wilhelm Kupke	RO	5.	X	C	†
20/8/44	*Fw.*	Heinrich Gräsel	FE	5.	X	C	†
20/8/44	*Uffz.*	Paul Fiekens	GN	5.	X	C	†
28/8/44	*Uffz.*	Xaver Roder	PT	4.	X	C	†
28/8/44	*Uffz.*	Karl Rath	OV	4.	X	C	†
28/8/44	*Uffz.*	Karl Meyer	PT	4.	X	C	†
28/8/44	*Uffz.*	Rudolf Strieder	FE	4.	X	C	†
28/8/44	*Obgefr.*	Manfred Frommhold-Treu	FE	4.	X	C	†

28/8/44	*Fw.*	August Hübner	AR	4.	X	C	†
28/8/44	*Uffz.*	Johann Bischoff	MCC	4.	X	C	†
28/8/44	*Uffz.*	Karl Förster	AR	4.	X	C	†
28/8/44	*Obgefr.*	Hermann Schachtebeck	CK	4.	X	C	†
28/8/44	*Obgefr.*	Hans Schultze	OV	4.	X	C	†
28/8/44	*Lt.*	Klaus Lüpke	OV	6.	X	C	†
28/8/44	*Uffz.*	Herbert Keller	RO	6.	X	C	†
28/8/44	*Uffz.*	Ludwig Loch	AM	6.	X	C	†
28/8/44	*Uffz.*	Friedrich Bialas	MCC	6.	X	C	†
28/8/44	*Obgefr.*	Christof Esser	RO	6.	X	C	†
28/8/44	*Lt.*	Fritz Will	PT	6.	X	C	†
28/8/44	*Obgefr.*	Hermann Deubner	MCC	6.	X	C	†
28/8/44	*Fw.*	Johann Scholl	PT	6.	X	C	M
28/8/44	*Fw.*	Waldemar Geyer	OV	6.	X	C	M
28/8/44	*Uffz.*	Ernst Brenner	RO	6.	X	C	M
28/8/44	*Obgefr.*	Heinrich Mette	FE	6.	X	C	M
28/8/44	*Fw.*	Franz Nowak	GN	6.	X	C	M
28/8/44	*Obgefr.*	Max Keilberg	MCC	6.	X	C	M
28/8/44	*Uffz.*	Ernst Hopf	AM	6.	X	C	M
28/8/44	*Uffz.*	Helmut Hartmann	AR	6.	X	C	M
28/8/44	*Uffz.*	Manfred Böhmerle	PT	6.	X	C	M
28/8/44	*Obgefr.*	Günther Klingbeil	OV	6.	X	C	M
28/8/44	*Uffz.*	Erich Schmidt	RO	6.	X	C	M
28/8/44	*Obgefr.*	Friedrich Fahrenbach	FE	6.	X	C	M
28/8/44	*Obgefr.*	Johann Groschan	GN	6.	X	C	M
28/8/44	*Uffz.*	Emil Ostermann	MCC	6.	X	C	M
28/8/44	*Fw.*	Bernhard Sedlmaier	AR	6.	X	C	M
28/8/44	*Uffz.*	Robert Hermann	GN	6.	X	C	M
28/8/44	*Obgefr.*	Karl-Heinz Kutsch	CK	6.	X	C	M
31/10/44	*Fw.*	Theodor Warwas	OV	4.	E	C	M
31/10/44	*Uffz.*	Julius Magin	OV	4.	E	C	M
31/10/44	*Uffz.*	Wilhelm Simon	RO	4.	E	C	M
31/10/44	*Uffz.*	Kurt Brendler	FE	4.	E	C	M
31/10/44	*Obgefr.*	Wolfgang Müller		4.	E	C	M
5/11/44	*Hptm.*	Heinz Zöllner	PT	4.	E	C	M
5/11/44	*Obfw.*	Karl Christmass	OV	4.	E	C	M
5/11/44	*Fw.*	Erich Schneider	RO	4.	E	C	M
5/11/44	*Obfw.*	Fritz Marhoun	FE	4.	E	C	M
5/11/44	*Fw.*	Leonhard Dollmeier	GN	4.	E	C	M
5/11/44	*Obfw.*	Fritz Jost	PT	4.	E	C	M
5/11/44	*Uffz.*	Alfred Hoffmann	OV	4.	E	C	M
5/11/44	*Uffz.*	Paul Schmidt	RO	4.	E	C	M
5/11/44	*Fw.*	Franz Breimeier	AM	4.	E	C	M

5/11/44	*Uffz.*	Johann Pöllhuber	GN	4.	E	C	M
5/11/44	*Obfw.*	Paul Flir	PT	5.	E	C	M
5/11/44	*Obgefr.*	Fritz Plöger	OV	5.	E	C	M
5/11/44	*Obgefr.*	Willi Marr	RO	5.	E	C	M
5/11/44	*Uffz.*	Hermann Andergassen	RO	5.	E	C	M
5/11/44	*Uffz.*	Herbert Hübsch	GN	5.	E	C	M
5/11/44	*Lt.*	Heinz Redde	PT	6.	E	C	M
5/11/44	*Obgefr.*	Herbert Jung	OV	6.	E	C	M
5/11/44	*Fw.*	Leo-Peter Weinand	RO	6.	E	C	M
5/11/44	*Uffz.*	Erich Bogen	FE	6.	E	C	M
5/11/44	*Obgefr.*	Richard Parzinski	GN	6.	E	C	M
5/11/44	*Uffz.*	Walter Schulz	PT	4.	E	C	M
5/11/44	*Obgefr.*	Günther Kudszus	OV	4.	E	C	M
5/11/44	*Obgefr.*	Werner Gassner	RO	4.	E	C	M
5/11/44	*Uffz.*	Helmut Reimann	FE	4.	E	C	M
5/11/44	*Uffz.*	Karl Kuchler	GN	4.	E	C	M
14/11/44	*Uffz.*	Georg Fiebig	GN	4.	E	C	†
19/11/44	*Fw.*	Rudolf Ripper	PT	5.	E	C	M
19/11/44	*Uffz.*	Klaus Henkel	OV	5.	E	C	M
19/11/44	*Obgefr.*	Günter Jaeger	RO	5.	E	C	M
19/11/44	*Obgefr.*	Hans-Horst Prochnow	FE	5.	E	C	M
19/11/44	*Obgefr.*	Johann Prochaska	GN	5.	E	C	M

III. Gruppe

23/10/39	*Gefr.*	Hans Kronier		7.		U	†
23/10/39	*Gefr.*	Helmut Baumann		7.		U	†
23/10/39	*Gefr.*	Eduard Hopperdiestel		7.		U	†
11/5/40	*Gefr.*	Richard Müller	OV	9.	F	U	†
11/5/40	*Uffz.*	Johann Zink	GN	9.	F	U	†
11/5/40	*Obgefr.*	Arthur Friebe	RO	9.	F	U	†
11/5/40	*Gefr.*	Franz Scholz	GN	9.	F	U	†
19/5/40	*Gefr.*	Erhard Gabler	GN	9.	F	U	†
19/5/40	*Gefr.*	Erich Ikert	GN	9.	F	U	†
19/5/40	*Fw.*	Hans Janker	PT	9.	F	U	†
19/5/40	*Uffz.*	Martin Männer	OV	9.	F	U	†
19/5/40	*Uffz.*	Horst Marotzki	RO	9.	F	U	†
19/5/40	*Obfw.*	Anton Gutschik	FE	9.	F	U	†
19/5/40	*Fw.*	Ludwig Mauter	FE	9.	F	U	†
1/6/40	*Uffz.*	Gerhard Leppin	PT	9.	F	U	†
14/6/40	*Uffz.*	Werner Scharfscheer	GN	8.	F	U	†
15/6/40	*Uffz.*	Josef Antholzner	GN	III.	F	U	†
10/7/40	*Uffz.*	Reimund Hoog	PT	7.	E	U	†
10/7/40	*Lt.*	Konrad Kupfer	OV	7.	E	U	†

10/7/40	*Fw.*	Emil Kunz	RO	7.	E	U	M
10/7/40	*Fw.*	Willi Erb	GN	7.	E	U	M
12/7/40	*Lt.*	Helmut von Brocke	OV	III.	E	U	†
12/7/40	*Fw.*	Bernhard Wlazlack	RO	III.	E	U	†
12/7/40	*Gefr.*	Alfred Mehringer	GN	III.	E	U	†
12/7/40	*Uffz.*	Heinz Zittwitz	OV	8.	E	U	†
12/7/40	*Gefr.*	Hekmut Tonn	GN	8.	E	U	†
12/7/40	*Gefr.*	Eugen Wagner	GN	8.	E	U	†
18/8/40	*Lt.*	Rudolf Woldmann	OV	8.	E	U	M
18/8/40	*Uffz.*	Gustav Gropp	PT	8.	E	U	M
18/8/40	*Uffz.*	Heinz Damm	RO	8.	E	U	M
18/8/40	*Uffz.*	Josef Schmitt	RO	8.	E	U	M
18/8/40	*Gefr.*	Wilhelm Damke	GN	8.	E	U	M
18/8/40	*Fw.*	Josef Wild	FE	8.	E	U	†
21/8/40	*Fw.*	Otto Henkel	PT	9.	E	U	M
21/8/40	*Hptm.*	Georg Pfeiffer	St.Kap.	9.	E	U	M
21/8/40	*Gefr.*	Fritz Nußbaum	GN	9.	E	U	M
21/8/40	*Uffz.*	Hans Kiauk	RO	9.	E	U	M
21/8/40	*Gefr.*	Kurt Christ	GN	9.	E	U	M
24/8/40	*Major*	Karl Ritscherle	OV	III.	E	U	†
24/8/40	*Uffz.*	Ludwig Dorn	GN	7.	E	U	†
24/8/40	*Uffz.*	Otto Schmieding	FE	7.	E	U	†
24/8/40	*Gefr.*	Willy Göllnitz	GN	7.	E	U	M
24/8/40	*Oblt.*	Gerhard Huhn	PT	9.	E	U	†
24/8/40	*Fw.*	Gottfried Ultsch	OV	9.	E	U	†
24/8/40	*Obfw.*	Josef Schmid	RO	9.	E	U	†
24/8/40	*Fw.*	Walter Jagher	FE	9.	E	U	†
24/8/40	*Flg.*	Erich Salomo	GN	9.	E	U	†
27/8/40	*Lt.*	Ullrich Weber	PT	III.	E	C	†
27/8/40	*Uffz.*	Anton Lehrhuber	GN	III.	E	C	†
27/8/40	*Gefr.*	Walter Eisenhöfer	RO	III.	E	C	†
27/8/40	*Flg.*	Wilhelm Federling	GN	III.	E	C	†
30/8/40	*Gefr.*	Leo Stilp	GN	7.	E	U	†
30/8/40	*Gefr.*	Fritz Rieß	GN	7.	E	U	†
30/8/40	*Fw.*	Hans Pallauf	OV	7.	E	U	†
5/9/40	*Fw.*	Erwin Anger	GN	7.	E	U	†
5/9/40	*Uffz.*	Rudolf Armbruster	FE	7.	E	U	†
5/9/40	*Gefr.*	Alexius Nowotny	GN	7.	E	U	†
5/9/40	*Fw.*	Karl Strobl	FE	7.	E	U	†
5/9/40	*Uffz.*	Fritz Bolz	PT	7.	E	U	†
5/9/40	*Fw.*	Hermann Bohn	GN	7.	E	U	†
5/9/40	*Uffz.*	Karl Bickl	RO	7.	E	U	M
5/9/40	*Uffz.*	Fritz Rosenberger	GN	7.	E	U	M

5/9/40	*Gefr.*	Kurt Haak	GN	7.	E	U	M
9/9/40	*Fw.*	Ernst Wendorff	FE	III.	E	U	†
9/9/40	*Fw.*	Wilhelm Wenninger	FE	III.	E	U	†
9/9/40	*Fw.*	Willi Döring	GN	III.	E	U	†
9/9/40	*Obfw.*	Ernst Pflüger	RO	8.	E	U	†
20/11/40	*Obfw.*	Wilhelm Weide	PT	8.	E	U	†
20/11/40	*Fw.*	Herbert Hebig	OV	8.	E	U	†
20/11/40	*Fw.*	Peter Wester	GN	8.	E	U	†
28/1/41	*Uffz.*	Andreas Bergmann		9.	D	U	†
19/2/41	*Lt.*	Werner Fischer	PT	9.	P	C	†
19/2/41	*Uffz.*	Otto Fischer	PT	9.	P	C	†
19/2/41	*Uffz.*	Karl Bernklau	GN	9.	P	C	†
10/3/41	*Hptm.*	Harry Giersch	PT	7.	R	C	†
10/3/41	*Fw.*	Hermann Schmenger	GN	7.	R	C	†
23/6/41	*Uffz.*	Gerhard Schulz	GN	9.	R	U	†
29/6/41	*Gefr.*	Joachim Dombrowski	RO	9.	R	U	M
29/6/41	*Fw.*	Jakob Burghardt	GN	9.	R	U	M
29/6/41	*Uffz.*	August Rothbauer	GN	9.	R	U	M
30/6/41	*Lt.*	Hans Bauer	PT	9.	R	U	M
30/6/41	*Uffz.*	Max Zink	OV	9.	R	U	†
30/6/41	*Gefr.*	Walter Böhme	RO	9.	R	U	M
30/6/41	*Obgefr.*	Josef Mondel	GN	9.	R	U	M
30/6/41	*Gefr.*	Manfred Wagner	GN	9.	R	U	M
1/7/41	*Obgefr.*	Rudolf Nitzsche	PT	9.	R	U	M
1/7/41	*Gefr.*	Franz Meister	OV	9.	R	U	M
1/7/41	*Gefr.*	Franz Leonards	RO	9.	R	U	M
1/7/41	*Obgefr.*	Günther Minke	GN	9.	R	U	M
1/7/41	*Gefr.*	Richard Wißmüller	GN	9.	R	U	M
2/7/41	*Fw.*	Josef Niggemann	PT	9.	R	U	M
2/7/41	*Gefr.*	Erwin Zabel	OV	9.	R	U	†
2/7/41	*Uffz.*	Paul Weck	RO	9.	R	U	M
2/7/41	*Gefr.*	Heinz Haase	GN	9.	R	U	M
2/7/41	*Uffz.*	Franz Hütter	GN	9.	R	U	M
17/7/41	*Fw.*	Josef Söller	PT	7.		FL	†
17/7/41	*Uffz.*	Ernst Goltermann	OV	7.	R	FL	†
17/7/41	*Gefr.*	Hans-Jürgen Reismann	RO	7.	R	FL	†
17/7/41	*Gefr.*	Josef Hauser	GN	7.	R	FL	†
17/7/41	*Gefr.*	Gustav Michel	GN	7.	R	FL	†
31/7/41	*Gefr.*	Heinz Wittorf	OV	7.	R	FT	†
31/8/41	*Oblt.*	Irmfried Leonhardt	PT	7.	R	FL	†
31/8/41	*Obfw.*	Leonhard Ebenbeck	OV	7.	R	FL	†
31/8/41	*Fw.*	Helmut Rosenberg	FE	7.	R	FL	†
1/9/41	*Obgefr.*	Ernst Menke	RO	9.	R	FL	†

2/10/41	*Obfw.*	Hermann Kindinger	GN	8.	R	FL	M
2/10/41	*Gefr.*	Hans Jais	GN	8.	R	FL	M
7/10/41	*Fw.*	August Kunz	PT	7.	R	U	M
7/10/41	*Gefr.*	Rudolf Rausch	OV	7.	R	U	M
7/10/41	*Uffz.*	Herbert Loh	RO	7.	R	U	M
7/10/41	*Uffz.*	Herbert Weil	GN	7.	R	U	M
7/10/41	*Obgefr.*	Kurt Snidt	GN	7.	R	U	M
22/10/41	*Uffz.*	Hermann Puschmann	GN	7.	R	U	M
23/10/41	*Uffz.*	Alfred Willnauer	GN	7.	R	U	M
23/10/41	*Lt.*	Georg Gade	PT	8.	R	U	M
23/10/41	*Gefr.*	Edwin Wagner	OV	8.	R	U	M
23/10/41	*Uffz.*	Hans Bräunlich	RO	8.	R	U	M
23/10/41	*Fw.*	Paul Hagedorn	GN	8.	R	U	M
23/10/41	*Uffz.*	Hugo Röllig	GN	8.	R	U	M
23/10/41	*Lt.*	Reinhard Puschmann	PT	7.	R	U	M
23/10/41	*Obfw.*	Werner Zartz	OV	7.	R	U	M
23/10/41	*Uffz.*	Helmut Klos	RO	7.	R	U	M
23/10/41	*Uffz.*	Louis Hommel	FE	7.	R	U	M
23/10/41	*Oblt.*	Oswald Gäbler	PT	7.	R	U	M
23/10/41	*Uffz.*	Heinrich Rudolf	OV	7.	R	U	M
23/10/41	*Obfw.*	Fritz Bayer	RO	7.	R	U	M
23/10/41	*Uffz.*	Adolf Hammann	GN	7.	R	U	M
23/10/41	*Uffz.*	Carl-Heinz Glaser	GN	7.	R	U	M
23/10/41	*Fw.*	Gustav Bode	PT	7.	R	U	M
23/10/41	*Uffz.*	Josef Rommel	OV	7.	R	U	M
23/10/41	*Uffz.*	Kurt Richter	RO	7.	R	U	M
15/11/41	*Fw.*	Franz Grave	PT	8.	R	U	M
15/11/41	*Uffz.*	Theo Markgraf	OV	8.	R	U	M
15/11/41	*Uffz.*	Werner Groppler	RO	8.	R	U	M
15/11/41	*Uffz.*	Friedrich Schmid	GN	8.	R	U	M
15/11/41	*Obgefr.*	Josef Hanisch	GN	8.	R	U	M
	Flg.	Heinz Margraf	AOC	7.	R	U	†
8/1/42	*Uffz.*	Erich Birkenhauer	OV	8.	R	EA	†
15/1/42	*Fw.*	August Puff	GN	7.	R	FL	†
15/1/42	*Lt.*	Gerhard Bumann	PT	9.	R	U	M
15/1/42	*Gefr.*	Fritz Rahn	OV	9.	R	U	M
15/1/42	*Gefr.*	Helmut Sabel	RO	9.	R	U	M
15/1/42	*Uffz.*	Jakob Keck	GN	9.	R	U	M
15/1/42	*Obgefr.*	Theodor Spielmann	GN	9.	R	U	M
18/3/42	*Gefr.*	Gerhard Beckmann	SC		R	EA	†
7/5/42	*Gefr.*	Helmut Gross		8.	D	EA	†
30/5/42	*Fw.*	Willi Fuhlendorf	AOC	7.	R	EA	†
29/7/42	*Lt.*	Willy Krieger	PT	7.	E	U	M

29/7/42	*Uffz.*	Otto Buhr	OV	7.	E	U	†
29/7/42	*Uffz.*	Werner Groth	RO	7.	E	U	M
29/7/42	*Uffz.*	Erich Michel	GN	7.	E	U	M
29/7/42	*Gefr.*	Josef Mayer	GN	7.	E	U	M
5/8/42	*Major*	Walter Brautkuhl	Gr.Kdr.	III.	E	U	†
5/8/42	*Uffz.*	Karl Worms	OV	7.	E	U	†
5/8/42	*Uffz.*	Werner Ißleib	FE	7.	E	U	†
5/8/42	*Obfw.*	Andreas Classen	PT	7.	E	U	M
5/8/42	*Uffz.*	*Franz Behrens*	*RO*	*7.*	*E*	*U*	*M*
5/8/42	*Uffz.*	Walter Knoppig	OV	8.	E	U	†
5/8/42	*Fw.*	Hans Birkmeier.	GN	8.	E	U	†
5/8/42	*Fw.*	Heinz Gilowitz	PT	8.	E	U	M
5/8/42	*Obfw.*	Rudolf Butz	OV	8.	E	U	M
5/8/42	*Uffz.*	Walter Haustein	RO	8.	E	U	M
5/8/42	*Uffz.*	Kurt Schulze	GN	8.	E	U	M
5/8/42	*Gefr.*	Hans Müller	GN	8.	E	U	M
9/8/42	*Uffz.*	Horst Große-Heitmeier	PT	7.	E	U	M
9/8/42	*Gefr.*	Günter Grüßner	OV	7.	E	U	M
9/8/42	*Obgefr.*	Wolfgang Richter	RO	7.	E	U	M
9/8/42	*Obgefr.*	Ferdinand Dolesal	GN	7.	E	U	M
9/8/42	*Uffz.*	Albin Kielmann	GN	7.	E	U	M
19/8/42	*Uffz.*	Wolfgang Zimmer	PT	8.	R	C	†
19/8/42	*Gefr.*	Ludwig Reinhardt	OV	8.	R	C	†
19/8/42	*Uffz.*	Anton Depfenhard	RO	8.	R	C	†
19/8/42	*Gefr.*	Horst Siedler	GN	8.	R	C	†
19/8/42	*Gefr.*	Hans Hass	GN	8.	R	C	†
19/8/42	*Oblt.*	Heinz Berkemann	PT	8.	R	U	M
19/8/42	*Obfw.*	Otto Kiesl	OV	8.	R	U	M
19/8/42	*Uffz.*	Werner Kiburg	RO	8.	R	U	M
19/8/42	*Uffz.*	Rudolf Brösdorf	FE	8.	R	U	M
19/8/42	*Uffz.*	Ernst Nüsser	GN	8.	R	U	M
28/8/42	*Gefr.*	Friedrich Pucig	GN	8.	R	FT	†
12/9/42	*Uffz.*	Max Friedrich	AOC	7.	R	U	†
13/9/42	*Hptm.*	Hans Waldforst	PT	III.	R	FL	†
13/9/42	*Obfw.*	Valentin Mayr	GN	III.	R	FL	M
13/9/42	*Gefr.*	Edmund Fiks	GN	III.	R	FL	M
1/10/42	*Lt.*	Rudolf Pohle	PT	7.	R	C	†
1/10/42	*Uffz.*	Walter Neumann	OV	7.	R	C	†
1/10/42	*Gefr.*	Herbert Klich	GN	7.	R	C	†
5/10/42	*Uffz.*	Edwin Wagner	PT	8.	R	FL	M
5/10/42	*Uffz.*	Otto Niemeyer	OV	8.	R	FL	M
5/10/42	*Gefr.*	Philipp Strom	GN	8.	R	FL	M
29/11/42	*Uffz.*	Friedrich Hillebrand	GN	9.	R	EA	†

29/11/42	Fw.	Heinrich Fenn	PT	8.	R	EA	†
29/11/42	Obgefr.	Reinhard Schüler	OV	8.	R	EA	†
8/12/42	Uffz.	Erwin Löpsinger	PT	8.	R	U	M
8/12/42	Gefr.	Rudolf Voß	OV	8.	R	U	M
8/12/42	Gefr.	Karl-Heinz Thormann	RO	8.	R	U	M
8/12/42	Gefr.	Karl Drefin	GN	8.	R	U	M
8/12/42	Obgefr.	Erich Hübschmann	GN	8.	R	U	M
25/12/42	Fw.	Hermann Gasser	OV	8.	R	U	M
25/12/42	Uffz.	Fritz Rudolf	GN	8.	R	U	M
25/12/42	Obfw.	Franz Türk	PT	8.	R	U	†
25/12/42	Obfw.	Albin Müller	RO	8.	R	U	†
25/12/42	Uffz.	Rolf Jakobs	GN	8.	R	U	†
25/12/42	Fw.	Bruno Mrozek	PT	7.	R	U	M
25/12/42	Uffz.	Paul Söll	OV	7.	R	U	M
25/12/42	Gefr.	Franz Müller	RO	7.	R	U	M
25/12/42	Gefr.	Ludwig Huber	GN	7.	R	U	M
25/12/42	Gefr.	Herbert Kepka	GN	7.	R	U	M
1/1/43	Gefr.	Eduard Merz	PT	9.	R	U	M
1/1/43	Lt.	Siegfried Heilsberg	OV	9.	R	U	M
1/1/43	Uffz.	Josef Koll	RO	9.	R	U	M
1/1/43	Uffz.	Georg Heinrich	GN	9.	R	U	M
1/1/43	Uffz.	Siegfried Leist	GN	9.	R	U	M
9/1/43	Lt.	Detlef Schulze	PT	8.	R	U	M
9/1/43	Gefr.	Gerhard Fischer	OV	8.	R	U	M
9/1/43	Uffz.	Paul Bingenheimer	RO	8.	R	U	M
9/1/43	Obgefr.	Anton Ruppert	GN	8.	R	U	M
9/1/43	Obgefr.	Rudolf Zill	GN	8.	R	U	M
28/1/43	Gefr.	Karl-Heinz Brix	OV	9.	R	FL	†
28/1/43	Uffz.	Josef Hartmann	RO	9.	R	FL	†
28/1/43	Gefr.	Heinrich Müller	GN	9.	R	FL	†
28/1/43	Obgefr.	Helmut Dornbach	GN	9.	R	FL	†
17/2/43	Uffz.	Helmut Matz	PT	8.	R	U	M
17/2/43	Lt.	Siegfried Eckert	OV	8.	R	U	M
17/2/43	Gefr.	Alfred Magiera	RO	8.	R	U	M
17/2/43	Fw.	Karl Hermann	GN	8.	R	U	M
17/2/43	Uffz.	Helmut Braunshausen	PT	8.	R	U	M
9/3/43	Obgefr.	Helmut Börner	GN	8.	R	FL	†
22/3/43	Obfw.	Johann Nowak	PT	9.	R	U	M
22/3/43	Uffz.	Helmut Droß	OV	9.	R	U	M
22/3/43	Uffz.	Hans Wiebusch	RO	9.	R	U	M
22/3/43	Uffz.	Walter Naddig	GN	9.	R	U	M
22/3/43	Gefr.	August Grühnendahl	GN	9.	R	U	M
26/3/43	Fw.	Erich Zippert	PT	9.	R	U	M

26/3/43	*Uffz.*	Paul Wagner	OV	9.	R	U	M
26/3/43	*Uffz.*	Erich Roehrig	RO	9.	R	U	M
26/3/43	*Uffz.*	Herbert Grützner	GN	9.	R	U	M
26/3/43	*Uffz.*	Helmuth Stenzaly	GN	9.	R	U	M
26/3/43		Hans-Joachim Kunze	WR	9.	R	U	M
27/3/43	*Fw.*	Richard Kayser	PT	8.	R	U	M
27/3/43	*Hptm.*	Franz Freyer	OV	8.	R	U	M
27/3/43	*Uffz.*	Walter Mann	RO	8.	R	U	M
27/3/43	*Obgefr.*	Gerhard Kauss	GN	8.	R	U	M
27/3/43	*Obgefr.*	Herbert Fleischer	GN	8.	R	U	M
21/4/43	*Fw.*	Georg Wobig	PT	9.	R	FL	†
26/5/43	*Uffz.*	Siegfried Thomas	PT	9.	R	FT	†
26/5/43	*Uffz.*	Harry Wermbter	RO	9.	R	FT	†
26/5/43	*Uffz.*	Hubert Franz	GN	9.	R	FT	†
26/5/43	*Uffz.*	Fritz Römer	RO	9.	R	FT	†
27/5/43	*Major*	Hubert Mönch Gr.Kdr.		7.	R	U	M
27/5/43	*Lt.*	Karl-Anton van Volxen	OV	7.	R	U	M
27/5/43	*Obfw.*	Paul Altrock	RO	7.	R	U	M
27/5/43	*Obfw.*	Helmut Stuhr	FE	7.	R	U	M
27/5/43	*Gefr.*	Friedrich Ständig	GN	7.	R	U	M
30/5/43	*Obfw.*	Götz Werner	GN	9.	R	FT	†
5/6/43	*Uffz.*	Erwin Seeber	GN	8.	R	FT	†
10/6/43	*Uffz.*	Wolfgang Miram	RO	8.	R	EA	†
13/6/43	*Oblt.*	Horst Weißart	PT	9.	R	U	M
13/6/43	*Uffz.*	Walter Schröter	OV	9.	R	U	M
13/6/43	*Obgefr.*	Gerhard Walzel	GN	9.	R	U	†
13/6/43	*Obgefr.*	Werner Asselmeyer	GN	9.	R	U	†
13/6/43	*Obfw.*	Josef Iblher	PT	9.	R	U	M
13/6/43	*Uffz.*	Andreas Emmerling	MCC	9.	R	U	M
18/6/43	*Uffz.*	Heinrich Klare	GN	7.	R	FL	†
21/6/43	*Uffz.*	Eugen Merz	RO	9.	R	FL	†
5/7/43	*Uffz.*	Herbert Beuche	OV	8.	R	FT	M
5/7/43	*Fw.*	Willi Riek	RO	8.	R	FT	M
5/7/43	*Uffz.*	Herbert Linssen	GN	8.	R	FT	M
5/7/43	*Uffz.*	Hans Klaus	GN	8.	R	FT	M
5/7/43	*Uffz.*	Kurt Friebe	OV	8.	R	FT	†
9/7/43	*Lt.*	Martin Ney	PT	8.	X	C	†
9/7/43	*Uffz.*	Erich Perplies	RO	8.	X	C	†
11/10/43	*Lt.*	Werner Lewitzki	PT	9.	X	C	†
11/10/43	*Obgefr.*	Franz Nuber	OV	9.	X	C	†
11/10/43	*Uffz.*	Reinhard Gräble	RO	9.	X	C	†
11/10/43	*Uffz.*	Josef Otzipka	GN	9.	X	C	†
11/10/43	*Obgefr.*	Josef Sumser	GN	9.	X	C	†

11/10/43	*Uffz.*	Franz Martin	MCC	9.	X	C	†
3/10/43	*Obfw.*	Jan Recke	PT	8.	X	C	†
17/11/43	*Lt.*	Erich Klöbel	PT	7.	X	C	†
17/11/43	*Uffz.*	Walter Moje	OV	7.	X	C	†
17/11/43	*Uffz.*	Hans Reiling	RO	7.	X	C	†
17/11/43	*Obgefr.*	August Hupe	GN	7.	X	C	†
17/11/43	*Obgefr.*	Anton Ihrlich	GN	7.	X	C	†
17/11/43	*Obfw.*	Paul Burmester	PT	7.	X	C	†
17/11/43	*Obfw.*	Helmut Lindemann	OV	7.	X	C	†
17/11/43	*Uffz.*	Walter Knobloch	RO	7.	X	C	†
17/11/43	*Oblt.*	Hans Großendorfer	OV	7.	X	C	†
17/11/43	*Obfw.*	Fritz Hartenstein	OV	7.	X	C	†
30/11/43	*Uffz.*	Ernst Baier	PT	7.	X	C	†
30/11/43	*Gefr.*	Gottfried Michel	OV	7.	X	C	†
30/11/43	*Uffz.*	Heinz Winkler	RO	7.	X	C	†
30/11/43	*Obgefr.*	Günter Barbig	GN	7.	X	C	†
30/11/43	*Obgefr.*	Paul Blosch	GN	7.	X	C	†
30/11/43	*Fw.*	Adolf Steiner	Ger. Verw.	7.	X	C	†
30/11/43	*Obgefr.*	Karl Vanek	MCC	7.	X	C	†
30/11/43	*Gefr.*	Walter Eichhoff	AR	7.	X	C	†
15/12/43	*Obgefr.*	Karl Redinger	GN	7.	R	EA	†
15/12/43	*Uffz.*	Oskar Szucsits	PT	9.	R	FL	†
15/12/43	*Obfw.*	Rolf Mehlsauer	OV	9.	R	FL	†
15/12/43	*Uffz.*	Walter Leis	RO	9.	R	FL	†
15/12/43	*Gefr.*	Franz Konrad	GN	9.	R	FL	†
15/12/43	*Gefr.*	Johann Radl	GN	9.	R	FL	†
21/2/44	*Fw.*	Helmut Gerdes	GN	8.	X	C	†
21/2/44	*Uffz.*	Kurt Seelow	GN	8.	X	C	†
16/2/44	*Uffz.*	Gerhard Lübbe	GN	III.	R	U	†
16/2/44	*Fw.*	Alois Kasper	PT	III.	R	U	†
16/2/44	*Uffz.*	Heinz Fischer	OV	III.	R	U	†
16/2/44	*Fw.*	Wilhelm Thöne	RO	III.	R	U	†
16/2/44	*Fw.*	Franz Steimer	GN	III.	R	U	†
21/2/44	*Fw.*	Kurt Lange	PT	8.	X	C	†
21/2/44	*Uffz.*	Ferdinand Groß	OV	8.	X	C	†
21/2/44	*Fw.*	Heinrich Brinkhoff	RO	8.	X	C	†
21/2/44	*Obfw.*	Alfred Ziesenböck	OV	8.	X	C	†
21/2/44	*Obfw.*	Johann Ullrich	MCC	8.	X	C	†
21/2/44	*Fw.*	Otto Wolters	CK	8.	X	C	†
16/3/44	*Uffz.*	Walter Hempe	OV	7.	R	C	†
21/3/44	*Uffz.*	Ottomar Fischer	PT/LS	9.	R	C	†
21/3/44	*Uffz.*	Werner Wörlein	GN	9.	R	C	†

31/3/44	*Uffz.*	Walter Telle	GN	7.	R	U	M
31/3/44	*Obgefr.*	Thomas Lübben	GN	7.	R	U	M
31/3/44	*Uffz.*	Hans Klinkenberg	GN	7.	R	U	M
31/3/44	*Obgefr.*	Clemens Kappen	GN	7.	R	U	†
31/3/44	*Uffz.*	August Diehl	PT	7.	R	U	M
31/3/44	*Uffz.*	Rolf Mahr	OV	7.	R	U	M
31/3/44	*Uffz.*	Hans Weidner	RO	7.	R	U	M
31/3/44	*Uffz.*	Heinz Wernicke	OV	8.	R	FT	†
31/3/44	*Fhj.Fw.*	Josef Genß	RO	7.	R	FL	†
31/3/44	*Uffz.*	Gottfried Endt	OV	7.	R	FL	†
5/4/44	*Uffz.*	Fritz Krull	PT	9.	R	C	†
5/4/44	*Uffz.*	Kurt Krukemeyer	OV	7.	R	C	†
5/4/44	*Uffz.*	Karl Henninger	RO	9.	R	C	†
5/4/44	*Flg.*	Bruno Möding	FE	9.	R	C	†
11/4/44	*Uffz.*	Otto Keßler	PT	7.	R	U	M
11/4/44	*Obgefr.*	Harry Fischer	OV	7.	R	U	M
11/4/44	*Obgefr.*	Erich Grießmayer	RO	7.	R	U	M
11/4/44	*Obgefr.*	Werner Matiske	GN	7.	R	U	M
11/4/44	*Uffz.*	Bernhard Lönneker	PT	8.	R	U	M
11/4/44	*Obgefr.*	Gerhard Trippner	OV	8.	R	U	M
11/4/44	*Obgefr.*	Friedrich Ostermann	RO	8.	R	U	M
11/4/44	*Obgefr.*	Günter Mau	GN	8.	R	U	M
11/4/44	*Obgefr.*	Helmut Petschulat	GN	8.	R	U	M
11/4/44	*Uffz.*	Werner Krumbholz	PT	7.	R	U	M
11/4/44	*Obgefr.*	Franz Meixner	OV	7.	R	U	M
11/4/44	*Uffz.*	Alfred Dehner	RO	7.	R	U	M
11/4/44	*Fhj.Fw.*	Friedrich Wilhelm Raffauf	GN	7.	R	U	M
11/4/44	*Gefr.*	Fritz Borchert	GN	7.	R	U	M
28/5/44	*Uffz.*	Karl Schenk	PT	9.	R	U	M
28/5/44	*Obgefr.*	Udo-Hans Dressler	OV	9.	R	U	M
28/5/44	*Uffz.*	Otto Mayer	RO	9.	R	U	M
28/5/44	*Obgefr.*	Florian Lorenz	FE	9.	R	U	M
28/5/44	Obgefr.	Franz Schmidt	GN	9.	R	U	M
11/6/44	*Uffz.*	Werner Schede	PT	9.	R	C	†
11/6/44	*Uffz.*	Arnold Wandzik	OV	9.	R	C	†
11/6/44	*Uffz.*	Ernst Bauer	RO	9.	R	C	†
11/6/44	*Obgefr.*	Günther Neuhaus	GN	9.	R	C	†
11/6/44	*Gefr.*	Franz Wenzel	GN	9.	R	C	†
9/7/44	*Obfw.*	Ernst Henseleit	PT	9.	R	C	M
9/7/44	*Uffz.*	Otto Finkener	OV	9.	R	C	M
9/7/44	*Uffz.*	Paul Lengfeld	RO	9.	R	C	M
9/7/44	*Uffz.*	Peter Sandlöbes	FE	9.	R	C	M

9/7/44	*Uffz.*	Gottfried Pelz	GN	9.	R	C	M
1/8/44	*Uffz.*	Heinz Bergander	OV	7.	R	FT	†
19/8/44	*Uffz.*	Eugen Finis	PT	7.	F	U	M
19/8/44	*Fw.*	Josef Wittmann	OV	7.	F	U	M
19/8/44	*Gefr.*	Günther Herbst	RO	7.	F	U	M
19/8/44	*Uffz.*	Erhart Schmalenberger	GN	7.	F	U	M
19/8/44	*Obgefr.*	Günther Menzel	GN	7.	F	U	M
20/8/44	*Gefr.*	Hanspeter Stephan	PT	9.	F	C	†
20/8/44	*Obgefr.*	Horst Dunst	OV	9.	F	C	†
21/8/44	*Fw.*	Rudolf Muschinski	PT	9.	F	U	M
21/8/44	*Uffz.*	Hermann Linke	OV	9.	F	U	M
21/8/44	*Uffz.*	Gustav Steinhofer	RO	9.	F	U	M
21/8/44	*Uffz.*	Lothar Fittkau	GN	9.	F	U	M
21/8/44	*Uffz.*	Heinz Gebhardt	GN	9.	F	U	M
22/8/44	*Uffz.*	Franz Lechner	PT	8.	F	C	M
22/8/44	*Obgefr.*	Josef Ziegler	OV	8.	F	C	M
22/8/44	*Uffz.*	Walter Hünlich	RO	8.	F	C	M
22/8/44	*Gefr.*	Albert Sames	GN	8.	F	C	M
23/12/44	*Uffz.*	Robert Rösch	PT	7.	E	C	†
23/12/44	*Obfhr.*	Alfred-Ernst Scholz	OV	7.	E	C	†
23/12/44	*Obgefr.*	Herbert Köchle	RO	7.	E	C	†
23/12/44	*Uffz.*	Werner Müller	GN	7.	E	C	†
23/12/44	*Uffz.*	Hans Gumz	GN	9.	E	EA	†
24/12/44	*Uffz.*	Herbert Neuber	PT	7.	E	U	M
24/12/44	*Obfw.*	Heinrich Kock	OV	7.	E	U	M
24/12/44	*Uffz.*	Fritz Reinhardt	RO	7.	E	U	M
24/12/44	*Fw.*	Otto Wieland	FE	7.	E	U	M
24/12/44	*Obgefr.*	Oswald Pfaffhausen	GN	7.	E	U	M
3/1/45	*Obgefr.*	Hubert Türks	GN	7.	E	C	†
3/1/45	*Uffz.*	Gerhard Tanner	RO	7.	E	EA	†
5/1/45	*Uffz.*	Emil Rydwal	RO	9.	E	C	†
5/1/45	*Obfw.*	Richard Mann	GN	9.	E	C	†
5/1/45	*Lt.*	Kurt Neuber	PT	7.	E	U	M
5/1/45	*Fw.*	Oskar Köhler	OV	7.	E	U	M
5/1/45	*Fw.*	Henry Aehlig	RO	7.	E	U	M
5/1/45	*Uffz.*	Bruno Burow	GN	7.	E	U	M
5/1/45	*Uffz.*	Adam Becker	GN	7.	E	U	M
5/1/45	*Hptm.* St.Kap.	Siegfried Jessen	PT	9.	E	FT	†
5/1/45	*Obfw.*	Alfred Beyer	OV	9.	E	FT	†
5/1/45	*Uffz.*	Wolfgang Gast	RO	9.	E	FT	†
5/1/45	*Fw.*	Hermann Fresken	GN	9.	E	FT	†
5/1/45	*Uffz.*	Gerhard Franke	GN	9.	E	FT	†

IV. Gruppe

9/6/40	*Uffz.*	Karl Leichenauer	AOC	4.	G	U	†
9/6/40	*Gefr.*	Joseph Stippel	AOC	4.	G	U	†
24/5/41	*Oblt.*	Hubertus Macha	PT	12.	G	U	†
24/5/41	*Obgefr.*	Reinhold Bulling	OV	12.	G	U	†
24/5/41	*Uffz.*	Franz Schmidt	RO	12.	G	U	†
24/5/41	*Fw.*	Otto Köhler	FE	12.	G	U	†
24/5/41	*Gefr.*	Alwin Siewert	GN	12.	G	U	†
25/5/41	*Lt.*	Wilhelm Tanke	PT	12.	F	U	†
26/5/41	*Uffz.*	Walter Keil	PT	12.	G	U	†
26/5/41	*Gefr.*	Hans Gebhardt	OV	12.	G	U	†
26/5/41	*Gefr.*	Ludwig Pfisterer	RO	12.	G	U	†
26/5/41	*Gefr.*	Rolf Borgsdorf	GN	12.	G	U	†
4/6/41	*Flg.*	Erwin Löhrke		11.	F	U	†
9/6/41	*Uffz.*	Richard Wächter	PT	11.	D	C	†
9/6/41	*Uffz.*	Hermann Wahn	OV	11.	D	C	†
9/6/41	*Gefr.*	Rudolf Zimmer	RO	11.	D	C	†
9/6/41	*Uffz.*	Herbert Weltchen	GN	11.	D	C	†
17/6/41	*Lt.*	Hayo Müller	PT	11.	X	U	†
20/6/41	*Uffz.*	Paul Schulte-Schrepping	PT	12.	F	C	†
20/6/41	*Gefr.*	Johann Wenth	OV	12.	F	C	†
20/6/41	*Uffz.*	Heinrich Siebert	RO	12.	F	C	†
20/6/41	*Gefr.*	Gerhard Dunkel	OV	12.	F	C	†
28/7/41	*Lt.*	Heinrich Egermann	PT	12.	F	C	†
28/7/41	*Gefr.*	Fritz Scheithauer	OV	12.	F	C	†
28/7/41	*Gefr.*	Egidius Rieger	RO	12.	F	C	†
28/7/41	*Gefr.*	Richard Müller	GN	12.	F	C	†
10/8/41	*Gefr.*	Werner Ay	GN	11.	F	U	†
8/10/41	*Fw.*	Stefan Breg	OV	10.	G	C	†
8/10/41	*Gefr.*	Günther Trautmann	GN	10.	G	C	†
14/10/41	*Lt.*	Hermann von Schleich	PT	10.	G	C	†
14/10/41	*Obgefr.*	Alfred Fuchs	OV	10.	G	C	†
14/10/41	*Obgefr.*	Richard Raßl	RO	10.	G	C	†
14/10/41	*Flg.*	Georg Wietschorke	GN	10.	G	C	†
23/10/41	*Fw.*	August Specht	MD	IV.	F	U	†
29/1/42	*Lt.*	Hermann Weger	PT	12.	G	C	†
29/1/42	*Obfw.*	Wilhelm Meißner	OV	12.	G	C	†
29/1/42	*Obgefr.*	Georg Hagmeyer	RO	12.	G	C	†
14/2/42	*Fw.*	Karl Selzan	PT	12.	F	C	†
14/2/42	*Gefr.*	Walter Tydecks	OV	12.	F	C	†
14/2/42	*Gefr.*	Karl Gaßmann	RO	12.	F	G.	†
14/2/42	*Uffz.*	Rudolf Just	GN	12.	F	C	†
14/2/42	*Gefr.*	Georg Schulz	GN	12.	F	C	†

7/5/42	Uffz.	Kurt Hätscher	PT	11.	G	C	†
7/5/42	Gefr.	Rudolf Wentigmann	OV	11.	G	C	†
7/5/42	Gefr.	Walter Schimansky	RO	11.	G	C	†
7/5/42	Obgefr.	Willibald Lugerbauer	GN	11.	G	C	†
10/8/42	Uffz.	Benedikt Bloier	PT	10.	G	C	†
10/8/42	Uffz.	Reinhold Karg	OV	10.	G	C	†
04/1/42	Gefr.	Johann Wohlmacher	DR	10.	F	U	†
11/4/41	Obgefr.	Helmut Rösler	DR	IV.	G	U	†
25/8/42	Fw.	Erwin Hoffmann	PT	10.	G	C	†
25/8/42	Uffz.	Wilhelm Haase	OV	10.	G	C	†
25/8/42	Fw.	Sigmund Weber	RO	10.	G	C	†
25/8/42	Uffz.	Franz Klindt	GN	10.	G	C	†
25/8/42	Gefr.	Albert Gerl	GN	10.	G	C	†
12/11/42	Lt.	Helmut Henkel	PT	11.	G	C	†
12/11/42	Obfw.	Wilhelm Oelker	PT	11.	G	C	†
12/11/42	Gefr.	Hans Raffel	GN	11.	G	C	†
22/11/42	Uffz.	Heinz Pieske	PT	10.	G	C	†
22/11/42	Uffz.	Adolf Jauernig	RO	10.	G	C	†
22/11/42	Obgefr.	Erwin Rapp	MCC	10.	G	C	†
14/12/42	Lt.	Helmut Karschewski	PT	12.	F	C	†
14/12/42	Uffz.	Franz Gütl	OV	12.	F	C	†
14/12/42	Gefr.	Werner Kollosche	RO	12.	F	C	†
8/1/43	Gefr.	Hermann Pieschl	PT	11.	F	C	†
8/1/43	Obgefr.	Kurt Abramowitsch	OV	11.	F	C	†
8/1/43	Gefr.	Friedrich Langeloth	RO	11.	F	C	†
8/1/43	Gefr.	Karl Kolbeck	GN	11.	F	C	†
8/1/43	Gefr.	Fritz Rademacher	GN	11.	F	C	†
5/2/43	Obgefr.	Walter Schwald	Four.	IV.	F	U	†
7/2/43		Hans Usinger	Insp.	IV.	F	U	†
7/2/43	Oblt.	Erich Horn	PT	12.	F	C	†
30/3/43	Uffz.	Johann Junker	PT	11.	F	EA	†
30/3/43	Uffz.	Hans Geister	RO	11.	F	EA	†
5/5/43	Uffz.	Johann Ruff	PT	10.	G	C	†
5/5/43	Obgefr.	Fritz Schutzbach	OV	10.	G	C	†
5/5/43	Obgefr.	Jakob Giroldstein	RO	10.	G	C	†
5/5/43	Obfw.	Ernst Bsdurek	FE	10.	G	C	†
5/5/43	Obgefr.	Gerhard Schneider	GN	10.	G	C	†
15/6/43	Uffz.	Johann Zimmer	PT	12.	F	C	†
15/6/43	Fw.	Waldemar Günther	OV	12.	F	C	†
15/6/43	Gefr.	Willibald Häntschel	RO	12.	F	C	†
15/6/43	Obgefr.	Albert Peissl	FE	12.	F	C	†
15/6/43	Obgefr.	Jakob Kessler	GN	12.	F	C	†
12/7/43	Uffz.	Alfred Stengel	PT	13.	F	C	†

12/7/43	*Fw.*	Erwin Koch	OV	13.	F	C	†
12/7/43	*Gefr.*	Gerhard Schwarz	RO	13.	F	C	†
12/7/43	*Uffz.*	Rudolf Lehmann	FE	13.	F	C	†
26/7/43	*Lt.*	Herbert Gerling	PT	13.	F	C	†
26/7/43	*Uffz.*	Heinz Kranhold	OV	13.	F	C	†
26/7/43	*Gefr.*	Günther Glaser	FE	13.	F	C	†
18/8/43	*Uffz.*	Herbert Schwedt	CK	13.	F	U	†
2/9/43	*Lt.*	Kurt Emmrich	PT	12.	F	C	†
2/9/43	*Uffz.*	Helmut Kohler	OV	12.	F	C	†
12/12/43	*Lt.*	Johann Renner	PT	13.	F	C	†
12/12/43	*Uffz.*	Viktor Lowak	RO	13.	F	C	†
12/12/43	*Obfw.*	Wilhelm Polacek	FE	13.	F	C	†
22/12/43	*Uffz.*	Karl Moser	PT	10.	F	FT	†
22/12/43	*Gefr.*	Otto Müller	OV	10.	F	FT	†
22/12/43	*Gefr.*	Walter Höhne	FE	10.	F	FT	†
22/12/43	*Obgefr.*	Robert Schneele	RO	10.	F	FT	†
24/1/44	*Fhr.*	Dieter Hartmann	PT	12.	F	C	†
24/1/44	*Gefr.*	Hubert Fleischmann	OV	12.	F	C	†
24/1/44	*Gefr.*	Manfred Topp	RO	12.	F	C	†
24/1/44	*Uffz.*	Artur Gauer	FE	12.	F	C	†
5/2/44	*Lt.*	Franz Schottmüller	PT	12.	F	U	†
5/2/44	*Uffz.*	Dagobert Schnetzler	RO	12.	F	U	†
5/2/44	*Obfw.*	Willi Engel	RO	12.	F	U	†
3/3/44	*Fhj.Uffz.*	Hubert Strobel	PT	10.	G	C	†
3/3/44	*Gefr.*	Ernst Döring	OV	10.	G	C	†
3/3/44	*Gefr.*	Ludwig Kalmar	RO	10.	G	C	†
3/3/44	*Gefr.*	Helmut Heinrich	GN	10.	G	C	†
18/4/44	*Uffz.*	Alfred Engler	PT	12.	G	C	†
18/4/44	*Gefr.*	Horst Kopp	OV	12.	G	C	†
26/4/44	*Obfw.*	Emil Kreuger	PT	11.	G	C	†
26/4/44	*Gefr.*	Dietrich Schmidt	OV	11.	G	C	†
26/4/44	*Obgefr.*	Heinz Zoschke	RO	11.	G	C	†
26/4/44	*Obgefr.*	Herbert Becker	GN	11.	G	C	†
26/4/44	*Obgefr.*	Alfred Degelmann	FE	11.	G	C	†
2/6/44	*Fw.*	Georg Uch	AOC	IV.	X	U	†
2/6/44	*Obgefr.*	Walter Lippig	AOC	IV.	X	U	†
2/6/44	*Gefr.*	Karl Knogl	RO	10.	X	U	†
10/7/44	*Gefr.*	Friedrich Ohm	RO	11.	X	U	†
25/7/44	*Gefr.*	Willi Reich	PT	11.	X	C	†
25/7/44	*Obfw.*	Willi Schmeißer	OV	11.	X	C	†
25/7/44	*Gefr.*	Josef Götz	OV	11.	X	A	†

Croatian Staffel

16/7/42	*Oblt.*	Ivan Boko	PT	15.	R	FL	M
16/7/42	*Lt.*	Mato Kreitner		15.	R	FL	M
16/7/42	*Stfw.*	Julije Batalo		15.	R	FL	M
16/7/42	*Obfw.*	Wjeskoslav Medić		15.	R	FL	M
25/8/42	*Oblt.*	Vladimir Smidt	PT	15.	R	C	†
25/8/42	*Ufw.*	Stjepan Ruzić	OV	15.	R	C	†
25/8/42	*Obfw.*	Nikola Pawlowić	RO	15.	R	C	†
25/8/42	*Fw.*	Pavao Gregurić	GN	15.	R	C	†
28/1/43	*Lt.*	Nikola Pindulić	PT	15.	R	U	M
28/1/43	*Stfw.*	Ferdinand Mekus	OV	15.	R	U	M
28/1/43	*Obfw.*	Ernst Gumhold	RO	15.	R	U	M
28/1/43	*Obfw.*	Dragan Dür	GN	15.	R	U	M

VII. KG Legion Condor 53: Recipients of the Knight's Cross

Rank	Name	Awarded On	Rank/ Position	Unit	Killed or Died On
Knight's Cross with Oak Leaves					
Major	Herbert Wittmann	11/2/1945	OV/Gr.Kdr.	II. *Gruppe*	26/07/2007
Knight's Cross					
Lt.	Georg Ackermann	28/2/1945	PT	II. *Gr.Stab*	16/12/2007
Obfw.	Georg Christmann	5/4/1944	OV	6. *Staffel*	5/11/1944
Lt.	Wilhelm Döring	19/2/1943	OV	2. *Staffel*	3/8/1955
Oblt.	Johann Dreher	5/4/1944	PT	5. *Staffel*	4/3/1945
Hptm.	Ernst Ebeling	20/3/1945	PT/Ops.	*Off.Geschw.Stab*	16/01/1999
Lt.	Otto Engel	28/2/45	PT	5. *Staffel*	30/01/2005
Hptm.	Ludwig Grözinger	25/11/1942	PT/St.Kap.	3. *Staffel*	15/2/1945
Oblt.	Hans Grossendorfer	19/4/44	OV	7. *Staffel*	20/11/1943
Oblt.	Heinz Gutmann	5/4/1944	PT	3. *Staffel*	3/3/1945
Oblt.	Alois Hulha	17/3/1945	OV	6. *Staffel*	07/05/1983
Lt.	Georg Juditzki	9/11/1944	PT	I. *Gr.Stab*	01/07/2007
Hptm.	Ernst-Ascan Gobert	27/4/1944	PT/St.Kap.	2. *Staffel*	2/11/1944
Oblt.	Dietrich Kornblum	9/6/1944	PT/St.Kap.	4. *Staffel*	27/11/1944
Oblt.	Rudolf Küster	17/3/1945	PT	6. *Staffel*	29/07/1991
Oblt.	Kurt Lehmann	19/2/1943	PT/St.Kap.	2. *Staffel*	25/06/1981
Fw.	Franz Lehner	22/5/1943	OV	6. *Staffel*	25/08/2000
Oblt.	Wolfgang Lührs	24/10/1944	PT/St.Kap.	2. *Staffel*	20/4/1945
Obfw.	Franz Mund	17/3/1945	OV	6. *Staffel*	21/12/1993
Major	Karl Rauer	29/2/1944	OV/Kdr.	I. *Gruppe*	07/05/1946
Oblt.	Siegfried Rehle	19/2/1943	OV	2. *Staffel*	30/12/1942

Obfw.	Willi Rein	5/9/1944	PT	5. *Staffel*	21/08/1944
Obfw.	Walter Richter	28/2/1945	FE	5. *Staffel*	17/11/1996
Obfw.	Fritz Steudel	28/2/1945	RO	II. *Gr.Stab*	25/08/2004
Obfw.	Waldemar Teige	7/6/1942	PT	6. *Staffel*	3/10/1942
Oblt.	Paul Weitkus	18/9/1941	OV/Kdore		09/11/1974
Fw.	Fritz Will	22/5/1943	PT	6. *Staffel*	28/8/1944
Hptm.	Herbert Wittmann	23/11/1941	OV/St.Kap.	*Stabstaffel*	26/07/2007
Hptm.	Heinz Zöllner	5/4/1944	PT/St.Kap.	6. *Staffel*	5/11/1944

Awarded after leaving the Geschwader

Oberstleutnant	Gustav Wilke	24/5/1940	*Kdr.*	*Kampfgruppe* z.b.V. 11
Oberstleutnant	Werner Koslinski	9/6/1944	OV	*Kommodore* KG 4
Lt.	Arnold Döring	17/4/1945	PT	10./NJG 3

VIII. KG 53 Command Position Staffing

Kommodore

Oberst Deßloch	1936-1937
Oberst Zoch	1937-1939
Oberst Erich Stahl	1/8/1939-Dec. 1940
Oberst Paul Weitkus	15/12/1940-31/10/1942
Oberst Karl-Eduard Wilke	1/11/1942-31/3/1943
Oberstleutnant Fritz O. Pockrandt	14/4/1943-April1945
(disbanded)	

Gruppenkommandeure
I./KG 53

Oberstleutnant Holzhauser	1937
Oberstleutnant Karl Mehnert	1938-10/5/1940
Oberstleutnant Erich Kaufmann	16/5/1940-Dec. 1941
Major Joachim Wienholtz	1941-30/3/1942
Major Fritz O. Pockrandt	11/4/1942-13/4/1943
Major Karl Rauer	17/4/1943-Sept. 1944
Major Martin Vetter	15/10/1944-April 1945
(disbanded)	

II./KG 53

Major Reinhold Tamm	23/7/1940-18/8/1940
Major Hans Steinweg	18/9/1940-1941
Oberstleutnant Hans Bader	25/7/1941-
Oberstleutnant Schulz-Müllensiefen	May 1942-14/4/1943
Major Herbert Wittmann	25/5/1943-March 1945
(disbanded)	

III./KG 53

Oberstleutnant Behrend	1938
Major Friedrich Edler von Braun	1939-1940
Major Willi Rohrbacher	1940

Major Richard Fabian	Feb. 1941-April 1942
Major Walter Brautkuhl	5/8/1942
Major Hans Waldforst	17/8/1942-12/9/1942
Major Hubert Mönch	21/10/1942-27/5/1943
Major Emil Allmendinger	24/6/1943-18/3/1945
(disbanded)	

IV./KG 53

Major Joachim Wienholtz	April 1941-Dec. 1941
Major Andreas Zahn	4/12/1941-April 1943
Major Ludwig Grözinger	April 1943-20/8/1944
	(disbanded)

Staffelkapitäne

Stabsstaffel

Hauptmann Ulrich Kleber	1/5/1938-30/6/1939
Hauptmann Herbert Wittmann	1/7/1939-14/10/1941
Hauptmann Jürgen von Horn	14/10/1941-March 1942

1. Staffel

Major Friedrich Edler von Braun	1939
Major Fritz Winkler	1/12/1939-August 1940
Hauptmann Karl Allmendinger	1/9/1940-Dec. 1941
Hauptmann Karl Rauer	14/2/1942-16/4/1943
Hauptmann Roth	Feb. 1944-May 1944
Hauptmann Werner Brandt	1944-Sept. 1944

2. Staffel

Hauptmann Herbold	1939
Hauptmann Joachim Wienholtz	1940
Major Karl Wolfien	14/5/1940
Oberleutnant Jacobi	1941
Hauptmann Kurt Lehmann	19/5/1942-1943
Oberleutnant Ernst-Ascan Gobert	1/3/1943-23/11/1943
Oberleutnant Wolfgang Lührs	24/11/1943-Sept. 1944
Hauptmann Horst Zander	Sept. 1944-April 1945

3. Staffel

Hauptmann Fritz Winkler	1936-1939
Major Alaric Hofmann	1939-1940
Hauptmann Bernhard Schwarz	1940-15/6/1940

Hauptmann Werner Hörenz	20/8/1940-16/4/1941
Hauptmann Otmar Hirschhauer	1941-23/6/1941
Hauptmann Ludwig Grözinger	1941
Hauptmann Heinz Gutmann	27/8/1943-19/7/1944
Hauptmann Kettel	
Oberleutnant Müller (Janusch)	1944-Sept. 1944
Hauptmann Werner Brandt	15/10/1944-April 1945

4. Staffel

Hauptmann Karl Wolfien	1939
Hauptmann Hans Waldforst	15/2/1940-20/04/1941
Hauptmann Rinza	June 1941-18/2/1942
Hauptmann Richard Klein	May 1942-26/1/1943
Hauptmann Franz-Josef Maubach	29/1/1943
Oberleutnant Gerhard Zabel	Sept. 1943-18/2/1944
Hauptmann Dietrich Kornblum	19/2/1944
Hauptmann Heinz Rehfeld	15/11/1944

5. Staffel

Hauptmann Ferdinand Muggenthaler	1939
Hauptmann Hubert Mönch	1/7/1939-31/1/1941
Hauptmann Köhler	1942
Hauptmann Erhard Schier	15/11/1944

6. Staffel

Hauptmann Fritz O. Pockrandt	10/10/1940-30/11/1940
Hauptmann Waldemar Mund	30/11/1940-1941
Hauptmann Andreas Zahn	1/6/1941-3/12/1941
Hauptmann Heinz Thierig	12/5/1941-Dec. 1942
Hauptmann Walter Spellig	Dec. 1942-15/3/1943
Hauptmann Heinz Zöllner	1/6/1943-26/9/1943
Hauptmann Wilhelm Bautz	15/11/1944-April 1945

7. Staffel

Hauptmann Heinz Zorn	1938-1940
Oberleutnant Irmfried Leonhardi	1940-31/8/1941
Oberleutnant Oswald Gäbler	1941-23/10/1941
Hauptmann Ernst Ebeling	October 1941-15/1/1944
Hauptmann Siegfried Jessen	14/1/1944-1944
Hauptmann August Lauerer	15/11/1944-10/1/1945
Hauptmann Kurt Bausek	10/1/1945-disbandment

8. Staffel

Hauptmann Richard Fabian	1939-1/9/1940
Hauptmann Joachim Wienholtz	1940
Major Willi Haster	Oct. 1941
Leutnant Berkemann	1941 (interim)
Oberleutnant Heinz Eicke	20/6/1942-2/5/1943
Hauptmann Artur Pfister	July 1943-4/4/1944
Hauptmann Josef Dengg	15/11/1944-April 1945

9. Staffel

Major Franz Reuss	1939-1940
Hauptmann Georg Pfeiffer	21/8/1940
Hauptmann Waldemar Mund	10/10/1940-30/11/1940
Hauptmann Fritz O. Pockrandt	1/9/1940-10/4/1942
(temporarily to 6. Staffel)	
Hauptmann Kurt Kindt	20/6/1942-2/5/1943
Hauptmann Alfred Bischowski	3/8/1943-Nov. 1944
Hauptmann Siegfried Jessen	Nov. 1944-5/1/1945
Hauptmann August Lauerer	10/1/1945-April 1945

10. Staffel

Hauptmann Gerhard Joachim	26/3/1941-20/12/1941
Hauptmann Alfred Bischowski	15/1/1942-2/8/1943
Hauptmann Kurt Kindt	18/7/1943-25/7/1944

11. Staffel

Hauptmann Karl Rauer	26/3/1941-14/2/1942
Hauptmann Kurt Lehmann	15/6/1943

12. Staffel

Oberleutnant Kobel	1943
Hauptmann Kurt Lehmann	1943
Hauptmann Franz Eicke	3/5/1943

13. Staffel

Oberleutnant Franz-Josef Maubach	29/1/1943
Oberleutnant Johannes Kowoll	15/7/1943
Hauptmann Walter Spellig	15/2/1944-25/7/1944

15. (kroat) Staffel

(A second *Staffel* and a *Gruppe* headquarters were later added under the German liaison detachment.)

Kommandeur: Major Gerhard Joachim   Dec. 1942-Aug. 1944
(disbanded)

Motorized Signals Company KG 53

Oberleutnant Lessing   1940-17/2/1942
Hauptmann Siebel   18/2/1942-March 1943
Oberleutnant Heinz Waldhecker   March 1943-disbandment

Airfield Operating Companies
1. FBK
Hauptmann Harald Lange   1938-3/7/1939
Oberleutnant Alfred Hufenreuter   July 1939-April 1940
Oberleutnant Werner Willmann

2. FBK
Hauptmann Samscha
Hauptmann Franz Landl   1/12/1939-14/1/1941

3. FBK
Hauptmann Otto Krug   1940

4. FBK
Hauptmann Dipl.Ing. Krebs   1938-October 1940
Hauptmann Theiß   1940-1942
Major Georg Flauger   March 1942-January 1943

5. FBK
Major Georg Pick   16/2/1940
Major Georg Flauger   20/3/1942-10/5/1942

7. FBK
Hauptmann Georg Pfeiffer   1939-1940
Hauptmann Seissler   1941-disbandment

8. FBK
Hauptmann Werner Klosinski   1939
Hauptmann Sattler   1941

9. FBK
Hauptmann Koch

IX. V 1 Operations by KG 53

This chapter begins with an excerpt from *Generalmajor* (Rtd.) Dr.-Ing. Walter R. Dornberger's foreword to the book *Damals in Peenemünde* by Ernst Klee and Otto Merk (1963):

"The first really big rocket experimental station was created in Peenemünde in 1936-1937 ... From a staff of no more than eighty men in 1936, the number of employees and workers rose to approximately 15,000 in 1943 ... When we think back of those days in Peenemünde, a unique period in the history of technology, and now witness the most powerful peoples on earth on both sides of the Iron Curtain in the first stages of realizing what was conceived and developed in Peenemünde, these events can only fill those who worked there as well as the German people as a whole with pride, but also with a certain sadness."

The bombardment of England, and especially London, with the Fi 103 (V 1) flying bomb was supposed to begin in early 1944. Construction of the ground organization in northern France – consisting of 8 large sites and 96 field sites – began in 1943. The sheltered launch ramps had to be well camouflaged. 35,000 workers, mainly Frenchmen, were used in the construction of the sites.

The V 1 launch ramps were installed in the forests and orchards of the Dunkirk-Abbeville-Tocqueville area and were supposed to be operational by the end of 1943. The first flying bomb did not fall on London until 12 June 1944, however, six months later than planned. The beginning did not go entirely according to plan, because many launch ramps were still not operational. Just ten missiles could be launched, of which only four reached England and just one London. But after a delay of three days, 120 to 190 missiles were being launched daily. Flak Regiment 155 under *Oberst* Wachtel operated the launch ramps and initially maintained this rate of fire. As the ramps were captured by Allied troops one after another, however, the launch rate dropped, and at the beginning of September 1944 this 'main offensive' came to an end. A total of 8,617 V 1s had been launched, of which 6,725 went on course. Of these, 3,463 were shot down by fighters, flak and barrage balloons, and 3,262 reached England, and 2,340 of those fell on London.

The loss of the launch sites resulted in the *Luftwaffe* employing the He 111 as a "flying launch ramp." The only *Geschwader* assigned to this role was KG 53, which employed about 100 aircraft on operations.

Hauptmann (Rtd.) Zander, then a *Staffelkapitän*, remembered:

"We were flying Hitler's miracle weapon! The *2. Staffel* of *KG "Legion Condor"* 53 was based at the airbase in Ahlhorn. The flying personnel were billeted in private quarters in Großenkneten in the district of Oldenburg. Relations with the civilian population were excellent, the accommodations outstanding.

The He 111 bombers, each loaded with one V 1 device, were parked in camouflaged aircraft pens at the edge of the Ahlhorn airbase.

Weighing 2200 kilograms, the V 1 device hung beneath the starboard wing and the aircraft fuselage. Thus equipped, the He 111s were watched over and guarded by pairs of sentries.

The *Gruppe* was ordered into action on 16 September 1944. Foxholes had been dug to the left and right of the Großenkneten – Ahlhorn road for protection against possible air attacks.

With the words 'Comrades, tonight we attack London,' the *Staffelkapitän* began the briefing. 'Remember that the He 111 is loaded asymmetrically. Trim your aircraft accordingly and don't lift off until you have sufficient speed.'

The weather in the drop zone and there at the airfield was very bad – ceiling 200-400 m, light rain, wind from 110-130 degrees at 40 kph. The ceiling was supposed to improve somewhat after nightfall.

The device's countdown timer number was set at 4800 and the V 1 control system was checked.

The *Staffelkapitän*'s aircraft took off at 20:45. The remaining machines took off at five-minute intervals.

Flight path: Ahlhorn-Den Helder radio beacon – radio beam to the Thames Estuary-London.

Release height: 500 meters above sea level.

The V 1 'wonder weapon' was 7.73 meters long and had a wingspan of 4.90 meters. Its gross weight was about 2200 kg, of which 500 kg was fuel. About 280 man-hours were required to build a V 1, which at the time cost several thousand *Reichsmark*.

The V 1 device (Fi 103) was capable of carrying about 1000 kg of explosives more than 250 kilometers. Cruising speed was roughly 600 kph at an altitude of 200 – 2000 meters. The intermittent pulse jet (pulsating athodyd) required the more oxygen-rich air present at lower altitudes for the combustion process.

The V 1 was released when the kilometer counter reached zero and its power plant achieved full power. The V 1 then headed west – to London.

Prior to launch, the releasing aircraft placed the V 1 on the general heading for the target. The precise flight path was determined by the two-axis autopilot, which had been set previously. The length of flight was determined by the amount of fuel. A small propeller was attached to the nose of the V 1. This powered a counting mechanism which determined the point at which the V 1 dove to the ground. The number of revolutions was determined and set prior to takeoff, and when it reached '0' it activated the elevator, causing the V 1 to dive into the ground at a predetermined angle.

The effect of this flying bomb was more moral than destructive in nature. One heard the sputtering sound of the pulse jet, then saw the exhaust flame and lastly the bomb itself. One never knew when the V 1 would begin its dive. In most cases the aircraft released the device in cloud. It then continued on through the cloud. This made the effect on morale even greater, especially as one ton of explosives produced a tremendous detonation.

After the successful invasion, the English population believed that air attacks were a thing of the past. The shock was considerable when bombs began falling from the sky randomly and without warning."

Because of the overwhelming British air defenses, the attacks almost always had to be made at night, at low altitude, below the British radar screen and in bad weather. These V 1 attacks, which due to the circumstances were flown irregularly, began on 16 September 1944 and for KG 53 ended on 5 January 1945. The last air-launched V 1 exploded near Hornsey on the northern outskirts of London on the morning of 14 January.

Overall, the results of the standoff raids by the He 111 bombers were quite modest. The *Geschwader* launched 1,200 V 1s from aircraft in the course of operations. Of these, 638 crossed the English coast. 71 were shot down by fighters, 331 by anti-aircraft fire, for a total of 403. This left 235 missiles, of which just 66 reached their target.

The reverse side of the air-launched V 1 campaign was that England had to employ 2,800 anti-aircraft guns, about 2,000 barrage balloons and 11 fighter wings to counter it, resources that were taken from the front.

The He 111 was converted for the role of V 1 carrier. With the weight of the missile it was overloaded. This of course affected handling characteristics, but despite considerable losses and overstress it was possible to increase the number of operational aircraft almost until the end.

Stab	I./KG 53	II./KG 53	III./KG 53	
20 Oct.	2/0	21/13	40/11	15/0
20 Nov.	2/2	26/21	22/15	29/20
20 Dec.	2/2	40/28	36/27	39/28
20 Jan.	1/1	37/25	33/29	30/24

1st number = actual number of aircraft

2nd number = number of serviceable aircraft

The *Staffeln* **operated from the following airfields:**

Geschwaderstab: Bad Zwischenahn

1. *Staffel*: Varelbusch
2. *Staffel*: Ahlhorn
3. *Staffel*: Vechta
4. *Staffel*: Bad Zwischenahn
5. *Staffel*: Jever
6. *Staffel*: Wittmund
7. *Staffel*: Leck
8. *Staffel*: Schleswig

To conclude the topic of the V 1, *Leutnant* (Rtd.) Walter Sticht, who joined the *Geschwader* in February 1939:

"I took part in many developmental tasks, the last during the air-launched V 1 program, when, at the Magnetic Field Observatory in Niemegk in the Mark Brandenburg, I took magnetic field measurements to be used in setting the magnetic compasses of the V 1s. When V 1 operations began, I became the *III. Gruppe*'s countdown timer officer. The V 1 device was designated the Fieseler Fi 103, while its tactical designation was FZG 76 (*Flakzielgerät*). In the summer of 1944 the former 1st Airfield Operating Company of KG 53, peacetime base Ansbach, was employed in the ground combat role in Artois and Flanders, suffering heavy losses.

III./KG 53 began launching V 1s in October 1944. Each *Staffel* was also assigned a FZG armaments platoon, which took charge of the V 1s from the manufacturer, fueled them and 'beat them into shape'. Because of the compass guidance system, the device had to be placed on its future heading prior to loading and shaken for a long time in a magnetically quiet place (vibrator or rubber chamber) in order to align the iron molecules. As well, the *Staffeln* were assigned so-called 'countdown timer officers', who calculated the launching data (approach course from the fixed point for the He 111 carrier aircraft, approach distance and length of run to the target) prior to takeoff based on the location of the target and wind conditions."

A He 111 modified to carry the Fi 103 (V 1) is illustrated on Page 305.

What became of the V 1? Some idea of this may be gained from two excerpts from the book *Zu Spät* by Werner Baumbach:

"The V 1 and V 2 triggered further developments in the postwar years, especially in the USA and Russia. A large portion of the German V 2 scientists continued working as a closed group at the big White Sands rocket site in Texas. After the war the American president, Harry S. Truman, declared that it was impossible to put a dollar value on these German inventions."

"A great deal of material about the V 1 fell into Russian hands, from which they were able to derive the complete state of this technology. Dr. Diedrich, the designer of the V 1's propulsion system, the 'Argus tube', had planned to switch to cheap coal dust emulsion oil for the V 1's fuel after successful preliminary tests with pure coal dust in 1944. It can be assumed that the Russians were aware of the results of these experiments, as the development department for the V 1 power plant as well as the workshops and test stands in Peenemünde fell into their hands. We know that the technical director of the Argus company is in Russia."

The detailed treatment in this chapter is intended solely to provide a complete description of KG 53's V 1 operations.

X. The Military Doctor

When the flying units were formed, the *Luftwaffe* command assumed that the air bases would provide adequate medical care. When the war began, however, it was soon realized that the flying unit, which was constantly on the move and which often had to fly from rudimentary airfields, required its own military doctor with medical service. Soon after the outbreak of war, therefore, the *Gruppen* received their own medical officers with a corresponding medical service. Within the *Gruppe* the medical services were designated Department IV b.

Dr. Gustav Mehlhorn, who took over the position of medical officer with the *I. Gruppe* of KG 53 soon after the outbreak of war and who was present for all of the *Gruppe*'s operations until it was disbanded, kept detailed diaries. Several extracts from these may enlighten the reader as to the nature of the military doctor's job:

"Before the war began in September 1939, I was called up to become the resident base doctor at the base in Roth, near Nuremberg. In addition to the personnel stationed there and their families, I was also responsible for treating the civilians and airfield workers. There were always around 6,000 persons. And as well there were the various units that landed there. At that time the combat units did not yet have their own military doctors and were looked after by the local base medical officers. The positions that I held in KG 53 were not created until later.

The first entries in my diary about I./KG 53 are from 25 February 1940, a Sunday. The new bomber unit arrived in my absence.

Sunday, 10 March 1940

Did aviation medical examinations all morning. I evaluated the results in the afternoon. On 16 March I gave the *3. Staffel* a lecture on high-altitude breathing. There was a topping out ceremony there with all sorts of good food and entertainment. Then I had to take the altitude test myself. I managed to hold out for twelve minutes at an altitude of 8000 meters. From 18-23 March I attended an aviation medicine course in Jüterbog. Apart from me, *Stabsarzt* Dr. Gerber from Straubing was the only other doctor from Air District 13 ordered to attend.

On Friday of the previous week I made a presentation to the officers about the medical problems of high-altitude flight. The next day *Oberarzt* Dr. Müller arrived with equipment for investigating the effects of high altitude. We conducted our experiments from morning until night all week, including on Sunday. He left yesterday, after having inspected all of the flying personnel.

Sunday, 28 April 1940: There was another Strength through Joy evening at the municipal hall on Friday evening, the presentations were rather meager. Yesterday morning a He 111 made a belly landing.

Roth airbase, Friday the 10th of May 1940. Since this morning the German Army's attack through Holland, Belgium and Luxembourg has been underway. This morning Dr. Goebbels read out the memoranda to these three states, explaining the alleged culpability of Holland and Belgium for working for the western powers against Germany. When I arrived at Roth in the afternoon, all sorts was going on. The *Gruppe* had moved.

Gelchsheim, 11 May 1940, Sunday.

Tonight I received my orders transferring me to I./KG 53, the *Gruppe* that had been based in Roth, as unit medical officer.

My last ray of hope for an early wedding was thus extinguished. In the afternoon a Ju 52 arrived to collect me and *Oberleutnant* Weber. A half-hour later we are in Gelchsheim, our new forward airfield. It consists of an estate and a large open field, nothing else. My questions as to quarters are answered quickly and simply: a bed and a cupboard are being installed in the local base doctor's room. It is very cramped, but the *Gruppe* could offer me less. In the barracks nine officers sleep in one room on straw mattresses, without a closet. The dispensary room is very small, serving simultaneously as an office, treatment room and sleeping area for three men. In the beginning it seems quite primitive compared to Roth, but it has the breath of the front.

There was great excitement when I arrived. Today four aircraft failed to return from a mission, including the commanding officer *Oberstleutnant* Mehnert and the entire command flight.

Gelchsheim, operations base, Pentecost Sunday, 12 May 1940.

This morning I was just putting away my things when the *Gruppe* returned from a combat mission. Two more aircraft were shot down, including that of *Lt.* Baron von Satzenhofen-Fuchsberg. As well, one man had a bullet wound in one hand, another a shoulder wound and a third frostbite in both hands. *Hauptmann* Schwarz's aircraft had sixty holes, *Oblt.* Sauer's eighty. Both aircraft had each shot down a fighter and landed here safely. *Oblt.* Sauer came back with his starboard engine shut down.

Operational base Gelchsheim, 14 May 1940.

The *Gruppe* has the morning off and moves into better quarters, Action in the afternoon. Targets: Verdun and Sedan. In the afternoon the stores sergeant from the air district arrives, bringing me my medical equipment. He also witnessed what is going on here. The *Gruppe* returned badly shot-up. Two aircraft, those of *Major* Wolfien and *Lt.* Anders, have been shot down. Last night I sat with the *Major* in the officer's club. He smiled as he spoke with his wife on the telephone and told them not to worry. Now 28-year-old *Hauptmann* Schwarz is leading the *Gruppe*. Two other machines had to come down in Giebelstadt, one with engine trouble, the other with a shot-up undercarriage. The latter machine made a crash landing. Schwarz's aircraft was hit by anti-aircraft fire several times, and the flight engineer had three fragments in his right leg. I drove with him to the hospital in Aub. My colleague there, Dr. Braun, is a very nice man. We took X-rays immediately and I assisted him in removing the fragments.

Operational base Gelchsheim, Wednesday the 15th of May 1940.

The *Gruppe* has the morning off, I drive to Aub and visit the wounded in hospital. Missions are flown in the afternoon. The aircraft return without loss. The first *Kette* with *Oblt.* Allmendinger is sent on a night flight.

Operational base Gelchsheim, Saturday the 18th of May 1940.

This morning we pack up and prepare to leave. Takeoff is scheduled for 10:00. I fly in a Ju 52. Adjutant *Oblt.* Großholz describes the military situation. Then a call comes that we have to turn back immediately. On the way back we learn the reason: our troops have advanced so far that supply difficulties have arisen. Every available Ju 52 is needed. After lunch a truck drives us to the senior base medical officer. We literally clean out the pharmacy there, and the friendly nurses also give us a piece of cake. In the afternoon the *Gruppe* takes off on a combat mission. After bombing railway targets all 18 of the *Gruppe*'s aircraft return safely.

Operational base Groß-Ostheim, Sunday, the 26th of May 1940.

In the morning I attended to a number of official matters. In the afternoon there is a mission against an airfield near Paris. All of the aircraft return empty-handed on account of bad weather.

Operational base Groß-Ostheim, Saturday, the 1st of June 1940.

I am fetched from bed at 05:30, as we have been ordered to Readiness Level I and action is imminent, but it is all called off at about 06:30. With Eisenberger and Böcklein, my medics, I spend the morning putting away our just-completed first-aid kits and recording the necessary materials. Then there is a mission in the afternoon and our aircraft return in the evening. The aircraft of *Lt.* Siegfried has been shot down by Swiss fighters, and most of the aircraft have taken not-insignificant hits. One dorsal gunner has a piece of glass in his eye, which I remove.

Operational base Groß-Ostheim, Friday, the 7th of June 1940.

I have to get up again at 04:00, because the aircraft are returning from a night combat mission. As everyone has come back happy and healthy, I go back to bed.

Operational base Groß-Ostheim, the 15th of June 1940.

The aircraft take off singly in hazy weather. No cloud over the target, easy meat for the enemy fighters. Three aircraft, those of *Hptm.* Schwarz, *Oblt.* Wegener and *Lt.* Schöppler, fail to return.

Operational base Groß-Ostheim, Thursday, the 20th of June 1940.

My bags have been packed for two days, ready for our next move. The *Gruppe* is supposed to be moving to Charleville. The advance party has been there for days setting things up, but we are still waiting. A flight is organized for me, but just before takeoff the order comes: 'Everything called off, advance party recalled.'

Operational base Groß-Ostheim, Saturday, the 22nd of June 1940.

The French have signed the ceasefire. I drive by the *II. Gruppe* in Schallhausen. Not finding my colleague Dr. Bekker, I carry on to the senior base medical officer in Langendiebach to organize a few things. I take Eisenberger and Böcklein with me.

Operational base Groß-Ostheim, Sunday, the 23nd of June 1940.

The *Gruppe* has been in Paris for two days now, and so there is nothing going on again tonight. *Oblt.* Dr. Knipping and I decide to drive to Mainz in my small Adler. *Inspektor* Zaus and *Waffenmeister* Bayer join us. In Mainz everything is festively decked for the celebration of the 500th anniversary of Gutenberg's invention of typography. At 01:00 a telex arrives. A stand-down has been ordered until 1 July 1940. My joy is indescribable. I resolve that I will marry during these eight days.

Operational base Wevelghem, Tuesday, the 2nd of July 1940.

I have to get up on time this morning. My things are quickly packed. Takeoff in the good old Ju 52 at 11:00. Großholz flies the machine himself. The base is a well-equipped Belgian airbase. The rooms are very well appointed, with hot and cold running water, mahogany paneling and comfortable Schlaraffia mattresses on the beds. I settle in and make contact with the base medical officer, *Oberarzt* Dr. Kennen. In the afternoon we drive into the city to set up an alternate dispensary in the practice of the Belgian doctor, who bolted.

In the evening a reunion celebration develops in the officer's mess with *Lt.* Siegfried and *Oblt.* Hufenreuter, who have returned from captivity. As the party is winding down, the door opens and in walks *Oblt.* Knipping with a bandaged head. He was leading the column in my Adler Trumpf Junior, which was being driven by Insp. Zaus, near Cambrai it was thumped in the side by a Mercedes and knocked over. Zaus suffered broken ribs. My medic *Uffz.* Eiesenberger and Dr. Knipping were thrown onto the street, Eisenberger sustained a concussion and Dr. Knipping head lacerations. Zaus and Eisenberger are in hospital in Cambrai. It is a great misfortune for me, first because Eisenberger, whom I need badly, is out of action, and second because my beautiful car is gone.

Operational base Wevelghem, Wednesday, the 3rd of July 1940.

Oblt. Willmann, commander of the 1st Airfield Operating Company, has become my knight in shining armor. Today he invited me to come along on a drive to the Dunkirk area, with the promise of acquiring a new car. Thousands of trucks litter the sides of the road, with every degree of damage. Many are undamaged, many others completely burnt out. At the Channel the vehicles are so wedged together that one has to climb over the wreckage. We find a Ford Prefect under an overturned truck. It has right side steering and is taken along for me. Then we return to Wevelghem.

Operational base Wevelghem, 4th of July 1940.

At this airfield, where Richthofen was once stationed, we have a wonderful life. The aircraft and the flying personnel are still in Groß-Ostheim, here is just the headquarters and the advance party. And so I borrowed a car and driver from headquarters in order to visit Insp. Zaus and *Uffz.* Eisenberger in Cambrai.

Operational base Wevelghem, Friday, the 5th of July 1940.

Oblt. Willmann arrives with the captured Ford, in order to turn it over to me as my new duty vehicle. The car is scarcely recognizable, with a fresh coat of paint and red crosses, it looks like new.

Operational base Wevelghem, Saturday, the 6th of July 1940.

Today *Hptm.* Landel, commander of the 2nd Airfield Operating Company, invited Dr. Knipping, Dr. Kennen and me to join him in a drive to Dunkirk. We are happy, because he owns a BMW, but he drives like a … We drive via Ypres to Langemarck and visit the memorial. Then we walk out into the broad square of the oak plantation, where thousands of the best German youth lie. I am overcome by a deep sense of awe.

Wevelghem, 9 July 1940.

Today the *Gruppe* flies a mission against oil tank farms on the Humber Estuary near Hull. Of the six aircraft that depart, the one with pilot *Oblt.* Kollmer and observer *Oblt.* Fritz fails to return.

Operational base Wevelghem, Thursday, the 11th of July 1940.

Yesterday my new ambulance made its maiden trip with us. I drove it to Cambrai and collected my old Eisenberger. As his concussion is just eight days old, I drive very cautiously. The car has an excellent suspension and *Uffz.* Eisenberger arrives none the worse for wear. He is much better resting on a wonderfully soft Schlaraffia mattress here than on the hard field cot of the military hospital in Cambrai. A *Gefreiter* from the *Gruppenstab* has a broken nose. As I cannot treat it here I take advantage of the opportunity to get to know Ghent. There is a specialist ward in the military hospital there.

Vitry en Artois, 12 July 1940.

The transfer order actually arrived last night. *General* Kesselring passed through here some time ago and complained about the airfield's inadequate camouflage. And so in the morning we packed up our things. Pity about the beautiful quarters and the lovely beds. The vehicle column forms up at 14:00. I drive my Ford myself, *Prüfmeister* Wirrel drives the ambulance. *Uffz.* Eisenberger still has to lie down on account of his concussion and makes himself comfortable in the ambulance. Vitry en Artois is a desolate area, without a tree or bush. It is situated between Douai and Arras. There is nothing whatsoever on the airfield. We stop there while we wait to be assigned quarters and look around. There is a large open field right next to the main road, and around it are the red lights that identify it as an airfield. A corrugated metal barracks on the west edge houses flight control. Around the field there are 20-mm anti-aircraft guns. From a distance the village of Vitry doesn't make such a bad impression. Not until we occupy our quarters do we see that it is a dirty, squalid village. The *Gruppe* headquarters is given two large houses next to each other. The command post is in the northern one, with my office on the second floor. In the other house are the officer's quarters. My office contains a desk, a chair and an old wardrobe. My bedroom is furnished with just a wide French family bed and a devotional picture. Wash basins, tables, chairs, etc. are quickly organized. It is a more miserable place than Wevelghem. Dreary.

Vitry en Artois, Monday the 15th of July 1940.

The base dispensary is in a house right next to the Vitry railway station, also a primitive place. But the base medical officer Dr. Onken is a very nice chap, from Oldenburg. On Saturday I was with the 3. *Staffel* in Douai. The city is completely wrecked in places, and only a small percentage of the residents have returned. Only a very few shops have opened. Apart from a few razor blades there is nothing to buy; I can't even scare up a cup of coffee. In the once elegant hotel, which is now half collapsed, we at least get an aperitif. Yesterday I had to look after the base, as colleague Onken wanted to visit his brother stationed nearby. Today I make a quarters inspection and issue several directives. In the afternoon I have to deliver a sick man to Arras. The city has suffered badly. The railway station is rather bent out of shape, parts of the city are completely destroyed while others are untouched. There's not much happening in Arras. The military hospital is located in the girl's school. It is a monastery-like structure. I get a terrific surprise there: all of the doctors are colleagues from Nuremberg and Erlangen. Dr. Jordan and Dr. Schubert from the surgery in Erlangen, Dr. Heumann, Dr. Heuler, Dr. Lützel, and so on and so on, all from Erlangen. There is a boisterous hello.

Vitry en Artois, Monday the 9th of August, 1940.

My request for leave came back from the corps doctor approved yesterday, but *Major* Kaufmann told me that he couldn't release me for military reasons. Is it starting?

Yesterday there was a going-away party for the *2. Staffel*. The *Staffel*, which is down to just three crews, is being sent to Giebelstadt to rest and reequip, along with the 2nd Airfield Operating Company. This morning the *3. Staffel* makes a formation flight to the coast. I go along and clamber into *Oberleutnant* Steinmann's crate. Five aircraft take off. We start out as the right outer aircraft in the second *Kette*, and later over the Channel Coast we assume the lead position. I have my camera with me and begin snapping photos. Lying up front in the nose I have an excellent view. It is cloudy, completely clear. We fly over Lille to Ostende, then out over the Channel and along the coast to Dunkirk. When we can clearly see the English coast ahead of us we change course. I exchange my camera for the machine-gun, but the Tommy doesn't stir himself. Off Calais we turn inland and soon afterwards land in Vitry.

Yesterday I was on the airfield because three aircraft were taking off on nuisance raids. In the evening there was a variety show, but just as I was about to go there I was summoned to the base dispensary. Of course the base doctor wasn't back yet and so I had to patch up a little French boy who had been run over by a car.

Nuremberg, Monday, the 1st of September 1940.

As compensation for my cancelled leave, *Major* Kaufmann authorized me to at least fly home for two days.

Vitry en Artois, Monday the 1st of September 1940, a Sunday.

A great week lies behind me, that is behind all of us. Monday night eight aircraft were sent to bomb the big oil storage facility near Hull on the Humber Estuary. All returned safely, but were unable to observe the results of their bombing due to heavy cloud cover. On

Monday I accompanied sick patients to Lille for examination by specialists and did paperwork. That night ten aircraft were sent to Hull. Numerous fires were observed. On the night to Wednesday ten aircraft were despatched to bomb the armament centers near Derby. Warehouses and the like could be seen in the glow of the numerous fires. At about 23:00 a report came from the *Fluko* that the English had set a large *Kriegsmarine* fuel dump ablaze in Dunkirk [*Translator's note: Fluko = Flugmelde-Kompanie, or aircraft reporting company, a unit of the aircraft reporting service*]. Our machines returned shortly after three in the morning. A1+CL, with pilot *Obfw.* Wolter and observer *Obfw.* Walter, crashed from a height of about 180 meters while turning onto finals and immediately caught fire. By then the fog had become so thick that I couldn't get there in my car without headlights and ended up in the ditch. The ambulance picked me up, but it became stuck in a turnip field. Meanwhile the firefighters had extinguished the fire and advised that all five crewmembers were dead. At 7 AM I went out to the crash scene with a recovery team and brought the bodies of our comrades, all well known to me, to the morgue in Arras. All had crushed skulls and broken bones. I returned in the afternoon with the chaplain to procure the caskets and discuss the postmortems with the pathologist. On the night to Thursday ten machines were sent to bomb armaments plants in Sheffield. Once again the visibility was restricted by haze. One of the pilots misjudged his height and struck the ground while maneuvering to land. Thank God the aircraft didn't burn. As the crash scene was close to the railway embankment that passed close by the town, we were on the scene quickly and with great effort we were able to pull the pilot *Uffz.* Brederer-Meyer and the observer *Uffz.* Büksch from the wrecked machine alive. Harrowing minutes of worry passed, as metal saws and axes had to be used to free the two from the tangled wreckage with. I applied emergency dressings and they were taken to the *Luftwaffe* hospital in Arras. The radio operator and flight engineer were dead. At dawn I and a recovery team took their bodies to the morgue in Arras. During the funerals several comrades were also sent against an airfield northwest of London. *Lt.* Lorisch's A1+IL failed to return from this flight. In the night to Saturday four machines were sent to Hull with good results.

Vitry en Artois, the 7th of September 1940, a Sunday.

Another busy week lies behind me, during which I was unable to write.

As a reprisal for ongoing raids by British aircraft against civilian targets in the Reich, the following night we sent eight aircraft to London.

On Friday afternoon I drove with *Oblt.* Ziegler to Arras to have his sprained hand x-rayed as a precaution. When I returned, my corps doctor, *Oberstabsarzt* Prof. von Willemshofen, was there. He inspected my shop and then departed in his Me 108. This morning I was at the *3. Staffel* conducting aero-medical examinations, when suddenly orders were received for a big mission against London that afternoon. Preparations were made quickly and the two other *Gruppen* flew in. 27 aircraft took off. I felt a twinge in my heart. By the skin of its teeth the entire *Geschwader* was only able to scrape together 27 aircraft. What a change that was from the French campaign, when each *Gruppe* would put up that number of aircraft day after day. Here you see the extent of our losses. All of the crates got away from the airfield safely; but when they returned we got a fright. One had a stationary propeller, one had a completely shot-up undercarriage, seven aircraft fired red flares, signaling that they had wounded on board or that the machine was in distress. I raced from aircraft to aircraft, applying emergency dressings and giving instructions to the medics. Even before reaching the target, the observer in *Fw.* Sünderhauf's crew had received large flesh wounds in both lower legs caused by shrapnel. The worst wounds, however, were suffered by *Fw.* Sünderhauf, the pilot, whose right femur was completely shattered. Despite his serious injuries and terrible pain he stayed in formation to the target and back to base. As I climbed into the aircraft and properly applied a dressing, a machine approached with one propeller stopped. A collision seemed imminent, as we were sitting in the middle of the airfield, whereupon Sünderhauf fired up the engines and taxied the machine off the field to where the workshop platoon was. Then we got him out with great effort and placed him in the ambulance. I examined the rest of the wounded, who were taken by ambulance to the *Luftwaffe* hospital in Arras. When the fuss was over we sat in the officer's club and breathed a sigh of relief. Three hours later news came that the commanding general had awarded Sünderhauf the Iron Cross, First Class and had immediately promoted him to *Oberfeldwebel*. He had also recommended him for the Honor Goblet created by the *Reichsmarschall*. Let us hope that the brave chap keeps his leg."

Dr. Mehlhorn was promoted to *Oberarzt* effective 1 October 1940. He experienced all of the *I. Gruppe*'s operations from France, especially during the Battle of Britain, as its medical officer. When the *I. Gruppe* was transferred to Russia in June 1941, Dr. Mehlhorn, since promoted to *Stabsarzt*, went with it. He was still there when the *Gruppe* returned to France after the invasion in 1944. The *I. Gruppe* was subsequently disbanded in Neuhardenberg in September-October 1944.

It remains to be mentioned that during his service with KG 53 Dr. Mehlhorn authored a scientific paper about "Pressure Balance in the Middle Ear while Flying." The paper was published in the magazine *Aviation Medicine* on 11 October 1944.

At the end of the war Dr. Mehlhorn was captured by the Americans in Bad Aibling. He was released eleven months later. Since 1949 he has been chairman of the medical profession in the Roth administrative district.

XI. The Geschwader Signals Company – LnKp (mot) KG 53

The *Kampfgeschwader* relied on the signals units at the air bases for signals support. Soon after the outbreak of war, however, it became necessary to furnish the *Geschwader* with their own air signals companies. In some cases, signals units were converted into motorized signals platoons and combined in motorized signals companies.

The signals company was directly subordinate to the *Geschwader* commander, only receiving technical directives from the signals commander of the *Fliegerdivision* or *Fliegerkorps*. The company commander was also the *Geschwader* signals officer.

The signals platoons provided the *Gruppe* with communications. Because of the threat of radio traffic being monitored, the units relied mostly on telex and telephone communications. However, if these lines were interrupted, overloaded or not available, ground radio communication was used. As well, contact was maintained with the aircraft in the air using short wave Morse code. In this way bombing results or information of a special nature could be transmitted between the formation leaders and the command post.

KG 53's motorized signals company remained fully intact even after the *Geschwader* was disbanded in April 1945. After serving the last Reich government under *Großadmiral* Dönitz, it was disbanded simultaneous with its release from internment in August 1945.

Brigadegeneral (Rtd.) Heinz Waldhecker, then an *Oberleutnant* and commander of KG 53's signals company, described its path in vivid, detailed fashion:

"In June 1940, the air signals corps began sending soldiers from various fields of the communications service – then called signals – one by one to the *Geschwader*'s signals unit, which was then supposed to be organized into a unit within the *Geschwader* in the Lille – Roubaix area. Some came from Schwerin, the radio operators were all from Bernau near Berlin, most of the telephonists and telex operators from Jesau in East Prussia. The formation was essentially completed in

December 1940 with the arrival of a complete signals platoon from Schleswig. The company retained its initial composition until 1945, apart from the departure of the 1st Platoon and the addition of the signals platoon from III./KG 3 towards the end of the war.

Most of the personnel were from northern, central and eastern Germany; there were only a few south Germans and Austrians. As long as the *Geschwader* had all its flying elements as per the wartime table of organization, total strength was about 350 men: 5 to 7 officers, 1 technical official, about 85 non-commissioned officers and at least 250 enlisted men. This was sufficient personnel to deal with all tasks assigned to the unit.

The new *Geschwader* signals Company was always available, because it was entirely at the *Geschwaderkommodore*'s disposal. As an integral part of the *Geschwader*, it soon showed itself capable of meeting the unit's needs, even under adverse conditions, with reliability and versatility. The signals corps remained responsible for providing replacement personnel and material, and the local signals commander (*Nafü*) also retained the right to issue directives and conduct inspections.

KG 53's motorized signals company was operational from the time of its formation. This was mainly due to the fact that most of its personnel were selected top-grade men.

In April 1941 the company began preparations for the *Geschwader*'s move east. Using means that were sometimes not entirely legal, it built up its stock of equipment far beyond what it was entitled, a step that would later prove very beneficial. Extended column marches were used to train drivers and provided the communications personnel with intensive, real-life training.

Later in the east, the period in France would be looked back on as heavenly. The man raved about the platoons' quartering areas in the red and white *chateaux* in Mouveaux, Virty and Vendeville. When, from the 2nd to the 5th of June, it finally left by train from Tourcoing for the Warsaw area, from where it drove by truck to the various frontline airfields, the company left a radio team in Mouveaux until winter. One of the radio operators related that, by means of coded radio messages, he had arranged additional supplies of 'scarce commodities' for his comrades in the east.

The supplies were delivered during the regular exchange of personnel, who travelled by rail. On one occasion a shipment of 'Soir de Paris' perfume broke in the luggage, which was appreciated on the train. But then, in freezing Shatalovka, the demi-company sought to be near the deliverer, in order to sniff his fragrant things and recall the past comforts of the Western Front.

In Russia the company immediately learned what this war was really all about. With the *Gruppen* of the *Geschwader* it was usually dislocated over large areas and great distances. From then on the company's platoons, one with each *Gruppe*, and the headquarters signals platoon with the *Geschwaderstab*, became semi-autonomous units. They were loosely led by the company, but there was little exchange of personnel. Most of the platoon leaders were *Leutnants* and *Oberleutnants*, trained radio operators and DF homing instructors. The company would not be reunited until towards the end of the war.

On 18 February 1942, company commander *Oblt.* Lessing was replaced by *Hauptmann* Siebel, who came from staff duty in the State Ministry of Aviation (RLM). He later returned to the ministry and was killed in the fighting in Berlin in 1945. I succeeded him in the *Geschwader* as the last company commander and *Geschwader* signals officer in March 1943.

Many signals officers pushed to go on operational sorties as radio operator. The crews usually agreed whenever their own radio operator was ill. Many of those who flew combat missions did not come back. Almost all were qualified officers who had gained recognition not just within their own platoons, but also in the *Gruppe* headquarters. In their capacity as *Gruppen-NO* (*Gruppe* signals officers), as they were called for short, they also performed a secondary function by regularly taking command post duty to relieve the operations officers.

Commanding the signals platoons taxed them little, because every soldier was accustomed to performing his responsible specialized task independently and without special supervision. This applied not just to the often outstanding NCOs, but also to the majority of the specialists in the enlisted ranks, the *Obergefreiten* who were gradually becoming 'ancient' in the proverbial sense, who became so experienced in handling their equipment that nothing could shake them. One can say that in this company the must-cited mission-type tactics became a reality of everyday duty.

With their individual teams of specialists, the signals platoons performed much differently. Each group included one light and one heavy short-wave radio squad, a telephone exchange squad, a field cable construction squad, a long-wave radio squad and a tuning squad – all fully motorized. The *Geschwader* headquarters signals platoon also had a DF Navigation squad, a radio receiver squad, two light navigation lighting squads, a light short-wave/long-wave radio squad, three field telephone construction squads, three teletype connection squads, a battery charger squad and a vehicle repair squad. The number of vehicles was never less than 80. It also had many special trailers and motorcycles; often the company had more than 100 vehicles.

The main functions of this extensive array of equipment are as easy to describe as it was difficult for the specialists in the signals squads to carry them out under field conditions.

When setting up the communications system at an airbase, telephone lines had to be set up so that the *Geschwader* or one or more *Gruppen* could receive their connections. In doing so the unit naturally relied on the local signals office, where one was present, but it was capable of doing the job without it. A telephone exchange was set up, sometimes two, and this was connected to the trunk lines of the general *Luftwaffe* communications system, probably the best available to any military force in this war.

The teletype machines were connected in a similar way, especially those of the *Geschwaderstab*, but also to supplement the airbase's teletype offices.

With the transmitters and receivers of the radio squad, the *Geschwader* maintained an internal radio net overlying the wire communications. In addition, it was connected to the higher-level radio system of the command authorities, and finally it maintained air-ground communications with the aircraft for tactical and air traffic control purposes. Everything happened in encrypted continuous wave transmissions; only air-ground communications saw the increased use of radio telephony.

The communications units had to be able to respond to the needs of the users in the setting up and operation of unit command posts.

Maintaining all of these systems required an excellent supply of spare parts and high-capacity workshops. It should not be forgotten that in most cases all of the electronic and mechanical technology had to be powered by dedicated electrical generators.

The administrative cohesion of the elements of the company was maintained by a company headquarters with its branches in the platoons. It was – and is – largely unknown that even then a functioning communications system, including what would now be called software, required careful, often very complex, planning work.

Moves were the operational focal point of the company. Signalmen were always the first at new airfields and command posts. Radio and telephone construction squads were usually sent ahead by air in order to achieve a limited state of operational readiness. The rest of the platoons followed in usually arduous overland transport. Later, when fuel became scarce, they were also transported by train, often through areas under partisan control with manifold incidents. No members of the company will ever forget these exciting transfers in all seasons through the expanses of the east, always pressed for time. Often it happened that, when the installation of communications at a new airfield was complete, the *Gruppe*'s air elements and headquarters never arrived, because the work had long since been overtaken by new operational plans. On several occasions advance parties from the company ended up in pockets and had to be flown out, or broke out with the army, or were surprised by Soviet breakthroughs. For many the events at Shatalovka are a somber high point in this respect. The communications systems and installations set up by the company in five years of war were often masterworks of improvisation and inexhaustible inventiveness. And as soon as everything was set up and functioning, came the unavoidable order to move. Dismantling the system was painful, for often enough it involved the personal destruction of the system, installations and improvised quarters.

When everything appeared to be over in March 1945, the disbandment of the *Geschwader* in no way meant the end of the signals company. Unforeseen tasks still lay before it.

For the signals company, the *Geschwader* disbandment order saw no more nor no less than that it should make its way from the platoons' various locations on the North Sea coast to Linz in Austria in order to bolster the 2nd Parachute Division there.

In fact, on the evening of 6 April 1945 the Headquarters and 2nd Signals Platoons were dispatched from Zwischenahn. Its journey by rail was temporarily interrupted in Scheeßel in Lowe Saxony.

Travelling by vehicle, the units crossed the Elbe near Lauenburg and took shelter in the dark forests on the east side of the Elbe near Boitzenburg. There they told us that *General* Heyser was setting up a defense line from Hamburg to Dömitz. It was said that the Air Fleet Command Reich was somewhere nearby. We located it and the operations officer of the senior signals officer, *Major* Gralka, later a *Generalmajor* in the *Bundeswehr*, was overjoyed to see us and immediately placed us under his command.

All of the surviving elements of the company finally arrived in Heidekamp near Reinfeld, not far from Lübeck between the 22nd and 26th of April. There they found quarters in the local area and took over the running of the air fleet command's communications system.

H. Willborn recalls of those days: 'To the senior signals officer of Air Fleet Reich we were a gift from heaven. We received radio transmissions from the *Führer* bunker. *Generaloberst* Ritter von Greim was summoned to Berlin as successor to the dethroned Reichsmarschall with instructions for him to be flown into Berlin by Hanna Reitsch.'

In those days *Oberleutnant* H. Kutzner was a radio officer at Herold 7. He remembered: 'Herold 7 was the radio relay system for Air Fleet Reich and everything it still controlled, to the Führer bunker and to all command authorities (southern Germany – Obersalzberg, navy in the north). I transmitted radio messages – always coded of course – that I could only look at briefly, whose significance I could not determine and whose contents I could understand even less. On one occasion Göring transmitted that the time had come for the Führer to designate his successor and requested confirmation that Hitler was no longer capable of functioning. Himmler gave orders for Göring to be tracked down and arrested – and vice versa.'

Our radio operators then also received what was probably Hitler's last operational order to the *Luftwaffe*. Its approximate contents: 'Beginning at dawn, Air Fleet Reich will attack enemy spearheads with all available resources.' I don't remember on which night the message was received, but in the command post a sleep-drunk *Oberst* took it gingerly and most unwillingly from *Oblt.* Willborn.

During the night of 2 May we heard the artillery fire in preparation for the British crossing of the Elbe. *Oblt.* Willborn came from the Herold 7 radio station with the latest message from Berlin: Hitler is dead.

On 3 May we moved to Ulsnis on the Schlei, where we destroyed our secret files. The Tommy is in Schleswig. We await him on Sunday, the 6th of May.

The air fleet command is now in a wood near Missunde, right beside the Schlei. We set up camp some distance away in a lovely dry stand of oak and beech trees in Ornum-Holz, alongside a farmstead.

What followed was something like Wallenstein's camp. There were no Tommies to be seen, beautiful weather, plenty to eat, and the evening the campfires burned. The squads manned the communications offices in Missunde according to the fixed duty roster, and there was still a sentry with rifle in front of the company area. This brief idyll ended abruptly. On the evening of 7 May the company commander was summoned to the air fleet. I heard this astonishing order for KG 53's motorized signals company: *Großadmiral* Dönitz wishes to establish direct radio communications with the *Wehrmacht* ceasefire delegations at Marshal Zhukov's headquarters in Potsdam, Field Marshall Montgomery's in Lüneburg and General Eisenhower's near Krefeld (KG 53's signal company had already done so).

From the provisional government of the Reich I receive sealed marching papers with orders for our heavy radio squad, which is to do the job. Who, for God's sake, is to go to the Russians? I decide that we will settle the matter with matches. The oracle decides: *Oblt.* Willborn and his platoon will go to Zhukov, *Oblt.* Kutzner to Eisenhower and I to Montgomery. Before the night is over we learn to our relief that the Potsdam job has been cancelled. So on the morning of 8 May *Oblt.* Willborn takes over the remaining elements of the company. Heinz Kutzner and I set off towards the south in a single column, about a dozen vehicles led by my faithful BMW with its huge wood gasifier on the back.

Outside Quickborn we leave the still unoccupied remnant of the Reich. Machine-gun positions of the *Großdeutschland* Division mark the spot. Immediately afterwards the first halt, an English checkpoint: our Dönitz papers work like sesame, the gate opens.

The column crosses the bridge over the Elbe in Lüneburg and finally reaches the English headquarters on "Victory Hill", a heather hill. There is a huge army camp of tents, at its center the tiny German enclave with *General* Kienzl and a few officers of a disarmament delegation.

They were having a rough time. While all around them the Tommies made tea and cooked meals, they had received no water for three days. When I entered the tent that had been assigned to me, I found an *Oberst* sitting there carefully shaving with red wine. They had enough of that.

I soon also had enough, for I learned that we were not permitted to establish radio contact with Flensburg. When that became clear and they began making veiled references to the nearest prisoner of war camp, invoking international law I asked for free passage for my column back to where we had come from, to the seat of the provisional government in Flensburg. It took a while but – we could scarcely believe it – the British accepted. I advised the taciturn *General* Kienzl that we were leaving. The next day he ended his life. On 11 May we rolled back across the Wilhelmsburger Bridge.

The rest happened very quickly. The company remained in fixed cohesion in its forest camp in those beautiful summer months of 1945. We lacked nothing, and the main thing was that we were spared captivity or internment.

There had long since ceased to be any communications traffic in Missunde. We gave away our equipment piece by piece. On 6 August the 1st Platoon packed up and Kutzner and Willborn accompanied it to the releasing camp. The air signals female auxiliaries had been in Rendsburg for some time and waited in the big anti-aircraft barracks for their release. At the camp gate Willborn and I silently watched the vehicles as they slowly disappeared from view in the pouring rain.

Now we three officers could also take off our uniforms, which happened on 29 August. On 6 September we bade each other farewell without saying much.

As the last commander, I, who twelve years later was to command a communications company of the new air force with a very similar structure, am permitted an appraising word.

This *Geschwader* signals company was a 'bunch' that the *Geschwader* could depend on. In this disastrous war it completely fulfilled its important but also unspectacular mission for KG 53."

Appendices

The Spanish Civil War 1936-39
The German "Legion Condor" in Spain – The Legend of Guernica. Quotations and Comments.

Pierre Broué and Emile Témime: Revolution and War in Spain. Extracts and preliminary discussion from the 11 December 1975 issue of Forward.

"Spain at the beginning of the Twentieth Century was in the western world a country crushed by history. 70% of the population was employed in agriculture, and the Spanish worked with the tools of the Middle Ages. The yield per hectare was the lowest in Europe, 20% of the cultivable land remained uncultivated. What little industry there was had barely outpaced the stage of manufactory. Another anachronism was the Spanish church with its 80,000 priests, monks and nuns. In its societal position and structure, the army was something unique. It was defeated whenever it was necessary to defend the last remnants of Spain's colonial empire, but it was nevertheless able to maintain its position as an independent political force in the theater of war of internal politics. For this army it was almost a matter of honor to overthrow the government and replace it with the military. Yet the officers humiliated by constant defeats blamed the respective governments for these defeats.

The election of 16 February 1936 resulted in a huge unexpected victory for the left-wing Popular Front, with 267 of 351 seats. The civil war began immediately after the election. The right feared an armed uprising by the Marxists, the left suspected the military of planning a coup. We now know that the Spanish government knew what the military was planning. In that July of 1936, which the military had chosen for its uprising, violence was the order of the day, and the Spanish government watched powerlessly. Not a day went by without clashes, shots, murder, demonstrations and street battles. Strikes rocked the already poverty-stricken nation.

In Morocco, however, the army felt at home as always, and the Moroccan officers knew exactly what they wanted. As well, the Moroccan troops were inhabitants of the Rif Mountains and were considered reliable fighters. At their side stood the so-called Spanish Foreign Legion 'Terico', which was made up largely of Spaniards. On 18 July the government admitted that parts of the army had revolted. The *Confederación National de Trabajo* and the *Unión General de Trabajadores* called a general strike. The government very quickly lost the capacity to act, the power lay in the hands of the military, the committees and the militias. Priests and monks were arrested, imprisoned and shot in mass executions. All confessional schools were closed.

At the beginning of August the generals on the mainland led only weak forces in the field, barely 33,000 men. Facing them were the militias and the troops that had remained loyal to the Republic. Both sides lacked money, weapons and war materiel. The militias exhibited chaotic confusion.

This was the opening state of the Spanish Civil War. Then in September the Communist Party and the *Partit Socialista Unificat Catalunya* became a decisive factor in the life of Republican Spain. The number of members rose from 30,000 in 1936 to one million in 1937. Already by the end of 1936 they were firmly in the hands of representatives of the Communist International party leadership and party organization.

The first Soviet weapons and inspectors arrived in Republican Spain on 12 October 1936. Soviet aircraft landed in Cartagena on 2 November.

They were followed in November 1936 by 6,500 German troops, who landed in Cadiz and later became the "Legion Condor." Also in November, powerful Italian units also arrived in Spain. The Italian troops included many men from South Tirol. Figures for the number of Italian troops fighting in Spain vary from 40,000 to 60,000. The number of Germans was 7,000, of whom about 1,000 were instructors and advisors.

In addition to the Soviet military, another category of foreign supporters was of special importance: the foreign Communists trained in the Soviet Union. They commanded the units of the "International Brigade", approximately 30,000 men, which included roughly 10,000 Germans. Many veterans of the International Brigade achieved high rank in Communist countries after the Second World War, such as GDR notables Rau and Staimer.

On the side of the generals there were three political forces: the monarchists, from whom Fal Conde, head of the Carlists, fled to Portugal after being charged with high treason. There were also the

Requetés (conservatives) and the Falangists, who emphasized the social issue and thus appeared more progressive. To bridge these differences Franco created his Unity Party and made himself its sole leader.

After several shifts in the fortunes of war, Catalonia fell when Barcelona was taken without a fight on 26 January 1939. On 28 March Franco's troops also occupied Madrid, again without a fight. Prior to this a second civil war broke out among the Republicans in the Madrid – Valencia area.

In the Republican camp so many had waited for reconciliation, but none came. The oppression of political opponents did not end with the war. The Spanish were instilled with loathing for the Red revolution and also any liberal system, and any work of liberal thought was condemned by the church. The Falangists, however, still waited for their national and at the same time social regime. And Pierre Broué and Emile Témine expressly state in their book that Franco's state had never been fascist.

But if he did do his nation one service, it was that Franco, who had shown himself to be a skilled juggler during the civil war, also knew how to exploit the different interests of the last war to his own advantage. Spain's commitment was limited to a gesture of good will. And so the deployment of the "Blue Division" under Muños was a skillful, calculated chess move, with which he appeased the German public and silenced the warmongers in his own camp."

Konrad Zuse: The Computer, My Life's Work.
"… In this circle I also met my friends, who helped me build the first models … One of them had been a member of the "Legion Condor", the German expeditionary corps in the Spanish Civil War. In Spain the young men of this legion felt like champions of a free Europe, just as the Americans in Vietnam today feel like champions of a free world. Such roles are always thankless, however. It would surely contributed more to a unified European spirit if we Germans had let things in Spain take their course. Either the other Europeans would have seen that an old European culture state was going communist, or they would have been forced to come together to take effective defensive action. In many respects we Germans were a generation ahead of our time. There was one difference, however: in the Germany of that time protests against participation in the Spanish Civil War, like the protests against the Vietnam War in Washington, would have been impossible. When my friend asked me when my machine would finally be finished, I said jokingly: 'When Franco has conquered Madrid', which in fact was roughly true."

Karl Otto Hoffmann: LN – The History of the Luftwaffe Signals Corps

"... On 25 April several towns west of Vergara (Elorrio) were taken and on 25 April the entire enemy front collapsed. Southeast of Bilbao it had been torn open on a width of 25 kilometers. The direction of new advance, with powerful air support, was northwest in the direction of Guernica, where an important bridge was supposed to be destroyed. On the 27th the commander's battle headquarters were in Zarauz, the command post in Deva, both situated on the coast west of San Sebastian. From the command post, the aircraft were summoned individually from their airfields and sent into action. Durango fell on 28 April and Guernica was taken on the 29th. An air attack on Guernica, the religious capital of the Basques, on 26 April 1937 was supposed to have cost the enemy 1,654 dead and 889 injured. Several waves of He 111s, Do 17s and Ju 52 bombers, so it was reported ... hit the transportation center and supply base hard. The first reports about it appeared in the London Star, submitted by George Lowther Steer, an independent writer of the international press. From there the reports made their way through the international press and were later reflected in the artist Picasso's Guernica and H. Kestens story The Children of Guernica. Everything was aimed against Germany and Franco's Spain ... In 1938 the French General Duval wrote about the lessons of the Spanish Civil War: 'The dismay of the Basques revealed itself in the invective they heaped upon the Nationalists for the destruction caused by artillery and aircraft, whose unfortunate victims had been Durango and Guernica. In the case of Guernica, it certainly cannot be claimed that the city had been evacuated before the arrival of the enemy.' Steer's reports, which were often contradictory and also embellished, prompted a group of foreign journalists to inspect Guernica for five days. They reported that serious devastation could not be found anywhere. After visiting Guernica, British military experts, among them the well-known wartime pilot Wing Commander Sir Archibald James, stated that no more than twelve light bombs had been dropped, that no traces of incendiary bombs were to be found anywhere in the city ... In the 'Guernica matter' it is certain that the target was a military object."

Wilfried von Oven, Hitler and the Spanish Civil War

"... After the successful conclusion of the Basque-Asturian campaign, Sperrle left his post as commander of the Legion Condor filled with bitterness which no letters of recognition and thanks and no decorations (including the War Merit Cross with Diamonds) could soothe. Neither the victors at Nuremberg nor the de-nazifiers in Munich could pin the 'war crime" of Guernica on him. Both had to find him innocent, even though the Basques brought the Guernica case before the International Military Tribunal … Not only the victors' tribunal in Nuremberg, but also every other official international body before it, had refused to take up the Guernica matter … The attitude of the victors was easy to understand, for after Dresden, Hiroshima and Nagasaki their air war conscience was too heavy to allow a trifling matter like Guernica to reopen a still-festering wound."

Television Broadcast 'Guernica – Pablo Picasso and Politics'
3rd Program 12 April and 11 October 1981

" … Pablo Picasso painted the picture in 1937 after the bombing of Guernica … The theme is the elementary destruction of man and animals … In 1937 in Paris, Picasso said to his friend, the Spanish writer Rafael Alberti: 'I am working on a big project for the Spanish government for the Spanish pavilion at the Paris World's Fair …' Picasso never concerned himself with the question 'hero or criminal' – war was the crime. The German legion in Spain was supposedly made up of volunteers, but in reality its members were career soldiers sent there. Guernica itself was just 20 kilometers from Franco's leading forces on 26 April 1937. They were advancing from the southeast. Guernica became a frontline area. *Oberleutnant* Karl von Knauer was the captain of a *Staffel* of K 88, the Legion Condor's bomber group. Knauer: 'As *Staffelkapitän* of 1./K 88, on 26 April 1937 I was given the mission of attacking the bridge at Guernica. My 1./K 88, with me at the controls of the lead aircraft and *Gruppe* commander *Major* Fuchs on board, came in from north to south from over the Bay of Biscay. In hazy conditions with a slight wind shift, we approached the target from east to west …' The order read: destroy the Renteria Bridge, which was right on the edge of the city and represented an important avenue of communication to the fighting front, and the roads leading to the bridge. Joseba Elosegi, then a Republican captain: 'I was in Guernica on the eve of the bombing. I and the company under my command had just arrived there. My company had suffered heavy casualties and was down to about 100 men. Of these, we lost anther 35 in the bombing. There were approximately 250 dead …' Reporter: 'You know that the communists spoke of 1,500 dead.' Elosegi: 'That number is not correct, it is wrong.' … In 1937 Picasso's 'Guernica' was considered 'decadent art' by the left, the right thought it 'degenerate'. As far as the head of the Basque National Freedom Party, Professor Javier Arzalluz, is concerned, Franco bears the main guilt for the destruction of Guernica … Picasso's cry against destruction and murder is equally applicable to Korea and Vietnam, to Rotterdam and Coventry, Dresden or Hiroshima."

Adolf Galland, The First and the Last

"… In the first months of their deployment the Condor bombers were given the task of destroying a road bridge, over which the Reds were moving their troops and large quantities of war materiel into the fiercely defended port and industrial city of Bilbao. The attack was made in conditions of poor visibility. When the smoke cleared it was found that the bridge was still intact but that the nearby town had suffered heavily. While war material must also have been destroyed in the Red-occupied town, the whole thing has to be seen as a failure. All the more so, as the supreme principle of our conduct of war was to completely destroy the enemy but to spare the civilian population if at all possible. When I arrived in Spain there was a certain despondency in the Legion Condor about it. No one wanted to talk about Guernica. It was just the opposite on the other side. The Reds made considerable propaganda capital out of the affair. Newspaper correspondents of all the friendly democratic powers were brought to Guernica. Soon there were huge headlines in papers from New York to Paris: 'Infamous attack by German air pirate son peaceful Spanish city', 'Open city of Guernica destroyed by Boche fliers', 'Cry of outrage of the civilized world: Guernica'. In fact Guernica was not an open city nor was it a target, but instead a regrettable mistake which was to be repeated countless times by both sides in the Second World War. Nevertheless it became a watchword for German nefariousness and barbarity. Even today after Rotterdam and Warsaw, after Hamburg, Kassel, Rothenburg and Berlin, yes even after the horror of Dresden, Guernica still spooks through the background of anti-German sentiments."

Airfields Used by KG 53

Agram (Zagreb)	Jever	Reppen
Agram-Gorica	Kauen (Kovno)	Rogoznica
Agram-Lucko	Kirovograd	Roth bei Nürnberg
Ahlhorn	Konstantinovka	Rotmistrovka
Alt-Lönnewitz	Korovye Selo	Sarajevo-Butmir
Ansbach	Landsberg am Lech	Shatalovka East
Bad Zwischenahn	Langendiebach/	Shatalovka West
Bobruisk	Gelnhausen	Schaulen
Briansk	Le Bourget	Schönfelde
Chartres	Leck	Schönwalde
Dnepropetrovsk	Liegnitz	Schwäbisch Hall
Dno	Lille-South-Vendeville	Sedan
Eggebeck	Lüben, Silesia	Seerappen

Evreux le Courdray

Frankfurt Rhine-Main

Freiwaldau

Gablingen near Augsburg

Gelchsheim

Gelnhausen

Gerdauen

Giebelstadt

Gomel-Pribitki

Gostkino

Greifswald

Grojek near Radom

Großostheim

Heiligenbeil

Insterburg

Jagel, Schleswig

Jesau near Königsberg

Manching-Ingolstadt

Miedzyrzee

Mielek

Minsk-Dubinskaya

Nancy

Neudorf

Ödheim

Orsha

Orleans – Bricy

Olsufyevo near Briansk

Pskov-South

Proskurov

Pukhovichi

Radom

Radzyn-Jedlanka

Rauchovka

north of Odessa

Sechinskaya

Smolensk-North

Stalino

Szolnok

Toul

Uman

Varelbusch

Vechta

Vitry en Artois

Wambrechies near Lille

Pskov-North

Wevelghem

Vinnitsa

Wittmund

Voroshilovgrad

Zellnhausen

Photo Section

The main street in Lipetsk, winter 1928-29.

An evocative photo of Voronezh, near Lipetsk, winter 1928-29.

Above: from left to right:
Oberst Deßloch, Kommodore of KG 355, Ritter von Epp, then Reich governor of Bavaria, Generalmajor Sperrle, commander of LKK VII (Later Luftflotte 3). Occasion: live bomb dropping by the III. Gruppe in 1936.

Lt. Klüter and crew with He 111 Bs in front of the 8. Staffel's building in Giebelstadt, 1938.

The same crew with a Do 23. The vulture talon painted on the aircraft later became a Gruppe emblem in KG 76.

Above: Change of command: in the spring of 1936, Otl. Speidel (brother of the later General Speidel of the Bundeswehr) hands the Fliegergruppe Giebelstadt over to Major Weber. Note that there are still no runways and that the unit is equipped with the Do 23.

The first He 111 Bs, photographed in front of the 8. Staffel's building, Giebelstadt 1939.

Left: the Allmendinger crew. From l. to r.: Sticht, Allmendinger, Peatau. The photo was taken in a park in Tripoli on 20 May 1939. At the time the crew was attached to the long-distance school in Köthen.

Right: Gustav Adolf Klüter as an Oberleutnant with III./KG 53, June 1940.

The port of Tripoli.

331

Top left: Flugkapitän Baur, Hitler's personal pilot, in conversation with Major Winkler, Kapitän of the 1. Staffel (was shot by terrorists in front of his hotel during the French campaign), during the fighting in Poland in early September 1939. Right: Oberst Stahl, Kommodore of KG 53 in 1939-40.

Center left: from l. to r.: Major Hofmann, Otl. Mehnert, General Sieburg, and Generalfeldmarschall Göring at the forward airfield in Mark Friedland, Sept. 1939. Center right: from l. to r.: General Sieburg, Hitler, Otl. Mehnert, unidentified, taken at the command post in Mark Friedland in Sept. 1939.

Kutno station in Poland after it was attacked by the 1. Staffel of KG 53, 1-10 September 1939.

Kampfgruppe I./53

++ KR - GSHL NR. 023 11.5. 0010 =

AN ROEM. EINS / K. G. 53 , GELCHSHEIM =

- G E H E I M -
EINSATZBEFEHL FUER DEN 11.5.40 -

1.) DER VORMARSCH DER DEUTSCHEN ARMEEN AM 10.5. WURD
PLANMAESZIG DUCHGEFUEHRT UND WIRD AM 11.5.
FORTGESETZT. -

2.) LUFTLAGE: DIE FEINDL. LUFTWAFFE WURDE MIT
TEILWEISE ERHEBLICHEN ERFOLG BEKAEMPFT. -
AM NACHMITTAG DES 10.5. ERHEBLICH GERINGE FLAK - UU.
JAGDABWEHR. -
FEINDL. LUFTWAFFE IM RAHMEN DER LFLM. 3 WIE FOLGT

3.) K. G. 53 SETZT AM 11.5. DIE ANGRIFFE GEGEN DIE
FEINDL.
FORT. =
ROEM. EINS / K. G. 53 ZIEL 10 168
ROEM. ZWEI / K. G. 53 ZIEL 10 175
ROEM. DREI / K. G. 53 ZIEL 10 174
ANGRIFFZEIT FUER ALLE GRUPPEN 07.00 UHR. -

4.) JAFUE 3 SCHUETZT MIT EINER ZERSTOERERGRUPPE DEN

ANFLUG DER KAMPFVERBAENDE IM RAUM SEDAN - ATTIGNY -
ST. MENEHOULD - VERDUN - VON 06.35 - 06.45 UHR DEN
AUSFLUG DER KAMPFVERBAENDE IN DEMSELBEN RAUM MIT
EINER ZERSTOERERGRUPPE VON 07.15 - 07.35 UHR .
AUSSERDEM AUFNAHME DER KAMPFVERBAENDE NACH DEM
FRUEHANGRIFF DURCH JAEGER IM RAUM ARLON - LONGVY -
VITRON - ROULLES . -

5.) AUFKLAERUNG: 1 HE 111 DER STABSSTAFFEL SCHLIESZT
SICH DEM ANGRIFF DER ROEM. DREI / K. G. 53 AN ZUR
ERFLIEGUNG VON ZIELWIRKUNKSBILDERN . -

6.) WETTER ZWISCHEN 05.00 U. 08.00 UHR VORRAUSSICHTLICH
WIE 10.5. MIT DUNST U. SCHLECHTER SICHT IST ZU RECHNEN .
- ANGRIFFSHOEHE ZWISCHEN 5 U. 6 000 M.

KAMPFGESCHWADER 53 , ABT. ROEM. EINS / A
NR. 624/40 GEH. ++

Geschwader mission order of 11 May 1940.

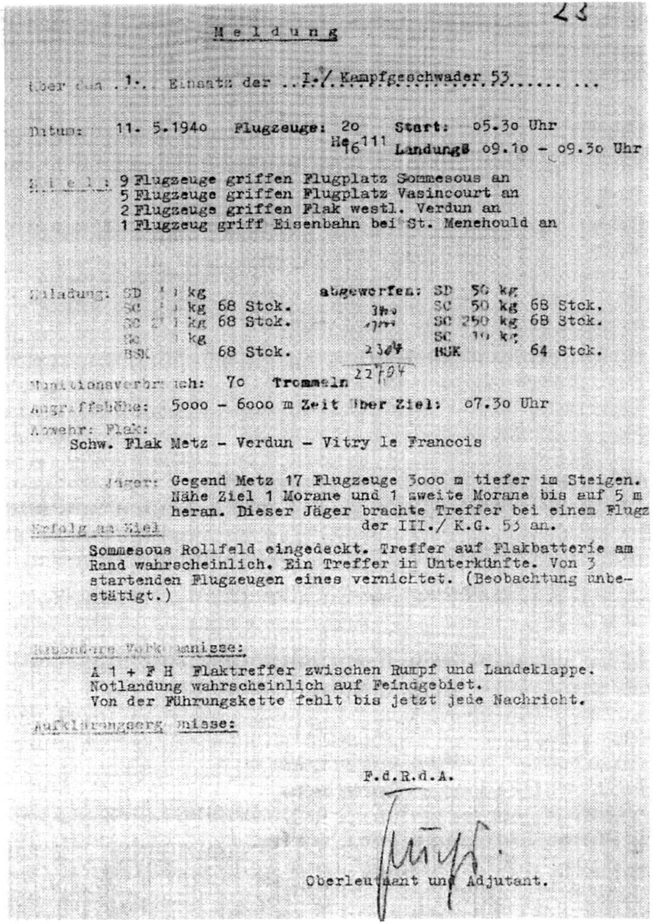

23

M e l d u n g

Über den .1.. Einsatz der ..I./ Kampfgeschwader 53...... ...

Datum: 11. 5.1940 Flugzeuge: 20 He 111 (16) Start: 05.30 Uhr Landung: 09.10 – 09.30 Uhr

Ziel: 9 Flugzeuge griffen Flugplatz Sommesous an
5 Flugzeuge griffen Flugplatz Vasincourt an
2 Flugzeuge griffen Flak westl. Verdun an
1 Flugzeug griff Eisenbahn bei St. Menehould an

Zuladung: SD ... kg · SC ... kg 68 Stck. · SC 2.. kg 68 Stck. · SC ... kg · BSK 68 Stck.

abgeworfen: SD 50 kg · SC 50 kg 68 Stck. · SC 250 kg 68 Stck. · SC 10 kg · BSK 64 Stck.

Munitionsverbrauch: 70 Trommeln 22794

Angriffshöhe: 5000 – 6000 m Zeit über Ziel: 07.30 Uhr

Abwehr: Flak:
Schw. Flak Metz – Verdun – Vitry le Francois

Jäger: Gegend Metz 17 Flugzeuge 3000 m tiefer im Steigen. Nähe Ziel 1 Morane und 1 zweite Morane bis auf 5 m heran. Dieser Jäger brachte Treffer bei einem Flugz der III./ K.G. 53 an.

Erfolg am Ziel

Sommesous Rollfeld eingedeckt. Treffer auf Flakbatterie am Rand wahrscheinlich. Ein Treffer in Unterkünfte. Von 3 startenden Flugzeugen eines vernichtet. (Beobachtung unbestätigt.)

Besondere Vorkommnisse:

A 1 + F H Flaktreffer zwischen Rumpf und Landeklappe.
Notlandung wahrscheinlich auf Feindgebiet.
Von der Führungskette fehlt bis jetzt jede Nachricht.

Aufklärungsergebnisse:

F.d.R.d.A.

Oberleutnant und Adjutant.

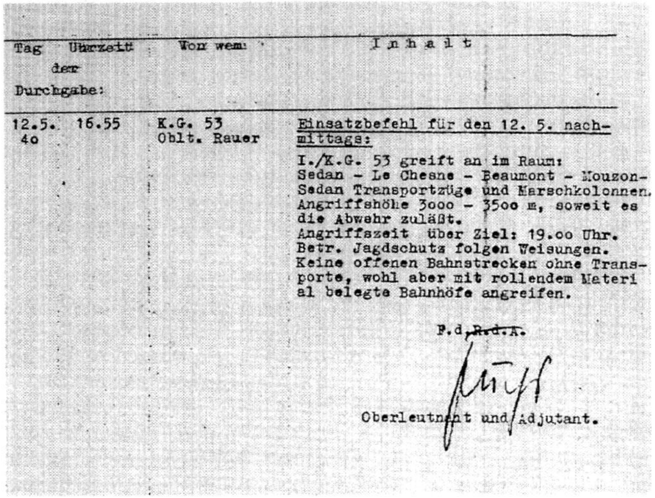

Tag der Durchgabe:	Uhrzeit	Von wem:	Inhalt
12.5.40	16.55	K.G. 53 Oblt. Rauer	Einsatzbefehl für den 12. 5. nachmittags: I./K.G. 53 greift an im Raum: Sedan – Le Chesne – Beaumont – Mouzon-Sedan Transportzüge und Marschkolonnen. Angriffshöhe 3000 – 3500 m, soweit es die Abwehr zuläßt. Angriffszeit über Ziel: 19.00 Uhr. Betr. Jagdschutz folgen Weisungen. Keine offenen Bahnstrecken ohne Transporte, wohl aber mit rollendem Material belegte Bahnhöfe angreifen.

F.d.R.d.A.

Oberleutnant und Adjutant.

The I. Gruppe's report on the mission of 11 May 1940.

Kurz vor Ziel 1 Morane wahrscheinlich abgeschossen (kippte mir schwarzer Rauch-
fahne steil ab) (Besatzung: Oblt. Sauer, 1.Staffel).
Kurz nach Ziel 1 Morane bestimmt abgeschossen (Uffz. Haas, 3.Staffel).

Besondere Vorkommnisse:
Uffz. Huber rechts Mittelhand Durchschuß. (Bordfunker, 3.Staffel),
1 Maschine (Lt. v.Sazenhofen - Fuchsberg) nördlich Mourmelon abgeschossen. Maschine abmontiert (2 Mann mit Fallschirm beobachtet
abgesprungen).
1 Maschine kurz nach Ziel mit 1 stehender Motor nach Norden abge-
dreht. Durch eigene Zerstörer aufgenommen.

Aufklärungsergebnisse: Aufklärungsergebnisse entlang Flugweg
Longuyon - Mourmelon:
1.) Bahnen von S nach N westlich der Maas geringer Verkehr.
2.) Flak bei Longuyon schoß außer schwarzen auch gelbe
    Sprengpunkte (wahrscheinlich Richtungsschüsse).
3.) An den Maasbrücken schoß keine Flak.
4.) Stützpunkt Mourmelon mit mindestens 50 Flugzeugen belegt.

P.d.R.d.A.

Oberleutnant und Adjutant.

A b s c h r i f t

Über den 1. Einsatz der .... I./ Kampfgeschwader 53....

Datum: 12. 5.40   Start: 05.55 Uhr ....18........ He 111
                  Landung: 09.19 Uhr ....16........ He 111
                           09.30 Uhr

Ziel: Flugplatz Mourmelon

Zuladung:		Stück	Abw. grafen:			Stück
SC	10 kg		SC	10 kg		
SC	50 kg	108	SC	50 kg	102	
SD	50 kg	108	SD	50 kg	102	
SC	250 kg	54	SC	250 kg	51	
SBe	50 kg		SBe	50 kg		
BSK			BSK	Brummeln		

Munitionsverbrauch: 236   Ziel über Ziel 07.55
Angriffshöhe: 5300 - 5800 m

Abwehr: Flak: Bei Verdun - Longuyon - (schwarze und gelbe
         Sprengpunkte) - Mourmelon - Reims
         Jäger: Suippes - Mourmelon - Somme Py - Monthois
         (Gesamt etwa 15 Morane und Potez).

Erfolg am Ziel: 1 Gruppe abgestellte Flugzeuge am Nordostrand gut
eingedeckt. 1 Gruppe abgestellte Flugzeuge am Südrand gut eingedeckt. 1 Gruppe abgestellte Flugzeuge am Nordwestrand eingedeckt. (Zusammen mindestens 50 Flugzeuge!)

The I. Gruppe's report on the first mission flown on 12 May 1940.

über den 2. Einsatz der ....I./ Kampfgeschwader 53

Datum: 12.5.40   Start: 17.40 ....Flur ....12 .... He ???
                  Landung: 20.25 - ...Uhr ....12 .... He ???
                           20.35

Ziel: Bahn- und Straßentransporte im Raum Sedan - Mouzon - Beaumont - Le Chesne - Poix Terron.

Zuladung:

		Stück	Abgeworfen:			Ohne
SC	10 kg		SC	10 kg		
SC	50 kg	72	SC	50 kg	42	
SD - 50 kg		72	SD	50 kg	41	
SC	250 kg	36	SC	250 kg	24	
SBe 50 kg			SBe	50 kg		
BSK			BSK	Trommeln		

Munitionsverbrauch: 27 Trommeln

Angriffshöhe: 4500 - 5000 m   Zeit über Ziel: 19.05 - 19.30

Abwehr: Flak: Schwere Flak sehr gut liegend bei
Longwy - Montmedy - Beaumont - Raum um Sedan.

Jäger: 1 Morane Angriff von rechts unten auf
Führerkette.

Erfolg am Ziel: 2 Volltreffer auf Straße Sedan - Vouziers.
Bahnlinie Charleville - Rethel Treffer eine 50 kg Bombe.

Besondere Vorkommnisse: 1 Bombe dicht, 1 Bombe weiter ostwärts
der Maas geworfen.
5 Flugzeuge Flaktreffer.

Aufklärungsergebnisse: Von 19.05 - 19.30

Bahnhof Mouzon wenig rollendes Material.
Straße Mouzon - Vendresse, Chemery - Sedan, Baalons - Flize
einzelne Lastwagen mit etwa 200 m großen Fliegerabständen. Fahrt-
richtung nicht erkennbar.
Bahnlinie Mouzon - Sedan , Mouzon - Baalons kein Verkehr erkannt.
Bahnhof Meziers stark mit rollendem Material belegt.
Starker Stellungsbau westlich der Maas zwischen Sedan und Charleville. Heftiger Erdkampf nordostwärts Sedan. Straßen und Bahnen
oistwärts der Maas unbelegt.

F.d.R.d.A.

[signature]

Oberleutnant und Adjutant.

The I. Gruppe's report on the second mission flown on 12 May 1940.

The phases of the Battle of Britain.

Der Führer und Oberste Befehlshaber
der Wehrmacht   18. Dezember 1940.

OKW/WFSt/Abt. L (I) Nr. 33 408/40 g. Kdos. Chefsache

G e h e i m e K o m m a n d o s a c h e.

Weisung Nr. 21.

„Fall Barbarossa".

Die deutsche Wehrmacht muß darauf vorbereitet sein, auch vor Beendigung des Krieges gegen England Sowjetrußland in einem schnellen F e l d z u g n i e d e r z u w e r f e n („Fall Barbarossa").

Das H e e r wird hierzu alle verfügbaren Verbände einzusetzen haben mit der Einschränkung, daß die besetzten Gebiete gegen Überraschungen gesichert sein müssen.

Für die Luftwaffe wird es darauf ankommen, für den Ostfeldzug so starke Kräfte zur Unterstützung des Heeres freizumachen, daß mit einem schnellen Ablauf der Erdoperationen gerechnet werden kann und die Schädigung des ostdeutschen Raumes durch feindliche Luftangriffe so gering wie möglich bleibt. Diese Schwerpunktbildung im Osten findet ihre Grenze in der Forderung, daß der gesamte von uns beherrschte Kampf- und Rüstungsraum gegen feindliche Luftangriffe hinreichend geschützt bleiben muß und die Angriffshandlungen gegen England, insbesondere seine Zufuhren, nicht zum Erliegen kommen dürfen.

Der Schwerpunkt des Einsatzes der K r i e g s m a r i n e bleibt auch während des Ostfeldzuges eindeutig gegen E n g l a n d gerichtet.

Den A u f m a r s c h gegen Sowjetrußland werde ich gegebenenfalls acht Wochen vor dem beabsichtigten Operationsbeginn befehlen.

Vorbereitungen, die eine längere Anlaufzeit benötigen, sind — soweit noch nicht geschehen — schon jetzt in Angriff zu nehmen und bis zum 15. Mai 1941 abzuschließen.

Entscheidender Wert ist jedoch darauf zu legen, daß die Absicht eines Angriffs nicht erkennbar wird.

Die Vorbereitungen der Oberkommandos sind auf folgender Grundlage zu treffen:

I. Allgemeine Absicht:

Die im westlichen Rußland stehende Masse des russischen H e e r e s soll in kühnen Operationen unter weitem Vortreiben von Panzerkeilen vernichtet, der Abzug kampfkräftiger Teile in die Weite des russischen Raumes verhindert werden.

In rascher Verfolgung ist dann eine Linie zu erreichen, aus der die russische Luftwaffe reichsdeutsches Gebiet nicht mehr angreifen kann. Das Endziel der Operation ist die Abschirmung gegen das asiatische Rußland aus der allgemeinen Linie Wolga—Archangelsk. So kann erforderlichenfalls das letzte Ruß-

land verbleibende Industriegebiet am Ural durch die Luftwaffe ausgeschaltet werden.

Im Zuge dieser Operationen wird die russische O s t s e e f l o t t e schnell ihre Stützpunkte verlieren und damit nicht mehr kampffähig sein.

Wirksames Eingreifen der russischen L u f t w a f f e ist schon bei Beginn der Operation durch kraftvolle Schläge zu verhindern.

II. Voraussichtliche Verbündete und deren Aufgaben:

1. Auf den Flügeln unserer Operation ist mit der aktiven Teilnahme R u m ä - n i e n s und F i n n l a n d s am Kriege gegen Sowjetrußland zu rechnen.

   In welcher Form die Streitkräfte beider Länder bei ihrem Eingreifen deutschem Befehl unterstellt werden, wird das Oberkommando der Wehrmacht zeitgerecht vereinbaren und festlegen.

2. R u m ä n i e n s Aufgabe wird es sein, zusammen mit der dort aufmarschierenden Kräftegruppe den gegenüberstehenden Gegner zu fesseln und im übrigen Hilfsdienste im rückwärtigen Gebiet zu leisten.

3. F i n n l a n d wird den Aufmarsch der aus Norwegen kommenden abgesetzten deutschen Nordgruppe (Teile der Gruppe XXI) zu decken und mit ihr gemeinsam zu operieren haben. Daneben wird Finnland die Ausschaltung von Hangö zufallen.

4. Mit der Möglichkeit, daß s c h w e d i s c h e Bahnen und Straßen für den Aufmarsch der deutschen Nordgruppe spätestens von Operationsbeginn an zur Verfügung stehen, kann gerechnet werden.

III. Die Führung der Operationen:

A) H e e r (in Genehmigung der mir vorgetragenen Absichten):

   In dem durch die Pripjet-Sümpfe in eine südliche und eine nördliche Hälfte getrennten Operationsraum ist der Schwerpunkt n ö r d l i c h dieses Gebietes zu bilden. Hier sind zwei Heeresgruppen vorzusehen.

   Der südlichen dieser beiden Heeresgruppen — Mitte der Gesamtfront — fällt die Aufgabe zu, mit besonders starken Panzer- und mot. Verbänden aus dem Raum um und nördlich Warschau vorbrechend, die feindlichen Kräfte in Weißrußland zu zersprengen. Dadurch muß die Voraussetzung geschaffen werden für das Eindrehen von starken Teilen der schnellen Truppen nach Norden, um im Zusammenwirken mit der aus Ostpreußen in allgemeiner Richtung Leningrad operierenden nördlichen Heeresgruppe die im Baltikum kämpfenden feindlichen Kräfte zu vernichten. Erst nach Sicherstellung dieser vordringlichen Aufgabe, welcher die Besetzung von Leningrad und Kronstadt folgen muß, sind die Angriffsoperationen zur Besitznahme des wichtigen Verkehrs- und Rüstungszentrums Moskau fortzuführen.

   Nur ein überraschend schnell eintretender Zusammenbruch der russischen Widerstandskraft könnte es rechtfertigen, beide Ziele gleichzeitig anzustreben.

   Die wichtigste Aufgabe der Gruppe XXI bleibt auch während der Ostoperationen der S c h u t z N o r w e g e n s. Die darüber hinaus verfügbaren

Kräfte sind im Norden (Geb. Korps) zunächst zur Sicherung des Petsamogebietes und seiner Erzgruben sowie der Eismeerstraße einzusetzen, um dann gemeinsam mit finnischen Kräften gegen die Murmansk-Bahn vorzustoßen und die Versorgung des Murmanskgebietes zu Lande und über See zu unterbinden.

Ob eine derartige Operation mit stärkeren deutschen Kräften (zwei bis drei Divisionen) aus dem Raum von Rovaniemi und südlich geführt werden kann, hängt von der Bereitwilligkeit Schwedens ab, seine Eisenbahnen für einen solchen Aufmarsch zur Verfügung zu stellen.

Der Masse des finnischen Heeres wird die Aufgabe zufallen, in Übereinstimmung mit dem Fortschreiten des deutschen Nordflügels möglichst starke russische Kräfte durch Angriff westlich oder beiderseits des Ladogasees zu fesseln und sich in den Besitz von Hangö zu setzen.

Bei der südlich der Pripjetsümpfe angesetzten Heeresgruppe ist der Schwerpunkt im Raum von Lublin in allgemeiner Richtung Kiew zu bilden, um mit starken Panzerkräften schnell in die tiefe Flanke und den Rücken der russischen Kräfte vorzugehen und diese dann im Zuge des Dnjepr aufzurollen.

Der deutsch-rumänischen Kräftegruppe fällt am rechten Flügel die Aufgabe zu,

a) den rumänischen Raum und damit den Südflügel der Gesamtoperation zu schützen,

b) im Zuge des Angriffs am Nordflügel der Heeresgruppe Süd die gegenüberstehenden feindlichen Kräfte zu fesseln und bei fortschreitender Entwicklung der Lage im Verein mit der Luftwaffe ihren geordneten Rückzug über den Dnjestr im Nachstoß zu verhindern.

Sind die Schlachten südlich bzw. nördlich der Pripjet-Sümpfe geschlagen, ist im Rahmen der Verfolgung anzustreben:

im Süden die frühzeitige Besitznahme des wehrwirtschaftlich wichtigen Donez-Beckens,

im Norden das schnelle Erreichen von Moskau.

Die Einnahme dieser Stadt bedeutet politisch und wirtschaftlich einen entscheidenden Erfolg, darüber hinaus den Ausfall des wichtigsten Eisenbahnknotenpunktes.

B) Luftwaffe:

Ihre Aufgabe wird es sein, die Einwirkung der russischen Luftwaffe so weit wie möglich zu lähmen und auszuschalten, sowie die Operationen des Heeres in ihren Schwerpunkten, namentlich bei der mittleren Heeresgruppe und auf dem Schwerpunktflügel der südlichen Heeresgruppe, zu unterstützen. Die russischen Bahnen werden je nach ihrer Bedeutung für die Operationen zu unterbrechen bzw. in ihren wichtigsten nahegelegenen Objekten (Flußüberfgänge) durch kühnen Einsatz von Fallschirm- und Luftlandetruppen in Besitz zu nehmen sein. Um alle Kräfte gegen die feindliche Luftwaffe und zur unmittelbaren Unterstützung des Heeres zusammenfassen zu können, ist die Rüstungsindustrie während der Hauptoperationen nicht anzugreifen. Erst nach

Abschluß der Bewegungsoperationen kommen derartige Angriffe, in erster Linie gegen das Uralgebiet, in Frage.

C) Kriegsmarine:

Der Kriegsmarine fällt gegen Sowjetrußland die Aufgabe zu, unter Sicherung der eigenen Küste ein Ausbrechen feindlicher Seestreitkräfte aus der Ostsee zu verhindern. Da nach dem Erreichen von Leningrad der russischen Ostseeflotte der letzte Stützpunkt genommen und diese dann in hoffnungsloser Lage sein wird, sind vorher größere Seeoperationen zu vermeiden. Nach dem Ausschalten der russischen Flotte wird es darauf ankommen, den vollen Seeverkehr in der Ostsee, dabei auch den Nachschub für den nördlichen Heeresflügel über See sicherzustellen (Minenräumung!).

IV.

Alle von den Herren Oberbefehlshabern auf Grund dieser Weisung zu treffenden Anordnungen müssen eindeutig dahin abgestimmt sein, daß es sich um Vorsichtsmaßnahmen handelt für den Fall, daß Rußland seine bisherige Haltung gegen uns ändern sollte. Die Zahl der frühzeitig zu den Vorarbeiten heranzuziehenden Offiziere ist so klein wie möglich zu halten, weitere Mitarbeiter sind so spät wie möglich und nur in dem für die Tätigkeit jedes einzelnen erforderlichen Umfang einzuweisen. Sonst besteht die Gefahr, daß durch ein Bekanntwerden unserer Vorbereitungen, deren Durchführung zeitlich noch gar nicht festliegt, schwerste politische und militärische Nachteile entstehen.

V.

Vorträgen der Herren Oberbefehlshaber über ihre weiteren Absichten auf Grund dieser Weisung sehe ich entgegen.

Die beabsichtigten Vorbereitungen aller Wehrmachtteile sind mir, auch in ihrem zeitlichen Ablauf, über das Oberkommando der Wehrmacht zu melden.

(gez.) Adolf Hitler.

Verteiler: ....

Hitler's "Directive No.21" for Case Barbarossa.

The buildup in the east.

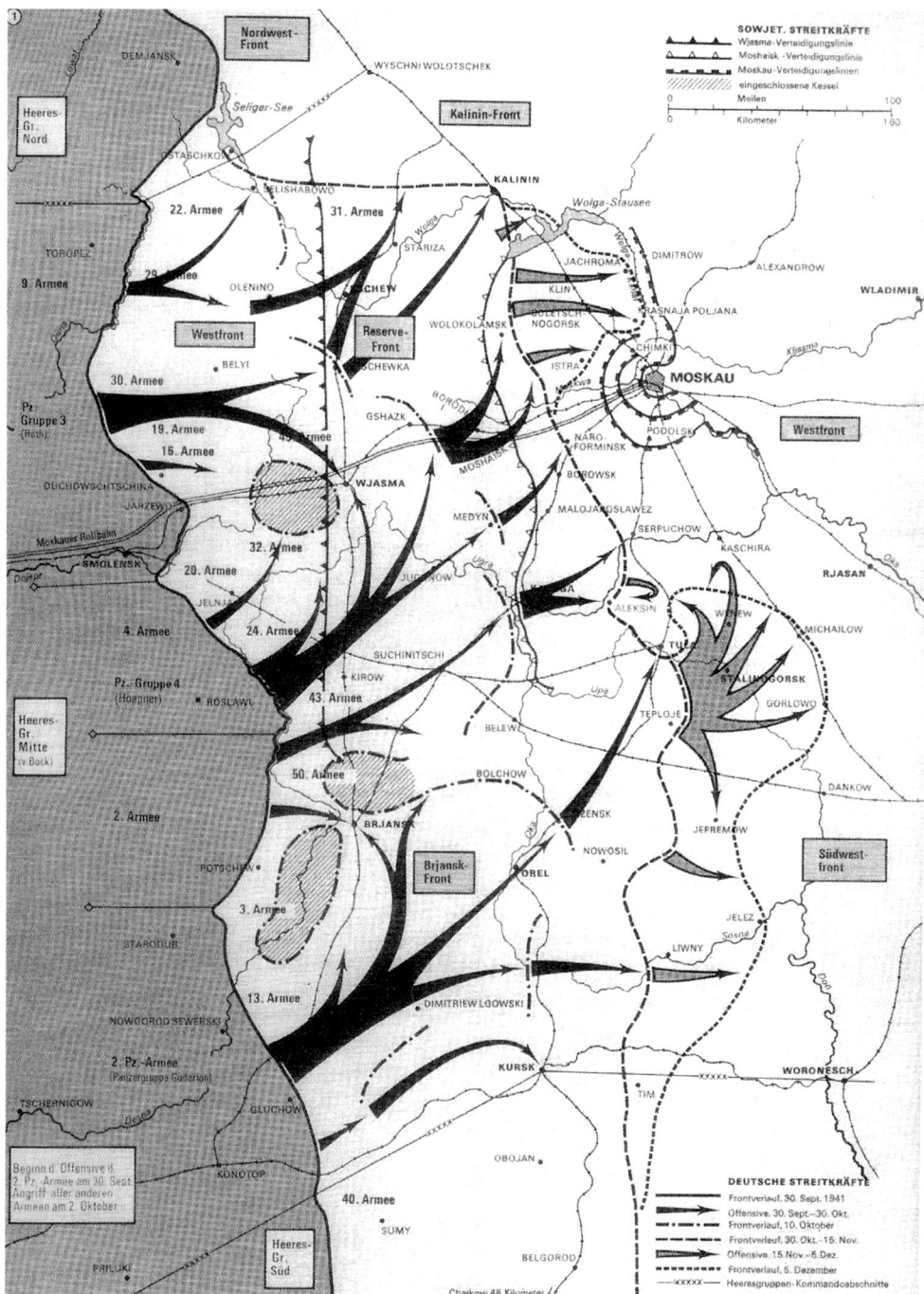

Areas of operations Kursk-Orel-Rzhev-Kaluga and Moscow.

Group photo: non-commissioned officers of the 8th Airfield Operating Company, November 1939.

Members of the 3. Staffel at Kattenbach airbase, Ansbach, in the winter of 1939-40. From l. to r.: Major Hofmann, Staffelkapitän, Oblt. Rauer, Uffz. Siebold, Fw. Ulrich, Uffz. Angermeier.

Roth airbase, March 1940. From l. to r.: Otl. Mehnert, C.O. I./KG 53, Feldwebel von Satzenhofen-Fuchsberg, Major Hofmann, St.Kap. 3./ KG 53.

General Loerzer in conversation with Hauptmann Seidel, Vitry en Artois, September 1940.

Großostheim, May 1940. From l. to r.: Oblt. Allmendinger, Lt. Müller, Oblt. Sauer, Oblt. Seidel.

343

Lt. von Glasow and his crew in front of their He 111 H-6, which is loaded with a 1000-kg bomb, Russia, Nov. 1941. From l. to r.: Köster, von Glasow, Knopping, Graf, Breuer.

The same crew in front of a He 111 H-5. Above right may be seen a side-mounted machine-gun, which was served by Köster. Russia, November 1941.

October 1941, Shatalovka. Wrecked Russian warplanes litter the edge of the airfield. Some of the aircraft were fabric-covered. In some cases this was even used to make bindings for our logbooks.

This map depicts the route taken by Lt. von Glasow and his crew during their trek through the Russian lines. Symbols: $\otimes$ = where the aircraft was shot down, ⱵⱵⱵⱵ = the front line on 23/11/41, xxx = path followed.

Left: Otl. Bader, C.O. of the II. Gruppe, 1941. Right: Orsha, September 1941, Generalfeldmarschall Kesselring visits III./KG 53.

Left: Summer 1941. Kommodore Otl. Weitkus (left) with Hauptmann Küster who, after being shot down, was hidden by a Russian farmer for six weeks and subsequently made his way back through the enemy lines. Right: Otl. Schulz-Müllensiefen at Shatalovka-East in the winter of 1941-42.

Aircraft mechanics at work.
Shatalovka, 1941.

The Stabsstaffel – transfer of command from Hauptmann Wittmann to Oberleutnant von Horn on 15 October 1941.

Members of KG 53 in a Canadian prisoner of war camp.

A similar picture to the one above, taken in another camp.

Officers of KG 53 wearing summer civilian clothing in a Canadian POW camp. From l. to r.: Lt. Leber, Oblt. Meinecke, Lt. Zipse, unknown, Lt. Lüttecken.

348

The aircraft flown by Hauptmann Hufenreuter and his crew. It made a forced landing in England (near Ashford, Kent) after bombing London on the night of 10-11 May 1941.

German air raid on Moscow on 26 July 1941. From Life Magazine, August 1941.

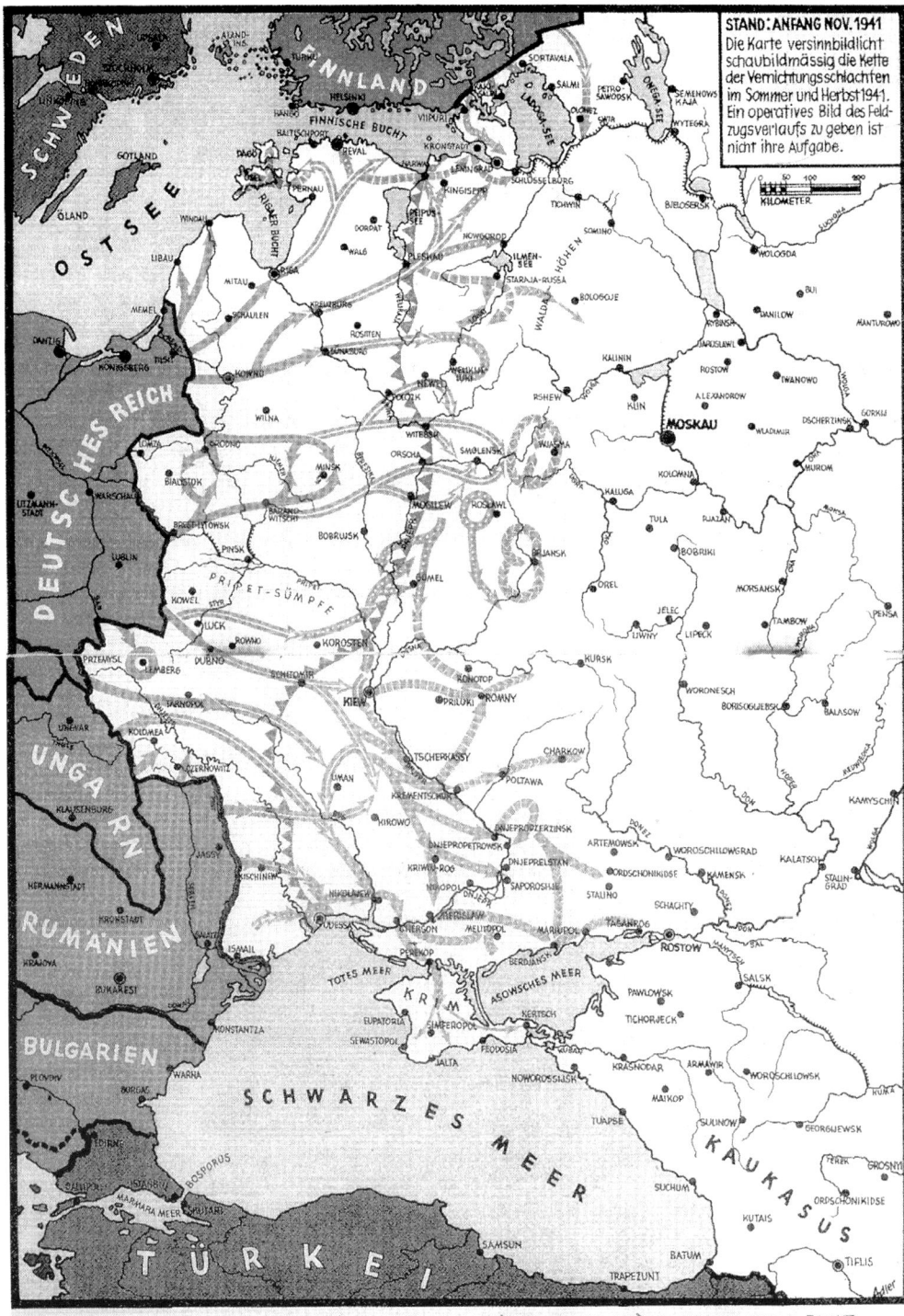

The German advance until 31 October 1941.

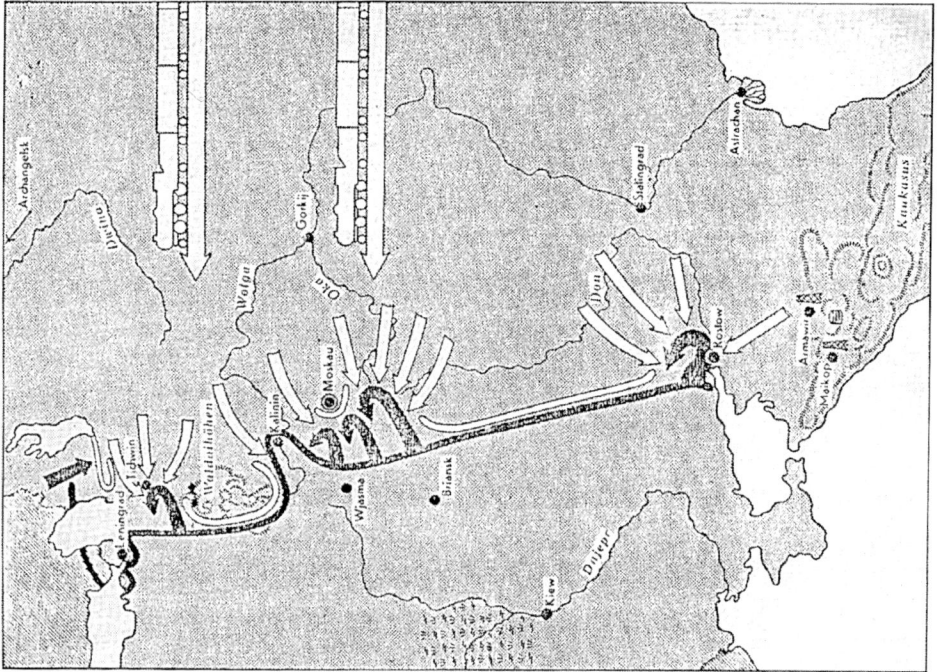

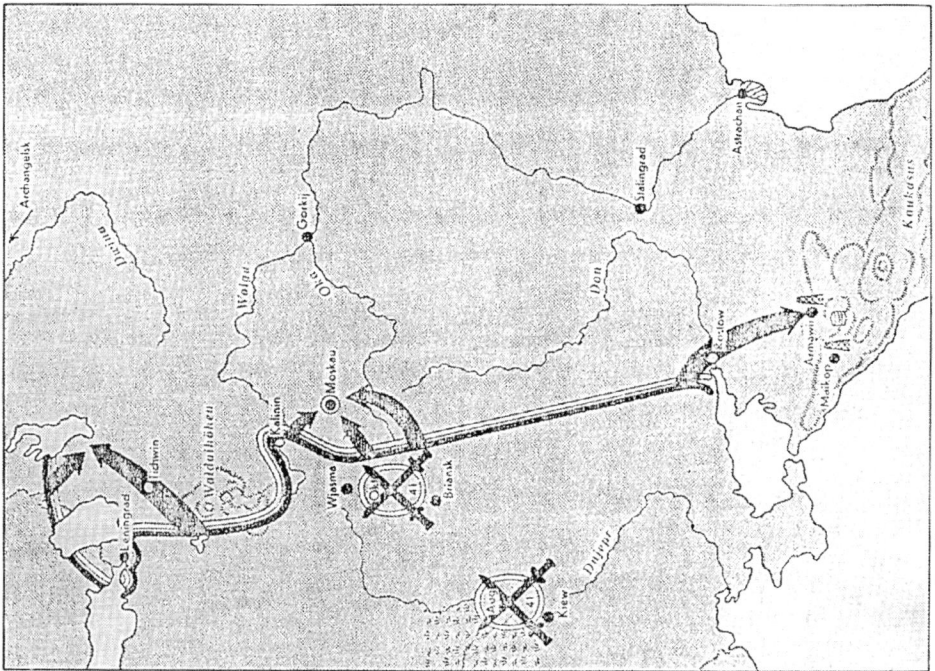

Plan for the German winter offensive of 1941 and its collapse (sketches by Bernhard von Loßberg).

1.) Lfl.Kdo. 1
2.) I./K.G.53
3.) Zahl: 3 He 111 (2 H 6 und 1 H 14)
4.) Start: 1o.52 - 1o.55
5.) Landung: 12.15 - 13.35
6.) Zeit über Ziel: 12.o5 - 11.4o
7.) Flughöhe: 3oo m
8.) Auftrag: Versorgung Welikije Luki (Zitadelle)
9.) Erfolg: 1 He 111 abgebrochen wegen Wetterlage (Ab Nowosokolniki 2-4/1o um 6oo m, Sicht 1o - 15 km)

1 He 111 nicht geworfen, da Ziel nicht gefunden.

1 He 111 Abwurf über befohlenem Ziel, 3 Behälter siehe im Ziel. Alle Zchirme haben sich geöffnet.

10.) Abgebrochen: 2 He 111
11.) Ausweichziel: Bahnhof Welikije Luki
12.) Behälter: 5
Munition: 5 Tr.MG., 1 MG./PF.
13.) Abschüsse: --
14.) Verluste: --
15.) Abwehr: MG. und leichte Flak westl. Werner
16.) Jagdschutz: --
17.) Wetter: Auf Strecke dünne Dunstschicht in etwa 3oo - 4oo m, ab Nowosokolniki aufgerissene Wolkendecke zwischen 3oo und 8oo m. Sicht etwa 5 km.
18.) Aufklärung: --
19.) Lichtbild: --

I.A.

[signature]

L e u t n a n t

1.) Lfl.Kdo. 1
2.) I./K.G.53
3.) Zahl: 6 He 111 H 6
4.) Start: 1o.55 - 11.1o
5.) Landung: 12.36 - 13.57
6.) Zeit über Ziel: 11.4o - 13.1o
7.) Flughöhe: 2oo - 3oo m
8.) Auftrag: Versorgung Welikije Luki (Bahnhof)
9.) Erfolg: 4 He 111 haben abgeworfen. Auftreffen der Bomben konnten wegen sehr schlechter Sicht nicht beobachtet werden. 1 Behälter nicht aufgegangen. Bei einer der 4 He 111 (A1+BL) hat sich infolge Beschuß der elektrischen Leitungen nur 1 Behälter gelöst.

2 He 111 konnten infolge der schlechten Sicht das Ziel trotz viermaligem Anfluges erst so spät erkennen, daß ein Abwurf der Behälter nicht mehr möglich war.

Sämtliche Behälter, die nicht abgeworfen wurden, wurden wieder zurückgebracht.

10.) Abgebrochen: --
11.) Ausweichziel: --
12.) Behälter: 16 Verpflegungsbehälter B 250
Munition: 93 MG.15, 2 MG./PF.
13.) Abschüsse: --
14.) Verluste: 2 He 111 (A1+BL) 1 Treffer in Kanzel, Hilfskompaß zerstört, Treffer im Instrumentenbrett, künstlicher Horizont und Variometer ausgefallen, Zündleitungen durchschossen.
15.) Abwehr: Mittlere und schwere Flak aus SW. von Welikije Luki.
16.) Jagdschutz: --
17.) Wetter: Über Ziel 5/1o Schleierwolken in 1oo m, nach Norden zunehmend im Süden und Westen auflösend. Sicht etwa 1 km.
18.) Aufklärung: Kriechino Quadr.BH 32 größeres Truppenlager und Stellung. Wm-41.89 im Quadr.BH65? w.W. 1-He-111-am-Boden-liegend.
19.) Lichtbild: --

D.E.

[signature]

Leutnant und Adjutant

1.) Lfl.Kdo. 1   2.) I./K.G.53
3.) Zahl: 9   He 111 H 6
4.) Start: o8.5o - o9.o5   5.) Landung: 1o.25-1o.5o
6.) Anr.Zeit: o9.43 - 1o.o5   7.) Anr.Höhe: Tiefstflug - 2oo m
8.) Auftrag: Versorgung Welikije Luki

9.) Erfolg: 2o Behälter wurden über dem Bahnhof abgeworfen. (4 He 111) 1 Fallschirm öffnete sich nicht.
Lage der Behälter im Bahnhof Welikije Luki.
Dabei 1 Maschine wegen Wetter die Zitadelle nicht ausmachen. Die beiden andern Maschinen, die die Zitadelle versorgen sollten, konnten den Auftrag nicht durchführen. (1 Maschine wegen Motorschaden abgebrochen, 1 Maschine überfällig).
Außerdem brachen noch 2 Maschinen wegen plötzlichen Absinkens der Wolkenuntergrenze auf 2oo m und Sichtrückgang auf 5o - 2oo m ab.
Die letzte Maschine dieses Einsatzes ist auch überfällig.

10.) Ausweichziel: --

11.) Abgebrochen: 3 Maschinen , 1 wegen Motorschadens, 2 wegen Wetter.
12.) Behälter: 2o Vers.Behälter (Verpflegung und Munition)
Munition: 55 Trommeln MG , 6 MG/PF
13.) Abschüsse: --
14.) Verluste: 2 Maschinen überfällig (Besatzung Lt.Bohalke, B2) Ufw. Donhauser , FL), 1 Maschine Flaktreffer.
15.) Abwehr: leichte Flak und Inf.Abwehr, heftig und gut liegend
16.) Jagdschutz: ---   19.) Bildrolle: ---
17.) Wetter: Wolkenuntergrenze stark wechselnd, zwischen 7o und 2oo m, Bodennebelfelder, Sicht 1-5 km, vereinzelt Schneeschauer.
18.) Aufklärung: ---

I.A.

[signature]

L e u t n a n t

Three reports by the I. Gruppe concerning supply flights to the Velikiye-Luki pocket on 31/12/42 and 1/1/43.

Korovye Selo ... another lucky escape. Flak damage.

Korovye Selo, awarding of decorations on 10 June 1942. From l. to r.: in foreground Otl. Schulz, Lt. Kornblum, Lt. Klinkel, General Keller, Lt. Blieweis, Lt. Geisendorfer, Lt. Dreher.

Staging base at Gostkino (near Luga), September 1942. Command post.

Above left: In Greifswald to rest and reequip. From l. to r.: Hptm. Klein, St.Kap. 6./KG 53, killed at Stalingrad on 26/1/43, Lt. Geisendorfer, Lt. Luchesig, missing at Stalingrad, Lt. Klunker, missing at Stalingrad.

Above right: Lt. Geisendorf and his crew. From l. to r.: Uffz. Stubbe, gunner; Fw. Schmauz, observer; Lt. Geisendorfer, pilot; Uffz. Kern, flight engineer; Uffz. Dürrnagel, radio operator.

Center: He 111 in winter camouflage over Voroshilovgrad, January 1943.

Below: Pskov, April 1943. Kommodore Oberst Wilke says goodbye to his officers. From l. to r.: Oblt. Zabel, adjutant II. Gruppe; Oblt. Wolf, technical officer; Lt. Kornblum, pilot; Lt. Geisendorfer, pilot; Lt. Dreher, pilot.

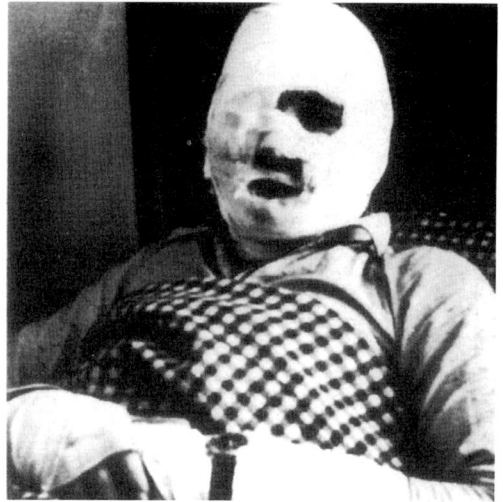

Above left: Voroshilovgrad, January 1943. Signpost with the names of towns in the homeland.

Above right: Oblt. Spelling, badly wounded after being shot down and making a forced landing, spring 1943.

Center: summer 1943, quarters at Olsufyevo airfield with military cemetery.

Below: Pskov, spring 1943. Oberst Wilke transfers command of the Geschwader to Major Pockrandt.

Above left: Obfw. Teige, the first non-commissioned officer of the Geschwader (6. Staffel) to be awarded the Knight's Cross. He received the decoration in Korovye Selo on 10 June 1942. Teige was awarded the Knight's Cross for shooting down twelve enemy aircraft while flying the He 111. At the time he had logged 220 combat missions.

Above right: Major Pockrandt with facial burns after his aircraft was shot down by a Russian motor torpedo boat west of Kronstadt, summer 1942.

Below left: Generaloberst Keller, commander of Luftflotte 1, in conversation with new Knight's Cross wearer Obfw. Teige and his crew.

Oberst Weitkus, Kommodore 15/12/40 – 31/10/1942.

Kämpfe um Welikiye Luki

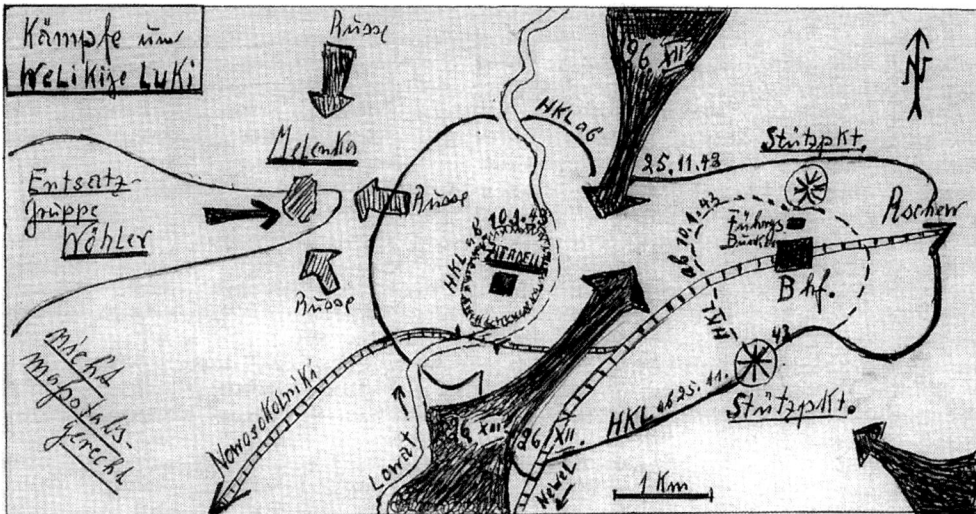

The situation in the Velikiye Luki pocket on 25 November 1942 and 10 January 1943.

Der Kommandierende General und H.Qu., den 22.1.1943.
Befehlshaber des Luftwaffenkommandos Ost.

Tagesbefehl!

Die langwierigen und überaus harten Kämpfe um den Stützpunkt Wel.Luki haben ihren Abschluß gefunden. Der Gefechtsverband
Wilke und die übrigen im gleichen Raum eingesetzten fliegenden
Verbände hatten entscheidenden Anteil an den Erfolgen des unerhört
schweren Abwehrkampfes, der stärkste feindliche Kräfte gebunden,
von anderen Schlachtfeldern ferngehalten und abgenützt hat.

Die Leistung des Gefechtsverbandes ist vorbildlich ge-
wesen für die Zusammenarbeit innerhalb des Verbandes, vor allem
aber für das taktische und kameradschaftliche Zusammenwirken mit
dem Heer. Der Einsatz von 4124 Maschinen, der Abschuß von 233
feindlichen Flugzeugen, sprechen ebenso für sich selbst, wie die
Versorgung von Wel.Luki durch Abwurf und Lastensegler.

Ich danke allen an dem Ringen um Wel.Luki beteiligten
Kampf-, Stuka-, Jagd-, Versorgungs- und Aufklärungsverbänden für
das, was sie mit Heldenmut, unermüdlicher Einsatzfreudigkeit und
beispielloser Härte trotz widrigster Umstände und häufig schlech-
testen Wetterbedingungen geleistet haben, um ihre Kameraden zu be-
freien und den angreifenden Entsatztruppen den Weg zu bahnen. Ganz
besonders möchte ich für alle Zeiten die heldenhaften Taten der
Führer der Lastensegler festhalten, die sich freiwillig geopfert
haben, um der Besatzung von Wel.Luki in schwerstem Feuer die letzte
Hilfe zu bringen.

Das Bewußtsein, der unter allerschwierigsten Bedingungen
gegen einen zahlenmäßig vielfach überlegenen Feind kämpfenden Erd-
truppe wirksam geholfen zu haben und ihren heldenmütigen Wider-
stand verlängert zu haben, ist der schönste Lohn aller Mühen und
Anstrengungen. Dieses Bewußtsein muß uns auch die schweren Opfer
ertragen lassen, die der Gefechtsverband, der Aufklärer und die
Lastensegler mit dem Verlust von insgesamt 28 Flugzeugen, 11 Go 242
und 6 DFS 230 erlitten haben.

Den toten und vermißten Kameraden gilt unser aller Dank
für ihr fliegerisches Soldatentum, das sie wohl meist mit ihrem
Tode besiegelt haben.

Ich weiß, daß die bisher dem Gefechtsverband Wilke un-
terstellten Verbände trotz des harten Einsatzes der letzten Zeit
für neue Aufgaben voll bereit sind.

Das tapfere Kampfgeschwader 53, das aus meinem Befehls-
bereich ausscheidet, verabschiede ich mit vollster Anerkennung
und meinen besten Wünschen für die Zukunft.

Dem Kommodore des Kampfgeschwaders, Oberst Wilke, danke
ich für die hervorragende Führung des Gefechtsverbandes.

Verteiler:
nur im Entwurf.

Oberst Wilke.

General der Flieger.

Order of the day acknowledging the efforts of those involved in the Velikiye Luki airlift, issued by General von Greim on 22 January 1943.

Oblt. Lehmann, Staffelkapitän of 2./KG 53, at the controls during a combat sortie, summer 1942.

Above right: Hauptmann Willmann, commander of the 1st Airfield Operating Company, at Korovye Selo in the summer of 1942. He has a shaved head after losing a race.

Center: Formation flight by the I. Gruppe, summer 1942, northern sector.

Right: Oblt. von Ehren and his crew after their 200th combat mission. Russia, winter 1942.

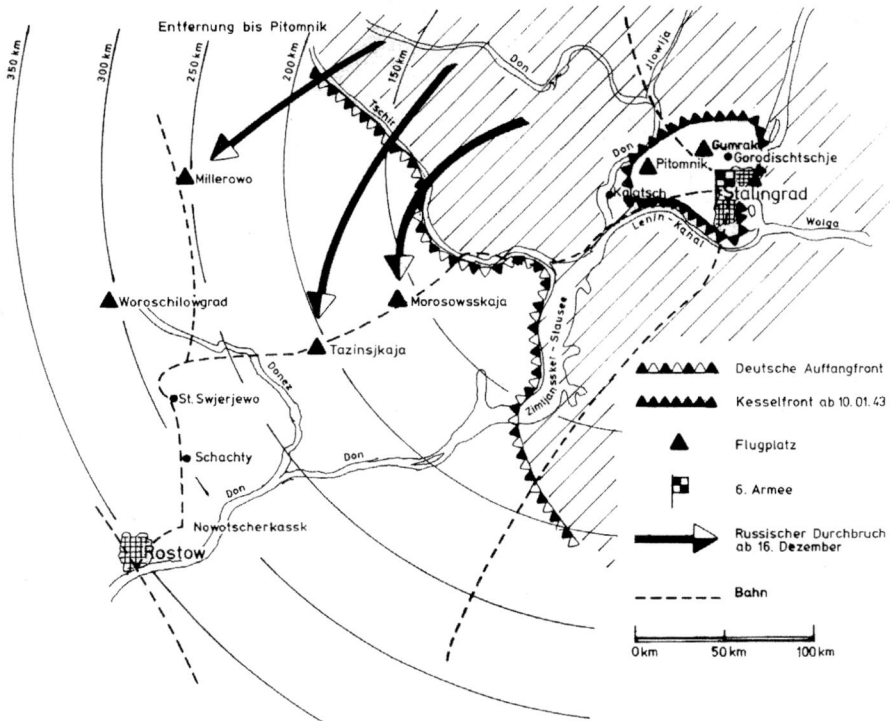

Airfields in the Stalingrad area.

Entfernung bis Pitomnik

350 km / 300 km / 250 km / 200 km / 150 km

Tschir

Don

Iiowlja

Don

Gumrak
Pitomnik
Gorodischtschje
Kalatsch
Stalingrad
Lenin-Kanal
Wolga

Millerowo

Woroschilowgrad

Morosowskaja

Tazinsjkaja

Zimljansker-Stause

St. Swjerjewo

Schachty

Donez

Don

Don

Nowotscherkassk

Rostow

▲▲▲	Deutsche Auffangfront
▲▲▲	Kesselfront ab 10.01.43
▲	Flugplatz
⊟	6. Armee
➤	Russischer Durchbruch ab 16. Dezember
---	Bahn

0 km   50 km   100 km

The Stalingrad Pocket.

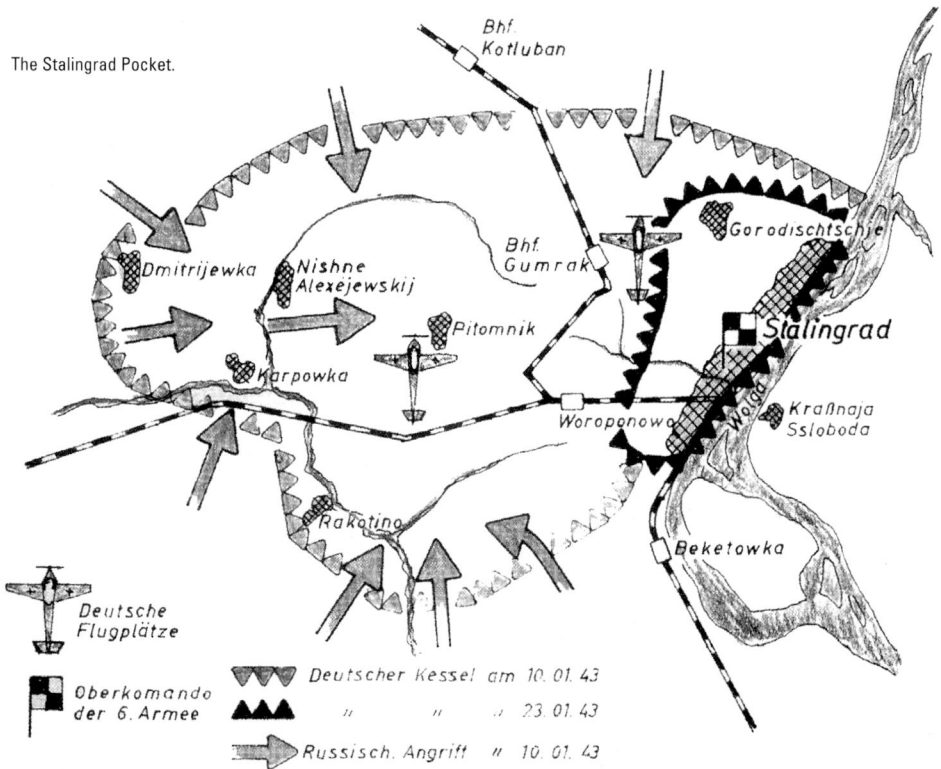

Bhf. Kotluban

Dmitrijewka

Nishne Alexejewskij

Bhf. Gumrak

Gorodischtschje

Pitomnik

Stalingrad

Karpowka

Woroponowo

Wolga

Kraßnaja Ssloboda

Rakotino

Beketowka

✈	Deutsche Flugplätze
⊟	Oberkomando der 6. Armee
▼▼▼	Deutscher Kessel am 10.01.43
▲▲▲	„ „ „ 23.01.43
➤	Russisch. Angriff „ 10.01.43

359

Missions to Kirovograd by the II. Gruppe from 24/2 – 8/3/1943.

Feldwebel Will and Feldwebel Lehner receive the Knight's Cross from the Kommodore on 22 May 1943. Right: Oblt. Werner, Geschwader technical officer, during the regeneration period in Gablingen.

Taken on the same occasion as the photo above. The two recipients received their decorations in front of the entire II. Gruppe of KG 53.

The new Knight's Cross wearers with the Kommodore and Kommandeur. From l. to r.: Fw. Will, Oblt. Pockrandt, Major Wittmann, Fw. Lehner Right: Oblt. Kurt Lohmann, Staffelkapitän of 2./KG 53, Knight's Cross on 19/2/1943.

The new Knight's Cross wearers with the Kommodore and Kommandeur. From l. to r.: Fw. Will, Oblt. Pockrandt, Major Wittmann, Fw. Lehner. Right: Oblt. Kurt Lehmann, Staffelkapitän of 2./KG 53, Knight's Cross on 19/2/1943.

The III. Gruppe's command post in Pskov, spring 1943. From l. to r.: (standing) Major d.R. Kürten, unidentified, Major Mönch, Kommandeur III. Gruppe; Oblt. Pfister, Geschwader technical officer.

Lt. Engel and his crew during preparations for the Geschwader's 30,000th combat mission in May 1943.

30,000th combat mission. Lt. Engel and his crew are presented with a gift basket.

Address to the II. Gruppe on the occasion of the 30,000th combat mission, Korovye Selo airfield, May 1943. From l. to r.: war reporter Ollig, Kommodore Major Pockrandt, Geschwader adjutant Hauptmann Thierig. In the background are Oblt. Lührs, adjutant I. Gruppe, and an unidentified officer. In foreground is Major Rauer, C.O. I. Gruppe, while Lt. Engel and his crew may be seen in the background.

Spring 1943. Visit by Oberst Joachim Helbig, Inspector-General of the Bomber Arm. In the middle is Oberst Wilke, then Hptm. Thierig (hidden) and an unidentified officer.

Visit by Generalmajor Rieckhoff, Luftflotte 1 Chief-of-Staff in the summer of 1943. On the right is Kommodore Major Pockrandt. Purpose of the visit: to discuss an upcoming major attack on the Volkhov bridges.

Farewell by Kommodore Oberst Wilke and Kommandeur II. Gruppe Oblt. Schulz-Müllensiefen, handover of the Geschwader to Major Pockrandt, Korovye Selo, April 1943. From l. to r.: Hptm. Thierig, Geschwader adjutant; Major Pockrandt, Oberst Wilke, Oblt. Schulze-Müllensiefen.

Korovye Selo, January 1943. Cheerful evening in the officer's mess of the Geschwaderstab. From l. to r.: (standing) unidentified; (seated) Lt. Neidhard; Hptm. Siebel, commander signals company and H.Q. signals officer; Oblt. Waldhecker, Geschwaderstab signals platoon; Major Mönch, C.O. III. Gruppe; Oberst Wilke, Kommodore, with unit mascot "Monk"; Major Pockrandt; Major Zahn, commander IV. Gruppe; base commander, unknown; Hptm. Thierig; (standing) Reg.R. a. Kr. Meinz; Hptm. Bake, BR Dr. Müldner.

Promotion to Hauptmann for, from l. to r. ,Oblt. von Ehren, Oblt. Kind, Oblt. Ebeling. III. Gruppe adjutant Oblt. von Ehren pins on their stars.

Technical personnel of the Geschwader staff flight (Stabsschwarm), 10/10/1943, central sector of the Eastern Front.

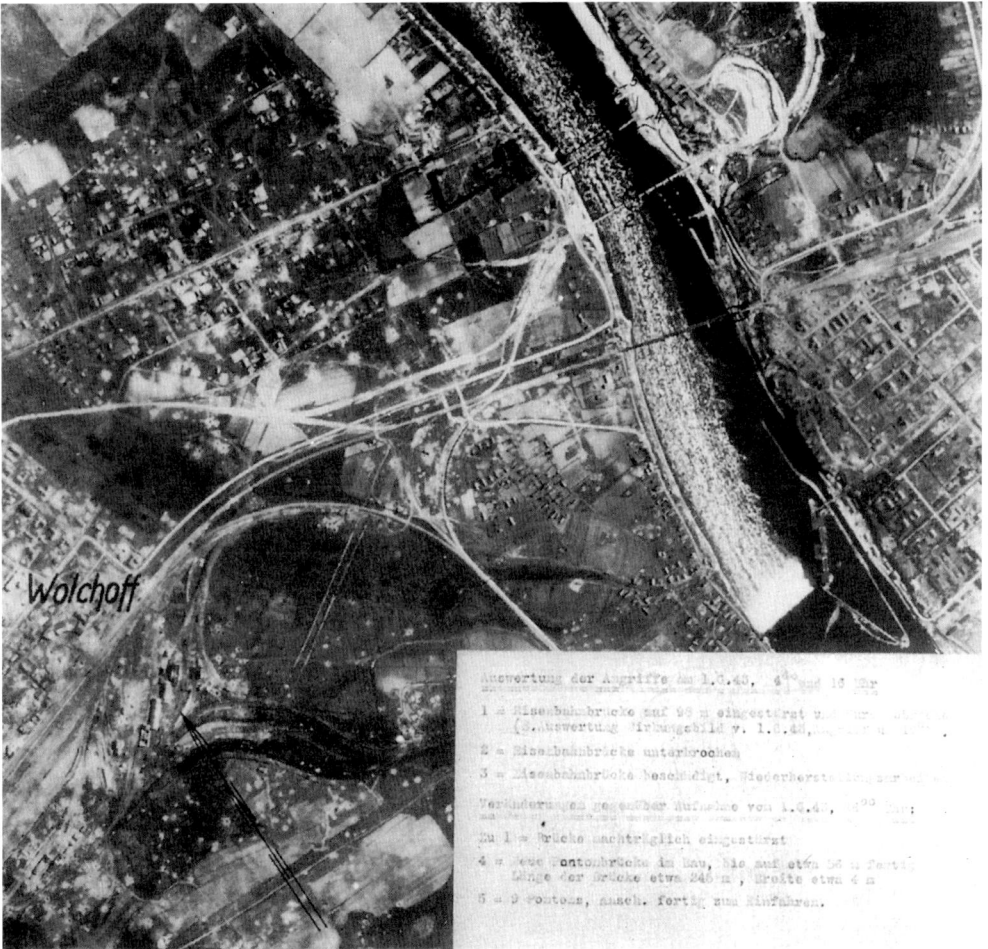

Aerial photo of the Volkhov attack, 1 June 1943.

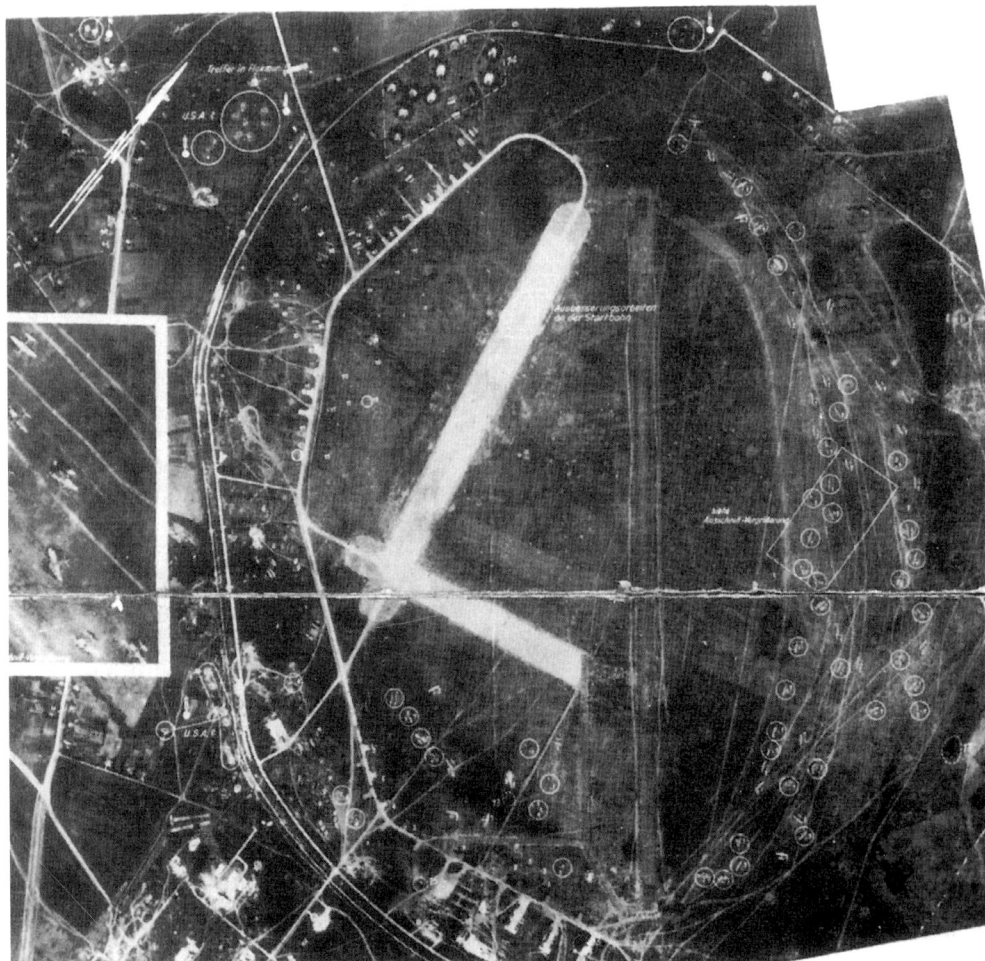

Gen. Kdo. IV. Flg. Korps — Fliegerbildstelle-Ost

egriffen in der Nacht vom **21./22.6.44** Zielwirkungsbild 2.(F)100 F 148/44 vom **22.6.44**

ch I, II, III./K.G.53 u. I, II, III./K.G.55 **Flugplatz Poltawa I** Maßstab etwa 1:5000
nd K.G.4 als Zielfinder Anf. Nr. 7.

Angriffszeit: 23,45 - 00,41 Uhr Ziel-Nr. **10375** □ 35 Ost 4044

Aerial photo taken before the raid on Poltava on the night of 21-22 June 1944.

370

General Meister, commanding general IV. Fliegerkorps, arrives to inspect the III. Gruppe, Schaulen, spring 1944. Major Allmendinger, Kommandeur III. Gruppe, greets the general.

May 1944 in Kauen, the awarding of five Knight's Crosses by Generalmajor Meister. From l. to r.: Obfw. Christmass, Oblt. Dreher, Hptm. Gobert, Hptm. Zöllner, Oblt. Gutmann.

General Meister decorates Major Rauer, Kommandeur I. Gruppe, and Oblt. Unruh with the Knight's Cross, Kauen, March 1944.

Above: Group photo of the 8. Staffel, Radom, May 1944.

Center: Radom, May 1944. Oblt. Dengg with just-decorated members of the 8. Staffel.

Aircraft mechanics at work … between landing and takeoff.

Major Joachim and his crew on their way to the Agram Gorica airfield, summer 1943.

Agram Gorica airfield, summer 1943. Visit by General Erdmann. Major Joachim reports.

Guest at a social evening with 8./KG 53. From l. to r.: Hptm. Tusche, Major Wittmann, Lt. Ackermann, Oblt. Zander, unidentified.

Sarajevo-Butmir airfield, summer 1943.

Over Montenegro, summer 1943.

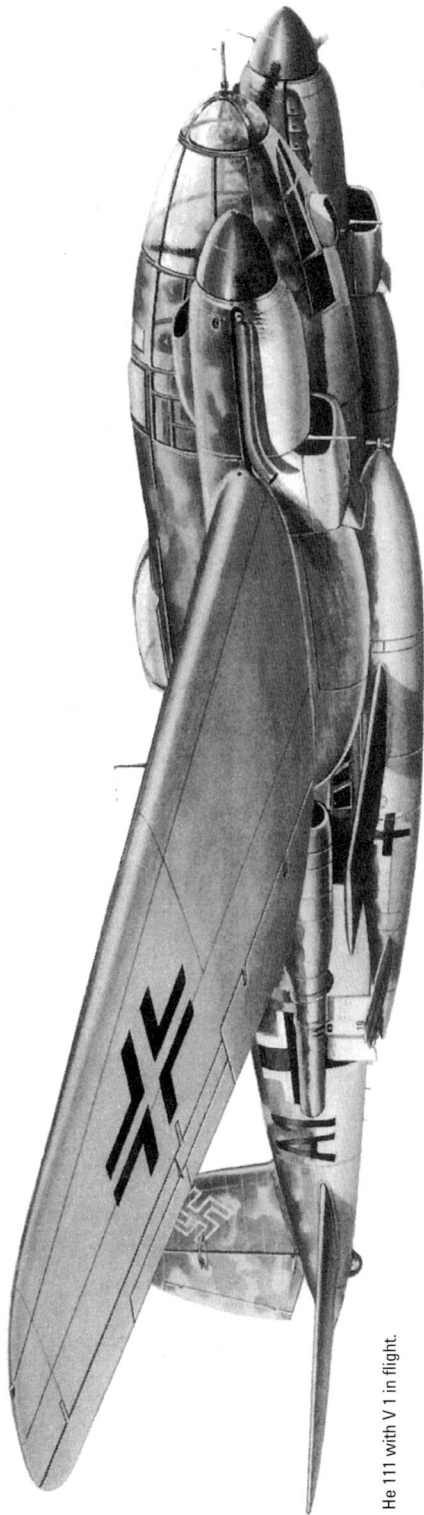

He 111 with V 1 in flight.

He 111 with Fi 103 (V-1)

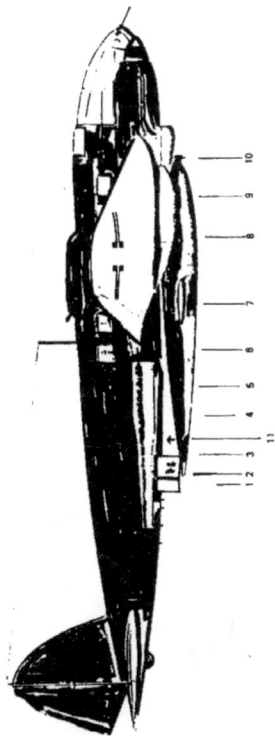

1. Vertical fin with rudder
2. Release chute for propaganda leaflets
3. Horizontal tail, elevator with covered footstep
4. Askania autopilot, pulse jet controls, altitude box
5. Aft cylindrical   compressed air bottle for control
6. Forward spherical   and fuel supply
7. Wings (no ailerons, fuel tank for kerosine in fuselage)
8. 'Cargo space' for up to 1000kg (TNT, Trialen)
9. Ground detonator for shallow landings
10. Fuselage nose, always Askania remote compass as backup for directional gyro,
countdown timer and forward detonator in front
11. Argus-Schmidt pulse jet power plant

V 1 range: 260-300km
Max. speed: 560kph
Takeoff weight: 2200kg
Thrust at 280 kph: approx. 800kg

Functional staff of the signals company, Russia 1943. Right: Oblt. Waldhecker, last commander of the signals company.

Signals company during the move from France to Poland, May 1941.

Hauptmann Artur Pfister, Staffelkapitän of 8./KG 53, who crashed near Ternopol on 4 April 1944.

Jesau airbase near Königsberg (East Prussia), August 1944. From l. to r.: Major Wittmann, C.O. II. Gruppe; Major Grözinger, C.O. IV. Gruppe; Otl. Pockrandt, Kommodore; Major Rauer, C.O. I. Gruppe; Major Allmendinger, C.O. II. Gruppe.

Lt. Rutte and crew, Lvov airfield, February 1944. From l. to r.: Uffz. Möller, flight engineer; Fw. Blazejovsky, observer: Lt. Rutte, pilot; Uffz. Hanck, radio operator; Obgefr. Lenz, gunner.

377

Major Allmendinger, commander of the III. Gruppe, gives a mission briefing at IV. Fliegerkorps in Radom, 1944. Beside him is Lt. Luksch, signals officer.

The Kommodore gives his final instructions. From l. to r.: Otl. Pockrandt, as guest commander of the IV. Gruppe Major Grözinger, and the former commander of the III. Gruppe Major Fabian.

Kauen. From l. to r.: Major Rauer, Major Wittmann, Major Grözinger, Major Allmendinger, Hptm. Ebeling, Major d.R. Kürten.

Takeover of the III. Gruppe of KG 3, Ahlhorn airbase. Kommodore Otl. Pockrandt, Major Vetter, commander III./KG 3 (then I./KG 53). October 1944.

Officer corps of I./KG 53 in Neuhardenberg at the time of the unit's disbandment, September 1944. From l. to r. top row: unidentified, Vitting, Neuber, Reiter, Kracht, Samscha, Hansen, Rüsing. Middle row: Renk, Olp, Braukmeier, Hullah, Küster, Berner, Rommel, Engel. Bottom row: Waldhecker, Mehlhorn, Müller, Brandt, Rauer, Lührs, Weiß.

The most highly decorated crew in KG 53. From l. to r.: Lt. Ackermann, pilot, Knight's Cross on 28/2/45; Major Wittmann, observer, Oak Leaves on 11/2/45; Obfw. Steudel, radio operator, Knight's Cross on 28/2/45.

The same crew 36 years later, photographed on 29 May 1981. From l. to r.: Fritz Steudel, Herbert Wittmann, Georg Ackermann.

Hauptmann Ebeling after receiving the Knight's Cross on 20 March 1945, Bad Zwischenahn.

The signals company's 1st Platoon's living quarters (Finnish hut) in Russia, summer 1942.

Jesau Signals Platoon on the move to Lille, summer 1940. The heavy transmitter's antenna truck.

The Headquarters Signals Platoon (II) in a forest camp near Orsha, August-September 1941. KG 53's telex section. In the foreground is Uffz. Beyer.

Luftwaffe memorial in Fürstenfeldbruck.